THE SONGS OF HUGO WOLF

by the same author

The Songs of Robert Schumann (1969: revised second edition, Eulenburg 1975)
Brahms Songs (BBC Music Guides 1972)

ERIC SAMS

THE SONGS OF
HUGO WOLF

Foreword by
GERALD MOORE

EULENBURG BOOKS
LONDON

Original edition first published by
Methuen & Co. Ltd
Revised and enlarged second edition
first published 1983 by
Ernst Eulenburg Ltd
48 Great Marlborough Street, London W1V 2BN

© Eric Sams 1961, 1983

ISBN 0 903873 32 X

Photoset in Sabon, printed and bound by
Redwood Burn Ltd
Trowbridge, Wiltshire

Contents

to Enid

Foreword by Gerald Moore

to the First Edition (1961)

This is the most important book in the English language on the songs of Hugo Wolf since Ernest Newman proclaimed the composer's genius in 1907. It is the first time, so far as I am aware, that every single song (except the posthumous which the author has rightly omitted) has been translated, examined and elucidated between the covers of one single volume.

To the English-speaking student this work is a treasure to which he will find himself returning again and again: it is indispensable to those of us anxious to gain a deeper knowledge of Wolf.

Through the author's penetration into and intimacy with this composer's style he is enabled to make clear to us how Wolf perceived the communicating function of music and its analogies with language. Yet it is this unique quality of inter-relationship of his muse with that of the poet for which Wolf is condemned in some quarters. Schubert, it is true, sang his songs to all the poetry he could lay hands on; he transfigured an unworthy poem by putting the most glorious music to it. To Wolf, the seed was the word; words inspired him. The finer the lyric, the finer his conception in terms of music. He was generally more discriminating in his choice of poet than any composer before him: his failures, and they undeniably exist, can often be traced to poems that were not worthy of his attention, of the labour – resulting in a 'contrived' composition – that they caused. But the greatness of some of his settings cannot be questioned.

An ardent Wolfian finds himself turning again and again to the Attic type of song, chaste in conception, simple in construction, and holding it in ever-increasing affection. He is seared by the sheer beauty of *Herr, was trägt der Boden hier; Grenzen der Menscheit; Sankt Nepomuks Vorabend; Anakreons Grab; Im Frühling; Um Mitternacht; Auf ein altes Bild*, which Sams in moving language sums up as 'eternal grief in an

vii

eternal summer.' He is charmed by the discreet wit and compactness of *Der Musikant*; *Das Ständchen*; *Begegnung*; and marvels at some of the miracles he finds in the *Italienisches Liederbuch*. To have written these songs alone was to have lived to some purpose; one senses their greatness instinctively and finds with pleasure this feeling endorsed by so eminent an authority as the author. Eric Sams, however, is no euphemist; he does not overstate his case. Thus he tells us that one may prefer the strong sweetness of Schubert's *Ganymed* to the blissful masochism of Wolf's, that the latter's *Philine* loses by comparison with Schumann's, that the popular *In dem Schatten meiner Locken* by no means eclipses that of Brahms (a statement which must surely make Hugo turn in his grave). These are suggestions, however, not edicts and the reader will draw from them his own conclusions and, more often than not, find himself in complete agreement.

Our guide will not lead us astray for he is not blinded by his hero and claims for him, in Frank Walker's words, 'a modest place among the immortals'. His judgement is fair, unclouded but not arbitrary. He induces us to think for ourselves.

The fruit of deep study and sympathy with his subject, this book should be on the shelf of every man who professes or calls himself musical.

It is a masterpiece.

Preface

to the First Edition (1961)

This book discusses all the 242 songs written for voice and piano published in the composer's lifetime, i.e. the contents of the invaluable Peters Edition in twenty-one octavo volumes.

In writing about each song I have tried to translate the German words, to comment on the music in general terms, and to add notes on points of detail. A word or two of explanation may be needed on each of these aims.

Some of the German texts are great poetry, some have no particular merit; some are long, others only a few lines. In some, individual words or phrases are important; in others, only the general mood matters. Accordingly the method of treatment varies. Sometimes it is a literal translation, sometimes a summary, sometimes a paraphrase; sometimes a mixture of all or some of these things. But the aim is always the same – to render in English prose the essence of the words as they appear in Wolf's music.

In the commentaries I try to describe each song, and, so far as possible in so brief a compass, to show the interconnection between the music and the poem. Inevitably, in so doing, I have also become involved in some attempt at evaluating the intentions and achievements of the songs. To describe music in words is already a difficult task, and the procedure adopted may well also involve a lack of proportion. For instance, there is little to say about some of the finest songs except that they are admirable, while others, less fine, may contain many points that can more helpfully be dealt with by verbal comment. In the last resort these commentaries are simply personal impressions of the songs, evaluated from their effect on one listener who has known them all, and loved most of them, for a long time.

The notes are mainly intended to illuminate various aspects of Wolf's 'musical language' (to use his own phrase). This topic sometimes raises technical points, and here textual references are included.

In the main, then, what follows is a series of separate discussions of particular songs. But one cannot altogether avoid generalization. So the opening chapter attempts a general account of Wolf's song-writing.

I have made no attempt at any serious consideration of Wolf's own personality and the tragic story of his life, important though these matters are to a proper understanding of his music. They have been definitively dealt with in Frank Walker's masterly biography *Hugo Wolf**, which should be read by everyone who is interested in Wolf's life and work.

Lastly, I would express my gratitude to all those who have helped me.

I am indebted to Max Hinrichsen for permission to quote and refer to the Peters Edition of Wolf's songs, and for his personal kindness to me.

To Robert Moberly I am grateful not only for the help he gave me by reading and commenting on the text in detail, but for his unfailing understanding and encouragement; and to David Mowatt also for his valuable assistance in critical comment.

---

* Dent, 1951 [revised and enlarged 2nd ed., 1968]

Preface to the Second Edition

The aims of this book remain unchanged; but the text has been very substantially revised and enlarged. For practical reasons the main sequence of subject matter remains centred on those 242 songs for voice and piano, in the same chronological order and numbering as before, that Wolf himself adjudged worthy of publication. For this new edition, however, I have added the three Ibsen songs composed by Wolf for voice and orchestra and published by him in his own piano arrangement.

The introductory essay on Wolf as a song-writer has been revised to include much new material; here I have drawn (by kind permission of Macmillan) on my articles 'Hugo Wolf' and 'The Romantic Lied' in the *New Grove Dictionary of Music and Musicians**. In the section on musical motifs, the original numbering has again been retained as the basic framework of reference, but fifteen more motifs, and many further examples, are now included. Factual information new in this edition includes the key and written compass† of each song, and the date of any orchestral version made by Wolf. The English translations have been completely revised so as to bring out, if possible without inversion or paraphrase, the literal meaning of the original German text. Square brackets now mark Wolf's repetitions of that text, while indentations denote a substantive piano prelude or interlude (in general, at least three bars) The revised commentaries assume no knowledge of German, and all their quotations from the original poem are duly translated. The detailed notes however, like the introductory essay, are intended for singers and

---

* Macmillan, 1980

† in the so-called Helmholtz notation, i.e.

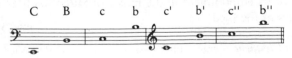

students, and here some knowledge of German is assumed. As a general rule, the notes begin with any textual points (including variant readings in current editions) and end with a reference to other major settings of the same words: here the many amplifications include some fifty further musical parallels between Wolf and his great predecessors and contemporaries, notably Schumann and Wagner. Finally the introductions to each of the major songbooks, together with the relevant commentaries and notes, have been expanded to include further background information about the poets and their sources. Here again I am obliged to Macmillan for permission to draw on my *New Grove* article on Mörike.

Since this book appeared in its first edition over twenty years ago, Wolf's art has gradually gained a wider following. All his major song-books and much of his other music have appeared in a new *Kritische Gesamtausgabe*, edited by Hans Jancik.* The recorded repertory has been very substantially extended by Lieder exponents of the stature of Gerald Moore, Elisabeth Schwarzkopf and Dietrich Fischer-Dieskau. In addition concert soloists such as Sviatoslav Richter and Daniel Barenboim have played a significant part in the interpretation of Wolf accompaniments. Further, outstanding pianists such as Graham Johnson, Geoffrey Parsons and David Willison in the English speaking world, in partnership with many gifted singers, have furthered the Wolfian cause by their advocacy as well as by their artistry. The greatness of Hugo Wolf as a song-writer is hence now more widely if not universally acknowledged. But the appreciation of his Lieder still remains a minority taste. This is no doubt largely due to the fact that his art is a hybrid between music and German, so that full appreciation demands some knowledge of that language.

But deep and detailed linguistic or literary competence is not essential; it may even prove something of a handicap, if familiarity detracts from the feeling that the German words are novel and exciting, with a meaning to be explored, a sound to be savoured, a poetry to be relished. It was exactly this alertness and receptivity of response, this sense of delight and discovery, which brought Wolf's songs into being, and which they in their turn still contain and communicate. It may well be therefore that the teaching of European language and literature, as well as of music, would benefit from increased attention to song-writing; and it is certainly arguable that studies of the German lyric are incomplete without some knowledge of its embodiment in the music of Hugo Wolf and the other great masters of the Lied.

Eric Sams, 1982

* *Hugo Wolf Sämtliche Werke*, Musikwissenschaftlicher Verlag, Vienna, 1960—

Wolf as a Song-writer

Born 13 March 1860 in Windischgraz, Austria (now Slovenj Gradec, Yugoslavia); given violin and piano lessons at an early age; was a music critic in Vienna from 1884 to 1887; early in 1888 suddenly found himself as a composer; and composed in that year alone nearly one hundred songs in rapid succession. These are among the few biographical details that Wolf himself sanctioned, in a letter to a friend (2 May 1890, to Oskar Grohe), which he ended by saying 'God grant me a long life and plenty of good ideas!'

This is tragic irony. To complete the summary biography:

1888–91: over 200 songs to words by Mörike, Eichendorff, Goethe, Geibel, Keller and Heyse.

1892–94: silence.

1895–97: an opera (*Der Corregidor*), another thirty or so songs, an unfinished opera (*Manuel Venegas*).

1897–1903: madness – death.

Wolf's creative life was among the shortest and most sporadic known to musical history. He did not achieve mastery until he was twenty-eight. In the nine years left to him his songs were written in irregular outbursts, at the rate of one, two or even three a day. These days add up to less than six months; the main creative periods add up to less than eighteen months. On the achievement of this short span his name and fame rest secure. At the same time his reputation has outstripped his popularity, and his praises are still sung more than his songs. Critics agree that his work is admirable; music-lovers are less unanimous about whether it is also enjoyable. These two points may be related. The reasons for which Wolf's songs are highly prized – their literary perception, their fastidious 'declamation' and so on – seem nicely calculated to put people off. It is human to ask what all this has to do with music.

The fact is no doubt that Wolf's songs have lived, and will live, because

1

of their musical excellence. It is also true that the music itself has a unique quality of intimate inter-relationship with words, with language, and with poetry. This introduction seeks to define and expound that quality. In brief, it is the compression of large-scale dramatic music within the miniature frame of German lyric verse, thus creating new springs of expressive power in the song form. Just as Schubert had distilled the essence of classical opera and oratorio (Mozart, Beethoven, Haydn) into the first Romantic Lieder, thus creating a new genre, so Wolf in his turn condensed the dramatic intensity of modern (i.e. Wagnerian) music-drama into voice and keyboard, lending fresh life and force to the Lied form and enhancing its expressive vocabulary to a pitch never since surpassed.

At first, however, his genius was neither foreseen nor foreseeable; so it could hardly benefit from tuition, let alone search for influences. As he later insisted, he was an independent and essentially self-taught composer speaking a new musico-poetic language of his own devising. He was also ready to acknowledge that these original ideas were deep-rooted in national tradition as well as personal temperament. But before they could flower and flourish they had to assimilate many different nutritive elements. Naturally the final harvest was agonizingly delayed; hence Wolf's doubt and despair. Naturally, too, when it at last arrived in 1888 it was commensurately rich and profuse; hence his astonishment and delight. Somehow, by instinct and sheer application, he had by his twenty-eighth year assembled the varied expressive components of a new musical style, and had also acquired the necessary wide range of artistic and human experience. Thus equipped, he could become almost overnight the final master of one of the most highly-developed and complex of all art-forms.

But most of his steps to that end seem to have been taken in the dark. To borrow, from the letter cited above, his own homely metaphor for his sudden spate of Mörike masterpieces in 1888, 'Eventually, after a lot of groping around, the button came undone' – a saying which agreeably defines the Wolfian blend of endeavour and change, simplicity and irony, earnestness and humour, bad fortune and good. His long and circuitous journey towards mastery began at fifteen, in 1875, when he first heard a Wagner opera. We know from his letters what a revelation that was; from his later music we can hear why. Orchestra and soloists sang aloud the secret that music could express not just the conceptual life of language but the enactment of drama. Thus Wolf's mind was early concentrated on musical techniques of characterization and atmosphere as well as expression. But his creativity was also deeply divided between the large-scale forms such as opera, tone-poem and symphony (in contemporary

2

practice, Wagner, Liszt and Bruckner) and the smaller song-forms perfected by his great predecessors (notably Schubert, Loewe and Schumann). Again, he was hampered by his own refractory temperament, with its innate defiance of authority, mistrust of instruction, and irregular mood-swings ranging from exaltation to despair. Upon all this were superimposed, from his eighteenth year, the severe physical and mental stress and trauma of serious illness (acquired syphilis) and the concomitant feelings of emotional frustration coupled with a sense of personal and artistic failure.

But there were corresponding compensations. The range of Wolf's experience and imagination, in dark or bright moods and moments, in sickness or remission, commanded a commensurately wide and contrasting range of musical expressiveness. His articulateness in verse and prose helped him in his work as a music-critic (1884–7), which in turn gave him some much-needed discipline, greatly enhanced his familiarity with the verbal medium, and afforded him unrivalled insights into the nature of operatic and other music. All these strains blended in the masterly *Italian Serenade* of 1887, the first of his major works to be wholly characteristic and successful. Here is opera without words; scene and character, dialogue and gesture, crystallized in one single sparkling movement for string quartet. Something of the same genius for musical compression and verbal expression had already been heard in the earlier D-minor Quartet (1878–84), with its overt homage to Goethe's *Faust* and unacknowledged indebtedness to Beethoven, Schubert and Wagner, and in the grand orchestral *Penthesilea*, directly inspired by Kleist's drama of that name and indirectly by the Lisztian symphonic poem in general. But those works and others were still in varying degrees diffuse and derivative. Only when form as well as content could be directly derived from a poetic source, without subjective intervention, could Wolf's genius shine out at its resplendent best. Then his musical sensitivity to poetic meaning and value was embodied in each separate aspect of song; form, rhythm, declamation, melody, counterpoint, harmony, tonality, modulation, key, programme music, piano texture and function, and motivic equivalents for verbal concepts and ideas.

In general, Wolf's songs contain a musical equivalent for the prevailing mood of a poem, or more than one if that mood changes. This concept governs and defines the whole Lied art-form; musical ideas suggested by words are embodied in a setting of those words for voice and piano, both to provide overall unity and to enhance details, e.g. when particular words or phrases are thrown into relief by musical means for particular effect. The total impression is thus one of diversity within unity. This, admittedly, is the essence of all musical form, and need not have any real

3

connection with the poem set. But Wolf (unlike his predecessors) rarely seeks to impose external musical form on the poem by restructuring the given text. He does so exceptionally, and the exceptions may be masterpieces. Thus the first verse of *Benedeit die sel'ge Mutter* is repeated without poetic warranty just to make a compelling peroration, and an indifferent stanza in *Geh' Geliebter* is omitted to make a viable song. In other ways too we may occasionally feel that the typical perfection of form has been arbitrarily contrived. But such instances are mainly confined to early or unpublished songs, e.g. the 1880 *Erwartung* or the 1882 *Andenken*. Elsewhere the form derives directly and objectively from the text Wolf found on the printed page of the source-book before him.

This does not necessarily argue a complete formal correspondence. Even where the poem is divided into regular stanzas, the music must feel free to develop and change if the verbal theme does. Again, the song-writer may choose to set the scene with a piano prelude, comment in an interlude, or have the last word through a postlude. But taken together the piano solo passages will be found to furnish a matching frame for the poem, both containing it and displaying it to the fullest advantage. Thus Wolf treats his lyrics as spirit, not letter; life and growth, not set pattern. He sees his task as the recreation of that life in musical terms. In the Mörike songs for example a strong central poetic image or idea evokes an iron logic of musical construction (*Auf eine Christblume II, Seufzer, Erstes Liebeslied eines Mädchens*) while a more diffuse poem, whether reflective or narrative, is transcribed into a more flexible and developing formal scheme (*Auf eine Christblume I, Auf einer Wanderung*). The structure of the setting thus reflects that of the poem; and within this general correspondence there is much subtle variation of each separate aspect of the music to re-create the finer details of the text.

Rhythm, in particular, can be expected to have a central part to play, since it is a factor common to poetry and music. It therefore includes an element of direct transference from one mode to the other; thus the basic compound time of *Der Soldat II* or *Liebesglück* is an involuntary response to Eichendorff's insistent dactylic or anapaestic beat, while the statelier measures of *Anakreons Grab* are closely calibrated to Goethe's classical metre. More typically still, rhythm is designed to provide formal shape and continuity throughout a song, as the effectively unobtrusive and unchanging background to explicit emotional colour and contrast, as in *In der Frühe* etc. In many songs it can yield additional meaning. Sometimes this is illustrative, as in the crisp elated rhythm of a song about the exhilaration of a morning walk (*Fussreise*) or the slow throbbing rhythm of a song about a beating heart (*Alle gingen, Herz, zur Ruh'*). A persistent figure can also be used evocatively to convey for example the idea of single-minded preoccupation (*Nun bin ich dein, Mühvoll komm' ich und beladen*). There is an even more intimate link with the moods and meanings of the poem in the rhythmic changes of such songs as *Auf eine Christblume I*, *Agnes* or *Grenzen der Menschheit*. The possibilities are endless, and Wolf exploits them without ever repeating them; each song creates and sustains rhythmically its own mood and its own world.

It is true that most are in duple or quadruple time, set out in regular two-bar phrases and four-bar sentences, and that this (just as in Wagner's music-dramas) can sometimes lead to squareness and monotony when the musical material is not of the finest. This very regularity however is one of the factors that enables Wolf to achieve his superlative perfection of formal construction; and as a technique of setting words to music it is not only defensible but almost inevitable. In German as in English, scansion is commonly by stress rather than by length of syllable; so the trochaic foot for example is most directly translated into equal pulses, thus ♩ ♩ rather than ♩ ♩. Because the whole of Wolf's music responds to poetry, this rhythmic translation will pervade the piano part as well as the voice. Not that Wolf"s vocal lines are monotonous; on the contrary, they are capable of the most delicate and subtle inflexions. But it is precisely the steady rhythmic feeling that makes this possible. Like a *danseur noble* it supports the voice part, which is then left free for rhythmic digression without sounding over-elaborate or impeding the forward movement of the song as a whole. This is one aspect of Wolf's declamation.

It has sometimes been supposed that Wolf takes great pains to match the actual speech-stress of the words he is setting to music, and that this practice is an essential part of his art. Such a view is wrong and misleading. The rhythm of spoken verse is so complex, and so individually variable, that it cannot be precisely transcribed in the more basic terms of musical notation. Even if it could, the feat would not after all be very musicianly. In fact, Wolf's melodic lines are rarely complex. Certainly he is often at pains to remove undue stress from inessential words, and in general to free the text from what has been called the tyranny of the bar-line. Very often indeed however his accentuation is obviously faulty from the point of view of prosody, just as it often is in Schubert, Schumann and Brahms. A glance through the vocal lines of the Mörike songbook for example discloses many a preposition set on a strong down-beat. Such anomalies are likely to happen to any song-writer who is doing something different from merely holding a mirror up to a poem. Wolf, in his declamatory as in his other procedures, aims far beyond this. From his first adolescent attempts at vocal writing, his word-setting has recitative inflexions with touches of cadential pointing and plainsong repetition perhaps influenced by his background of church school and choir. This thrust towards verbal expressiveness led him to explore choral composition at the same time (c. 1876) as the earliest songs. In both genres he strives for linear independence and significance; the vocal melodies are keenly expressive of poetic stress, cadence and meaning. In his mature song-writing, whenever his voice part hesitates over certain words, or prolongs others, its purpose is to enhance them musically and thus to add expressive effect or even new ideas. On occasion Wolf uses sustained high notes as Wagner does, e.g. in *Tristan und Isolde*, to signify wild and passionate outcries. The vocal line of *Erstes Liebeslied eines Mädchens* for example gasps and clamours most realistically and effectively in this way. But such vocal climaxes as those on the word 'Sieg' (victory) in *Der Genesene an die Hoffnung* or *Morgenstimmung* often have as much lyric as dramatic significance and owe more to Schubert than to Wagner. Like the former's 'ewig' (eternal) sustained for ten bars' duration in his *Elysium*, they embody poetic expression. Their model is not so much the pitch or duration of emotive cries as the cadence and significance of spoken verse; they are essentially declamation rather than exclamation. In such typically Wolfian utterances as the prolonged 'geflügelt' (winged) towards the end of *Die ihr schwebet*, the lift to 'geträumt' (dreamed) in *Das verlassene Mägdlein* or the heightened curve of 'süsser noch' (sweeter still) in *Um Mitternacht*, the melodic line draws our attention to the beauty of the lyric verse in a wholly un-Wagnerian way. This tender solicitude for the expressiveness of poetic vocabulary appears very early in Wolf's vocal writing, e.g. in the 1881 *Sechs Geistliche Lieder* for unaccompanied chorus, where the word 'ruht' (rests) relaxes on to a sustained note held over a bar-line. No doubt this sensitivity of response was an inborn trait; but such effects could have been heard in both middle-period Schubert ('Düfte', scents, slowly diffused through three bars in *Dass sie hier gewesen*) and late Schumann ('hingst', hung, suspended over a bar-line in *Der leidige Frieden*).

When in moments of especial poetic intensity two or three words are expressively stressed thus within the same phrase, the result is the wholly Wolfian fluid melodic line, e.g.

An die Geliebte

tief ge-stillt, mich stumm___ an dei - nem heil' - gen Wert ver-gnü - ge

Wenn du zu den Blumen gehst

müss __ test __ du dich sel - - ber pflük-ken

Such effects re-create a mood which Wolf has either read in the poetry (as in the first example above) or has read *into* the poetry (as in the second). They are rarely complex, and never merely artificial; nor are they at all obtrusive or even prevalent. They offer a special case of the declamation that is at the heart of all Wolf's song-writing – the flexible vocal line which is, in Byrd's majestic phrase, 'fram'd to the life of the words'. Even in a strophic song the melody does not necessarily follow set patterns of repetition but is sensitively deployed to match a changing mood (as in *Der Rattenfänger*) or a new poetic image (as in *Um Mitternacht*).

Declamation of this kind, part recitative and part cantilena, had already been adumbrated by Schubert, e.g. in *Die schöne Müllerin*. Wolf's further refinements exemplified above are quite new in the Lied. But of course he would have heard the similarly fluid melodic lines that drift and eddy through the violin parts of Wagner's operas and Schumann's later chamber music. In his own work they are first heard in the youthful D-minor Quartet, begun in 1878. The early songs serve to confirm that the concept is instrumental in origin. It first appears in the piano part, not the voice – tentatively and discreetly in the 1881 *In der Fremde I*, more robustly in the dance measures of *Wohin mit der Freud'* and with increasing assurance in *Wiegenlied im Sommer* (both 1882), where it emerges as a fully-fledged expressive device. In this latter lullaby the melodic line leans over a rocking and weaving movement in the piano part, making a music of song and cradle together; and we hear that the keyboard image contains a small separate melodic life of its own which dreamily stretches and relaxes with each repetition of the refrain 'Gut' Nacht'. Thus a melodic line can be used for figure- or character-drawing.

Naturally there is no question of deliberate musical imagery here, Wolf's counterpoints like his other procedures are drawn intuitively from the poetry; they colour the music with the varied shades of meaning inherent in each strand of melody. The function of two melodic lines as a basic image of duality yields a wide range of musical metaphor, from close proximity to complete separation. Not only do parallel thirds brought together in the right hand make a lively image of travelling companionship (described later as motif 16); at the other extreme a single left-hand melody offers a vivid equivalent to the idea of loneliness or isolation, as in the prelude to *Lied eines Verliebten*. Similarly the voice may be divided from the piano, and one played off against the other, for expressive purposes. Thus an independent vocal counterpoint to an instrumental melody further distanced by being set in a separate conceptual frame of its own (e.g. in the style of a Chopin mazurka or ballade) conveys the idea of two different worlds and hence of total and irretrievable separation, whether of lover from lover (as in *Mein Liebster singt*) or of the singer from the world (*Tief im Herzen*) or both (*Bedeckt mich mit Blumen*). The two voices may also suggest an imagined dialogue or colloquy, as in *Seltsam ist Juanas Weise*, where the vocal and keyboard melodies are put out of step and out of joint, like the two lovers in the poem. Conversely, two melodies though ostensibly quite separate may be audibly made for each other, thus implying that a reconciliation between the two voices or characters is either imminent (*Auf dem grünen Balkon*) or at least negotiable (*O wüsstest du wieviel*, and perhaps *Tretet ein, hoher Krieger*).

It may be observed that in adopting and perfecting these melodic styles Wolf could be said to be making a virtue out of necessity. He is not among the world's most popular melodists. But he could of course write broad swinging tunes whenever his text required them (*Fussreise* is a peerless example). Furthermore, the melodic language of French and Italian opera, as of Austrian, Italian and Slovene popular song, had been familiar to him since childhood; and these influences remained strong and vital throughout his creative life. At eight years old he had been entranced by a Donizetti opera; at eleven, his staple piano repertory was French and Italian opera overtures and selections. Even in middle life he doted on the homely tunes and verses of the Austrian folk-singer and song-writer Johann Kain; later he became obsessed with the swinging strains of *Funiculi, funicula*. All those melodic styles were ready to be adapted at need, as in the long quasi-operatic cantilena of *Ach im Maien war's* or the rollicking student song (Wolf's own description) that breaks out at the end of *Nimmersatte Liebe*. His real genius however lay in the creation of melodic ideas, whether in transient intervals or long lines, that are not only appealing or beautiful in themselves but serve to match and enhance the meaning and emotive power of words, to conduct a current of poetic feeling. In this respect there is hardly his equal in the whole world of music. Sometimes the voice may leap or drop in wide intervals for special effects, whether serious, e.g. the grandiloquent tenths at the final climax of *Grenzen der Menschheit*, or comic, as in the graphic illustrations of braying (*Lied des transferierten Zettel*) or snoring (*Der Tambour*). More typically, the melodic lines are tranquilly drawn and spun out in long curves to match the movement and sense of the verse. Perhaps the finest examples are in the Italian Songbook (e.g. *Der Mond hat eine schwere Klag' erhoben*, or *Wenn du mich mit den Augen streifst*); but almost every song of Wolf's maturity has some such delight to offer. For these reasons the vocal compass of a Wolf song, the melody's general pattern of movement, whether by step or by leap, and the words to which its highest and lowest notes are sung, are all worth close study as guides to the mood and meaning of the music as a whole. It will not be by mere coincidence for example that the assured peace and quietude of *Anakreons Grab* and *Nun lass uns Frieden schliessen* are both mirrored in a confined compass of one octave from tonic to tonic in a major key.

The memorably penetrating quality of Wolf's melody must have owed much to the intense acuity of his own aural perceptions. He had absolute pitch, and was a skilled and enthusiastic piano-tuner. He expects from his listeners a sense of tonal values as exact and exacting as his own, in which the slightest inflexions can be charged with significance. But all his melody, whether in the vocal line or the piano themes that are often extended and developed quasi-independently throughout a song (*Auf einer Wanderung, Alles endet, was entstehet*), is inseparable from its harmonic context; so harmony is all-important in Wolf's work.

In his own lifetime he was, like many another composer, attacked for his 'dissonance'. His own comment on this (in a letter of 21 May 1890 to Emil Kauffmann) was 'The fact that I have been reproached for perpetrating chains of unresolved discords leaves me wholly unmoved, for I am in a position to demonstrate how each of my discords, however bold, can be justified by the most severe criteria of the theory of harmony'. In case this sounds alarming it should be said that Wolf's music is notable for its concord, and that its occasional dissonances rarely sound especially daring nowadays. But his proposed rejoinder to his critics shows how deeply he felt himself rooted in the classical tradition; as indeed he was, though no composer of his time could have failed to take advantage of the extended harmonic possibilities so richly exploited by Wagner. Wolf could have replied instead that all his harmonic resources – and they are always lavish, and often original – are invariably deployed to match the mood of the poem; and this is not only true but vital to his artistic integrity. Of course he has mannerisms and 'fingerprints'; not everyone will share for example his predilection for augmented fifths and cadential second inversions within the framework of academic four-part harmony, which was the basis of such training as he had. Nevertheless the abiding impression left by Wolf's harmony is not one of mannered novelty, still less of mere scholastic conformity, but of deep and original intuitive response. Even the identifiable fingerprints can be traced to the effect of recurrent and definable poetic ideas. Thus the basic four-part

9

accompaniment style is mainly manifest in settings of poems on religious or devotional themes, such as *Gebet*. The gifted song-writer Robert Franz explicitly acknowledged his personal indebtedness to the Protestant chorale; Wolf's own musical background was dominated by early experience as an organist and chorister. Within the accustomed four-part frame, altered chords such as the augmented fifth signify increased intensity of feeling or vision, whether wholly serious (*Das verlassene Mägdlein*) or quasi-parodistic (*Nimmersatte Liebe*), while the six-four chord indicates an approaching peroration or climax point (as at 'da bin' in *Wohl denk' ich oft*).

This intuitive use of harmony stems from two related sources. First, it clearly corresponds to a musical translation of language, a mode in which any skilled song-writer in most epochs would perforce be innately proficient. Secondly, it could also have been heard in, and absorbed from, vocal music in the German tradition, such as Bach's church cantatas, Mozart's Singspiels, Schubert's and Schumann's songs. Thus Wolf's separate major and minor glosses on the words 'froh und traurig' (glad and sorry) in *Alles endet, was entstehet* were foreshadowed by Schubert in his *Wehmut* at the words 'wohl und weh' (happy and sad). Similarly Wolf is harmonically indebted to Schumann, not merely in such youthful acts of frank homage as the questioning final dominant seventh of *Die Spinnerin*, with its audible echo of *Im wunderschönen Monat Mai*, but also in more subtle ways. For example, Wolf's use of modal harmonies to evoke the mood of a remote past in *Auf ein altes Bild* offers a parallel to Schumann's *Auf einer Burg*, while the *tierce de Picardie* predicting peace and repose in *Nun wandre, Maria* was anticipated in Schumann's *Mein Herz ist schwer*, Op. 25 no. 15. In such instances the concept of influence may be misleading; each composer translates his chosen poem, and a fortuitous similarity of poetic theme may suffice of itself to account for a certain musical kinship.

Much the same may apply to Wolf's much-discussed and well-documented harmonic affinity with Wagner. But even without Wagner, a German song-writer of the later nineteenth century would inevitably have evolved such a style for his own purposes, just as Liszt and Schumann had. It is related to word-setting. Wolf's expressive independent melodic lines with their ubiquitous falling tones and semitones in appoggiaturas adapted to the normal disyllables and feminine rhymes of German words and lyrics would inevitably have led, in contrapuntal combination, to chromatic clashes and recoils, tensions and resolutions; and the resulting idiom would be the natural medium for expressing complex poetry, such as Mörike's. The unity of the small-scale Wolfian song-form however requires that all such effects are recognizably related (whether by affinity or contrast) to some definable tonal centre; hence no doubt Wolf's already-quoted insistence on the essentially traditional nature of his harmonic language. This is used to translate poetic meaning in two main contrasting ways. Either there is a definite well-established home key or keys from which the tonality diverges at moments of stress or tension; or else, conversely, there is a fluctuating tonality, corresponding to a basic poetic mood of complexity or stress, from which a definite tonality emerges as the tension is resolved. *Der Mond hat eine schwere Klag' erhoben* is a good example of the former, *Mir ward gesagt* of the latter. Each type is of course only one particular aspect of a general procedure, an instinctive response in harmonic terms to the emotional tensions and relaxations of poetic language and structure.

Again, such effects are not new; they can readily be exemplified in Schubert, as in *Wehmut* and *Dass sie hier gewesen* respectively. But in Wolf they are all-pervasive; and they are among the most subtle and evocative of all his many correspondences between music and words. They have perhaps particular relevance for interpretative purposes; the harmony is often more helpful than the marked dynamics in determining the emotionally climactic moment of a song. There is for example a whole category of songs in which the introduction or reintroduction of the major tonic chord is delayed, so that its eventual appearance or reappearance will convey an ineffable sense of coming home, of peace and repose (*Verborgenheit, Wir haben beide*). Similarly in several songs the later introduction of the major form of a minor tonic suddenly lights up the music, throwing a word or idea into bright relief (*Wie sollt' ich heiter bleiben, Ob der Koran von Ewigkeit sei, Mignon III*). Examples of Wolf's evocative uses of harmony and tonality are endless. They may pervade a whole song, as in the major-minor contrasts of *Wohl denk' ich oft*, and more delicately in *Zitronenfalter im April*, and more subtly still in *Heut' Nacht erhob ich mich*, or in the moving contrast between chromatic richness and diatonic simplicity in *Anakreons Grab*. They may be reserved for special moments within a song, as in the harmonic play at the refrain 'Ach nein' of *In dem Schatten meiner Locken*, the musical pun that illustrates the verbal pun at the beginning of *Elfenlied*, or the single poignant dissonance for the sudden shadow that falls in the last line of *Auf ein altes Bild*. They can also be used quasi-pictorially for effects of chiaroscuro (e.g. *Verschwiegene Liebe*, but very many songs have something of this quality) and of colour (*Auf einer Wanderung*). Similarly, chromatic harmonies are deployed to symbolize e.g. the changing hues of the rainbow in *Phänomen*, or the blurred thought-processes of dreamy reverie on the last page of *Der Tambour*.

That latter passage can also serve to exemplify Wolf's modulatory procedures, which create musical form by re-creating poetic form. Mörike's wish-fulfilment fantasy, confronted by reality, cries to dream again: we hear this as clearly in the final piano interlude as in the poem. Similarly towards the end of *Fussreise* the modulatory interlude rejoins the original tonic just as a winding road leads back home, which is exactly the sense of the verses. Again, in *Komm, Liebchen, komm* the successive key-changes serve to symbolize the winding of material into a turban, a service which in both setting and poem is meant to have its own further symbolic overtones of devotion and love. In studying a Wolf song it is always rewarding to speculate on ways, however subtle or recondite they may appear, in which his harmony and tonality are moulded and shaped by the significance of the words.

So it is not surprising that Wolf, just like Schubert and Schumann in their song-writing, seems to have definite verbal associations with certain keys, key-signatures, or even accidentals. Many people imagine, or even actually hear, sharps as relatively brighter or more colourful than flats. Wolf, with his sense of perfect pitch, certainly had such associations. Sometimes his musical notation itself takes on an almost visual quality, as if extreme flat keys written in sharps, or conversely, were not just a matter of convenience but corresponded to some notion of dark or bright sonorities, as in *Komm, o Tod* or *Deine Mutter, süsses Kind*. Again, his favourite mediant key-sequences for brightening effect add four sharps to (or take four flats from) the key-signature with each change. Many examples are far more specific. Thus Wolf tended to use A major for spring songs (e.g. *Frühling übers Jahr, Wandl' ich in dem Morgentau, Gesegnet sei das Grün* as well as the spring choruses in *Das Fest auf Solhaug* and *Manuel Venegas*). Perhaps he heard this as a bright tonality; that would explain e.g. his sudden brief excursion into A major on entering the shining candlelit room of *Peregrina II*. Then A minor, conversely, would have a veiled or wistful quality; and this often seemed apt for women's songs in various moods of distress or bereavement (*Mignon III, Die Bekehrte, Das verlassene Mägdlein*). E♭ or A♭ major on the other hand embody moods of serene assurance, especially in love-songs (*An die Geliebte, Sterb' ich, so hüllt in Blumen*). Wolf often chose C major for plainness and directness of character or expression (*Der Soldat I, Gesellenlied, Königlich Gebet*), D major for moods of blissful contentment or elation, such as the euphoria induced by the freshness of a dewy morning (*Fussreise, Ganymed, Morgentau*), D minor for discontent or anger (*Das Köhlerweib ist trunken, Prometheus*) and D♭ (or C♯) major or minor, depending on mood, for music of night and dream, or death (*Um Mitternacht, Alles endet, Komm, o Tod*). The B-minor songs, especially those ending on the dominant, have a lingering indefinable bittersweet (*Lied eines Verliebten, Sagt ihm, dass er er zu mir komme*), while the tonality (not, strictly speaking, the key) of F sharp major is felt to be appropriate to a certain rollicking or boisterous mood (*Erschaffen und Beleben, Nein, junger Herr, Gudmunds zweiter Gesang*). That last correlation is so often and so clearly in evidence as to qualify it for motivic status. Even so, there are of course apparent exceptions to it, as to all these generalizations. Nevertheless a study of key-associations in Wolf will prove helpful for interpretative purposes, for example in considering the question of transposition. Wolf, like most other song-writers, sanctioned transposed versions of his songs, whether to suit particular singers or more generally to facilitate performance. Yet his sense of pitch and tonality was so finely-tempered, and so closely integrated with verbal connotation, that any departure from his original keys will fall short of the ideal or even falsify the composer's intentions.

Thus far the evidence suggests that Wolf's musical language, as he called it, has a vocabulary which is both deeper and more precise than ordinary tonal illustration or depiction. These are of course also found in abundance. Thus there are many, often brilliant, keyboard evocations of other instruments, whether singly (e.g. guitar in *Ein Ständchen euch zu bringen*, lute in *Das Ständchen*, violin in *Wie lange schon*, harp in *Gesang Weylas*, bagpipe in *Storchenbotschaft*, tambourine in *Klinge, klinge mein Pandero*) or in combinations (flute and drum in *Was in der Schenke*, fife and drum in *Der Schreckenberger*), culminating in complete military bands (*Der Glücksritter, Sie blasen zum Abmarsch*). There are several equally frank examples of the sonorous re-creation of movement. In addition to soldiers marching, and travellers walking, *passim*, there are people running (*Unfall*), writhing (*Wo find ich Trost*), sidling (*Harfenspieler II*), tiptoeing (*O wär' dein Haus*), whirling (*Was in der Schenke*), and thronging (*Der Feuerreiter*). Cats leap (*Die Zigeunerin*), rats scamper (*Der Rattenfänger*), deer step delicately (*Auf eine Christblume I*), butterflies, birds and bees fly (*Zitronenfalter im April, Die Spinnerin, Der Knabe und das Immlein*). Horses trot and canter (*Der Soldat I, Der Gärtner*, perhaps *Auf einer Wanderung*), gallop and race (*Der Feuerreiter, Der Soldat II*). Sound itself is freely translated. Donkeys bray (*Lied des transferierten Zettel, Schweig einmal still*), bells peal (*Zum neuen Jahr, St. Nepomuks Vorabend*), bees buzz (*Der Knabe und das Immlein*), guns fire (*Unfall, Der Jäger*), cocks crow (*Nixe Binsefuss*), nightingales trill (*Philine, Singt mein Schatz*), winds blow (*Begegnung, Lied vom Winde*), treadles whirr (*Die Spinnerin*), sleepyheads yawn (*Der Schäfer*), thunder resounds (*Der Jäger*) and there is even the swishing of whips (*Gesellenlied, Selbstgeständnis*). All this, and much more, belongs to the song-writer's stock-in-trade, and Wolf sets it out very attractively

13

and entertainingly. Such overtly onomatopoeic effects, though not always very subtle, are undeniably very close to language. But this is only the beginning; there are many deeper interconnections between sound and sense, such as the widely-spaced chords that suggest heights, depths and echoes, and hence hollowness and reverberation (*Cophtisches Lied I, Der Feuerreiter*), the processional exits that fade away in the distance (*Epiphanias, Nun wandre Maria*) or the analogous disappearing trick which makes the music vanish upwards into thin air (*Waldmädchen, Lied vom Winde*).

All these effects belong to a grand theatrical design of three-dimensional symbolism in several different modes. Just as differences of pitch convey ideas of height or depth in the vertical plane, so dynamics and texture add a further dimension of near or far, large or small, while rhythm and tempo suggest movement in the lateral plane, as it were across the field of vision. *Elfenlied* is a good example of such components and their possible permutations. Similarly the notion of 'vanishing into thin air' is made audible by a combination of musical metaphors. Movement is conveyed by upward runs, disappearance by diminuendo, thinness by bare fifths, airiness by a high register. Here *Nixe Binsefuss* offers a graphic illustration. Each of these spatial dimensions has a quasi-visual equivalent, with its own special feeling-tone. Thus if high staccato notes can signify an intermittently bright or twinkling effect, then low sustained notes may be expected to evoke darkness and depth whether as it were literally in the music of underground springs (*Frage und Antwort*) or night-time (*Um Mitternacht*), or figuratively for the depths of despair (*Alles endet*) or perhaps of the subconscious mind (*Fühlt meine Seele*). Similarly the upper reaches of the keyboard symbolize lofty thoughts, spiritual aspirations, the starry sky (*An die Geliebte*), while the left hand has rather more worldly gestures (*Geselle, woll'n wir uns*). In all these various modes and dimensions, repetition acts as an intensifier, creating a mood of trance or dream by the hypnotic effect of iteration, whether of phrases (*Im Frühling*) or notes (*Auf eine Christblume I*) or chords (*Gesang Weylas*). Again, the piano accompaniment can be quasi-vocal, as if it were singing or speaking the words already sung, in a reprise of their melody, with greatly heightened effect; as in *Ganymed* or *Komm, Liebchen, komm*. Keyboard autonomy also permits a quasi-symphonic motivic development reflecting the changing moods of a poem (*Auf einer Wanderung, Im Frühling*). Piano interludes can link contrasting sections of a song and so suggest continuous action, whether in narrative or ballad forms (*Ritter Kurts Brautfahrt*) or more rarely in the lyric mode (*Fussreise*). Often, as in both those examples, the postlude is akin to a stage exit, usually with a touch of character-study in the music. Not only do piano preludes set the scene, but their absence or curtailment can imply a breathless impatience, an eagerness to begin (*Die Spinnerin, Peregrina I*). Similarly, accompaniment structure not only provides a satisfying formal framework but enables significant inferences to be drawn from audible variations and departures from the expected design. Thus phrase-lengths may be interrupted or interchanged to suggest confusion (*Was in der Schenke*), or extended to make more room for expressive words (*Treibe nur mit Lieben, Auf dem grünen Balkon*); other such changes can symbolize different rates of passing time, e.g. by suggesting mental lethargy (*Im Frühling*) or eager anticipation (*Mein Liebster singt*). Again, these are dramatic or theatrical images of action and character. Keyboard marches or dances tell us what steps were taken, and with what air. Because of their individual independence, Wolf's piano parts can create not only décor and perspective (by distinguishing foreground from background, as in *Mein Liebster singt*) but also dramatic irony (by presenting two different levels of involvement simultaneously, as in *Bei einer Trauung*). It is not surprising then that the independent keyboard writing so often seems to have been the composer's primary inspiration, sometimes even taking precedence over the verbal stress, as exemplified in *Tretet ein, hoher Krieger* (181, note 2). This degree of independence or primacy recalls the orchestral writing in Wagner. In Wolf's own operas, the piano reduction often sounds more compelling than the orchestral version; and the same applies with even greater force to his scoring of his own songs (twenty of which were arranged for solo performance, two for incorporation into *Der Corregidor*, and two into *Manuel Venegas*). The resulting genre is intermediate between what might be called the compressed opera of his songbooks and the expanded songbooks of his operas. This hybrid has not proved fertile, and the works are rarely performed. Yet Wolf himself thought highly of them, and most of them date from 1890, one of his most prolific song-writing years. Their purpose was not only to reach a wider public but also to deploy even greater expressive power and device than the solo song-form could contain, whether by broadening the scene-painting (e.g. the thunder and lightning effects in *Prometheus*) or brightening the sound-painting (e.g. the added chromatic runs in *Der Rattenfänger*). But Wolf also invoked the orchestra for further depths of feeling (e.g. the horn counterpoints in *Gesang Weylas*). In general his aim was to convert his miniatures into oil paintings suitable for wider exhibition, whether in the concert hall or better still, the opera house. In his own creative imagination, his songs belonged not only in an auditorium but behind a proscenium arch.

In all this a major share of the musical expression inevitably falls to the pianist, not only in the ballad tradition of pictorial interludes, in which

Wolf was no doubt influenced by Loewe, but also in the newer vein of grandiloquent quasi-orchestral device found in Wagner transcriptions. That in turn led Wolf to the direct exploration of quasi-Wagnerian resonance and reminiscence, in quest of his own new concept of the Lied as a multi-dimensional singing theatre of the imagination, where everything is made of music – construction, action, character, plot and sub-plot, irony, narrative, gesture, mime, dance and song, costume, scenery and even stage properties and effects, including lighting. From all these copious solutions to the problem of sonorous equivalence, certain clear-cut musical ideas are heard crystallizing out, just as analogous ideas occur in Wagner, in the form of specially significant motifs.

But Wolf remains within the song tradition; the keyboard was always the foundation of the Lied form. Before Schubert could write his first great songs, it was first necessary for the piano to evolve so that it could render orchestral sound-effects, and thus enable Lied composers to compress the intensity of large-scale musical expression within the more personal and intimate frame of voice and keyboard, household and drawing-room, friends and lovers. That task of compression was dramatically eased for Wolf by the techniques of piano reduction used by Karl Klindworth and other fine pianists, including Liszt, in their vocal scores of Wagner operas. Wolf's own Wagner paraphrases (c. 1882) often presage the piano parts of his later songs, both in their part-writing and in their transcription of orchestral effects such as string runs or tremolandos. Thus the flashing brilliance of massed strings is metamorphosed into the wildly ebullient (and difficult) postlude to *Ich hab' in Penna*. The vibrating or pulsating effects of tremolandos express a powerful intensity of emotion, whether directly personal as in the postludes to *Wenn du mein Liebster* and *Wohl denk' ich oft* or mediated through such nature-symbols as the thunder in *Prometheus* and *Der Jäger*. In Wolf's earlier songs the independent piano part is sometimes derivative; thus a Heine setting *Wenn ich in deine Augen seh'* of 1876 has an accompaniment in the style of a Schubert impromptu. Again, Wolf soon adopted the Schumann style of a lyric piano solo, the melody of which also serves as vocal line; *Morgentau* of 1877, the earliest song Wolf adjudged worthy of publication, is a very successful example. But far more important was his timely discovery that real keyboard independence can confer a new dimension of meaning. For example the piano may depict a convivial scene, the singer's sad exclusion from which is expressed in the voice part, as in *Sie haben heut' Abend Gesellschaft* of 1878. This example too was obviously derivative (from Schumann's *Das ist ein Flöten und Geigen*) and not wholly successful. But it led to such supreme evocations of mood and character as *Mein Liebster singt*, where the independence of the piano part embodies the excluded

16

lover and his haunting serenade, while the vocal melody is the sad song of the lonely listener. Such works are *tableaux vivants* on which an imagined curtain rises. As Wolf told his friend Emil Kauffmann, he always imagined a background to each of his songs; and examples he gave (the goddess sitting on a reef in the moonlight, playing her harp, in *Gesang Weylas*; a chorus of wise men joining in the refrain of *Cophtisches Lied I*, to the sound of clinking glasses) go well beyond anything described in the text. It is this dramatic embodiment of the lyric moment that creates Wagnerian resonances in Wolf's mind, especially when the words of the poem he is setting run parallel with passages or phrases in Wagner's libretti. In *Die Geister am Mummelsee* for example, where the poem speaks of a funeral procession ('Totengeleit') the piano part is reminiscent of the cortège of Titurel ('Geleiten wir') in *Parsifal*. Again, the opening of *Auf eine Christblume I* has a certain kinship with the appearance of Erda in *Siegfried*, e.g. at 'kräftig reizt der Zauber'; Mörike's poem too describes a magic flower-like apparition and speaks of a 'Zauberreich'. Not only are the verbal and visual links with Wagner always vividly present to Wolf's creative imagination; Wolf himself, as the most complete and perfect Wagnerite of his time, was always ready to introduce deliberate Wagnerian allusions (for example to *Die Meistersinger von Nürnberg* in *Gesellenlied*) in accordance with contemporary ironic or parodistic convention. Furthermore, as we have seen, his own essential medium of keyboard style and texture had been strongly influenced by the piano reductions of Wagner's operas. Unsurprisingly, then, the resemblances between Wolf and Wagner are sometimes strong. But they are usually general, not specific. Wolf's detailed knowledge of Wagner's scores and stage action, which so strikingly informs his critical writings, helps to protect him against involuntary allusion and unconscious plagiarism. The affinity goes far deeper, down to the very roots that both music and language have in common. It is the same kinship that Schubert shared with Mozart. The masters of song learn from the masters of opera; the motive power of music-drama is converted into the lyric mode.

In this way the expressive elements of music, described above, had already been taken very close to language in the earliest songs of the nineteenth century, notably those of Schubert and Loewe. The latter's work is mainly illustrative and depictive; his ballads with their characteristic piano interludes are the sonorous equivalent of a storybook with pictures. Schubert's verbo-musical ideas are much deeper; they are more lyric than narrative, more poetry than painting, and include clear musical equivalents for the inner life of feeling. Wagner's motifs combine and expand ideas from both those sources. Wolf shared this common ancestry of a musical idiom already saturated with language. From this matrix, when poetry is added, the Wolfian song-motif crystallizes out. It has two main functions; to symbolize feeling, and to create structure. But it may take many different forms. Some of Wolf's musical equivalents have a clear verbal counterpart; others are more puzzling. Some have a long tradition; others are more personal. Many are difficult to define. But each is open to verification by direct experience of the music; and all are worth close attention for whatever they can tell us about the meaning or interpretation of a particular song.

They are also relevant to a closer study of the expressive or communicative powers of music and its analogies with language in those respects. But that would go beyond the present purpose. The following list, in no special order, is intended only to exemplify. Many further instances of these and other such correspondences will be found in the notes to the songs, though of course it is not possible to mention each motif each time it occurs.

Motifs

1. *Worship, submission, self-surrender*

A syncopated rhythm e.g. ♩♪♩ ♪♪♩ ♪ often appears, usually in open fifths in the left-hand piano part, in songs of which the words express the idea of worship, whether of God (*Zum neuen Jahre*, middle section) or of the loved one (*Wenn du mich mit den Augen streifst*). The reason for this correspondence is not readily apparent. Yet these persistent figures somehow seem to convey the impression of submission or self-surrender; it is as if the tonic stress had taken refuge by hiding away within the bar-line. Certainly this effect is elusive, and is likely to be lost if there is any suspicion of overt syncopation, thus ♪♩ ♪ or too strong an accent on the main beats. But the resemblances among songs otherwise as diverse as *An die Geliebte* and *Und willst du deinen Liebsten* seem directly attributable to this rhythmic consanguinity. A more complex and very compelling example of this motivic syncopation is heard throughout the bass part of *Sterb' ich, so hüllt in Blumen*, where the effect of rapt self-surrender is unmistakable. In that context, and no doubt in others, the idea has Wagnerian parallels: cf. the 'Liebestod' syncopations of *Tristan und Isolde*.

2. *Childishness, weakness*

An analogous rhythm, thus ♪♪♪♪ or ♪♪♩♪ etc is frequently found in association with the idea of childish helplessness or weakness. The reason behind this equivalence is much clearer. These are the weak beats of the bar, and the allusive use made of them is very striking. Thus on the last page of *Der Genesene an die Hoffnung*, at the mention of the word 'child' ('wie ein *Kind*' etc) the piano rhythm is displaced by a semiquaver, and hence weakened, solely for the one bar in which that word occurs. Similarly in *Peregrina II* the off-beat accompaniment seems to respond to the word 'Kindersaal'. Other examples of this verbal association are in the opening bars of *Der Freund* ('ein sanftgewiegtes Kind') and again in *Nimmersatte Liebe* (at the word 'Mädchen', where the symbolism of emotional helplessness is particularly close and apt). More subtle, and movingly, the off-beat rhythm is heard all through the Harper's song *An die Türen*; the poem depicts a frail old man who has become 'still und sittsam', quiet and docile. Again there are Wagnerian analogues, as for example when the dead swan's wings hang limp ('matt hängen die Flügel') in *Parsifal*.

3. Smallness

This idea is conveyed by the repeated interval of the minor second, with the two notes played either together or consecutively, usually high in the right hand with small note-values, and often staccato or *pp*. The idea of the smallest possible interval lasting the shortest possible time is sufficiently clear. The motif in its basic form is used to illustrate an elf both in *Elfenlied*:

and in *Auf eine Christblume I*:

and is of course heard throughout *Mein Liebster ist so klein*.

4. Laughter, mockery, criticism

Another related effect, this time frankly burlesque, is that of the sharply rising or falling semitone, often in the form of an acciaccatura; and sometimes a mordent. This stands for the idea of laughter not wholly free from malice, as throughout *Rat einer Alten*. In that song and others such as *Abschied* it is also used to suggest the notion of criticism. Its elaborations include downward chromatic runs, whether in chords as at 'er aber lacht' in *Unfall* or in single notes as in the postlude to *Das*

Köhlerweib ist trunken, depending on the quality of laughter depicted. Even at its most mirthful it has a characteristically Wolfian bite and snap from its earliest appearance (in the 1878 piano piece *Scherz und Spiel*, evocative of children's games).

5. Unrest, unease

In other contexts, the inclusion of a sharply rising semitone conveys an entirely different idea. A repeated piano figuration of this kind

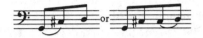

often corresponds to a mood of unrest, whether physical (*Genialisch Treiben*, piano prelude etc) or mental (*Storchenbotschaft*, piano, bar 34) or both (*Der Jäger*, left hand *passim*).

6. Manliness

That previous motif in turn is related to what seems to be an equivalent for the idea of manliness or virile force. Here the basic concept is a strongly ascending bass line, sometimes chromatic and sometimes diatonic, usually in a jerking dotted rhythm and almost always rising by step rather than by leap. Its simplest form could be exemplified thus:

It is perhaps revealing that Wolf sounds ill at ease with this motif in the 1888 songs. There its use is mainly light-hearted or mock-heroic, as in many of the Eichendorff songs; and when it is intended seriously, its effect can be bombastic and unconvincing, as in *Der Freund*. But in 1889 an analogous idea achieves a true and powerful expression. In the climbing octaves of *Prometheus*

(octaves in both hands)

Wolf conveys a supremely impressive effect of manly pride and determination. With this he said almost his final word on the subject; the motif is never heard again in the solo songs, and recurs only as the orchestral prelude to a rousing patriotic chorus, *Dem Vaterland*. No doubt it tended to sound too obviously representational for regular or extended use. The idea is a commonplace in Wagner; both he and Wolf could have heard it in Schubert (e.g. in *Lied eines Kriegers*) and earlier sources, where dotted rhythms in two- or four-time commonly imply military marches and hence doughty deeds.

7. *Gaiety, élan*

In Wolf's many songs in light-hearted vein there is an irresistible sweeping vitality and exultation. Among his most typical musical equivalents is the simple idea of a scale-passage rising to an accented tonic, usually in the piano treble, thus:

This is put to many fresh and pleasant uses, even expressing various shades of meaning, from swaggering, as in *Der Glücksritter*, to suavity, as in *Spottlied*. Its appearance is often significant. In *Gutmann und Gutweib* and *Ritter Kurts Brautfahrt*, for example, it tells us quite plainly early in the song that the high-flown style is burlesque or mock-heroic. In all contexts it is an indication that the composer is in high spirits, enjoying the humour of the verses and his music-making.

8. *Freedom, release*

The use of the rising horn passage, thus:

is almost a history, in itself, of musical equivalence in Wolf's songs. There is an immediate association with the chase, the huntsman, the open air; and sure enough the first extended deployment of this motif occurs in the *Jägerlied* of 1888. Towards the end of Wolf's creative life, the same quasi-literal association figures in *Gesegnet sei das Grün*. In between, the idea takes on a variety of illustrative meanings with the same verbal concepts of freedom, or release from constraint, underlying them. A clear example is found in *Verschwiegene Liebe*, where the brief appearance of this motif at the word 'frei' in the first verse serves to underline the poetic concept of thoughts flying free. In two songs in which a shot is fired (*Die Zigeunerin*, *Unfall*) the trigger is released to the sound of this motif, in an unmistakably significant metaphor, also no doubt related to the same basic concepts of hunting and the open air ('im Freien', in German). In Wagner, analogous motifs take on powerful overtones of nature-myth, as in the prelude to *Das Rheingold*; Wolf's influences were no doubt more firmly rooted in the field of Lied-composition, notably Schumann, Schubert, and their own earlier German-speaking folk-tradition.

9. *Contentment, the open air*

The ebullience of motif 7 above is an evident feature of Wolf's song-writing. Less apparent but no less real is his series of vocal melodic counterparts for the idea of serenity or happiness which, like motif 8 above, is usually found in association with the idea of the open air. It is perhaps relevant that Wolf himself was never happier than when out walking in the countryside; his typical outdoor tunes are readily harmonizable in the horn passages of motif 8. The following examples (among others) occur in verbal contexts of open-air elation. All are transposed for ease of comparison.

10. *Singing*

When Wolf has in mind the idea of singing as such, a different equivalent appears, a chain of rising and falling sixths in the voice part, thus:

This pattern, or a melodic line based upon it, occurs typically in songs within songs; whether those that have the word 'song' in the title (*Jägerlied*, *Spottlied*), or those that are about someone singing (*Der Musikant*) or even about birds singing (*Der Scholar*, at the words 'singen alle Vögelein'). The melodic curves of *Lied eines Verliebten* and of *Das Ständchen* also have something of this quality. We may think perhaps of the typical waltz or ländler, with which Wolf was wholly familiar. It is clear from the final section of *Abschied* how easily and pleasantly this motif, with its hint of yodelling, can be turned into a popular song and dance refrain. Again it embodies a feeling or frame of mind, rather than the actual sounds of singing. These have a related equivalent, treated with more bravura and breadth, as in the far-flung phrases of 'sing, sing' in *St Nepomuks Vorabend*. The notion of a rising vocal sixth as a symbol of an inward singing may perhaps have been absorbed by Wolf from such Schumann Lieder as *Wehmut*, Op. 39 no. 9.

11. *Adoration*
A close analogue of this 'singing' motif – basically thus:

is put to different though related uses. The sixths, in either the voice or the piano part, rise and fall more quiescently, more acquiescently; the singing is transfixed. The contexts in which this motif occurs show its meaning; all are songs of adoring love. Its significance is perhaps plainest in the postludes of *Frage und Antwort* and *Und willst du deinen Liebsten sterben sehen*. The latter song is built up from this idea in masterly fashion.

12. *Longing, yearning*
This feeling-tone is suggested by a recurring snatch of melody in the right-hand piano part, thus:

It is first heard in the ecstatic culmination of *Auf einer Wanderung*. This last page, beginning 'Ach, hier' cost Wolf much effort and revision. The motif he eventually devised to match Mörike's intensely yearning lines is not an independent construction. It is derived from previous material, as described in the notes to that song (27). But it evidently seemed so right for the trance-like mood it depicts that it was used again throughout the later Mörike song *Im Frühling* with transcending effect. The feeling of both these songs is one of rapt absorption; and the motif recurs in two Spanish songs of similar stamp, *Bedeckt mich mit Blumen* and *Nun bin ich dein*.

13. *Love I*
This is a direct musical metaphor. In Wolf's love-music, two strands of

melody (often in the piano right hand) converge, moving in two-part harmony towards unison. A simple example

occurs in the early and rather trifling little allegory of love *Das Vöglein* of 1878. Its later uses however are far more finely wrought, and highly charged with meaning. Their Wolfian source may well be the postlude of *Lebe Wohl*, in which the sad theme of farewell (cf. motif 22) sounds downward in the treble while the tenor voice strives upward to meet it. In the *Peregrina* songs this idea is extended into the passionate music that links the two as the postlude to the first song and the prelude and main thematic material of the second.

In this more complex form it recurs in the last song of all, *Fühlt meine Seele*.

In one guise or another it is a marked feature of many a fine love-song, as of the passionate duetting music in *Der Corregidor*. So manifest a metaphor needs no antecedents; but Wolf was no doubt familiar with, and may have been influenced by, the converging lines of Schumann's love-song *Nichts Schöneres*, Op. 36 no. 3.

14. *Love II*
The evidence for a second related love theme is offered with more

diffidence. But there is a recurrent strain of quasi-inversion of the idea of motif 13, so that two melodic lines diverge, e.g. in the simplest form

It happens that, musically speaking at least, inversion gives like results. If these ideas are in fact used thematically, we would expect them to mean another kind of love. There is some ground for conjecturing that such expressions may be an equivalent for what the Greeks called 'storge', the love between parent and child, as distinct from 'eros'. For example, these diverging but euphonious melodic lines occur in *Selbstgeständnis* (e.g. piano postlude), a song about a parent-child relationship, and in *Der Genesene an die Hoffnung* (piano at the last words 'in deinem Arm') where Hope is personified as a maternal and comforting figure. The motif also pervades the music of *Und steht ihr früh*, a song of ineffable physical tenderness but far removed from Wolf's typical passionate love-music. It might also be hazarded, for what it is worth, that the piano part of *In dem Schatten meiner Locken* is saying in Wofian terms that the singer feels towards her sleeping lover as tenderly as a mother towards her sleeping child.

15. Isolation, separation, loneliness

This is another example of primary musical metaphor. Again it is a piano figuration. The right hand has repeated chords, from which the left hand moves away downwards, usually in single notes. It is difficult to find a precisely apt verbal equivalent for this motif; yet the passages in which it occurs are clearly related in meaning. To mention first a generalized example—the descending bass of *Im Frühling* seems unlikely to bear any particular thematic significance, though the song is in fact about isolation. This is followed by some interesting, if vague, associations in the Goethe songs. Little is heard of this motif for over a year (no song that might have been felt to demand it was written during the interval). Then in *Schmerzliche Wonnen* it falls pat on the words 'when the soul is separated from the body'.

Perhaps Wolf's associations were becoming more definite from this moment on. At any rate there is no mistaking the meaning of the motif that goes grieving through the piano part of *Mir ward gesagt*, a song on the sole theme of the sorrow of parting. This is deeply felt music; and so we may feel justified in ascribing the same mood to *Auch kleine Dinge* and, even after an interval of another five years, to *Wohl kenn' ich Euren*

Stand. As with motif 13, the musical metaphor is manifest enough to need no model; but Wolf was certainly familiar with Schumann's *Ich grolle nicht*, Op. 48 no. 7 which conforms *passim* to the basic tonal pattern described above, and is also designed to express cognate verbal ideas.

16. *Companionship*

In songs expressing the idea of companionship, togetherness, Wolf sometimes makes effective use of chains of parallel thirds in the piano right hand. This motif is mainly concentrated in the one supreme example *Nun wandre Maria.* But it has a wider range; thus two songs about young soldiers marching off to the wars – *Sie blasen zum Abmarsch* and *Ihr jungen Leute* – have the piano's consecutive thirds in common while remaining in other respects musically dissimilar. The basic motivic metaphor of close harmony moving in step is clear enough, though rare in other Lied sources. Perhaps Wagner had an analogous imagery of parallelism in mind, though in a very different context, for the consecutive thirds of his 'Ring' motif, which as it were describe the segment of a circle.

17. *Night and wakefulness*

This motif occurs infrequently but so characteristically as perhaps to exemplify a deep interconnection between Wolf's creative inspiration and his personal experience. For many years he suffered from insomnia; and poetry about solitary wakefulness and movement at night evoked a definable though varied musical response. Repeated notes or octaves in the piano right hand are underlined by a wandering left-hand theme, also in single notes or octaves, as in the following three examples:

The first is from *Auf eine Christblume I* and the words are about movement in a nocturnal scene, as the deer graze in the twilight; the same music is later used to accompany the activities of an elf at midnight. The second is from *Gutmann und Gutweib* and the words are about the old folk lying in bed, deliberately keeping awake. The third is from *Alle gingen, Herz, zur Ruh* and the words are about the beating heart of a sleepless lover in the night. In *Lied eines Verliebten* the whole song is about being awake at night; much of the piano part assumes the basic pattern described. This motif first appears in embryo in the Körner *Ständchen* of 1877, the opening words of which describe the silence of the night; lovers' thoughts alone are awake. At the following idea of being surrounded by nocturnal phantoms ('mich umschleichen ... nächtliche Gespenster') the left-hand single notes surround the repeated right-hand chords, on both sides. The same association persists in Wolf's mind as late as 1895 when in Act II of *Der Corregidor* Frasquita keeps her nocturnal vigil (scene 3) or Manuela gropes her way in the dark (scene 10). The same Gestalt clearly informs each example.

18. *Night and sleep*
This is another manifest metaphor. A rocking, lulling movement (not unrelated to motif 12 above) usually a shifting semitone in cross-rhythm,

e.g. 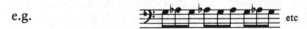 etc

in the middle register of the piano, regularly occurs in songs about night, sleep, dream, nocturnal reverie. We glimpse this movement in the early song *Die Nacht* (1880). But it is already fully-fledged by 1887 in *Nachtzauber*; and in its simplest and most basic form quoted above it evokes the idea of Night herself dreaming in *Um Mitternacht*. In *Der Freund* only the opening words are about sleeping – and only the opening bars contain this motif. Its use is evident in *Verschwiegene Liebe*, about night-time, and *St Nepomuks Vorabend*, a nocturnal scene. It requires no very lively sense of metaphor, whether in words or music, to pass from the idea of sleep and night to that of the serenity of death; an analogous motif is heard throughout *Komm, o Tod*. Unproblematical though this metaphor is, it has few clear antecedents. But similar cross-rhythms occur

27

in related contexts by Schumann (e.g. *Nachtlied*, Op. 96 no. 1, *Abendlied*, Op. 107 no. 6) and Wolf may have heard them there.

19. *Mystery, magic*

This is essentially a chordal progression, often dominant sevenths, in slow time, involving a chromatic shift in which two unrelated tonalities are juxtaposed. The corresponding voice part often moves up and down by octaves or fifths. There are also many instances of a change of keyboard register to point the contrast between the two tonalities. The effect is basically thus:

This idea is given a bewildering variety of treatment in contexts of which the common factor is musically apparent enough but impossible to define precisely in verbal terms, e.g. the music that greets the mysterious apparition of the storks in *Storchenbotschaft* (bar 16) and of the mermaid in *Seemanns Abschied* (bars 13–16). The mystic refrain of *Cophtisches Lied I* is also analogous. Among many related examples, one of the clearest occurs at the word 'magisch' in Act 1 of *Der Corregidor*. In addition to its textual correspondence with the poems, the motif is also found in association with the composer's own directions 'heimlich' in *Heimweh* and 'geheimnisvoll' in *Der Feuerreiter*, as if this were indeed his way of saying 'misterioso' in music. Schumann uses a similar chord-progression in the same sense, with impressively mysterious effect, in his song *Auf das Trinkglas eines verstorbenen Freundes*, Op. 35 no. 6, which Wolf greatly admired. A similar idea is conspicuous in Wagner's *Ring*. The juxtaposition of unrelated tonalities characterizes both the 'Tarnhelm' motif and that of Loge, god of fire and lies, all flickering flame and forked tongue. This in turn may have influenced the connection in Wolf's mind between this motif and the next.

20. *Deception*

A semitonal shift akin to the 'mysterious' motif 19 above, but less solemn and lighter in texture, may suggest the idea of deception or falsity. A good example occurs in *Geselle, woll'n wir uns*:

The point is not well documented, but for what it is worth similar chromatics are also heard in other songs, e.g. *Lass sie nur gehn* (bars 2–4) in passages where 'pretence' or 'deceit' is the idea behind the words.

21. *Narration, reflection*
A harmonic progression on these lines

although perhaps more of a mannerism than a motif properly so called, offers a revealing comparison with the 'singing' motif (10 above). Instead of lilting sixths in the voice part we have a rather ordinary formula consisting of a gradual shift in four-part harmony. The contrast is complete; nothing could be less like 'singing'. This piano motif shows a general correspondence in certain of its uses to the idea of 'thinking'. It occurs in particular where the voice part is about to introduce a new thought – *Der Knabe und das Immlein* (bars 20–1) – and in general in the opening bars of many songs in reflective mood, e.g. *Gebet*. For reasons already given (p. 10) the basic concept of four-part harmony in Wolf tends to reflect a meditative or overtly devotional mood, no doubt because of its association with the church music of hymn or chorale.

22. *Sorrow*
As with all these motifs, in particular 15 above, to which it is closely akin, this is not precisely definable in words despite the similarity of musical effect common to all the contexts in which it occurs. The basic idea is sorrow or despair induced by loss or deprivation; its musical expression is a recurring downward-tending melodic line, usually in the piano right hand, moving by step, in tones or semitones (mainly the latter), rarely more than three or four notes, rarely traversing more than a major third, thus:

This motif is present throughout Wolf's creative life and is heard in all four major songbooks. One of the first and finest examples is the deeply-felt *Lebe wohl*. Here the falling phrase

echoes the sound and sense of this sad word of farewell. In the Goethe volume this motif is prominent in the three Harper songs; despair is the theme of them all. It resounds throughout the only Mignon song which is specifically about deprivation – *Nur wer die Sehnsucht kennt*. In its later uses this motif has great simplicity and effect, as in the sad slow crotchet octaves that begin *Wir haben beide*. In the 1896 masterpiece *Wie viele Zeit* it is introduced, again in a simple form, at the end of the song (in the postlude) as a new idea. The unmistakable sadness of its presentation there may help with the interpretation of the song as a whole. There are also many examples of its use in a lighter vein; thus it is parodied in the opening section, where despairing love is derided, of *Frech und Froh II*. Of course this motif has obvious onomatopoeic overtones. Among Wolf's immediate precursors, both Schumann and Wagner use a falling semitone to convey the sound of a groan and hence the sense of affliction – Schumann in e.g. *Warte, warte, wilder Schiffmann*, Op. 24 no. 6, to illustrate the exclamation 'Oh!', which he has himself added to Heine's text for extra expressive effect, and Wagner in his so-called 'Wehe-motiv' in *Das Rheingold* and throughout the *Ring*. But the extension of this idea into (so to speak) meaningful phrases rather than exclamatory sounds is characteristically Wolfian.

23. Pathos, bathos

'Übermässig', the German technical term for 'augmented', also means both 'extreme' and 'extravagant' in common parlance; and chords of the augmented fifth, e.g.

are frequently heard in songs of powerful feeling. Like the previous motif its use may be serious or parodied; it illustrates both tense emotion and maudlin sentiment. Two examples of its serious application are *Grenzen der Menschheit* (bar 44 et seq.) and *Das verlassene Mägdlein* (e.g. bars 23–6); and two of its burlesque function: *Zur Warnung* (bars 1–2) and *Bei einer Trauung* (*passim*). Again the wide-ranging allusiveness of this particular chord is typically Wolfian; but the basic feeling-tone may well be related to the augmented fifth of Wagner's 'Nothung' motif expressing a concentrated longing for the liberating sword.

24. Light I

This idea is motif 23 writ large. Instead of (say) the notes C, E, G♯ together, passages in the tonalities of C major, E major, G♯ (= A♭) major are heard consecutively in ascending order. This effect is clearly associated in

Wolf's mind with the idea of increasing brightness, as in *In der Frühe* and *Morgenstimmung*. The culminating vision of *Auf einer Wanderung* and the transfiguration of *Ganymed* are also stated in these terms. This association of ideas perhaps lends added significance to other examples, e.g. *Die ihr schwebet*, *Das Ständchen*, and *Schon streckt' ich aus*.

25. Light II

The idea of light emitted at the same level of intensity, whether steady or discontinuous, shining or twinkling, is conveyed by sounds at the same level, whether sustained or staccato. Thus the high E on the third syllable of 'Mondenschein' in *Mausfallen-Sprüchlein* measures out two full minims of bright moonlight. In the piano right hand, high chord-clusters evoke the night sky graced by moon (*Wie glänzt der helle Mond*) or stars (*An die Geliebte*) beaming or sparkling respectively in slower or quicker repetitions, with lesser or greater staccato (cf. the equally nocturnal motif 17). The same musical imagery lights up the lamps in *Philine*, the candles in *Peregrina II*, the torches in *Die Geister am Mummelsee*. The equivalence of staccato notes or chords with points of light can be traced back to Haydn's *Creation* (e.g. at the moment when stars are created) and thence no doubt to earlier sources. This motif was thus well-established in the Lied from its inception, e.g. in Schubert's *Adelaide* (at 'im Gefilde der Sterne').

26. Detachment

Staccato notes can have further extended significance. Sometimes this is as it were literal, as when five separate notes symbolize five crimson drops in *Auf eine Christblume I*. Such equivalence is found copiously illustrated elsewhere in the Lied, notably by Brahms, who seems habitually to have imagined falling tear-drops as separate descending notes, usually in the right hand of the piano part. But Wolf's staccato can also be much more metaphorical; thus the light touch of the accompaniment in *Der Scholar*, and perhaps also in *O wüsstest du*, signifies ironic detachment.

27. Accusation, insistence, defiance

A different set of physical equivalents, perhaps related to notional gestures of hand or foot, arm or finger, is also conveyed by separate repeated notes or chords, this time strongly underlined or heavily accented. Into this category fall the four emphatically accusing crotchets in the piano part of *Sagt, seid Ihr es*, or the vocal phrase 'du falsche Renegatin', as if italicized by repetition, in *O wüsstest du*. Most characteristic is the two-fisted hammering and pounding in e.g. *Cophtisches Lied II*. But these ideas are powerfully combined in the punitive self-accusations of *Mühvoll komm' ich*.

28. Soothing, stroking

The converse of motif 27 is the gentle arpeggio idea of hands used in calm or serene gestures, whether of fingers straying upon an instrument as in *Gesang Weylas* and *An eine Äolsharfe* or in a symbolized combing of hair, as in *Und willst du deinen Liebsten sterben sehen* and *In dem Schatten meiner Locken*. These latter applications may well have been influenced by Schubert's *Versunken*, where also the hand on the keyboard offers an image, again directly derived from the verses, of a 'five-pronged comb'.

29. Wielding, carrying

Assured gestures of command are conveyed by falling left-hand octaves as in the kingly bidding of *Der Sänger*, or the creating power of *Gesegnet sei, durch den die Welt entstund*. By extension, octaves and chords in contrary motion can illustrate e.g. how it feels to have the width and weight of the world within one's hands, like the king in *Königlich Gebet*.

30. Simplicity, directness

When piano octaves are in unison with the voice, the effect is of naive or unfeigned utterance, whether of statement (*Der Schäfer*) or question (*Ob der Koran von Ewigkeit sei?*). It makes a typical narrative beginning in folk-tale or fairy-story vein, as in *Epiphanias* or *Elfenlied* respectively. There are some Lied precedents, notably the outset of Schumann's *Frühlingsfahrt*, Op. 45 no. 2, and also in the ballad style of Loewe and Schubert.

31. Questioning I

The opening phrase (motif 30) of *Ob der Koran* ends on the fifth note of the scale, which the textual question-mark invests with implied dominant harmony. Elsewhere in Wolf, and very frequently (just as in Schubert and Schumann), a poetic question evokes a musical dominant, and conversely. This tonal association begins early, e.g. at and after 'was soll ich tun?' in *Die Spinnerin* of 1878. It is so clear and strong that a well-defined transition to dominant harmony, e.g. at the last chord of a piano postlude, can as it were leave a question-mark hanging over the music, to show that the tone is enquiring or the outcome uncertain.

32. Questioning II

An added seventh serves to increase the intensity of interrogation, by seeming to insist on the need for an answering and resolving tonic chord. The dominant seventh (again as so often in Schumann) implies an enhanced sense of questioning, sharpened to the point of pleading or yearning, as repeatedly in *Wo wird einst*. As that example also shows, further nuances of meaning are achieved by the relation of those dominant sevenths to the home tonic key of the song.

33. *Frustration, discomfort*
The harmonic tensions of motif 31 and 32 can be tightened another notch into feelings of unassuaged frustration expressed (again in a highly Schumannian way) by dominant sevenths in third inversion, or by diminished sevenths. Here the unresolved questioning becomes so intense as to sound not only unanswered but unanswerable. Sometimes the result is just puzzlement or bewilderment, whether deliberately ironical (as at 'aber keine Ochse' etc in *Epiphanias*) or frankly comic (as at the impact chord in the last page of *Elfenlied*, which conveys the concussed effect of running one's head into a brick wall). But the feeling can also be one of self-inflicted punishment, as in *Mühvoll komm' ich und beladen*; and there the diminished seventh chords are memorably meted out in the two-handed hammering style of motif 27, as also in the postlude to *Blindes Schauen*.

34. *Pain, torment*
Motif 33 is only metaphorically painful, in its serious use. Literal pain, or spiritual anguish, are expressed by the active dissonance of semitonal clash. Sometimes this remains unresolved for extra effect, as at 'O weh', with the direction 'schmerzlich', in *Ein Stündlein wohl vor Tag*. More generally, as at the last word of *Auf ein altes Bild*, the dissonance occurs within a diminished or dominant seventh chord and is closely resolved downward, i.e. the essential component of the sorrow motif 22 is built into the tension of motif 32 or 33.

35. *Emptiness, transparency*
Motifs 31–34 derive from various ways of filling up or completing a given chord. When the harmony remains unfilled, and only the so-called bare octave or bare fifth is employed, usually in the upper right-hand register of the piano, the effect is one of emptiness or transparency whether metaphorical or literal. To these strains the diaphanous water-nymph dances in *Nixe Binsefuss*; they express the essential vacuousness of the vapid verses inset in *Zur Warnung*. And the unfilled sound of this chord has its own way of expressing an unfulfilled feeling or question, as at 'warum schreibt Er aber nicht?' in *Auftrag*.

36. *Enhanced awareness, awakening*
Of course all musical tensions, including those described in motifs 31–35 above, are relaxed or resolved by a movement towards tonic or other consonance. But there are several especially Wolfian aspects of this general procedure which seem to have quasi-verbal equivalents. Thus a movement from a chromatically inflected chord via a tonic six-four and added dominants towards a full close, as at the last three bars for voice

and piano in *Wenn du mich mit den Augen streifst*, conveys in its context a clear impression of outward or upward movement. The words at that point are about a metaphorical expansion or breaking-out of the heart in love, 'wenn es ausbrechen will'. It will not be mere coincidence that the same music in the same key recurred to Wolf's mind as a suitable setting for the end of *Wohl denk' ich oft*, where the same idea is presented in a more literal form as the singer's fame and stature grow and are recognized. The analogous idea of awakening is treated in the same basic progression each time the soul awakens, at the words 'Zeit ist's, dass sie sich ermuntre' in *Ach wie lang die Seele schlummert*. The moment of recall from sleep in *Schon streckt' ich aus* occurs on a six-four chord ('dein Bildniss').

37. Diminished awareness, falling asleep
The converse idea is audibly related by Wolf to the flattened sixth or seventh of the major scale. Thus, again in *Schon streckt' ich aus*, the F flats in the opening A♭ major bars lend added drowsiness to the verbal idea of relaxing tired limbs; the same harmonic inflexion has a similar function in *An den Schlaf*.

38. Unsteadiness, fluctuation
The waking sensation of losing control, or being overcome, whether by waves of bliss as in *Ganymed* or by surges of drunkenness as in the *Westöstlicher Divan* songs, has a rhythmic rather than a harmonic equivalent. Spiritual exaltation tends to divide common time into 3 + 3 + 2 quavers; mundane intoxication results in an even more syncopated movement.

39. Serenity, assurance
Rhythmic continuity and steadiness on the other hand conveys the contrary of motif 38. In particular the quiet sustained note is eloquent of peacefulness, whether in the voice ('still' at the end of *Morgentau*, 'stille ruh'n' in *Um Mitternacht*) or in the piano accompaniment, usually low in the left hand (the repeated semibreves that appear at the words 'süsser Friede' in *Wanderers Nachtlied*, or at the equally tranquil close of *Frage und Antwort*). This idea, like 37, is occasionally heard in Schumann; but such metaphors, in these instances as in others, belong to the general musical language of European tradition.

40. Euphoria
An expression that seems wholly personal and peculiar to Wolf however is so striking and pervasive as to qualify for motivic status despite its difficulties of precise musical definition; this is the persistent association of F♯ major (rarely G♭ major) with moods and feelings of ebullient

excitement, euphoric elation. Examples abound.

So do many other kinds of musico-verbal equivalence or congruence; the canonic movements of following or overtaking, the contrary motion of opposing ideas or forces, the chromatically drooping chords of diffidence or shyness, the harmonic or rhythmic expansion symbolising growth and development, and many another such tonal analogue. Some wholly defy verbal description; others, such as the rising-octave figure that graces the words 'Scherz und Liebe' in *Philine*, or the elongated nose-motif in *Abschied*, are clearly word-related but are confined to the one song in which they occur. The fertility and freedom of their invention, the concision and integrity with which they are subjugated to the Lied form; these are among Wolf's supreme strengths as a song-writer.

Thus far we have considered particular aspects of Wolf's idiom as they appear throughout the songs. The characteristic quality of his song-writing however lies in the way in which certain of these several aspects are combined in the music of each particular song. The Mörike *Jägerlied* setting is a clear and typical example of one possible result. Its date, early in 1888, shows that all the elements of Wolf's style were present from the very beginning of his maturity as a composer. That style impressed critics and connoisseurs, as well as ordinary music-lovers, by its originality. All the contemporary essays had the word 'new' in their titles. Heinrich Rauchberg's 'Neue Lieder und Gesänge' in the *Österreichisch-Ungarische Revue* of late 1889 was followed by Joseph Schalk's equally laudatory and far more influential 'Neue Lieder, neues Leben' in the *Münchener Allgemeine Zeitung* of 22 January 1890. Others refer to a new springtime, a new renaissance. These were no mere journalistic clichés. Nor were such reactions confined to musicians; the poet Detlev von Liliencron hailed Wolf as 'a king of the new art'. Wolf himself wrote, more modestly, of the novel aspects of his musical language. Yet he nowhere defined them; and the evidence of contemporary comment taken as a whole suggests that their essential originality was not wholly grasped, perhaps not even by their creator, much of whose song-writing is manifestly and avowedly in the main Lied tradition. He and his audiences felt that he was continuing the line of Schubert and Schumann, without radical departure; and indeed there are obvious similarities, including the notable intensity and spontaneity of composition that characterized Wolf's spate of song-writing in 1888 no less clearly than Schumann's in 1840 and Schubert's in 1815. Basically similar too, despite the superficial differences much exaggerated by later commentary, are his choice and treatment of words. Well over half his texts have no pretension to poetic supremacy or even

35

excellence. Even the great poets can be treated cavalierly; not only can the accentuation go astray, as so often in the Mörike volume, but the subtler declamatory effects are quite often second thoughts inserted at proof stage. Again in the Mörike volume, *Er ist's* has repeated phrases and *Das verlassene Mägdlein* uses an unauthentic text, no doubt under the influence of Schumann in both instances. On occasion Wolf could repeat a whole strophe (*Benedeit die sel'ge Mutter*) or tacitly omit one (*Geh', Geliebter*), without any textual justification. He could embellish poems with his own insertions or inventions (*Die Zigeunerin*) or simply mistranscribe them (there are several textual errors in the manuscripts and first editions). He could deliberately add a new meaning unintended by the poet or translator (*Wer rief dich denn?*). Even his much-discussed practice of calling his songbooks 'Gedichte von' (poems by) Mörike, Goethe or Eichendorff was anticipated and perhaps prompted by Schumann. The same applies to his choice of translations, for example from the Spanish.

Nevertheless Wolf was indeed original, and in four main ways. First, he seems to have planned in advance the contents of each volume (e.g. the Spanish Songbook, as described in a letter of 12 November 1889 to his sister Käthe) rather as if the artistic unit is not only the chosen poem but the songbook considered as representative of the poet or source. Secondly, it was his practice to preface a performance of each song by a recital of the text; thus the words were separately acknowledged as a vital part of the artwork's content, as well as of its form. Thirdly, Wolf was reluctant to set a poem which he considered had already been successfully composed – a view which (like the title 'Gedichte') presupposes that a musical setting is more like a translation or objective critique than a purely personal commentary. His songbooks are thus perhaps designed as anthologies, as homage, and also as critiques or translations. They make no sense, have no being, apart from the words which have breathed their life and essence into the music. Fourthly, this essence is dramatic. Wolf's art is a means of framing, embodying, presenting, enacting, the life of words. Hence no doubt his lifelong obsession with the search for suitable opera libretti, his constant preoccupation with Wagner, his feeling that he was after all 'only a song-writer'. At the very moment when his true genius was first becoming manifest to himself and the world, he could still write 'For the moment they are admittedly only songs'.* On the very day when his inspired Mörike outburst began, he could still be busying himself with the task of extemporizing a whole comic opera at the keyboard.† Even

---

* letter to Josef Strasser, 28 March 1888
† letter to Edmund Lang, 22 February 1888

with three great song-books completed he could still lament 'I'm beginning to think I have reached the end of my life. I can't go on writing songs for another 30 years'.* And in a further letter to Grohe comes the astoundingly anguished cry 'I really and truly shudder at the thought of my songs. The flattering recognition as "song-writer" disturbs me down to the very depths of my soul. What does it signify but the reproach that songs are all I ever write, that I am master of what is only a small-scale genre?'.† Six years later, Wolf's eventual madness took the form of, and was probably precipitated by, a megalomaniac obsession with operatic composition and performance.

There were perhaps three main reasons for this fixation. Songs were still generally held to be an inferior art-form, a belief that had earlier inhibited Schumann. Secondly, Wolf as an expressive and communicative composer craved the maximal audiences attainable only through opera and symphony. Lastly, and most significantly, his genius was in fact for drama in music, though in a condensed form. No wonder he arranged his songs into composite volumes comprehensive enough to yield extended recitals and programmes of planned contrasts, with at least a potential appeal to a mass audience. Further, each major songbook contains linking motifs designed to integrate the single songs into a larger conceptual scheme (as with Eichendorff songs 9–10, Mörike 2–3, Goethe 39–40, Spanish sacred songs 8–10, Italian 42–3). The songbook is thus itself the large-scale dramatic form; and in consequence the musical style changes with each songbook.

In the majority of the Mörike songs for example it is the verbal music of the words that seems to be the essential inspiration, and the vocal and instrumental melodic lines that carry the primary musical current, in response to the poetry. In the Goethe volume the proportion of such songs is significantly less; and with the Spanish songs the trend away from verbal music is even more marked. Rhythmic ideas, accompaniment figures, formal constructions, begin to dominate the musical expression. It seems that this aspect of Wolf's art, like all the others so far considered, is directly related to the texts he selected for setting.

A hypothetical example may make this clearer. Let us imagine some Wolf settings, for voice and piano, of English poetry; say Shakespeare's sonnets. Some of these have a verbal melody to which Wolf would surely have responded in terms of musical melody as the basic inspiration.

> Shall I compare thee to a Summers day?
> Thou art more lovely and more temperate:

---

* letter to Oskar Grohe, 1 June 1891
† 12 October 1891

Those lines might have begun to sing in his mind, taking shape as a melodic line following the questioning and answering inflexions of the words and bringing out their emotive content – perhaps by prolonging each 'more' on a higher note so that the melody can curve down and hesitate gently before 'lovely' and 'temperate'. The idea of a tenderly lulling accompaniment, say in the worshipping rhythm of motif 1 above, might then have presented itself. The noble serenity of the sonnet could have suggested a primary tonality of E♭ or A♭ major, perhaps with a brightening allusion to a sharp-sounding tonality (say C♭ or F♭ major) at the word 'Summers'. Against this background we can imagine an endearingly evocative musical treatment of the next line:

> Rough windes do shake the darling buds of May,

and so on to a fine ringing conclusion at

> So long lives this, and this gives life to thee.

This would be Wolf in the Mörike songbook.

Other sonnets however might have been translated in terms of a rhythmic idea in the first instance.

> Alas 'tis true, I have gone here and there,
> And made my selfe a motley to the view,

We can imagine how those lines might have suggested a glumly clownish piano figuration. Its interest would of course be partly melodic, since it would have to leap up and down, here and there, and generally make itself a motley to the ear. But the primary idea would have come in the shape of a repeated rhythmic piano figuration, quite independent of the stress of the words, which could be left to make their own way along a melodic line following their spoken inflexions. The piano part might easily be a self-contained solo, of great formal perfection. The bittersweet mood of the sonnet could have suggested the key of B minor, with harmonic tensions moving towards a hopefully inquiring dominant in the piano postlude after the last line:

> Even to thy pure and most most loving breast.

This would be Wolf in the Spanish Songbook.

The first example assumes a melodic response, the second a rhythmic response, to a poetic idea. Each was imagined as being direct and immediate. In the second example however the music might easily sound less emotionally involved, more deliberately concerned with creating a mood of its own to match the poem, and so more dominant in the partnership with words.

With these points in mind we can trace a development in Wolf's song-writing. What may be called the primary melodic impulse is a striking feature of most of the Eichendorff and Mörike songs and many of the Goethe songs. In the mature Eichendorff-Lieder it is as if the characters bring their own melodies with them; they begin with the soldiers' songs of *Der Soldat* and continue with a seaman's chanty, a students' chorus, the serenades and minstrelsy of assorted musicians. People and places are conceived as actors and scenes in the Mörike volume also; but there the characters and landscapes are drawn with far more depth and definition, often with an added narrative element in such extended ballads as *Der Feuerreiter*. The music is correspondingly more intense and diversified, and the evocations of folk-song (*Das verlassene Mägdlein*) and other simple and popular strains (e.g. student song in *Nimmersatte Liebe*, Viennese waltz in *Abschied*) are used, not as ends in themselves, but as a means of adding new dimensions and perspectives. The resemblances among songs of this first mature period however are mainly melodic; even the favoured four-part harmony is quasi-vocal in character, as in *Gebet*. The songs are almost invariably in two- or four-time, in direct correspondence with the prevailing metres. The music is thus a continuous response to the verbal music and emotion of the words; in particular there are identifiable musical equivalents for poetic concepts. To match Mörike, Wolf had not only to become motivically more inventive but also to devise larger-scale themes and structures designed to convey a sense of panorama and movement both spatial (*Auf einer Wanderung*) and temporal (*In der Frühe*). In consequence, some of the piano accompaniments seem orchestral in range and scope (*Neue Liebe, Der Feuerreiter*). This sense of extended musical frontiers and horizons, almost entirely absent from the Eichendorff songs of later 1888, becomes even more manifest in the Goethe settings of 1888–9.

Here the lyric style is just as intense, just as motivic, even within the one-page miniature frame (*Blumengruss, Gleich und Gleich*). But the ballad style, conversely, has become more extended and diffuse (*Ritter Kurts Brautfahrt, Gutmann und Gutweib*) and the piano writing even grander in conception (*Prometheus, Mignon 'Kennst du das Land'*). Further, Goethe's poetry offers a new rich source of quasi-dramatic background and effect. Both Eichendorff and Mörike had incorporated their lyrics into their *Novellen* or prose tales. Wolf set several such examples. But these poems are separable entities, whereas the interspersed lyrics in Goethe's *Wilhelm Meister* are integrally related to plot and character, so that Wolf's music designedly sets context as well as text. Much the same is true of the *Westöstlicher Divan* poems. The characters of Hatem and Suleika are not merely costume parts assumed by the poet and his mistress; they also inhabit a whole secondary world, a notional Orient peopled with other characters from cup-bearers to sultans. Thus Goethe's poetry in Wolf's representative selection has a greater range of ideas and thought than Mörike's, and far greater than Eichendorff's. The musical style undergoes a corresponding transition. This collection is both musically and poetically the least homogeneous of all. There is no clearly definable Goethe style, as there is a Mörike or a Spanish style; the music inclines to one or the other. For example, the late Goethe song *Die Spröde*, which dates from the same period as the first Spanish songs, is like them in style. Similarly from the Persian and Mohammedan world of the *Westöstlicher Divan*, with its strong sense of external influence enriching the German poetic tradition, there is no great journey to the Spanish songbook, which not only contains fine verse by great foreign poets (e.g. Cervantes, Lope da Vega, Camoens) in skilled translation (by Heyse and Geibel) but also offers the elements of national character and local colour that Wolf increasingly needed for his musico-dramatic projections.

At the same time his stylistic development undergoes a further change. He had now exhausted German poetry of the necessary quality and quantity. But the translations to which he turned were no longer, despite their technical excellence, so fertile a source of direct verbal inspiration. In the Spanish songs Wolf is confronted with a series of rather flat lyrics, each mainly on one invariant theme or idea, each in its way formally perfect, often with a cunningly intricate rhyme scheme. Thus it is less the lyric as such than the substructure of ideas and concepts that serves as the foundation for musical setting. The result (already foreshadowed by some of the *Westöstlicher Divan* songs, such as *Was in der Schenke waren heute*) was a new autonomy for the composer, who now became less dependent on an intuitive response to poetry. Wolf the partial poet was gradually supplanted by Wolf the complete musician. Rhythmical motifs, dance patterns, accompaniment figures, recurrent refrains, formal structures, begin to dominate the musical expression. The piano parts of some of the songs (including some of the very finest, e.g. *Auf dem grünen Balkon*) stand up as self-contained instrumental solos. Sometimes, as in that song, the vocal melody is a brilliant embroidery on the piano part; sometimes it is tacked on less dexterously. The similarities among the songs are harmonic rather than melodic. Musical equivalents for poetic ideas are fewer and less conspicuous. Triple time makes its first large-scale appearance, showing that the metre of the words is (rightly) regarded as of secondary importance. Folk music, nature studies, broadly humorous songs, ballads, all gradually disappear. The themes and styles that persist in the Spanish volume are the religious (the first ten songs) and the erotic

40

(almost all the rest); and these two strands become more personal, more intense, and more closely interwoven.

The six Keller songs that followed in May and June 1890 reverted to the previous themes of character study and psychology, with occasional symbolic allusions to nature (as in *Wandl' ich in dem Morgentau*). Here, as before, poetry is the main source of inspiration. But in these songs Wolf was working against the grain of his own development, which may help to account for the sometimes perceptible effort entailed in their composition. Six months later we come to the first Italian songs. Here, in what may be called Wolf's third and last creative period, the two previous styles achieve an unexpected and resplendent synthesis. Most of the verses are insubstantial, and again the instrumental character of the music is unmistakable; indeed in the later Italian songs the texture suggests string quartet writing. But the affinities among the songs of this volume are now again melodic as well as harmonic and, in the later works, rhythmic. What seems to have happened is that Wolf is once again emotionally involved in the words as such, especially in the love songs. All the lyrics are anonymous; all have the same translator, Paul Heyse (as compared with only about two-thirds of the Spanish Songbook, in each respect). They thus present the composer, by his own instinctive choice, with a polished and uniform poetic style that has no strong creative personality of its own. The verses are a smooth blank page on which to inscribe Wolf's knowledge of human feeling. There are no religious themes; all the poems are in some sense love songs. In consequence the style becomes unified and integral. The music in overwhelming the words raises them to its own level of exaltation. They then demand and receive a treatment in terms of primary melodic impulse, much as in the Mörike songs. At the same time the musical technique has become refined. The keyboard is far less dominant. The piano interlude disappears; motifs are unobtrusively scaled down to fit the miniature frame. In general, the simplest of means are used; melodies moving by step or in repeated notes, a basic four-part style with plain harmonies and restrained dynamics, often culminating in a few murmured words and a quiet postlude. The emotive force of the Mörike style is here allied to the formal perfection of the Spanish style; and the result, in the brief compass of the short Italian lyrics, is often transcending.

Thus Wolf's development, in his tragically short creative life, traversed a world of the imagination so wide that two great poets once divided it between them. In their *Lyrical Ballads*, Coleridge wrote of 'persons and characters supernatural or at least romantic' and Wordsworth of 'such feelings as will be found in every village and its vicinity'. Those contrasts might very well serve to define Wolf's range from the Mörike volume to the Italian Songbook; and at all stages he is capable of a truly Wordsworthian sense of 'the loveliness and wonders of the world before us'.

This introduction has sought to give some general account of the innumerable and complex ways in which Wolf's music responds to different aspects of a poem and to different kinds of poetry.

This is a rare phenomenon, and one that may still present difficulties of appreciation from the purely musical point of view, just as it did in Wolf's own day. Yet it is also real and rewarding, as anyone who has felt the force of its twofold impact can testify. Wolf's music at its best has a quality of bright wounding beauty, better felt than described. This quality is no doubt derived from the way in which the songs came into being – the intuitive precise penetration that reaches the heart of a poem and absorbs and re-creates its essence in an illumination of music. Compared with the whole range and resource of all that music has to offer, this may be a limited gift. Yet it is surely precious and enduring. Wolf expressed the truth about the human condition as he apprehended it, as keenly and as stringently as he could. It was his assigned task, he thought, to cultivate that gift to the furthest limit of his powers.* When he could no longer compose, as he told Rosa Mayreder, he was fit only to be thrown on the dung-heap.

It was his sense of purpose and mission that gave Wolf's life and art their fierce concentration, their characteristic burning intensity of expression. His vision was limited by its close focus on those points where words and music intersect or coincide. But within that specialized lyric field he has claims not only to greatness but supremacy. Thus Hugo Wolf has attained, in Frank Walker's words, 'a modest place among the immortals, in the hierarchy of musicians, and the grateful love of inarticulate humanity, for whom he sang of truth and beauty'.†

---

* letter to Wilhelm Schmid, 14 June 1891
† Frank Walker, *Hugo Wolf* (Dent, 1951)

The Songs

I. The first published songs

At the beginning of 1887 Wolf's life was at crisis-point. He had promised much as a composer, and achieved little. He had shown temperamental incapacity to profit from academic training, or to make a living as a teacher of music. He had worked for three years as a critic on the fashionable weekly *Wiener Salonblatt*; and this function, though useful as a vocation and a discipline, had somewhat inhibited his creativity. But in May 1887 he composed his most original and successful work of this first period, the *Italian Serenade* for string quartet. At least he was then aware of his genius, though its actual nature remained unclear to him. Wolf's first masterpiece closely followed his last critique; no doubt he sensed the development of new musical skills and powers. But then his father was suddenly taken ill, and died on 9 May. Hugo was inconsolable; his cyclic disposition reverted to depression and inertia. From these doldrums he was rescued by Friedrich Eckstein, whose library and conversation had enriched and influenced the young Wolf in his earlier student days in Vienna and who now performed the further signal service of persuading a publisher (perhaps with some financial inducement) to bring out some of Wolf's songs. From his manuscripts of many years the composer selected the following twelve. They contain a few favourites, and much fine music, but no masterpieces. Yet this timely publication, by inducing a glow of creative euphoria and focusing it firmly on song-writing, must have helped to set off the blaze of achievement that followed throughout 1888.

43

Six songs for a woman's voice

1 Morgentau (*Morning dew*)

6–19 June 1877   D major   e'–e''

Morning breezes have fanned away the sultry night, and the meadows laugh blissfully in their spring array; from the dark tree a bird sings its sweet dawn-song softly, as if in a dream. The rosebud lifts her head uneasily, for the sweet song has thrilled her through; her profusion of petals unfolds more and more, and from them a drop of dew flows like a secret and silent tear.

The poem is described as being taken 'from an old song-book'. It has no great merit or originality, and we need not regret its anonymity. But the seventeen-year-old Wolf was evidently much pleased with it, and our first introduction to his work is a charming one. The young composer, though evidently writing under the influence of his great predecessors, especially Schumann, shows in this unpretentious song an original and authentic talent of a high order.

The melody is beguiling, and the ostensible simplicity of the accompaniment conceals much deft art. Towards the end, for example, at 'mehr und mehr enthüllet' (more and more unfolds) there appears a new melody, extended by a new unfolding harmonic progression. These lead gracefully into the final word 'still' (silent), which is lovingly prolonged for two whole bars while under it the right-hand piano part recalls the opening vocal melody to round out the picture and round off the song. This delightful passage, and indeed the whole work, evoke the unaffected freshness of youth as well as dawn; the song is well named.

NOTES 1. On Wolf's manuscript the text is ascribed to 'Albert Reinhold'; in the first edition this is amended to 'aus einem alten Liederbuch'. Frank Walker suggests that the source may well have been a book of handwritten poems copied out by Wolf's father for his mother in their courting days.* One such collection dated 1849 (two years before the marriage) was preserved by Wolf among his own books.

---

* op. cit.

2. The Schumann influence is manifest both in the general piano-song technique (melodic line doubled in voice and keyboard) and in the specific echoes of *Dein Angesicht*, op. 127 no. 2, in the semiquaver movement of the accompaniment. Despite the surface disparity of the two poetic themes, life in Wolf and death in Schumann, there is sufficient congruence in their underlying sadness of mood and especially in their identity of vocabulary ('Traum' and 'mild' juxtaposed in both texts) to account for the musical links.

3. But there are more interesting affinities between this song and Wolf's own incomparably greater *Fussreise* (22) written eleven years later. The basic mood is similar – enjoyment of the freshness of the morning. *Fussreise* too is in D major, ends with the same rising scale passage to the keynote, and has as a special feature the progression from a dominant to a tonic on the mediant of the keynote to the dominant and tonic of the keynote itself (i.e. C♯, F♯, A, D). In *Morgentau* this progression occurs briefly at the word 'Lenzespracht' (spring array); in *Fussreise* it forms the essence of the piano interlude that reintroduces the main theme on the last page, in each case leading back into the original melody. None of these points is common in Wolf's music and the last two are rather rare. This may be just coincidence, or at most an involuntary reminiscence, as in note 2 above. But there is another and not unpersuasive explanation, namely that the idea of morning freshness suggested to Wolf a musical expression of the kind described.

4. The sustained 'still' is motif 39.

2 Das Vöglein *(The little bird)*

2 May 1878 E major c♯'–f♯''

The bird flutters down from the branch, and then in the same instant flies gaily back again.

Now it is near to you, now hiding; now it comes close again, playing and teasing.

Try to touch it, and you'll be tricked; off it flies, in a flash, mockingly away. But just be quiet and wait. Soon it will come hopping round your hand again; and then if you're quick it really can't escape you.

And is it really so hard just to await that moment? Look around you; see the flower-filled garden.

Never despair; let the bird have its own way. You can manage without it until you catch it.

Even then it won't bring you very much; but how very sweetly it can sing.

Hebbel was a dramatic poet of some importance. His lyrics are for the most part well-turned and original in form and imagery, and sometimes (as in the much-anthologized *Abendgefühl*) beautifully singable; but their allegorical content can tend towards the ponderous. The intended significance of this early lyric about the elusive nature of happiness is rather heavily obtrusive; yet the neatly-rhymed short lines with their atypically lively rhythm invite a correspondingly light and deft musical setting. The words thus present a mild technical problem which the young composer solves with some distinction. The vocal melody has an engaging lilt; the music combines graphic allusions to flight and song with a youthful wistfulness that still appeals. The accompaniment flutters and trills, swoops and soars, or alights and hops (at 'hüpfen') and generally suits the musical action to the word with an engaging felicity that lends wings to the poet's metaphor. It is perhaps not irrelevant that Wolf himself at this time had just met the first love of his life, Vally Franck.

NOTES 1. The lyric was entitled *Das Glück* (Happiness) in the earliest editions of Hebbel's poems. No doubt the bird's symbolic connotations included love, for both poet and composer; and the theme proposed in the very first bar of the piano prelude is a fledgling form of Wolf's main musical equivalent for the idea of love (motif 13), from which he was later to fashion so many phrases of exquisite refinement.

2. Similarly the staccato hopping is a forerunner of the more subtle and more integral treatment of the same image in *Jägerlied* (16). Note too how the vocal line is made to hop, skip and jump at 'hüpfen', 'versteckend' etc, by means of a quaver rest inserted between the syllables – the kind of operatic effect to which Wolf very rarely resorted.

3. A particularly neat piece of musical equivalence, this time not merely rare but unparalleled in the Wolfian repertory, occurs at the word 'still!' (be silent); this injunction to be quiet and wait evokes three quaver rests and an extra bar deftly spliced in among the otherwise wholly regular four-bar pattern.

4. Cf. Schumann's duet setting Op. 79 no.15 – perhaps Wolf's source for the text as for the 3/8 rhythm, though the latter is in effect imposed by Hebbel's dactyls.

3 Die Spinnerin *(Spinning song)*

5–12 April 1878   A minor   d#'–f#''

Oh my dear mother, I can spin no more, I can sit no longer in my little room, in this narrow house.

The wheel stops, the thread breaks; I must go outside, mother dear.

The spring sun peeps brightly through the panes; who now can sit indoors, who can stay in and be busy? Oh let me go; let me see if I can fly like the birds.

Oh let me see, let me hear how the brooks flow, the breezes blow, the flowers grow.

Let me pluck them and garland my brown hair with bright green.

And if young men come by in wild gangs then I'll trot, I'll run, not stand still;

I'll hide myself here behind the hedge until they've gone by on their noisy way.

But if one quiet young man should happen to bring me the very flowers I want for my garland, what should I do?

Might I not give him a nod and a friendly smile, dear mother, and rest by his side?

There are several Rückert settings by Schubert; all are superb. This early Wolf setting offers mainly some interesting anticipations of the mature composer; yet we can share the eighteen-year-old's exhilaration in weaving his contrasting ideas together so cleverly within a frame of theme and variations, matching the naïve passion of the poem by fiery outbursts with a highly original turn of musical phrase. As Wolf commented later in life on other examples of his early work – 'man spürt schon das kleine Wölferl darin' – you can tell it's a Wolf-cub. Many of the effects are brilliant and novel, such as the way in which the voice begins without preamble, like an involuntary cry of impatience and frustration. Again, the idea of scoring the springtime music for crossed hands (in the piano interlude after 'fliegen wie Vögelein') so that the left hand sketches out its flight motifs in the upper reaches of the keyboard, could have occurred to no one but Wolf; nor could the notion of so arranging a selection of themes in the postlude as to give a nine-bar summary of the poem – pent-up passion, springtime yearning, hesitant indecision. But the total impression is of self-conscious display rather than transmuted poetry, and the finely-woven tapestry contains too many loose ends.

NOTES 1. Half the song is highly original, half rather unenterprisingly derivative. The running and trotting triplet semiquavers for the idea of boys and girls coming out to play (bar 43ff.) are the property of Schubert, *passim*, while the idea of ending a song of unstilled longing on the dominant seventh (motif 32) is an infringement of the copyright established by Schumann in *Im wunderschönen Monat Mai*. Either of those mentors might also have suggested the questioning and drawn-out dominant (motif 31) as the apt treatment of 'was soll ich tun?' (bars 68–9).

2. More specifically Wolfian, however, is the use of two converging voices as a theme of yearning (motif 13), first modestly in the opening bars and then more outspokenly in left hand chord and right hand octaves (bars 12–13) in the passionate accents of the Spanish Songbook. Similarly the fluttering wings of bars 24–5 later become the piano part of *Bitt ihn, o Mutter* (162), also an address to a mother about the wayward ways of young men and perhaps involving some degree of involuntary reminiscence.

3. The older Peters edition omits to tie the first two C sharps in bar 14.

4. Cf. Loewe Op.62 (I) no.3.

47

4 Wiegenlied im Sommer *(A summer lullaby)*

17 December 1882   F major   c'–f''

The last rays of the setting sun are now sloping down from the hillside; my child lies in its cradle, all the birds are in their nests, all save one small songster trilling far out into the twilight 'Good night, good night; dear child, good night!'

The cradle rocks gently, the clock ticks to and fro, the flies are softly humming. Leave my child in peace, you flies; what is it you are humming so secretly? 'Good night, good night; dear child, good night!'

Birds and stars and all things, all around, love my child so dearly, and so do the angels, even more; they cover my baby with their wings and sing softly 'Good night, good night; dear child, good night!'

No doubt Wolf was closely acquainted with the lullabies of Mendelssohn (Op. 47 no. 6) and Schumann (Op. 25 no. 14) as well as the far more famous exemplars of Schubert (D498) and Brahms (Op. 49 no. 4). In none of them do the words count for very much; the endearing tenderness of the music is the main theme. Wolf's song worthily follows this great tradition. The sugary mawkishness of the verses is not permitted to seep into the music, which is clear and fresh in structure and harmony. At the same time one essence of Reinick's poem is distilled into Wolf's setting, namely the idea of regular swing and sway, rock and return, which is not only explicit in the subject-matter and secondary imagery (rocking cradle synchronized with ticking clock) but also implicit in the rhyme-scheme and repetitions. Wolf's accompaniment figure duly twines two strands of single notes into a gently rocking background above which the maternal voice sings its own sweet melody with a special quality of regular rise and fall, both in phrases (the first four bars fall to the lowest pitch and rise to the highest) and in single notes (at the clinching final refrain in each verse).

NOTES 1. The whole vocal line, especially in the refrain, is among the earliest examples of the lifting and dipping melody that the idea of 'singing' often suggested to Wolf (motif 10). Equally typical of his later procedures is the technique of highlighting one particular verbal phrase (here 'die Engel noch viel mehr' in the last verse) by such devices as an unexpected variation of the otherwise unchanged strophic melody, further enhanced by a sustained soft high note.

2. Also highly predictive of Wolf's maturity are the ways in which the bass semibreves of stillness (motif 39) dissolve into a more animated high register at the mention of the sole sound to break the silence of the first verse (the songbird heard at bars 10ff.) and these singing strains in turn are made more melting and fluid by the languid syncopations of the piano right hand (bar 14 etc).

5 Wiegenlied im Winter *(A winter lullaby)*

20 December 1882   A♭ major   e♭ '–a♭ ''

Sleep, sleep, sleep, my sweet child, sleep, my sweet child. Outside, the wind is blowing; it knocks on the window-pane and peers in, and if it hears a baby crying anywhere, it scolds and moans and roars and then brings in its own bed of snow to cover the cradle, if baby won't lie quiet.

Sleep, sleep, sleep, my sweet child, sleep, my sweet child. Outside the wind is blowing, it shakes the fir-tree and out flies a beautiful dream that comes flying through snow and night and wind so fast, fast to my dear child and sings of the lights and the wreaths that will soon be shining on the Christmas tree.

Sleep, sleep, sleep, my sweet child, sleep, my sweet child. Outside, the wind is blowing. Yet it shall blow your cheeks red when the sun cries 'Good morrow and God bless you!'; and it shall blow the whole earth awake when springtime says 'Good day!' and what has lain quiet until then shall leap for joy all around.

[But now sleep, now sleep, now sleep, my sweet child. Outside, the wind is blowing; but you must sleep, my sweet child, sleep.]

This companion piece to the previous song has much of the same charm and invention; but here the latter is far less original and appropriate than before. The piano prelude sounds as if it aims to become a Chopin ballade, an impression not entirely dispelled by what follows. Wolf has to re-create the poem in musical terms; so the winds of Reinick's inflated verses blow through the music, which as a result is full of sudden fortes and sforzandos that seem to jeopardise if not forfeit its lullaby status. But in the welcome moments when the piano stops puffing and blowing there are some wholly Wolfian passages of beatific tenderness, notably the last page with its repeated (and, as the postlude tells us, successful) appeals to sleep.

NOTES 1. The textual repetitions on the last page are Wolf's own, not his poet's, and are designed to serve musical structural purposes – a practice he would hardly have countenanced in late songs.

2. The persistent flattened sixth (F♭ in A♭ major) is here used as passing harmony or colouring; in the Mörike *An den Schlaf* (41) it is a more integral part of the tonal structure. But it will not be mere coincidence that both songs are in the same key and both consist of invitations to sleep: motif 37.

3. We may also compare this lullaby with *Die ihr schwebet* from the Spanish Songbook (14), as another song concerned with chill winds and a cradled child; the latter though written only eight years later is far richer in musical resource and accomplishment.

4. Yet the invention here is already far from negligible. Thus the structure is, perhaps deliberately, related to the previous lullaby pattern of No. 4, e.g. in the

initial tonic pedal and its modulation to the dominant and beyond at the first mention of contrasting external sound and activity, whether late songbird or chill nightwind. In this song however, with its wider range of ideas and topics in need of illustration, the depiction is not equally apt from verse to verse; thus the joyous lefthand two-octave leap for 'springt lustig' (bars 70–1) is less clearly relevant at bars 46–7.

5. Again the mature Wolf is presaged, as shown e.g. by a comparison between the piano part in bars 15–24 and 39–48 (=63–72); the original material has been specially let out to incorporate gusts of weeping and wailing, in conformity with the poetic text.

6 Mausfallen-Sprüchlein *(Mousetrap magic)*

18 June 1882   F major   d♭'–g''

(The child is to walk three times round the trap and say:)

Little guests, little house; dear Mrs or Mr Mouse, just pop boldly in tonight in the moonlight! [moonlight, moonlight!] But be sure to close the door carefully behind you, do you hear? [do you hear?] And in doing so watch out for your tail! [Do you hear? Do you hear? Your tail!]

After supper we'll sing, after supper we'll leap and dance a little dance! Look out! Take care! [Take care!] My old cat will probably be dancing with us too, [do you hear? Do you hear?]

It is easy to hear why this delightful miniature has become so popular. The charm, in every sense, of Mörike's verses is manifest in the gaiety and delicacy of the music, which independently conveys a graphically convincing account of the mouse-charming process. The piano has a series of tiny phrases that come popping up in the treble, like the emergence of a tentative whisker; and the alluring vocal incantation tempts them to venture out very slightly further each time. After the final repetition of 'Mondenschein' (moonlight), specially sustained over two tied minims before fading away, so as to depict a steady glow, we hear inquisitive quivering in the left-hand trills and scampering in the right-hand runs, with a hint of apprehension at the thought of the sharply-closing door. The menaced tail, the communal dancing and singing, the menacing cat, are all treated in music as appealing as it is witty; and its integration of the manifold motifs within a mere thirty-nine bars is masterly. But it arguably takes too many liberties with the text to be wholly successful as a setting, though delectable as a song.

NOTES 1. The song might have been even shorter; but Wolf chose to expand Mörike's fifty-one words into seventy-two by repetitions designed to achieve either purely musical patterns and symmetries ('hörst du?' in bars 16–17 and 20–

21) or special quasi-verbal effects of his own to be superimposed on the poem (motif 25 at 'Mondenschein' in bars 9–11). Prominent among the latter is the repeated 'Witt witt!', presumably intended by Mörike as an allusion to the nonsense syllables frequently found in German nursery rhymes and children's games; Wolf's direction 'rauh' (hoarse, harsh) together with the emphatic vocal accents and the piano's trills and augmented fifths (motif 23) leaves no doubt that the repeated monosyllable is to be interpreted as a croaked warning – one that interestingly anticipates the croakings of the later Mörike song *Zur Warnung* (61).

2. Another anticipation worth noting is the reappearance in *Gleich und Gleich* (110) of the musical material in the piano interlude here after the second 'Dein Schwänzchen' (bars 22–4); the two songs are linked by the notion of minuscule activity, expressed here more by the high register and light texture of motif 3 than by its characteristic minor seconds (though these also appear, e.g. in the upper left-hand part, bars 1–7).

3. The interpretation of this song presents problems; the element of innocent merriment has to be compounded with the mischief, indeed malice, that is manifest in Mörike's poem and much intensified by Wolf's music.

4. Cf. Hugo Distler, Op. 19 (SA).

Six songs to words by
Scheffel, Mörike, Goethe and Kerner

7 Wächterlied auf der Wartburg (Neujahrsnacht des Jahres 1200) *(Watchman's song from the Wartburg (New Year's night of the year 1200))*

24 January 1887 (arranged for chorus and orchestra 1894; unfinished)

E♭ major   c–f'

Soar on high, ye massed trumpets; let the Lord God hear a song of praise resounding from the lofty watch-towers through the star-bright night. His hand guides the planets on their sure courses through space and time and leads the soul to eternity through the strifes of this world.

    One century is about to vanish, and a new one is dawning; happy now is he who goes on his settled way with a pure heart and mind! Though the times are now clad in steel and iron, yet a golden age will follow this age of baser metal, and a manly heart shall win its way through to the promised salvation.

    So let each man address himself vigorously to his duty, as is right and seemly, whether he wears a cowl or bears arms, whether in the workplace or at the plough; and to this end, Lord, pour out Thy blessing on this Thy castle, on mountain and meadow, here at this turn of the century bedew them with Thy grace.

Wolf's two songs (this and No. 9) to words by the once popular historical romancer Joseph von Scheffel, now remembered if at all for his versified tale *Der Trompeter von Säkkingen*, were completed shortly after the poet's death in 1886. They were no doubt intended as a special commemorative tribute. This song, though not among Wolf's greatest, is vigorous and striking. There is much to admire in the stirring vocal melodies, the first of which later reappears in an effective counterpoint that recalls the opening words with which it is associated, so that the piano is heard as it were declaiming the opening words 'Schwingt euch auf, Posaunenchöre' while the voice salutes the New Year in the last verse.

But the poem despite its protestations is not good enough to sustain for long at a time the impression of staunch devoutness that it seeks to convey, and the same is true of Wolf's music. In both, the efforts to scale the ultimate heights of nobility and grandeur are rather too apparent; and without superlative artistry of performance, the results will sound less like the dawn of a new century than the start of a new school term.

NOTES 1. Both the Scheffel poems (this and No. 9) come from his collection *Frau Aventiure* (1863) which offers versified homage to the time of the Minnesingers. The archaic expression 'Sälde' in the last line means 'bliss', or 'salvation'. The collection is subtitled 'Songs from the time of Heinrich von Ofterdingen', who was a leading figure in the song contest described in the Middle High German poem *Der Wartburgkrieg*. No doubt the Wartburg of Scheffel's poem too is the castle of the Landgraf Hermann of Thuringia, who recurs in the same setting and story in Wagner's *Tannhäuser* (cf. also No. 9, note 2). Not surprisingly, Wolf has Wagner in mind. There are general affinities in the bold harmonic changes and the quasi-orchestral effects of left-hand tremolandos as well as the trumpeting octaves that resound throughout. More specifically, the key, rhythms, march tempo and processional bass octaves of Wolf's reprise here (at 'Rüstig mög' drum jeder' etc) all recall the chorus of knights at the end of Act I of *Parsifal*. Typically, the kinship is not only musical but verbal and conceptual; Wagner's themes too are those of mediaeval Germany, religious dedication and knightly resolve to fight the good fight.

2. Similarly Wolf's piano part in the interlude after 'ein männlich Herz' adumbrates his manly motif 6, which recurs on the last page in an E-major form evocative of the similar peroration in *Der Freund* (66). The progressions at 'Ein Jahrhundert will zerrinnen' (One century is about to vanish) are much akin to the music later used by Wolf in verbal contexts suggestive of mystery or magic (motif 19), while the idea of happiness in a settled and assured way of life is greeted by the G♭/F♯ tonality (bar 29 etc) which later came to be regularly associated with exuberant cheerfulness: motif 40.

3. Ten years later Wolf used a motif which has much in common with the music of this song to express the quintessential nobility of Manuel Venegas, hero of the unfinished opera of that name.

4. There is a typical uncertainty of verbal accentuation of the half-bar which suggests that the piano part was the primary inspiration.

8 Der König bei der Krönung *(The king at the coronation)*

13 March 1886   E major   A♯–f♯'

Dedicated to your service at the altar, my fatherland, how I am yours! Now let me be either a priest or a sacrifice for the right and the truth. Anoint my head, Lord, from Thy chalice, with the precious oil of peace, so that I may shine like a sun over my fatherland and my house.

Mörike's deceptively simple poem is, as ever, full of deep resonance; it evokes from Wolf an earnest of the enriched harmonic style that was to characterize his Mörike songbook of 1888. The hymn-like quality of the slow melody and its chordal accompaniment, in conjunction with the very unhymnlike harmonic progressions, again suggests Wagner. But mainly we hear Wolf's own authentic and original lyric voice. The strong independence and appeal of the melodic line; the slight stress by prolongation on the first word as well as the last in '*wie* bin ich *dein*' (how I am yours) to underline the sense of how whole-hearted the service to the fatherland is to be; the way in which this simple idea, simply stated, is musically transformed into an idea of correspondingly greater complexity and richness at the closing words 'dass ich wie eine Sonne strahle' etc: these features are admirable and characteristic. There is good opportunity here for effective and compelling singing.

NOTES 1. This song was written on Wolf's twenty-sixth birthday; it has an air of personal exhortation, as if he were dedicating himself anew to the service of music. The dates of composition, choice of texts and arrangement in the songbook of all three songs 7, 8 and 9 alike suggest a solemn mood of pledge and affirmation.

2. The subject of Mörike's poem is also that of Goethe's *Königlich Gebet* (116). Perhaps neither the poems nor their settings are among the best or most typical work of their creators; but a comparison may prove rewarding.

3. Cf. Reger, Op. 70 no. 2.

9 Biterolf (im Lager von Akkon 1190) *(Biterolf (in camp at Acre, 1190))*

26 December 1886   F major   d–f'

Battle-weary and sunburned, far away on a heathen shore, I think of you, my green-forested Thuringian homeland. Soft bright starlight, you shall be my messenger; go you and greet my homeland far over the sea!

The bronze of my weapons defies enemies from every quarter, but there is no shield to protect me against the pangs of my longing. Yet despite the heart's lament I shall endure undaunted; he who has ventured forth in God's cause bears his cross uncomplaining.

As before (No. 7) Scheffel's theme is the high chivalry of mediaeval Germanic literature and legend. But this account of the knight-errant Biterolf as a crusader seems to have moved Wolf in one respect only, and that the subsidiary one. Love and longing for a far homeland and an absent lady are emotions that Wolf could understand and transcribe. The piano prelude tempers resolution with tenderness, and the vocal melody begins memorably. From 'waldgrünes Thüringland' (green-forested

Thuringia) to 'weit über Meer' (far over the sea) voice and piano combine in a melting strain that is all longing and sweetness.

Then the song suffers a decline. The notion of being a doughty and uncomplaining warrior in God's cause may have made some transient appeal to the composer, but it evokes no deep response; even the strongly-accented chords and wide-ranging harmonic progressions emblazoning the knight-errant can do little to help this lost cause. There are still enjoyable moments, whenever the text relapses into wistfulness, as at 'wider der Sehnsucht Schmerz' (against the pangs of my longing) etc. But the contrast between the appropriateness of this music and the inadequacy of the rest disturbs the balance of the song.

NOTES 1. A similar patchiness – exquisite treatment of tender sentiments, comparatively banal rendering of forthright sentiments – may be found in some of the Eichendorff songs (66, 77, 83). The next song is also of interest from a similar point of view. The pattern of response may be relevant to Wolf's own temperament and its development.

2. The verses become increasingly bellicose. If Wolf's source was indeed *Frau Aventiure* (see No. 7, note 1) he has tactfully omitted a third verse about the imminent resumption, at daybreak, of hostilities against the Saracen.

3. Unlike the Minnesinger Heinrich von Ofterdingen, Biterolf may be more of a fictional character than a literary figure; but he too reappears, duly restored to his beloved Thuringia, as a knight in *Tannhäuser*.

10 Beherzigung *(Counsel)*

1 March 1887   G minor/G major   d'–g''

The timid uncertainty of cowardly thoughts, womanish hesitation, anxious lamenting; these cannot avert misery, cannot make you free!

But bidding defiance to all external forces, never yielding, showing oneself tough and strong; these will call forth the arms of the gods in your support! [call forth the arms of the gods!]

This is the first of Wolf's published settings of Goethe, universally acknowledged the greatest of all German poets. Like the earlier Mörike song (8) it foreshadows the greatness to come; but here the music seems to aim at greatness rather too selfconsciously. Considered as a purely musical argument the setting displays much invention and power; as a restatement of poetic thought in musical terms it is less convincing. The piano prelude has chromatically drooping right-hand chords, indicating uncertainty and diffidence. There is a hectic intensity in the music which suggests that these are envisaged more as culpable personal failings than as common human feelings. The unifying rhythm $\mathbf{c}$ ♩ ♩ ♩.♩♩ is reiterated in the left hand while the voice contributes its troubled phrases rising, for no very clear reason, to a massive climax at 'macht dich nicht frei' (does not make you free). Out of the previous turmoil the piano evolves a new theme in the same rhythm, now in both hands together as a musical image of active determination. Then the vocal phrases ring out with great vigour and confidence, the last ('rufet die Arme der Götter herbei') being declaimed through an accompaniment of decisively emphatic chords that continue to hammer the point home throughout the piano postlude.

NOTES 1. The verbal repetitions on the last page are Wolf's, not Goethe's; and the music as a whole perhaps tells us more about the composer than the poem. It is reasonable to suppose that Wolf intended to give an objective account of the meaning of the text; but the music so exaggerates and arguably distorts the simple contrast of the verses that some special explanation seems called for. Instead of weakness and strength, irresolution and fortitude, we are given a convoluted shyness and an aggressive brashness, thematically related as if to illustrate the point that they are two aspects of one personal inferiority feeling. This is done brilliantly well; but it is hardly what the poem means.

2. The contrast in the poem is a recurrent motif in Goethe's work; and one has only to compare this song with later settings of similar poems, e.g. the later *Beherzigung* (103) and the second *Cophtisches Lied* (100), to appreciate the amazing rapidity of Wolf's development from 1887 onwards.

3. It may be felt that the idea of a thematically unifying rhythm is here carried too far; compare the later use of this device in the far finer song *In der Frühe* (36).

4. A rather odd feature of Wolf's work is the use of the chord or tonality of F♯ major, often quite arbitrarily, for feelings of extreme exuberance: motif 40. Here at 'frei' this chord appears in force. The two-handed hammering home of the point is motif 27. Some older Peters editions, and the *Kritische Gesamtausgabe*, omit the B natural needed in the right-hand crotchets at bar 9.

11 Wanderers Nachtlied *(Wanderer's song in the night)*

30 January 1887   G♭ major/B major   d♯'–g''

You who are from heaven, who soothe away all grief and pain, doubly refreshing him who is doubly afflicted – oh, I am weary of this journeying! Why all this pain and joy? Sweet peace, [sweet peace], come, oh come into my heart! [come, oh come into my heart!]

Goethe's poem is so strongly yet simply self-sufficient that musical commentary seems superfluous. The only real chance for a composer is to find a melody as limpid and moving as the words themselves, and sharing the same patterns of tension and relaxation. This Schubert achieved in his memorable setting. Wolf's music is colourless in comparison, despite its striving for effect. His melodies are neither resilient enough for the powerful emotional content of the verses, nor wholly congruent with them. Atypically, an arbitrarily repeated phrase ('süsser Friede', sweet peace) is accentuated quite differently on its second appearance. Yet the song has moments of beauty and inventiveness. Thus the tired drooping figures that typify weariness ('ach, ich bin des Treibens müde') emerge refreshed in a brighter tonality in the final invocation (at 'komm in meine Brust'), while at the first 'süsser Friede' the piano musingly repeats the melodies allotted to the voice for the opening description of the nature of peace; and that nature is now made more graphically manifest by the addition of long slow bass semibreves.

NOTES 1. The phrase-repetitions are Wolf's, not Goethe's.

2. At bars 1–2 the prelude has the reflective idea of motif 21, which then gives place to a forerunner of the worshipping motif 1. At 'Schmerz und Lust?' appears the longing dominant seventh of motif 32.

3. Much of the musical essence of this song, including the opening motif 21, is recaptured in the Mörike Gebet (40) in a more precise form.

4. Cf. Reichardt; Zelter; Loewe, Op. 9; Schubert, D224; Schumann, Op. 96 no. 1; Liszt (two versions); Pfitzner, Op. 40, no. 5; Medtner, Op. 15 no. 1; Joseph Marx.

12 Zur Ruh', zur Ruh' *(To rest, to rest)*

16 June 1883   A^b major   b–a^b ''

To rest, to rest, weary limbs; eyelids, firmly close. I am alone, the world is left far behind; the night must come so that I can find the light.

O inward powers, lead me away where in the darkest of nights a light is shining, forth from this earthly realm with all its sorrows through night and dream to a mother's heart.

A moving oration was spoken by Dr Michael Haberlandt at Wolf's funeral. It described the composer's short and tormented life, his dedication to his art, and his achievement – for which, the speech concluded, 'take the late, the all too late, thanks of the world with you into your last resting-place. And now, as you sang in one of your loveliest songs...' – and the speaker quoted the first two sentences of Justinus Kerner's poem above. So the song has a special claim on the attention of all those who admire Wolf's music. Its basic concept is undeniably fine; and a restrained performance can invest it with a mystic solemnity not unworthy of the last rites of a composer who was buried beside Schubert and Beethoven. Nevertheless, it is not among Wolf's most outstanding successes. The highest level of achievement is not to be expected from him at the age of twenty-three; he was still serving his apprenticeship. Further,

Kerner's typical mysticism made no deep appeal to Wolf at any age; his too palpable effort to share it here leads to bombast.

The first page of the song is impressive, with its appealing vocal melodies and sensitively modelled accompaniment; the two components are independent (thus the twice-three-bars piano pattern has no clear counterpart in the voice) but most deftly integrated. Unfortunately for that appealing first page, the second section of the poem is much weaker than the first. It has nothing of substance to add; and its sentiment is a liability. The young composer worked too hard at restoring the balance by sheer weight of musical effect. In later years he would hardly have relied on the sequential treatment of melody to such an extent as here at 'O führt mich', (lead me) etc, and would have recoiled from the idea of proceeding through night and dream to a mother's heart by way of a crescendo up to a fortissimo six-four chord and a sustained swelling top $A^\flat$.

NOTES 1. By a clear enough train of no doubt involuntary association, the sequences follow much the same lines as the pilgrims in *Tannhäuser*; this and the over-dramatized climax suggest a Wagnerian influence still unassimilated and hence to some extent detrimental.

2. In this early use of the brightening mediant modulation of motif 24 it is noteworthy that the first shift of tonality moves in the other direction, namely down a major third from $A^\flat$ to E major, after the words 'Nacht muss es sein...' only to recover again to $A^\flat$ as the visionary gleam is duly restored.

II. The Mörike songs

Eduard Mörike (1804–75) has been reckoned with Goethe and Rilke among the greatest of German poets. Yet his lyrics are limited in quantity if not in range, and like his life as clergyman and teacher they are outwardly uneventful. He has little of Goethe's outgoing intellectual vigour, or of Rilke's passionate quest for inward self-awareness. Instead, his poetry offers a quiet and seemingly passive quality which is easy to perceive but hard to describe. Imagination, religious devotion, realism and humour in the content of the verses, folk-song and the classical tradition in their forms, are some of the more evident components of this quality. But its precise definition has been the despair of students and examiners for years; and also of commentators and critics, to judge by the comparative paucity of published Mörike studies.

Something of its indefinable essence was conveyed by another of Wolf's poets, Gottfried Keller, who when Mörike died said that it was as if a fine June day had passed away with him; 'es ist als ob ein schöner Junitag dahin wäre mit Mörike'. That choice of simile was not merely conventional. Mörike was a painter and pastor as well as a poet; his pages are characteristically bright with coloured or shining pictures or visions of this world or the next. His drawings and sketches too, like his sermons and letters, are full of quirky yet warm-hearted insights into human feelings, expressed in vigorous and often homely images from daily life and the natural scene. This quasi-pictorial sense of communication also illuminates the vocabulary and imagery of Mörike's main writings in poetry and prose, to give Keller's 'June day' effect.

Goldenness, to take just one example, is a highly-valued quality. Gold bell-notes are set floating through the air in *Auf einer Wanderung* to symbolize outward serenity, while in *Peregrina I* inward and spiritual grace is compared with the hidden gleam of unmined gold. The image of the golden grape in *Fussreise*, receiving the impression of sunlight and storing it for future expression, beautifully blends both those ideas, external and internal, divine creation and the human creature. Similarly in Mörike's novel *Maler Nolten* (Nolten the Painter) a fulfilment of mind and mood is seen as sunlight reflected through a glass of golden wine; while at the climactic lines of the short lyric *Septembermorgen* (not set by Wolf) the metaphor takes on universality as the whole world flows and glows in warm gold.

None of these images or their many analogues implies a mere one-sided or superficial geniality. Mörike has also a dark and daemonic aspect, especially noted and commented upon by Wolf in correspondence (e.g. about his own settings of *Der Feuerreiter* and *Erstes Liebeslied eines Mädchens*). Mörike's own intuitive awareness of the occult and erotic worlds of ancient pagan worship and ritual, witchcraft and legend, had been further enhanced by daily experience of rural life in remote communities. The pastoral poet, like his parishioners, was close to the instinctive springs of feeling; and these too find their own typical diction and imagery in the dark flowing of subterranean streams, the irresistible surge of storm-winds. Between the two realms of bright open day and dark secret night lies the much-prayed-for Mörikean resting-place, his 'holdes Bescheiden' or golden mean of *Verborgenheit*. In his poetry, time itself stands still in contemplation at dusk or dawn, as so memorably in the moment of equipoise contained in *Um Mitternacht*.

In all this Mörike displays clear temperamental affinities with Wolf. Their unworldliness often left them both dependent on the bounty of friends or the hazards of circumstance. Their creative minds shared a similar polarization of mood-swing from dark trough to bright crest, from apathy and inertia to frenzied and elated composition. Each felt a strong affinity with nature and intuitive feeling; each rejected anything contrived or mechanical; each identified with patterned contrasts of storm and calm, flowering and fading, travel and homecoming; each saw human life and experience in visual and dramatic terms. And all this was as readily expressible for Wolf in musical as for Mörike in poetic structure and imagery.

It is not surprising then that the verbal warmth and fire discerned by Keller in Mörike should have inspired Wolf to his sudden quasi-Pentecostal release of creative genius in 1888. The surprise is rather that other song-writers in former years, or Wolf himself at an earlier stage, should not have been similarly inspired. After all, Mörike's poetry had by then been in print for well over half a century; composers from the pioneering Schumann and Robert Franz onwards, including Brahms, had already set it to music.* By the time that Wolf first read Mörike, in the 1870s, the words of *Das verlassene Mägdlein* had appeared in some fifty published settings, and those of *Agnes* in more than eighty. Yet very few

---

* cf. Eric Sams, 'Homage to Eduard Mörike', *The Musical Times*, July 1975

of those compositions had achieved any real symbiosis between words and music. All the other main lyricists of the Lied had elicited durable or definitive settings soon after the publication of their poems, while they were still young men; Goethe in Mozart and Beethoven, Müller, Heine and Rückert in Schubert. Only Eduard Mörike failed to find any comparable fulfilment; and he died in 1875 at the age of seventy-one without ever having heard a note of Hugo Wolf. And even Wolf had needed a gradual eight-year Mörike induction course; in addition to the 1882 *Mausfallen-Sprüchlein* and the 1886 *Der König bei der Krönung* there had been the 1880 début *Suschens Vogel* and the 1884 *Die Tochter der Heide*, neither of which was adjudged worthy of publication. The conclusion from these facts is surely that Mörike's lyrics, so far from being eminently settable and singable, demanded (and indeed helped to create) a new tonal language for their satisfactory translation into musical terms. For Mörike's creative mind and environment were saturated with music of their own, both in general and in detail. He was himself a practising musician with a social circle that included the amateur pianist Wilhelm Hartlaub and the amateur composer Friedrich Kauffmann. As a priest and pastor in the Protestant tradition, he was closely familiar with the metres and themes of hymns and folk-songs. His lyrics were often conceived in avowedly musical terms. At least one poem (*Zum neuen Jahr*) was written to an existing tune ('Wie dort auf den Auen', from Salieri's *Axur*); another (*Chor jüdischer Mädchen*) was part of an unfinished opera libretto; a third (*Ach, nur einmal*) is prefaced by a Mozart melody quoted from *La Clemenza di Tito*. Again, the justly renowned novella *Mozart auf der Reise nach Prag* is as notable for its critical insight as for its beauty of form and phrase. Thus Mörike is deep-rooted in classical tradition; he often reads as if Mozart had been reborn as a poet.

Wolf often sounds as if Mörike had been reborn as a musician. He too was always keenly aware of artistic continuity. It seemed apt that Mörike's friend Moritz von Schwind should also have been the friend of Schubert; and more fitting still that Emil Kauffmann, son of the Friedrich Kauffmann who had made the first Mörike settings from manuscript copies of the poems, should have been Wolf's devoted patron and sponsor. It was from Emil that Wolf in his turn had received the cherished gift of a Mörike manuscript (*An Longus*). But Wolf's feelings for the poet were already on the further side of idolatry. The published songbook begins, at the composer's earnest and repeated stipulation, with a picture of the poet; it is called (again following the admired precedent set by Schumann) *Gedichte von Mörike*, a way of announcing the translation of poetry into music by means of quasi-verbal equivalence.

To achieve that equivalence, Wolf had had to elaborate and perfect what he himself called a new musical language. As we have seen, it owed much to the examples of Schumann and Wagner. But its essential *raison d'être* was a transfusion from the deepest veins in Mörike, at a time when words and music were attaining their most intense interpenetration in the whole history of Western art. The verbal music of Mörike may be briefly classified into melody, declamation, rhythm, harmony and motif. In the first place, devices such as poetic echo-refrains (as in *Agnes*) or puns (*Elfenlied*) or deliberate vowel-patterns and cadences (*passim*) evoke an analogous turn of melodic phrase. Similarly, Mörike's practised familiarity with classical verse-forms and metres made him a master of the stress and placement of key words; his scansion is often by length as well as by stress of syllable, again with clear musical implications. Next, he greatly extends the Goethean use of relevant rhythms to unify a lyric, as in the cantering amphibrachs of the prancing pony in *Der Gärtner*, or the insistent metrical feet that take their morning walk in *Fussreise*. Again, his Goethean penchant for compound words and concepts, such as 'mitleidschön' (literally 'pity-beautiful'), in *Peregrina II*, builds up as it were a chord or modulation of meaning in the composer's mind. Finally the favourite unifying devices or images that proclaim Mörike as the first great symbolist poet are either directly musical (the bell-notes of joy, the harp-notes of lamentation) or are readily translatable into sonorous terms (the birds and breezes that signify various aspects of love and longing) or else are in an infinite variety of other ways amenable to Wolfian expression. Thus the particulars of poetry are, in the 1888 Mörike songbook, memorably subsumed into the universals of music.

Mörike's poems had first appeared in his *Gedichte* of 1838. This volume was enlarged and revised in three subsequent editions during the poet's lifetime culminating in the final reprinted collation of 1873. The sixth edition of 1876 was Wolf's constant companion. As he once told a friend, he could not bear to part from it, even for an hour. It contains some 275 poems, many of which are wholly unsuited, whether in length or style, to solo setting. Of the remaining 200 or so, Wolf eschewed all epigrams, all the personal poetic addresses and letters to friends and family, and almost all the poems in classical metre. Of the 100 left, Wolf set more than half; and the poems he chose are not only fully representative but, with very few exceptions, contain a complete collection of Mörike's finest lyrics. This songbook as a whole is unique for its absorption of the essence of one great poet's work into music of comparable quality.

13 (M 1) Der Genesene an die Hoffnung (*To Hope, on recovering from illness*)

6 March 1888   F# minor/G♭ major   b♭ –a♭ ''

Day dawned deathly pale. But already my head lay hidden, how sweetly, in your lap, O hope, until victory was assured. I had made sacrifice to all the gods, but you were forgotten. You stood aside from the eternal saviours and watched the ceremony.

Oh forgive me, thou ever-faithful! Stand out from your twilight, so that I may for once with all my heart look up, like a child and free from grief, at your eternally renewed moonbright face; oh take me, just once without pain, into your arms.

Wolf chose this song to stand at the head of the published volume of the Mörike songs, no doubt because the poem had a deep personal significance for him. In 1888 he knew, after long delay, the joy of great achievement.

The prelude begins with slow bleak bass octaves that come groping menacingly up the scale and are heard still questing as the voice enters with its similar theme. The first syllable of the first word, 'tödlich' (deathly), is stressed by prolongation over the bar-line, to show that the sickness was nearly mortal. Then the octaves soften into warm comforting chords, with a broader vocal line; the first signs of hope. Voice and piano soon swell exultantly towards a high G#, at the repetition of 'der Sieg gewonnen hiess' (victory was assured). Hushed chords now introduce pleading recitative in voice and piano, where an interlude seems to sing its plea for forgiveness before the corresponding words are heard. At a second climax, contrasting in its quietude and restraint, the top G# (now notated as A♭) is again touched upon, this time very softly, at 'mondenhelle Angesicht' (moonbright face), in a vocal phrase fully as compelling as the poetic phrase. Finally the voice falls in a long fluctuating melodic line through nearly two octaves humbly and prayerfully down to the last low notes at 'deinem Arm'; heartfelt amens from the piano end the song.

NOTES 1. Wolf's corrections to his own copy of the Mörike-Lieder, as described by Walter Legge (see *Music Review*, August 1941) include the amendment of bar 24 (left hand) to read

instead of

as first printed; the addition of a slurred staccato to the last three right-hand quavers in bar 28, and the deletion of G natural (right hand) and upper D♭ (left hand) in the penultimate chord of bar 34. The *Kritische Gesamtausgabe* (1963) has adopted these readings, with the unexplained exception of the staccato markings, and has also incorporated an amendment communicated personally by the composer to his friend Paul Müller, namely

instead of

at the end of bar 11 (see *Peters Jahrbuch*, 11 Jahrgang, 1904). In this last instance however it seems permissible to prefer the original text, especially since Wolf's judgement was arguably impaired at the time (September 1896). An amendment that needs to be made to the older Peters Edition is the reading of A not F♯ as the lowest note of bar 2 (conformably with bar 4) and similarly in transposed versions.

2. In general Wolf is among the most objective of song-writers; but he is human enough to allow his personal emotions to colour his interpretations of the text from time to time. This may mar the music considered as a setting of the poet's words. Here, for instance, the repetition of 'bis der Sieg gewonnen hiess', all set about with fanfares, has little obvious justification in the poem despite its undoubted relevance to Wolf's own jubilant mood. So the music of exultation may seem at odds with the poetry of repentance. However, the poem may itself express the double triumph of recovery from physical illness, and pride in artistic achievement; it was written in 1838, the year in which Mörike published the first edition of his poems.

3. The music left a lasting imprint in Wolf's mind. Thus the ominous bass octaves recur as a *memento mori* in *Alles endet* (241), also in the prelude, while the high G♯ at the word 'Sieg' illuminates that same syllable in *Morgenstimmung* (234); each echo retains a similar harmonic and tonal content, even after nine years or more.

4. A less clear echo arises from the slow ascending semitones that accompany the visitation of Hope. These reappear in e.g. *Auf eine Christblume* (32: right hand, bars 14–19), *Schlafendes Jesuskind* (37: left hand, bars 19–20) and *Anakreons Grab* (114: piano, bar 11) – each time, as it happens, in a poetic context concerned with the growth and development of flowers. The idea was

first heard in *Morgentau*. Perhaps the musico-poetic mind imagined Hope as springing from a process of germination. On any analysis the idea of continuous development is deeply implanted here. In contrast to the regular quatrain patterns of Mörike's poem, the music treats each line quite separately, with hardly a trace of formal repetition.

5. The piano interlude after 'Feste zu' with its two voices suggests an image of duality and apartness; cf. the analogous duetting in the postlude to Schumann's *Intermezzo*, Op. 39 no. 2, also about a consolingly bright face seen in vision.

6. At 'einmal schaue' etc the piano part assumes the worshipping rhythm of motif 1, which is varied, just for the one bar containing the phrase 'wie ein Kind', to the childlike motif 2. For the diverging melodic lines in voice and piano right hand at the last words 'deinem Arm', see motif 14.

14 (M 2) Der Knabe und das Immlein (*The boy and the bee*)

22 February 1888   G minor/G major $c^{\sharp\,\prime}$–$a^{\prime\prime}$

In the vineyard on the hill a little house stands so precariously, with no door or windows; and time hangs heavy on it. And when the day is so sultry that all the birds are mute, one lone bee goes humming round the sunflower.

'My sweetheart has a garden, with a pretty beehive in it; have you flown thence, did she send you out to find me?' 'Oh no, my fine lad, no one sent me on any errand. That child knows nothing of loving; she has hardly ever set eyes on you. And what could girls know when they've only just left school! Your adored sweetheart is still a mother's pet. I'm bringing her wax and honey; farewell! – I've got a whole pound. How the little darling will laugh! Her mouth is watering already.' 'Oh, I wish you would tell her that I know something that's much sweeter still; there's nothing on earth so delightful as hugging and kissing!' ['nothing on earth so delightful as hugging and kissing!']

This delectable song begins with the melancholy strain heard again throughout the following song of betrayal and heartbreak. Its effect is one of veiled wistfulness, to suit Mörike's rather mysterious first verse; and this minor mood lightens as soon as the imagined dialogue begins. We need not assume that a bee is actually discoursing here, in the style of a Lafontaine fable; it may well be more like a bee in the bonnet. In this enchanting music, in any event, it shares the same bright melodies as the boy's thoughts of his longed-for sweetheart, as if to make the point that he is talking to himself about her. Of course Wolf seizes the opportunities for musical illustration. Little delicate persistent trills buzz in the piano part, which later adds a charming comment on the prickling foretaste of honey in the staccato quavers that join in with the trills at 'ihm wässert schon der

Mund' (her mouth is watering already). Meanwhile the right hand sketches out a lyric flight high in the keyboard at 'kommst du daher geflogen', and choreographs a triumphant honeycomb dance to express the bee's glee at scoring off the boy ('was wüssten auch die Mädchen' etc, what could girls know?). The lad is thereby stung into an effective rejoinder, which suddenly clarifies all the preceding content of both verse and music as the erotic symbolism already well known to the Elizabethan lyricists: 'Love guards the roses of her lips/And flies about them like a bee'. So under all the semi-descriptive writing there is the exquisite portrayal of the hopes and hesitancies of young love. These contrary feelings are blended at the repeated last lines of the poem, 'nichts Lieblichers auf Erden als wenn man herzt und küsst!' Each time these words are sung the music begins with passionate elation and then drifts into a wistful shyness, expressed first in the uncertain harmony and then in the faltering rhythm, yet without ever disturbing the flowing shapeliness of the vocal line. The blend of emotion is summed up in the final four bars of piano postlude – two of ecstasy and exultation, two of uncertainty and diffidence. The same blend is heard in Wolf's own comments in his letters to Dr Edmund Lang. On the same day he writes:

I have just written out a new song. A song for the gods, I tell you! Quite divinely wonderful! Good Lord, there will soon be an end of me at this rate; my competence is increasing from day to day. How much further can I take it? I'm frightened at the thought... What does the future still hold in store for me, I wonder? This question torments and frightens me, preoccupies me, waking or sleeping. Have I been called – perhaps even chosen? God forbid the latter. That would be a nice mess!

NOTES 1. Walter Legge (see 13, note 1) gives a left hand slur from E (bar 53) to C (bar 54), and a minim D natural (a fourth below the stave) added at the half-bar in 55: these changes have been incorporated in the *Kritische Gesamtausgabe*.

2. Mörike's first verse seems oddly detached. No doubt the 'Häuschen' is a beehive; but opinion is divided on whether 'windebang' means 'afraid of the wind', e.g. because rickety, or exposed on a steep slope, or is just a dialect intensive form of 'bang' (anxious). The former reading seems rather more Mörikean.

3. The final repetition of the text is Wolf's, not Mörike's. So is the idea of a thematic link between this song (bars 1–19) and the next (*passim*). Both were composed on the same day. But any hint at the possibility of a tragic sequel to the present poem seems gratuitously pessimistic; the two songs are best kept separate.

4. At 'Mein Lieb hat einen Garten', where the whole mood changes from depiction to colloquy, there is the narrative harmony of motif 21. The right-hand flights at 'geflagen' anticipate *Zitronenfalter* (30). The bee's scherzando semiquavers at bars 36ff. have the diminutive quality of motif 3, in its *Elfenlied* form. The idea of boyish infatuation is implied in the use of the weak motif 2 and

the passionate motif 13. At 'süsser ist' and 'herzt und küsst' the heartfelt music misses a beat, while in the postlude the melodic lines passionately converge (at the composer's direction 'leidenschaftlich').

5. Cf. Distler, Op. 19 (SATB).

15 (M 3) Ein Stündlein wohl vor Tag (*Just before dawn*)

22 February 1888   G minor   a♭'–g''

As I lay sleeping, just before dawn, a swallow sang to me from a tree by my window; I could hardly hear it, just before dawn.

'Listen to what I'm saying to you; I'm accusing your lover; while I'm singing this he lies snug abed beside another love, just before dawn'.

'Alas, say no more; be silent, I don't want to hear any more. Fly away, fly away from my tree. Oh love and faith are like a dream just before dawn'.

The simple words and their sad overtones that pervade the poem are perfectly mirrored in Wolf's strophic setting with its plaintive harmonies that pervade the music. The melody suggested by Mörike's refrain 'Ein Stündlein wohl vor Tag'

is heard some twenty times in this short song. Monotony is avoided by subtle variation of pitch and rhythm, e.g. in the truncated version which occurs in the tiny prelude and postlude (broken off to make a musical equivalent of 'oh say no more'), and in canon in the left hand throughout. Each verse is tuned a semitone higher to match the gradually mounting emotion of the poem in its transition from sleep to wakefulness. Yet the vocal melody is so organized that the last repetition of this refrain theme is at he same pitch as its first appearance, suggesting an endless and universal sorrow.

So, too, with the treatment of the word 'Stündlein' (a little while) within the refrain. The first time we hear it, there is a plain simple harmony to suit sleep; thereafter, a semitonal clash of half-waking grief. Lastly the same plaintive harmony is separated and accented and placed in a lower register at the final moment of clear realisation and overt acceptance. Meanwhile this same discord, in an even more sharply stressed form, has been incorporated into the last verse as a pang of felt pain, at 'O *weh*! nicht weiter sag!' (*Alas*, say no more!). At this moment, where the words for the first time directly express sorrow, the entry of the voice occurs a bar earlier than the corresponding passage in the second verse, as if grief had compelled its utterance.

NOTES 1. In Mörike's text the refrain of the last line is not preceded by a comma. In a reading of the poem this omission suddenly extends the expected meaning from 'Love is like a dream, just before dawn' to 'Love is like a dream just before dawn'. It is important to preserve this effect in sung performance, by permitting no perceptible break between 'Traum' and 'ein'.

2. The recurrent theme is also used to introduce *Der Knabe und das Immlein* (see 14, note 3) written on the same day.

3. The device of varying the strophic form and increasing the tension by transposition from verse to verse, later so popular with song-arrangers, has hardly any precedent in the Lied. Wolf is unlikely to have known the *Don Gayseros* songs of Schubert (D93) where a similar idea is tried out with far less sophistication.

4. Cf. also the admirable early setting of Mörike's poem by Franz, Op. 28 no. 2, to which Wolf may well have been indebted; and Distler, op. 19 (SATB).

5. The tensions remains unresolved at the end of the song, on a dominant chord, motif 31.

16 (M 4) Jägerlied (*Huntsman's song*)

22 February 1888   A major   e'–a''

How delicate is the tread of a bird in snow when it walks on the mountain top; more delicate still is my love's dear hand, writing me a letter from far away. A heron soars high into the air, far beyond the reach of shot or shaft; the thoughts of true love are a thousand times as swift and high.

A time-signature of 5/4 is unique in Wolf's song-writing. He wrote exultantly to Edmund Lang:

> No sooner had I posted my letter than I found myself, Mörike in hand, writing a second song, and what's more in 5/4 time, and I think I may safely say that such a time-signature was seldom more aptly in place than in this composition.

This seems an odd assessment, since on a literal interpretation the accentuation and tempo would be manifestly awry ('in' and 'die' fall heavily on down-beats; accents, pauses and ritenutos constantly interrupt the rhythmic flow). But Wolf was composing in a molten glow of inspiration, to adapt his own description in the same letter; and his instinct was wholly sound. The intuitive craftsmanship here is exquisite; the blend of simplicity and subtlety charged with emotion exactly akin to that of the poem is Wolf at his most characteristic.

Mörike's mountain scene presents the composer with a picture of virgin inaccessibility; cold and pure, distant and lofty, with an unbroken whiteness of snow or brightness of air. Yet there is also an element of intimacy in the warm love-letters, which like the bird's tracks are dark hieroglyphs on a white background. This linking idea, the tracings or tracks of hand or claw, yields the further comparison that the bird is out of its element when walking, the girl out of hers when writing. Typically, Mörike's meaning is expressed in the unaccustomed mode of trochaic pentameter; even the metrical feet are made to halt and hop, pause and poise. All this coalesces in the sound and sense of the first five-beat line: 'Zierlich ist des Vogels Tritt im Schnee', by which Wolf, like any reader of the German text, must have been wholly captivated. This idea is given musical shape in the piano prelude:

and the rhythm and texture plus the final accent brilliantly convey the needed hint of slight awkwardness. Then that motivic idea is used as the basic structure of the whole song. The quoted phrase is repeated, to make a two-bar prelude which introduces the singing voice with its new theme; the same two bars then reappear as an interlude to reintroduce the voice; then the main vocal theme is echoed with heartfelt sighs in a four-bar postlude. Thus half the song's sixteen bars are for piano solo, which serves both as picture and as frame. This Wolfian power of re-creating poetry in musical terms is so typical and so revealing as to be worth dwelling on in more detail in the notes below.

NOTES 1. There are several other aspects of the music which offer a verbal or conceptual connotation. Thus piano and voice in bar 3 have the engaging lift and dip found in many other Wolfian melodies in association with the idea of singing – here a song within a song (motif 10). The piano left-hand harmony at bar 4 occurs elsewhere in reflective or narrative passages (motif 21). The mediant key-changes in bars 9–11 are thematic in contexts suggesting yearning or aspiring, particularly in association with the idea of increasing intensities of light (motif 24): cf. *In der Frühe* (36) with its analogous association of ideas. Finally the postlude's horn passages are elsewhere used to convey the idea of freedom and the open air (motif 8).

2. On such bases the interplay of musical and verbal concepts, showing how each reflects and enhances the other, could be charted (bearing also in mind the composer's expression marks) as follows:

Bar	Wolf's music	Mörike's words
1 2 }	A bird walking on the snow!	
3	The sight sets me singing about	a bird walking on the snow
4	which in turn makes me think	here on the mountain
5	with an especial tenderness, of	her hand, even more delicate
6	and just as unaccustomed	writing to me from far away.
7 8 }	like a bird walking on snow.	
9	And if a bird were to rise,	a bird high in the air
10	soaring into the bright sky	remote and free [thoughts
11	high and sunlit, it would still be	far less high and swift than my
12	of my own sweetheart,	and of her true love.
13	Lost in those thoughts I go on singing	
14	and sighing as I sing,	
15	out here in the open air;	
16	a huntsman's love-song.	

3. Other relevant points are the ways in which (a) the singing curve of the voice part for a bird in the snow (bar 3) is counterpoised by the upward trend curve of the melody for a bird in the air (bars 9–11, each culminating on the word 'Höh' or 'hoch'); and (b) the duetting melodies of voice and piano become more articulate, while the harmony becomes disturbed at the thought, and imagined touch, of a loved hand (bars 5–6).

4. Cf. Schumann, Op. 59 no. 3 (SATB), and Distler, Op. 19 (two settings, SA and TTB).

17 (M 5) Der Tambour (*The drummer-boy*)

16 February 1888   E major   b#–g# ''

If my mother were a witch and could cast spells! Then she'd go with the regiment to France and everywhere with us, and be the vivandière.

In the camp, at about midnight, when no one is about except the guard, and everyone's snoring, steed and man, then I'd be sitting in front of my drum. The drum would turn into a dish heaped with steaming sauerkraut, the drumsticks would be knife and fork, and my sabre a long sausage. My shako would be a fine tankard that I'd fill with red Burgundy. And because I'd lack light the moon would shine into my tent. Even though it would shine in French I'd still be reminded of my dearest love – oh dear, [oh dear ... oh dear ... dear] there's an end to my fun.

But if only my mother could cast spells ...

[If my mother could cast spells!]

Mörike's engaging little wish-fulfilment fantasy of the drummer-boy posted to France in the Napoleonic wars (still quite recent history in 1837, when the poem was written) would not be the most obvious match to ignite Wolf's creative fire of 1888; nor is the result one of his greatest songs. But it is bright with promise of the greatness to come. It is especially notable for prodigality of thematic material. In four pages there are enough march tunes and rhythms, enough musical allusions and comments for half a dozen songs. Also notable are the deftness and wit that can compress all this fertility of invention into a unified narrative and embellish it on every page with apt and colourful illustrations of the text like a story-book with pictures. The music shows how much Wolf must have enjoyed these unpretentious and good-humoured couplets, with their vivid yet unobtrusive scene- and character-painting that corresponded so closely with his own creative gifts.

The drum-roll in the piano that begins the song and conveys its central character is obvious enough, and so is the drum-beat that accompanies the later mention of 'die Trommel'. But such special Wolfian touches as the vocal line's sudden double lapse into snoring ('alles schnarchet' etc); the piano's delighted dance at the thought of heaped sauerkraut; the sad echoes at the repeated 'ach weh' (oh dear); the way in which the tonality finally loses itself in a dream on the last page as the bewitching mother-motif slips vaguely from key to key in a reverie of home and beauty, particularly the latter – all these are evidence of a new and lively impetus in song-writing, of compelling originality and power.

NOTES 1. The setting has not yet attained to Wolf's final standards of fidelity to the text; thus the repetitions of 'ach weh' with an added 'weh', and of the last phrase in a form that reverts to the first line, are not well designed to express Mörike in musical terms, undeniably effective though they are.

2. The elatedly rising piano phrase at 'Marketenderin' (here vivandière or sutler, hardly a 'camp-follower' as some dictionaries and translators have it) is motif 7. Elation also evokes the euphoric F$^{\sharp}$ major response (motif 40) at 'vor meiner Trommel' etc. The horn passages at bars 23 and 25 are an analogue of motif 8, decorated with swift gesturing scale passages, as in *Der Schreckenberger* (74), here standing for the imagined plying and brandishing of drumsticks.

3. Fertility of invention is a constant feature of those Wolf songs that initiate a new cycle of creativity. There is another example in the Eichendorff songbook (74, note 3); the Italian song *Dass doch gemalt* (195) is even more striking.

4 Cf. Distler, Op. 19 (TTBB).

18 (M 6) Er ist's (*Spring is here*)

5 May 1888, orchestrated 20 February 1890　　　　　　G major　　d'–g''

Once again Spring sends his blue ribbon fluttering through the breezes;
sweet well-known scents drift propitiously over the countryside.
　Violets are already dreaming, and want to come soon.
　Listen! from far off, the soft sound of a harp. That must be you, Spring
[that must be you, Spring]; it is you I have heard [it must be you].

As a setting of words, this song is hardly among Wolf's outstanding successes; his music paraphrases and adapts rather than translates this famous lyric, the inward feeling-tone of which is further underlined by the context later provided for it by the poet in his novel *Maler Nolten*. There it is presented as being sung by a girl working in the garden under the window of the convalescent hero. The text then continues: 'The verses wholly depicted that mood of tender excitement with which the new season is accustomed to invest people, and affects the convalescent more deeply than the healthy man'. Perhaps Wolf chose to read into this poem, as into *Der Genesene an die Hoffnung* (13), something of the fervour and triumph that he himself presumably felt in this particular springtime of 1888, and the full flowering of his own creativity after so many dormant years. Such a response might help to explain the arbitrary repetitions of the text, and the way in which a shy and tender evocation of the personified spirit of Spring is concluded by a sustained top G over a thunderous accompaniment. Yet the effect is one of the utmost brilliance and energy, and the song remains a splendid *tour de force* for gifted performers. Setting Mörike's poem to one side, the music can be greatly enjoyed for its own sake – the racing pulse of the accompaniment, the soft treble harp chords, the excited dipping and soaring and final quietude of the postlude, and the free melodies and strong climaxes of the voice part. All these emphatic underscorings of the verses are still further intensified by the orchestral version, which seems finally to divorce Mörike and espouse Wagner.

NOTES 1. Perhaps this was an earlier sketch refurbished for the new songbook; the idea of illustrating the poet's one harp-note by eight spread chords and then forcing an expressive vocal line to take a final operatic curtain-call (much as in *Zur Ruh* of 1883) seems altogether too jejune for the mature Wolf. So does the repetition of 'Frühling, ja du bist's' followed by another gratuitous 'ja, du bist's'; this suggests the unfortunate influence of Schumann's Op. 79 no. 23. Cf. also Franz, Op. 27 no. 2; Schoeck, Op. 51 no. 4; Reger, Op. 111b (SSAA); and Distler, Op. 19 (SA).
　2. Another influence is Wagner; the opening melody has the air of Siegmund's 'Auflach' ich in heiliger Lust', also a harbinger of spring, in *Die Walküre*, Act I.

3. At 'Veilchen träumen schon' etc both voice and piano have something of the 'mystery' of motif 19.

19 (M 7) Das verlassene Mägdlein (*The forsaken servant-girl*)

24 March 1888   A minor   e'–f''

Early at cockcrow, before the faint stars fade, I must stand at the hearth, must kindle fire.

The flames shine beautifully, the sparks fly; I gaze at them sunk in sorrow.

Suddenly it comes to me, faithless boy, that I have been dreaming of you all night.

Then tear on tear pours down. So my day dawns – would it were over.

Mörike's few folk-song lines evoke a whole world of love and loss. The warm brightness of flames and dreams, the cold darkness of the house and the truth, paint a poignant contrast which is blended into one single emotion as the poem passes from night and unawareness to daybreak and tears, evoking in this brief transition a lifetime of joys past and sorrows now and to come. This is among the great lyrics of the world, and the task of finding music to match it is a daunting one.

We know from a letter* something of how Wolf came to attempt it.

On Saturday I wrote, without having intended to do so, a setting of *Das verlassene Mägdlein*, already set to heavenly music by Schumann. If, despite that, I too composed the same poem, it happened almost against my will; but perhaps for the very reason that I let myself be suddenly taken captive by the magic of this poem, something outstandingly good has resulted, and I think that my composition can stand comparison with Schumann's.

It is not easy to see how any musical setting could do full justice to the fusion of contrasting moods and scenes in Mörike's lyric. But Wolf has no doubt rendered as many aspects of it as are simultaneously translatable into musical terms, and the result is indeed a masterpiece. The music, like the verses, is similar in inspiration to *Ein Stündlein wohl vor Tag* (15) and *Agnes* (26); all three songs are dominated by rhythmic and melodic variants of one plaintive theme. This one begins graphically in A minor with a small dragging and drooping figure. Then it turns warmer and brighter with major chords, a rising melody, and a slightly livelier vocal rhythm as the shining sparks fly. In the third verse, beginning 'Plötzlich,

---

* to Friedrich Eckstein, 27 March 1888

da kommt es mir' (Suddenly it comes to me), new wistful harmonies, underlined with stresses and sighs, are added in the piano part, together with a new hopeful rising motif. The enduring love which is hinted at but not directly expressed in the poem is similarly adumbrated in the music, e.g. at the word 'geträumet' (dreamed). Here the voice part lifts and lightens and hushes; with only the slightest of changes in texture or mood, a sudden tenderness invades the song. But then the hopeful and questioning motif in the right hand falters and fails, as the bleak cold music of the dawn returns to confront warm memory with chill reality. As Mörike says when introducing this song in his novel *Maler Nolten*: 'The melody resounded through the silence of the dark dawn with infinitely moving effect.'

NOTES 1. 'Wann' in the first line is a dialect form of the expected 'wenn'.

2. This lyric, like *Er ist's* (18), is introduced into *Maler Nolten* in the guise of the overheard words sung by a servant at work, this time in the downstairs kitchen. The device reminds the hero, and the reader, of the adored but deserted *Agnes*, whose own song (26) also appears in the novel.

3. As so often in Wolf, the augmented chord conveys pathos (motif 23), while the dominants (after 'habe') impart a yearning inflection (motifs 31–2). The key of A minor is often associated with an especially wistful mood, mainly in songs for a woman's voice.

4. It was Wolf's general rule never to set words which had already, in his judgement, been successfully composed by earlier masters. His exception here suggests a special relationship with Schumann's setting Op. 64 no. 2, which is valuable both as a comparison and in its own right. The extent of Wolf's indebtedness to it can be judged from the fact that Schumann's minor alterations or mistranscriptions ('schwinden' for 'verschwinden', 'darein' for 'drein') occur in both settings. This, in conjunction with the evidence quoted above that Wolf had not intended to set the Mörike poem, yet had Schumann's song in mind at the time, would confirm that the latter, not the former, was his textual source.

5. Cf. also Franz, Op. 27 no. 4; Pfitzner, two settings, no. 5 of *Sechs Jugendlieder* and Op. 30 no. 3; Distler, Op. 19 (SSAA).

20 (M 8) Begegnung (*Encounter*)

22 March 1888   E♭ major   d'–g♭ ''

What a storm there was last night, until the morning finally appeared! How clean that uninvited broom has swept chimneys and alleys!

Already a girl comes down the street, looking around half-startled; like roses blown apart by the wind, so the colour changes in her cheeks.

A handsome lad goes up to her, delightedly seeks to approach her; how awkwardly yet how joyously the two unaccustomed rogues look at each other!

*He seems to be asking if his darling has tidied her plaits that were
disbevelled by a storm last night, in a bedroom with its windows open.*

*The lad is still dreaming of the kisses the sweet child exchanged with
him; he stands enchanted by her charm as she rustles off round the corner.*

One imagines that a chance encounter witnessed by Mörike from his
window one morning gave rise to the idea of this fresh and colourful lyric,
with its typically vivid and intense erotic symbolism, which here as in
Erstes Liebeslied eines Mädchens (54) strikingly anticipates Freud. In
particular, the idea that love is as wayward as winds in their power and
gentleness is a recurrent image in Mörike's verse and prose. Another song-
writer might have gone in for good solid storm-effects in the piano part, in
order to make additional play with the already obvious significance of the
storm, in all senses. Wolf's understanding of his poet impels him far
beyond this, to find a unity of theme and concept that refreshes and
rarefies the poem still further. The gentle sighing accompaniment, even at
its most dramatic, in the prelude

never rises above *f*, and reaches that level only eight times in over sixty
bars. All is restraint, discretion and allusion. A slightly different
figuration, a new tonality, a shift from minor into major, and the
remembered night storm quietens and brightens into voice and piano
melodies well suited to express the morning's freshness and the girl's
charm, as she appears at 'Da kommt ein Mädchen' etc. The sighing and
moaning winds reappear in the piano interludes, and at the mention of
delight ('voll Entzücken') and are delicately recalled as a pianissimo
memory or metaphor while the brief encounter and imagined question are
described at 'Er scheint zu fragen' etc (he seems to be asking). In the last
verse voice and piano resume their duetting; the vocal counter-melody
lingers dreamily on the same note, at 'der Bursche träumt noch von den
Küssen' (the lad is still dreaming of the kisses), and then wells up in
delight. The postlude, with typically Wolfian felicity, takes the piano's
melodies that heralded the girl's arrival on the scene, and adapts them to
her departure; they are set sighing in the same way as the main wind-
theme already quoted, as the girl whisks round the corner and out of sight,
herself a breeze.

NOTES 1. The verbal accentuation of this song is inexact, a feature which often suggests that Wolf is deliberately subordinating the natural stress of the words to an instrumental preconception, here no doubt the main accompaniment figure. This in turn may well have been inspired by Schumann's *Lust der Sturmnacht*, Op. 35 no. 1, which exploits the same tonalities and similar textures to express another text about pleasure taken in a night of storms. We know (from 19 above) that Schumann was in Wolf's mind at the time. An earlier Wolfian version of the same musical metaphor is found in his Heine setting *Das ist ein Brausen* of 1878.

2. The necessary hesitance and shyness of musical as of poetic expression demand unusual restraint from both pianist (no added dynamics) and singer (no added meaningfulness, least of all at the key-phrase 'ein Sturm in Unordnung gebracht').

3. Cf. also Reger, Op. 62 no. 13.

21 (M 9) Nimmersatte Liebe (*Insatiable love*)

24 February 1888   A♭ major   e♭ '—a♭ ''

This is how love is, this is how love is, not to be stilled with kisses: who is such a fool as to try to fill a sieve with mere water? You could pour water in for a thousand years, you could kiss for ever and ever, and never find love's fulfilment.

For love, love has new and strange desires at every hour; we bit our lips sore when we kissed today. The girl kept quite still, like a lambkin under the knife; her eyes were pleading, go on, the more it hurts, the better!

This is how love is, and always was, ever since love has existed; and not even Solomon himself, for all his wisdom, ever loved in any other way. [and not even Solomon himself, for all his wisdom, ever loved in any other way.]

'Yet another new song' wrote the delighted Wolf to his friend Edmund Lang on the day of its completion. 'You'll go wild with delight when you hear it.' One reason for this reaction, he explained, was that at the end it bursts out into a rollicking student song. So indeed it does, with splendid effect, after the music has duly explored, with rather more subtlety than the poem, one aspect of amorous experience. The piano prelude begins with a repeated phrase

Very moderate

which so clearly mimics speech that we are surprised not to find words written in. Since they are not, the precise sense remains conjectural; but the general impression of pleading is apparent enough. The vocal line looks as if it should be taken quite fast. But Wolf asks for a 'very moderate' tempo; the words are meant to be heard. Indeed, they begin with a nuance of declamation unusual even for Wolf, perhaps intended to add a new inflexion to the poem; 'so *ist* die Lieb', *so* ist die Lieb'. But for once the effect seems a little strained and unconvincing, as well as difficult to interpret with complete clarity. At first the piano shares in the melody, but soon – to enhance the idea of vain endeavour towards a love fulfilled or a sieve filled full – there are softly syncopated chords which proceed in increasingly yearning leaps ranging from an initial fifth to two octaves at 'tust ihr nie zu Willen' (never find fulfilment). Here the voice has a characteristic phrase of small compass but great effect. The brief piano interlude is again akin to speech; this time the sense is easier to follow since the right hand is playing a broader variant of the vocal phrase just heard. Excitement grows with the search after new delights in the next verse. The melodies become more chromatic and intense; the pulse of the piano part quickens with repeated semiquaver chords. The accompaniment to the following expressive phrases that link pain with pleasure is masochism itself in its musical weakness – repeated notes, in augmented fifths, shifted off the beat; and this weakness of melody, harmony and rhythm is all graphically devoted to the idea of willing submissiveness.

Finally the promised student song arrives, contrived with brilliant poetic insight and technical assurance as a musical equivalent for Mörike's claim to universality on behalf of his own highly personal thesis. Wolf provides, without a trace of self-consciousness or condescension, a rousing, beer-drinking chorus to typify this view of the average sensual man. This section is marked 'Mit Humor'; and we may safely assume that one point about Solomon had not escaped the attention of either poet or composer – namely that he is popularly known for the number of his wives as well as the extent of his wisdom. Here Wolf preserves the unity of the song by so reorganizing the material of the first part as to display its latent possibilities for the depiction of forthright jollity as well as romantic yearnings. The piano postlude offers the same pleading comments as the prelude, this time with a quiet but decisive full close.

NOTES 1. The poem seems particularly startling as the expression of the transient affection of a twenty-four year old curate (as Mörike then was) for the village schoolmaster's daughter Josephine (also the recipient of the related *Frage und Antwort*, cf. 47, note 2) in 1828. But the erotic equation of love with pain, or passion in a religious sense (even the sacrificial lamb has a Paschal flavour) clearly found a ready response in the future composer of the Mörike and Spanish sacred songs such as *Auf ein altes Bild* and *Wunden trägst du, mein Geliebter*.

2. So, for similar reasons, did the references to Solomon in the last lines (the repetition of which is Wolf's, not Mörike's). Both poem and song suggest a highly unorthodox sermon on Old Testament texts: 'But King Solomon loved many strange women ... and he had seven hundred wives, princesses, and three hundred concubines...' (I Kings XI, 1–3) and 'Let him kiss me with the kisses of his mouth...' (The Song of Solomon I, 2).

3. The striking passage at 'Das Mädchen hielt in guter Ruh' etc combines two typical aspects of Wolf's thematic procedures; the chains of augmented fifths, here standing for maudlin sentiment (motif 23) and the chords on the off-beat conveying childish helplessness (motif 2). The expressive rhythms throughout the song make an interesting study; for ♪♩ ♪ in particular see motif 1.

Wholly characteristic is the epitome of the first two bars for voice and piano; much as in *Wie lange schon*, the apparently simple idea takes an unusual turn, here by the unexpected harmonic inflexion of the flattened sixth.

4. Cf. Distler, Op. 19 (SSATB).

22 (M 10) Fussreise (*A country walk*)

21 March 1888   D major   c#'–e''

When I set off early like this, with a fresh-cut walking-stick, through the woods, uphill and down;

then, like a bird singing and stirring among the leaves, or like a cluster of golden grapes sensing the spirits of delight in the first morning sun:

so too my dear old Adam feels the fever of autumn and spring, the God-emboldened, never forfeited, primal bliss of Paradise. So you are not, after all, old Adam, as bad as austere teachers say;

as if each day were one of the Creation, eternally renewed, you still love and praise, you still sing and exalt your dear Maker and Preserver.

By His grace my whole life would be, in a light stride and sweat, just such a morning journey!

The euphoric Wolf wrote to his friend Edmund Lang:

I have to retract the opinion that the *Erstes Liebeslied eines Mädchens* [54] is the best song I have ever written; for what I wrote this morning, *Fussreise*, is a million times better still. When you have heard this song, you can have only one wish – to die.

This is an odd way of putting it, but one sees what he means. The music creates and communicates a very real sense of release, exaltation and abiding delight. It may be that Wolf's vision, here as elsewhere in the Mörike songs (e.g. *Neue Liebe*, 42) is more secular and less devout than that of his poet. But the sheer physical vitality of the musical response is an apt match for the sensuous imagery of the young Mörike, which (as traditionally in the *Song of Solomon*, cf. 21 above) is freely used to embody erotic as well as spiritual experience.

The brief prelude, with its easy melodic lilt and unifying rhythms that sound throughout the song's eighty-three bars, sets the scene. This, one recognizes, is just how a man might feel, walking at peace with himself and the world, in love with life (or just in love), invigorated with the morning air, humming a little tune, about to break into a song. Then, at the inevitably right moment, the voice strikes in with its fine swinging melody. The piano, not to be outdone, joins in zestfully at the same moment; and the two set off together with a light step, their tunes blending into one exhilaration as the melodic curves go gently lifting and dipping into the words 'Hügel auf und ab' (uphill and down).

The freshness and immediacy of this music, achieved by the simplest of means, have an irresistible forward impetus. This, like the thought of the words, carries through and over the piano interludes; the song walks on air. When the prelude theme resumes, lively in the higher octaves, the voice strikes in as before, alighting gently on the word 'dann' (then) as if it had never really left off – an effect also demanded by the sense of the words. The song sweeps on through the same long sentence in the same melodies, now lovingly extended and brightened, first to 'Morgensonne' (morning sun) and then, via an interlude now delicately altered to suggest small stirrings of exaltation in nest or vine, to the memorable comparison with the first flush of dawn in Eden at 'Erstlings-Paradiesewonne' (primal bliss of Paradise), further brightened by a joyous echo from the piano.

After having thus re-created the fresh feelings abroad in the morning air, the voice drops in pitch, and the musical mood becomes quieter and more reflective. As before (21), the curate Mörike is thinking in terms of texts and sermons. But his vindication of unregenerate man, 'old Adam', as being not so bad after all ('also bist du nicht so schlimm') is decidedly heterodox; and here the music is harmonically uncertain and lacking in conviction. It gradually regains its elation once the depressing doctrines of the austere teachers and preachers, 'wie die strengen Lehrer sagen', have been refuted and rejected. The accompaniment, having thoughtfully echoed those words, is ready to join in the singing again at 'liebst und lobst du immer doch' (you still love and praise), moving on to a strongly affirmative F$^\sharp$-major climax at 'deinen lieben Schöpfer und Erhalter' (your dear Maker and Preserver). And with this thought, as the voice ends its melodic curve, the brisk walking accompaniment is entirely content. For eight bars it breathes pure delight, returning happily to the original key of D major in a memorable musical metaphor of a winding road that leads back home. It rejoins the voice in a repetition of the opening themes with which, in a paean of rejoicing, the song ends. In the postlude the swinging tunes stride past and away with a light heart, leaving lightened hearts behind them.

NOTES 1. The correct tempo of this song is a matter of some uncertainty, not helped by Wolf himself, whose direction 'ziemlich bewegt' (quite quick) is hard to reconcile with his own reported testimony. He is said to have expounded the tempo by reference to the Styrian dialect expression 'schlenzen', meaning to stroll or saunter.* Much depends on taste and technique; but perhaps the tempo is less important than the texture. The music is clearly idealized; it is not so much about the act of walking as about the feeling of walking on air. This is reflected in the use of quaver and semiquaver rests throughout, and single notes rather than chords in the continuous rhythmic figure in the left hand. The music should surely sound as light and crisp as it looks on the printed page. Once the sturdy plodding of hobnailed boots gets into this song, the exhilaration dies forlornly out of it.

2. At 'Hügel auf und ab' is a fine example of the lilting melody that moments of outdoor contentment suggested to Wolf (motif 9); equally apt is the occurrence (at bar 7 etc), in this song of freedom and the open air, of the horn passages of motif 8. The climax at 'lieben Schöpfer' etc has the tonality of F♯ major, which Wolf often reaches at moments of special elation (motif 40).

3. Some parallels between this song and the much earlier *Morgentau* (1) and also the contemporary *Gebet* (40) and *Selbstgeständnis* (64) are suggested in the notes to those songs.

23 (M 11) An eine Aeolsharfe (*To an Aeolian Harp*)

15 April 1888   E major   c♯'-g♯''

Leaning against the ivied wall of this old terrace, you, mysterious lyre played by a Muse born of air, begin, begin once again your melodious lament.

You winds come hither from far away, oh! from the fresh-greening mound of the boy who was so dear to me. And brushing spring blossoms on your way, surfeited with fragrance, how sweetly [how sweetly, how sweetly] you grieve this heart! [how sweetly you grieve this heart!] And you murmur here into the strings, drawn by their sweet-sounding sorrow, growing in response to my yearning and then dying away again.

But all at once, as the wind gusts more strongly, the harp's gentle cry echoes, to my sweet terror, the sudden stirring of my soul; and here the ripe rose, shaken, strews all its petals at my feet!

Aeolian harps were dear to the nineteenth century; there is something romantic in every sense about a stringed instrument played by the wind. But Mörike's poem, and Wolf's music, go far beyond mere romance. The

---

* see Anton Tausche, *Hugo Wolf's Mörike-Lieder*, 1947, p. 53

song begins without prelude, in soft invocation. Coaxing arpeggios provide the accompaniment, as if a real harp were appealing to the wind to play it. All this is beautifully drawn, in melodic recitative of the utmost quietude; the piano's spread chords avoid the first beat of the bar, and this absence of rhythmic impulse confirms that there is at first no breath of wind in the air. But the appeal is answered. After 'Klage' (lament) the most delicate of breezes strays into the song. Successive harp notes drift up slowly and softly from the left hand, barely audible at first (*pppp* is the composer's direction) but then gaining slightly in strength and intensely in sweetness as slow chordal melodies are added high above them. In between, the voice weaves its own independent lines. At every turn the music mirrors the rich sweet melancholy of the poem, compounded of grief for a dead brother, surrender to the radiance of summer, and over and through all the wind-blown music latent in the words that Wolf finds and releases and sets singing anew. In the long postlude the soft breeze is stripped down whisper by whisper to the total silence from which the song first emerged.

NOTES 1. On a walking holiday in the summer of 1888 Wolf visited the castle of Hoch-Osterwitz and heard an Aeolian harp, set in a window. He was delighted with the sound, which, he told his companions, was exactly as he had imagined it in his song, even though he had never heard it in his life before. But he very likely knew the next best thing, namely Brahms's very similarly conceived and wholly comparable setting (Op. 19 no. 5) of the same poem. This too repeats 'wie süss', though only once; all the other repetition here is Wolf's.

2. But Wolf, unlike Brahms, saw the need to reproduce, as part of his song, Mörike's Latin epigraph to the poem, viz:

> *Tu semper urges flebilibus modis*
> *Mythen ademptum: nec tibi vespero*
> *Surgente decedunt amores*
> *Nec rapidum fugiente solem.*

You ever in tearful strains dwell on Mythes taken away: your loving laments cease not when the evening star rises, nor when it flees the swift sun.

The classical scholar and translator Mörike would certainly have known that these words in their context (Horace, *Odes* II no. 9) convey a reproach, even a reproof to one Flavius for the unreasonable duration and intensity of his mourning. No doubt the quotation was selected for that very reason. Mörike's beloved brother August had died in 1824, at the age of seventeen, in Ludwigsburg. There in 1831 the poet had heard an Aeolian harp; and as he wrote to his then fiancée Luise Rau (14 May 1831) 'The sweet tones brought all the past welling up in me'. There too, another six years later, he wrote this poem. The ingrained and obdurate grief confers a Tennysonian richness and satiety upon the elegiac rhythms and imagery of the verses and hence, via Wolf's vivid intuitive faculties, upon the music.

3. Note the falling semitone used for the repeated words 'wie süss'. The same

interval appeared in a similar rhythmic and harmonic context for the same words at bar 8 of *Der Genesene an die Hoffnung* (13) dated only five weeks earlier.

4. One of the prevailing rhythms, ♩♪ ♩ 𝅗𝅥 ♩♩♩ , is akin to the self-surrendering of motif 1. The mystery of motif 19 is heard in the piano at 'geheimnissvoll'.

24 (M 12) Verborgenheit (*Seclusion*)

13 March 1888   E♭ major   d'–g''

Let me be, O world, let me be! tempt not with gifts of love, leave this heart to know alone its own bliss, its own pain. I cannot tell why I grieve; it is unknown sorrow. Through tears I still see the sun's dear light.

Often, when I am lost in thoughts, a bright joy flashes, through the heaviness that oppresses me, blissfully in my breast.

Let me be, O world, let me be! tempt not with gifts of love, leave this heart to know alone its own bliss, its own pain.

One can see why this famous song should already have attained widespread popularity in Wolf's lifetime, and also why he himself came to express dissatisfaction with it in later years. Both these responses result from the atypical touches of overt sentiment in the music, which in turn may well derive from Wolf's personal reaction, in a setting written on his twenty-eighth birthday, to a lyric that exactly describes his own cyclic creative experience and temperament. The music sees its own face in the poem with just a hint of self-consciousness; and without the utmost restraint in performance its expression can easily suggest a drawing-room ballad cosiness which is false to Mörike and unfair to Wolf. For *Verborgenheit* is not unworthy of its composer, despite his own misgivings. It has tenderness, even nobility; its melodies are memorable, its structure shapely and effective; it epitomizes the deep and intense personal affinity between poet and musician.

A repeated bar of quiet prelude leads to the entry of the voice with a simple melody entwining and interchanging with a new countermelody in the sustained top notes of the right hand. The image of contented self-communion is graphically vivid; the nature of inward feeling is made apparent to the outside observer. There is a quiet climax at the word 'Wonne' (bliss) and a brief reflective ritenuto to point the instant transition to 'Pein'; but the harmonies remain serenely diatonic, to show that both joy and sorrow feel settled and at home within the frame of mind here described. The more conflicting emotions of the next verse are reflected in an increasing intensity of harmony, though the strong melodic impulse never falters. As joy finally triumphs, at least for a time, the real climax is reached in an extended version of the first; at 'wonniglich' (blissfully) the earlier music of 'Wonne' is writ large. The tonic chord of E♭ major shines out splendidly, an effect greatly heightened by the fact that it is being heard for the first time since then, after a delay of sixty deliberate crotchet beats. Then quietude supervenes; and the song ends as it began, in gentle intercession. The last word is left not with joy but with the sadness that is seen (here as in *Gebet*, 40) as a necessary part of true peace of mind.

NOTES 1. The repetition of the last verse is Mörike's own.

2. The music has interesting affinities with Schumann's *Du Ring an meinem Finger*, Op. 42 no. 4, also about a private joy and sorrow and also composed by a song-writer with as intensely cyclic a temperament as Mörike and Wolf. Both songs are marked 'innig'; they also have key, texture, rhythm, and a melodic phrase ('Lass, o Welt' = 'Ringelein') in common.

3. The musico-verbal equivalence of bars 11–19 is worth separate study. As perplexing sorrow yields place to illuminating sunlight, so the harmonic clashes and tensions on key words ('traure', 'Wehe', 'Tränen', 'Licht') become progressively less poignant; the questing left-hand figure lapses into silence; and is caught up in the repeated chords that suggest effulgence to Wolf, motif 25, whether of sunlight as here or starlight as in *An die Geliebte* (44).

4. Meanwhile the tonic chord is consistently avoided and delayed, giving enhanced effect to its eventual appearance; this feature of Wolf's song-writing becomes especially noteworthy in the Italian songs, e.g. *Wir haben beide* (205) and *Wenn du mich mit den Augen streifst* (224).

5. Other motivic points are the unobtrusively-touched and unique low F in the left hand at 'Brust', to show how deeply yet unwittingly the heart is suddenly and briefly filled with joy; the epigrammatic construction of the 'innig' prelude from the harmony at 'alleine'; and the rising and falling sixths of motif 10 – the inward singing of the solitary mind.

6. Cf. Franz, Op. 28 no. 5; Distler, Op. 19 (two settings, SA and TTBB).

25 (M 13) Im Frühling (*In Spring*)

8 May 1888   F♯ minor   b–g''

Here I lie on the hill of spring. The clouds become my wings, a bird flies ahead of me. Oh tell me, one and only love, where you live, that I may dwell with you. But you and the breezes have no home. Like a sunflower my mind stands open, yearning, expanding in love and hope. Spring, what is it you want of me? When shall I be stilled?

I see the cloud moving, and the river; the golden kiss of the sun drives deep into my veins; my eyes, wondrously enchanted, close as if in sleep. Only my ears still catch the hum of the honey-bee.

I think of this and that, I yearn without quite knowing why. It is half pleasure, half lament. Tell me, my heart, what memories you are weaving here in the darkling shade of golden-green boughs? Old unnameable days.

In this typically Wolfian masterpiece the radiance of a great poem is rekindled in music. Mörike's lyric mood whether closed as in the previous song or sunflower-open as here remains poised between pleasure and pain. When he introduced this poem into his only full-length novel *Maler Nolten*, he strove to clarify its feeling-tone with a phrase or two of explanation. His hero feels overcome by a 'powerful yearning ... a sweet impulse towards a nameless good, which seemed to speak to him with such tender allurement on all sides from the deeply-moving aspects of Nature and yet to vanish again into an infinite remoteness. So he became lost in his dreams. Let us come to their aid – for they would often melt into melodies of their own accord – with a suitably loving strain' – and then follows the text of the poem.

Wolf might have taken Mörike's last sentence above as his own motto. His song flows in an endless stream of dreamy melody from start to finish, and every bar testifies to the depth and authenticity of the composer's response to the poet's mood. The first four bars offer a directly sensuous equivalent to the opening line, as to the piano's musing reveries the voice adds its own – 'Hier lieg' ich auf dem Frühlingshügel'. Then voice and piano pursue their own separate dreaming and wistful ways. All the music grows from the terrain of these first few bars, branching and flowering out into new yet related melodies. The last of these contains the brief persistent yearning phrases which are the heart and joy of this song, symbolizing the poetic concept of 'all-einzige Liebe', the unique essence of love. Before the word 'Liebe' occurs, those phrases are kept disguised or veiled or separated within the piano part; thereafter that word releases them in explicit and repeated clusters that fade and wilt sadly at the phrase 'ihr habt kein Haus' (you have no home). The opening strain resumes; and at the sunflower simile, 'Der Sonnenblume gleich', the initial melody is opened out into right-hand octaves and new left-hand counterpoints. The phrases are expanded, the vocal line is extended; the harmonies are higher and brighter; voice and piano flower as before. At the next mention of love, now quickened with hope, 'Lieben und Hoffen', the yearning motifs return to sing on and on in the right hand, eager to be heard, unwilling to cease, all through the invocation to spring at 'Frühling, was bist du gewillt' etc. Then they move lullingly down into the left hand as if moving into the tranced or visionary state that the poem describes, beginning with the words 'Die Wolke seh' ich wandeln, und den Fluss'. Here the main motif comes to rest on a dominant pedal of fifteen bars, while the right hand has chords with new melodies and arpeggio figures for the slow broad movement of clouds and river. The total hypnotic effect induces the visionary trance that now follows in the poem; closing dazed eyes 'als schliefen sie ein' (as if falling asleep), hearing only the distant hum of bees, as in the piano interlude the melodies go drowsing and daydreaming on, in a state of suspended animation further depicted by the left hand's barely audible seven-fold insistence on the key-note. Finally this interlude stirs, rouses and drifts gently back to the first strain again. Now, at 'ich denke dies' the voice enters a whole bar later than at the outset; awareness is returning only gradually. The mutual flowering and brightening in voice and piano follow as before, and grow once more into the all-pervasive main theme of yearning. The culminating question 'was webst du für Erinnerung' (what memory are you weaving) is asked and answered in a broad vocal recitative to slow solemn harmonies that have been at the heart of the song throughout, as the answer lies at the heart of the poem: 'Alte unnennbare Tage', past days, lost beyond recall, too deep for words. But not too deep for this marvellous music.

NOTES 1. Some older Peters editions have 'wenn' in bar 38; it should be 'wann'.

2. The unified structure is masterly. Here is the musical four-bar frame devised by Wolf for Mörike's expressive landscape of free verse.

		I		II		III
A	openness	1–4	=	23–6	=	72–5
B	yearning	5–8	=	27–30	=	76–9
C	love	9–12	=	31–4	=	80–3
D	reflection	13–22	=	35–42	=	89–94

The transition from II to III is, the trance-interlude 43–71; the 'memories' coda 95–8 recalls 1–4.

3. The verbal links fall neatly into place. Thus AI is the hill of spring, AII the sunflower image, AIII thinking this and that; all begin at the same pitch. Similarly BI is cloud and bird, BII is 'sehnend', BIII 'ich sehne mich'. BII is a semitone higher than BI; further, each consists of a two-bar phrase repeated a tone higher, intensifying the feeling from 'sehnend' to 'sich dehnend'. CI is 'all-einzige Liebe', CII 'Lieben' und Hoffen', CIII 'halb Lust, halb Klage'. The D-form extracts, repeats and develops the main motif as the poetic thought is developed through time: love and fulfilment are (I) unattainable in the present and (II) uncertain in the future, so after deep musing, (III) sadly, yet joyously, one dreams of the past. And indeed these last four bars go as far back in time as is musically possible, namely to the first four, while the last bar looks forward questioningly to the future in the dominant chord of motif 31.

4. The Wolfian weaving of the vocal line into this structural pattern inevitably entails the occasional kink of declamation, as at 'auf' in bar 3; but these can readily be smoothed out, e.g. here by singing the first three vocal bars as two of 9/4 rather than three of 6/4.

5. The main theme equated with 'yearning' in the comments above (piano right

hand, bars 13–20ff) is found in similar contexts elsewhere (motif 12). Its daydream or lullaby use here emphasizes its musical affinities with the themes that Wolf also found appropriate in contexts expressive of nocturnal reverie (motif 18). Throughout the song, motif 12 is found in association with a steadily falling bass line in the piano – an expression which in later songs comes to connote the idea of loneliness of separation (motif 15). The repeated bass F sharps before 'Ich denke dies' have the repose of motif 39.

    6. See 37, note 4.

26 (M 14) Agnes

3 May 1888   F minor $f^{b\,\prime}-g^{b\,\prime\prime}$

Time of roses! alas, how swiftly by, swiftly by, you have sped! If my lover had kept faith, kept faith, it would not grieve me so.

The reaping women sing contentedly, contentedly at the harvest. But I am sick, sick at heart; no more happiness for me.

So I creep through the meadow vale, so through the vale, as if lost in dreams, up to the hillside where a thousand times, a thousand times, he vowed to be true.

Up there on the hill's edge, turned away, I weep by the lime-tree; in my hat the rose-red ribbon, the one he gave me, plays in the wind.

At first hearing, the vocal melody takes precedence and the piano 'accompanies' in traditional fashion. Wolf naturally feels that the gracefully cadenced folk-song style repetitions of the lyric –

> Rosenzeit, wie schnell vorbei,
> Schnell vorbei
> Bist du doch gegangen! –

call for this treatment. No doubt he was also well aware of the poem's ironic function and detailed description when included in Mörike's novel *Maler Nolten*, where the heroine is asked to sing. We are told that her voice is strong and gentle, yet (*sic*) more at home in the lower than the upper register. She selects this song as a plea to her lover Nolten for constancy, which he duly vows. But the reader is meant to feel that the choice, and the probable outcome, are alike unhappy; Agnes will live her own song. Mörike suggests that we try to infer from these simple verses, as he calls them, some approximate notion of the music, especially from the echo-refrain, when 'the melody always took a turn impossible to describe, which seemed to express every element of sadness and sorrow that could possibly lie hidden in the bosom of an unhappy creature.' Wolf responds admirably to this stipulation. The vocal line is full of wistful appeal; and when the lyric is allowed to speak in terms of simple melody, plainly harmonized, as at 'Schnitterinnen singen' the result is enchanting. But the composer feels that he must also extract the latent grief and find a manifest equivalent for it. So the piano part is deliberately though sensitively inflected to that end. The wide rising discordant intervals (minor ninths) heard in the slow prelude constitute the bass of the piano part throughout the first verse. The right hand has light chords that follow the rhythm of the vocal melody, mainly in contrary motion, perhaps as an intuitive image of paths sundering and diverging. In the second verse the minor ninths disappear, and are replaced by a new falling motif in the right hand, sounding out the new rhythm 𝄴 ♪♩ ♪♩ etc, with a suggestion of an echo of the vocal line in the first verse, at the word 'gegangen'. It is as if, while the voice is singing of the cheerful reapers at the harvest, the accompaniment were saying to itself 'gone, gone', softly and insistently, a nagging pain. The rhythm is now incorporated into the left hand for the third verse, making the recurring leaps of the minor ninth more poignant and desperate than ever. In this verse the falling phrase already noted occurs at the word 'verloren' – and the piano reverts to this strain again in the last verse, with similar effect. 'Lost, lost', say the repeated drooping right-hand phrases that resound throughout the verse and bring the song to a close in a short postlude.

NOTES 1. Walter Legge tells us that in Wolf's own copy of the first edition, the ⎺⎺⎻⎼ signs in the voice at bar 15 were added in the piano part (see *Music Review*, August 1941): so in the *Kritische Gesamtausgabe*.

2. The poem's extreme sensitivity and sophistication include a deliberate use of folk-song idiom, in diction and metre as well as the echo-device. The resulting amalgam presents a problem to composers. Wolf's setting is arguably over-stylized. Brahms's pleasant treatment of the same lyric (Op. 59 no. 5) goes to the other extreme; it is homespun. The contrasting essences of the poem are perhaps not wholly captured by either.

3. Wolf's minor ninths again recall Schumann's setting of *Das verlassene Mägdlein* (see 19, note 3), a poem similar in style as well as content; and also the poignant upward leaps of the upper voice and piano in the Schumann duet *Liebesgram*, Op. 74 no. 3.

4. The pervading rhythm 𝄴 ♪♩ ♪♩ with its missing or failing prime pulse is an analogue of helplessness; cf. motif 2.

5. Cf. Franz, Op. 27 no. 5; Distler, Op. 19 (TB).

27 (M 15) Auf einer Wanderung (*On a journey*)

11–25 March 1888   E♭ major   c♭'–g''

*I arrive in a friendly little town, with red evening light lying in its streets.
Just then, from an open window away across the richest riot of flowers,
gold bell chimes come floating, and one voice seems a choir of
nightingales, making the blossoms quiver, the breezes quicken, and the
roses shine out in a brighter red.*

Long I stood in amazement, oppressed by joy.

How I passed through the town gate, I myself truly cannot tell.

*Oh here, how light the world lies! The sky surges in a tumult of
crimson, the town lies behind me in a golden haze. How the stream purls
among the alders, how the mill clacks in the valley! I am as if intoxicated,
confused.*

O Muse! you have touched my heart with a breath of love!

Mörike's poems often take place in a timeless world or a timeless moment
(as also in e.g. *Im Frühling* and *Um Mitternacht*). This poem (inspired by
the beautiful singing voice of Marie Mörike, a cousin's wife) distils an
essence of pure joy in one such moment, and Wolf finds for it a musical
equivalent of matchless perfection.

The music grows out of the lilting four-bar prelude, which brings the
singer jauntily into town to the rhythm of springing steps whether of
notional heels or hooves, on foot or on horseback. This motif determines
the mood of the first part of the song – light and carefree, yet somehow
expectant and incomplete. It is essentially an accompaniment figure, and
is so used throughout. But as in so many of Schubert's songs, it also
contains subsidiary melodies, e.g. in the tune formed from the first and
fourth right-hand quavers throughout the main theme and also in its four-
part decorations. Into this cheerful background one of the melodies (the
tenor part) enters as the vocal line – 'In ein freundliches Städtchen tret' ich
ein'. Then the harmony darkens flatwards while the voice finds warm low
tones for the sunset glow at 'Abendschein'. The tonality brightens into D
major for the riot of flowers, 'den reichsten Blumenflor', and then
mellows again into D♭ for the golden bell's notes, the 'Goldglockentöne'.
At the crucial words 'eine Stimme scheint ein Nachtigallenchor' (one
voice sounds like a choir of nightingales) the music enters briefly into the
neutral C major, where the piano's melody shifts off the beat to the half
bar like a catch in the breath; and its first three notes are made to sing out
and then falter and stammer a repetition as if overwhelmed. This feeling
of being overcome and indeed almost daunted by delight now sounds out
in E major, at the first climactic moment of the song. The voice swells and

shines on the sustained first syllable of the word 'Nachtigallenchor' over a *pp* accompaniment, creating a vivid image of rapturous song and intent listening. The very considerable emotive force of the music is now concentrated on the notion of utter amazement and joy that a circumstance so mundane and naive as hearing a voice singing at sunset could on this one occasion seem so sweet to one listener.

All this is touched in with the utmost restraint and delicacy. Only at the following words 'dass die Blüten beben' (making the blooms quiver) is the pent-up emotion allowed to come out; and then it bursts out, overflowing with excitement and gratitude. It needs an extended piano interlude in which to recover. Here the moment of singing is savoured again, with chromatic sighs repeated in the left hand; the sustained chords anticipate the following explanation in the voice part at the extended first note of 'Lang hielt' ich staunend' (Long I stood in amazement), and this is further illustrated by long held chords. Meanwhile the piano has gradually regained the capering or cantering movement of the prelude, to show that the journey has been resumed. But now that movement is no longer jaunty; it has been affected by the experience, and emerges transformed by slight but telling changes into a mood of ineffable dreaminess. This wandering tranced music again anticipates and illustrates the voice's explanation: 'Wie ich hinaus vors Tor gekommen, ich weiss es wahrlich selber nicht' (How I passed through the gate, I myself truly cannot tell).

Again the mood changes, this time from dream to vision. A new though related theme is heard in the piano. As the voice sings in expressive phrases of the crimson sunset, the golden haze, this theme is extended over sixteen bars, shifting along Wolf's characteristic bright chain of mediant key-change from B♭ through D and F♯ to B♭ an octave higher. The tumultuous excitement mounts, then subsides as the piano rediscovers, for the first time since the opening bars, the home tonic of E♭ major, and there broadens into spread harp-chords, to herald Mörike's final invocation to his Muse. The postlude softly resumes all the musical themes that we have heard, now made richer by their verbal associations. The piano part is as it were reliving the poem, like an inward voice whispering 'surprised by joy'.

NOTES 1. There should be a decrescendo sign in bar 40, as in 42; the inter-stave rests are otiose in bars 50 and 52. These points are confirmed by Walter Legge's study (*Music Review*, August 1941) of Wolf's own copy, which also contained the following changes, all in the piano part.

Bar 23, delete *ppp*; 47–8, change left hand from

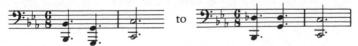

53, 59, change *ppp* to *pp*; 63, add ⟋ under *p(ausdrucksvoll)*; 64, add *mf* on first beat, then ⟍ to end of bar; 65, add *p* on first beat, then ⟋ to *mf* on last quaver; 73, add *p* at beginning; 85, add ⟍ after *dim.* to end of bar; 98, delete *ppp*; 102, amend *pp* to *p*; 103, add ⟋ above G and *dim.* above A♭; 105, replace *ppp* by ⟍ to end of bar; 106, add *pp* at half-bar.

All these amendments have been adopted in the *Kritische Gesamtausgabe*

2. Like the poem, the music is a single essence undergoing changes. The journeying theme of the prelude

is shifted half a bar and made to falter thus, at bars 21–2

yielding a new theme of which a further variant (bar 26) is

This in turn becomes

for the visionary climax from bar 63 onwards, and finally in augmentation

for the invocation to the Muse, bars 82–3.

(Essential notes only are shown, in the same key and register for ease of comparison.)

3. The first of these themes might suggest, if the rhythmic resemblances to *Der Gärtner* (29) are a sound guide, that Wolf has imagined a traveller on horseback, despite such contra-indications in the text as the initial 'eintreten', with its pedestrian connotations.

4. This song offers a paradigm of Wolf's expressive harmonic procedures. Here he uses key-change and -contrast as a painter uses a palette: a warm C♭ tint for sunset red, a bright D major for flowers, a mellow D♭ major for gold, a clear E major for nightingales. The result has a chromatic look on the page, but a diatonic sound in performance. Of the sixty-four notes sung by the voice up to the quiet climax of 'Nachtigallenchor', only *two* fail to belong to the ordinary major scale

of the key being used at each successive moment. These are the B flats on the word 'Stimme' – the idea whence all the emotion of the poem derives.

5. The trancing effect of the fourth example above so appealed to Wolf that he used it again, transformed but recognizable, in other songs where the mood is also one of something approaching auto-hypnosis (motif 12) –notably in *Im Frühling* (25). The fifth example, when it appears in the postlude (at 'ausdrucksvoll') recalls the invocation to the Muse with the harmonies of motif 14, which may imply the idea of quasi-filial affection. Mediant key change (B♭, D, F♯, B♭, in bars 63 ff), for effects of increasing radiance, is motif 24. There is some affinity between the opening vocal line here and the open air contentment of motif 9 in its *Fussreise* form.

28 (M 16) Elfenlied (*Elf-song*)

7 March 1888   F major   d'–f''

At night in the village the watchman cried 'Eleven'.* A very small elf was asleep in the wood, just at eleven.

And he thinks that the nightingale must have called him by name from the valley, or Silpelit might have sent for him. So the elf rubs his eyes, comes out of his snail-shell house, and is like a drunken man, his nap was not finished; and he hobbles down tip tap through the hazelwood into the valley, slips right up to the wall; there sits the glow-worm, light on light.

'What are those bright windows? There must be a wedding inside; the little people are sitting at the feast, and dancing about in the ballroom. So I'll just take a peep in!'

Shame! he hits his head on hard stone! Well, elf, had enough, have you? Cuckoo! [Well, elf, had enough, have you?] Cuckoo! [Cuckoo! cuckoo! cuckoo!]

This dazzling *tour de force* crackles with wit and invention. As in *Der Tambour* (17) there is material enough for half a dozen songs; and again we hear some particularly revealing examples of Wolf's intuitive skill in underlining textual details without marring the unity of the whole. Thus in the first two lines the composer seeks and finds the musical equivalent of a contrast of meaning (the pun on 'Elfe'*), a contrast of states of being (ponderous watchman, airy elf), and a contrast of distance (village in a valley, coppice on a hill). These are respectively rendered by a change of key, a change of texture, and a change of dynamics, all within the infinitely simple thematic framework of a rising scale and a falling octave (for the word 'Elfe'). Then, when the voice describes the first confused thoughts of the waking elf, the octaves persist in both hands in the piano part as if to say 'someone's calling my name'. As the elf rubs his eyes

---

* Elf = eleven

('reibt sich der Elf die Augen aus') the piano indicates some small dazed activity, in the right hand, while in the left the octaves continue to call out. Then their top notes are peremptorily accented, implying 'someone *did* call my name: I'm *sure* of it'. As the elf leaves his home and stumbles down into the valley, the hitherto unchanged octaves also leave the home tonic and hobble downwards, still interspersed with small-scale uncertainties. Meanwhile the right hand has become gradually clearer and more distinct in texture as consciousness returns, and now goes brightening into G major as the piano takes on a soft sparkling appropriate to glow-worms. The elf's subsequent enthusiasm and painful disillusion are graphically illustrated; and the song ends with a page of teasing comment from the poet or singer.

NOTES 1. Mörike's poem finishes 'Elfe, gelt, du hast genug?/Kuckuck! Kuckuck!' In some editions of the *Gedichte* the last word has the dialect form with an initial G; but the spelling 'Gukuk', as well as the copious repetition, may be Wolf's own contribution. The sense of the cuckoo-call here is one of mockery or teasing; the children for whom Mörike wrote this and other elfin fantasies would have used the word thus in their hiding games: 'peep-bo'.
2. There is a very subtle touch at the mention of 'Silpelit', who in Mörike's private mythology is a lady elf; so her name evokes a *poco rit.* of affection, or respect. Character and poem were both incorporated in *Maler Nolten*, in the third and ninth scenes respectively of the shadow-play *Der letzte König von Orplid*, which is also the inspiration of Mörike's *Gesang Weylas* (58) and the textual source of his *Die Geister am Mummelsee* (59).
3. The treble minor seconds in e.g. bars 22–5 are characteristic; motif 3. The opening octaves and unisons are motif 30.

29 (M 17) Der Gärtner (*The Gardener*)

7 March 1888   D major   a'–g''

On her favourite mount, as white as snow, the loveliest of princesses rides down the avenue.

Upon the path that her steed prances so delicately down, the sand I have strown glitters like gold.

You rose-coloured bonnet bobbing up and down, throw me a feather on the sly! And if you would like a bloom from me in return, take a thousand for one, take them all! [Take a thousand for one, take them all!]

The delightful poem has two aspects, picture and mood. Wolf's painting is deftly done, with an immediate charm and appeal that have made the song well-known. Its freshness is never spent; it catches to perfection one fleeting and gracious moment, like a Fragonard canvas in white, gold and rose. But the Minnelied frame of mind, all submission and devotion, somewhat eludes the music. True, the curvetting rhythm of the prelude dominates the song, and tells us, hardly less explicitly than the opening words, of the princess riding elegantly and capriciously down the avenue. But there is little musical equivalent for the hopeless and humble adoration of the unseen gardener, who is after all both the subject and the speaker of the poem. In the verbal mode, the chasm that sunders his lowness from Her Highness is subtly and sensitively conveyed by his absence from her presence. The sand is in every sense beneath her notice; its strower keeps a respectful distance; only her headgear is addressed, and then only in inaudible or unspoken words. But the hero's corresponding absence from the song, apart from its title, carries no such clear implications in the musical mode. Wolf is reduced to indicating the singer's feelings by marking two expressive ritenutos in the last verse, at 'Blüte' (bloom) and 'alle' (all); and certainly the song needs to be performed with more consciously heightened feeling, and more deliberate underlining of the text, than is normally necessary in Wolf, if the music is to achieve its full emotive effect. The usual and not unacceptable alternative is to perform the work as if it were a nursery-rhyme or fairy-tale of a fine lady upon a white horse; and a very enchanting one it makes.

NOTES 1. The repetition is Wolf's, not Mörike's. Perhaps one reason for the apparent emphasis on pictorial effect is the superimposition by the piano of an extra caracoling figure on the vocal line's own equivalent of Mörike's amphibrachs, which are already intended to convey the prancing rhythm. Wolf seems over-influenced by this strongly-marked metre, to the extent of misaccentuation ('Leibrösslein ... reit't *durch* die...'). Interestingly, Mörike's correspondence (letter to Wilhelm Hartlaub, 29 December 1842) tells us of a setting by Friedrich Kauffmann, whose son Emil was later a close friend of Wolf's:

[He] has set it quite simply ... the accompaniment has a very pleasant imitation of a gentle gallop, which keeps in step with the melody and stands out with especial distinctness when the latter leaves off.

2. The poetic mood may perhaps be permissibly inferred from what seems the obvious inspiration of the verses, namely a passage in Eichendorff's *Novelle Aus dem Leben eines Taugenichts* (From the Life of a Good-for-Nothing) (1826), also known to Wolf (see 77, note 1). There in Chapter II the hero, who is a gardener, hears hoofbeats and sees his adored high-born lady in a green hunting-habit, and with plumes nodding on her hat, riding slowly down the avenue. He becomes intoxicated with fear, palpitations of the heart, and great joy; and cries out involuntarily 'Loveliest and most gracious of ladies, take this bouquet of flowers from me, and all the flowers from my garden, and all I have'.

3. Wolf's setting has perhaps somewhat unfairly eclipsed Schumann's Op. 107 no. 3, also in D major and no doubt among the sources of his own inspiration. Cf. also Distler's three settings Op. 19 (SATB, SSAA, TTB).

30 (M 18) Zitronenfalter im April (*Brimstone butterfly in April*)

6 March 1888   A minor/A major   e'–a''

Cruel spring sun, you wake me before my time; my delicate food does not flourish until the bliss of May.

If there is no dear girl here to offer me a droplet of honey from her rosy lips, then I must perish miserably, and May will never see me in my yellow dress, [in my yellow dress].

The grave delicacy and grace of this music make a perfect match for the elusive beauty of the poem, with its mood of lingering wistfulness perfectly matching its picture painted in the as yet non-existent but hoped-for colours of green, rose and yellow. But as in *Der Gärtner* (29) the manifest charm will remain more apparent than the latent poignancy unless the latter is especially instilled in performance. Then the music will take wing. The prelude is already evocative of a striving and pining for flight in its repeated jerky yet dainty phrases suggesting the tentative movements of a newly awoken butterfly. As the voice enters, the piano part moves higher and takes on a hopeful upward lilt. The tonality lightens into the major to greet an imagined girl, with the piano's right-hand phrases assuming occasional downward inflexions, as if the dream were unlikely to come true. But it continues in a notional flight, most delicately drawn in high, drifting staccato lines that rise, float, fall and gradually fold at the last words. The hesitant and lingering tone, the postlude's reversion to the prelude's more static theme, varied by one tiny extra effort, seem to take a dubious or pessimistic view; but the final dominant chord leaves the question still hovering in the air.

NOTES 1. The repetition is Wolf's, not Mörike's. A 'Zitronenfalter' is the brimstone butterfly *Gonepteryx Rhamni*, presumably imagined as emerging after hibernation.

2. In other contexts (e.g. *Das verlassene Mägdlein*) A minor suggests a damsel in distress; A major, springtime (e.g. *Frühling übers Jahr*). Both the theme of the verses and the minor/major changes make this song a perfect companion piece to Schubert's *Die Rose* (D745).

3. The right-hand flights recall those of the bee in *Der Knabe und das Immlein* (14); the final dominant is motif 31.

31 (M 19) Um Mitternacht (*At midnight*)

20 April 1888   C♯ minor   g♯–e''

Night came serenely ashore, and leans dreaming against the mountain side. Her eyes see the golden balance of time now at rest in equipoise.

And the streams rush out more boldly, they sing in the ear of their mother the night about the day, the day it has been today.

She heeds not that old, age-old, lullaby; she is tired of it. The blue of the sky sounds sweeter still to her, the equal-swung yoke of the fleeting hours.

But the streams go on telling their tale, the waters still sing in their sleep about the day, the day it has been today.

Wolf's strophic setting is a fine match for Mörike's masterpiece. The piano begins in a low register with a gently-rocking quaver rhythm that goes on murmuring its lullaby of night and dream throughout the song, like the streams that sing in their sleep. From this background the slow calm rising melody of the voice comes in as inevitably and serenely as Night herself. Piano and voice rise and brighten at the first mention of the singing streams, their boldness unobtrusively emphasized by sustained accented notes in the right hand as pitch and harmonies deepen and darken again into the word 'Tage', with a pang of regret for the bright day ended. The piano echoes lingeringly – 'Tage'. Now the music has found the lower register again. The shades close, the memory merges into the night, as at 'vom heute gewesenen Tage' (the day it has been today) the voice twice falls in octaves, ending on a deep dominant; an evocative and moving moment.

In the second verse the variants of the voice part though slight are most memorable and effective. At 'klingt des Himmels Bläue süsser noch' (blue of the sky sounds sweeter still) the vocal line arches up to reach the highest and brightest note in the song. Again, at the last word of 'gleichgeschwungenes Joch' (equal-swung yoke) the long note heard at 'ruhn' (rest) at the end of the first verse is held longer still, in an image of sustained equipoise. In the postlude the lullaby themes of the prelude sing themselves to sleep.

NOTES 1. The characteristic accompaniment theme (tones and semitones alternating in cross-rhythm) is often found in association with the idea of sleep, dreams of night (motif 18); so is the key of C♯ minor. The sustained vocal notes on 'ruhn' and 'Joch' exemplify the serenity of motif 39.

2. The falling octaves at the end of each verse recall those at the end of Schumann's *Im Walde*, Op. 39 no. 11 – also about a day's events recalled at nightfall.

3. Cf. also Bruch, Op. 59 no. 1; Franz, Op. 28 no. 6 (where the first word 'bedächtig' derives from an earlier edition of Mörike's poems); Distler, Op. 19 (SAB).

32 (M 20) Auf eine Christblume I (*To a Christmas rose I*)

26 November 1888 (orchestrated 25 September 1890; unfinished)

D major   c'–f''

Daughter of the forest, you close kin to the lily, sought by me for so long, unknown; in an unfamiliar churchyard, bleak and wintry, here for the first time I find you, beautiful flower.

I do not know whose hand tends your blossoming, nor whose grave you watch over; if it is a young man, he has found salvation, if a maiden, her lot was happy. In the darkling grove overspread with snowlight, where the innocent roe deer pass by you as they graze, near the chapel, by the crystal pool, there I sought the magic kingdom of your homeland.

Beautiful you are, child of the moon, not the sun; what is bliss for other flowers would be death for you; the food for your virginal body, full of ripeness and scent, is the balsam-sweet air of a cold heaven.

In the golden fullness of your bosom dwells a barely perceptible fragrance, like the scent diffused by the Blessed Mother's bridal robe touched by an angel's hand. Five crimson drops, portending the Passion, would become you fair and uniquely; but like a child you adorn your white dress at Christmas-tide with a touch of light green.

The elf, on his way to dance at the midnight hour in the moonbright glade, stands in awe at your mystical glory from afar, in inquiring silence; and flits by.

Mörike found his hellebore or Christmas rose in the churchyard at Neuenstadt. In a letter to Wilhelm Hartlaub* he describes his discovery, the elation and wonder of it, in vivid phrases that freely anticipate the poem. The mystic bloom, as he called it, had 'looked at him with so fascinating a strangeness' that he was 'filled with yearning'. The symbolism of the Christmas rose, rooted deep in his complex creative personality, yields a multiple flowering from the worlds of folk-mythology, visionary Christianity, and sensual human experience. Each of these aspects is treated with the same high order of poetry, and they can be conceptually unified by the shared concept of mystery and by familiarity and sympathy with Mörike's mind and art. But they are not perhaps wholly fused in these recondite and elusive quatrains. Wolf's music faithfully re-creates not only the beauty of the verses but their diffuseness; and this long song is more a succession of exquisite moments than an organic musical whole.

Mörike's imaginative musings on a mystic symbol are matched by richly inventive variations on an intangible theme. The slow semibreves

---

* 29 October 1841

that accompany the opening invocation to the Christmas rose are gradually unfolded by the unobtrusive introduction of successively shorter note-values, repeated until the rhythm is totally transformed into staccato quavers at the third verse, beginning 'Im nächt'gen Hain' (In the darkling grove). This metamorphosis, almost a rhythmic modulation, is one expression of the change of inward mood and movement from the rapt motionless contemplation of the first line to the idea of a delicate-footed deer picking its way cautiously past. Meanwhile the melody and harmony have superimposed further contrasting patterns and colours on the musical texture; their warmest and most varied moments are attained in the second verse, which turns aside from the cold flower to mourn and bless the dead in a mood of tender melancholy. Perhaps Wolf knew that the ostensible unfamiliarity with churchyard and grave was poetic licence; Mörike was in fact visiting a family burial-ground, as he told Hartlaub. The slow opening strains resume at 'Schön bist du', as the flower is again directly invoked. But with the arousal of interest the pulse quickens; the movement here is already in minims, and the further diminution process begins earlier than before. Now the music in voice and keyboard is made to spread out smoothly, like the fragrance and raiment described, with corresponding vocal peaks in the top notes at 'Wohlgeruch' and 'Brautgewand'; in similar imagery each of the five crimson drops ('fünf Purpurtropfen') has the same staccato note, marked 'zart' (tenderly). In the final verse the motifs of the earlier nocturnal scene reappear with the repeated quavers of the grazing deer now transformed into high semiquaver triplets for the wondering elf. As that slight figure finally stops, dwindles and vanishes from the poem, so does its figuration in the music.

NOTES 1. The poem's last line will fail of its effect unless we share Mörike's knowledge (imparted in *Elfenlied*, 28) that all elves are insatiably inquisitive; only the most awe-inspiring beauty could have spared this or any flower a thorough investigation.

2. The five staccato notes (motif 26) in the piano part seem so designedly evocative of five crimson drops in bars 66–7 and 67–8 that one wonders whether the last three right-hand quavers in bars 65 and 68 should not also be staccato in conformity with the same pattern.

3. At 'so geschah ihm Heil' is the mystery motif 19 (cf. 'Veilchen träumen schon' in *Er ist's*, 18). The piano part at 'im nächt'gen Hain' etc and again on the last page, 'in mitternächt'ger Stunde', is the nocturnal movement of motif 17; in the latter elfin context the right hand is aptly embellished with the minuscule minor seconds of motif 3 in the last two notes of the semiquaver triplets.

4. The rising semitones that characterize Hope in *Der Genesene an die Hoffnung* (13) play a full part in this song (e.g. right hand at bars 14–16) and are found again associated with the Christ child in *Schlafendes Jesuskind* (37). From the same motif is spun the peace and beatitude of *Anakreons Grab* (114). All four

songs have related feeling-tones of fulfilment or redemption. Similarly the vocal melody at 'lieblich fiel ihr Teil' here is akin to that found in *Auf eine Christblume II* (33) at 'nie soll er kosten deinen Honigseim'; again there is some kinship between the verbal contexts, with their common idea of acquiescence in fate.

5. The opening semibreves hint at Erda in *Siegfried*, Act III, e.g. at 'kräftig reizt der Zauber'. There too a mystery has grown from the ground, glowing in a cold light; Mörike's 'Zauberreich' provides a specific verbal link.

33 (M 21) Auf eine Christblume II (*To a Christmas rose II*)

21 April 1888   F# major   c#'–g''

Within the wintry ground there sleeps, itself a flower seed, a butterfly that will rock its velvet wings over bush and hill in the nights of the coming spring. Never shall it taste your honey-dew.

But who knows whether some day when all the beauties of summer are faded and gone, its frail ghost, invisible to me, may not be circling, dizzy with your faint fragrance, around you as you bloom?

Mörike's letter about his discovery of a Christmas rose (see 32 above) also contains the seed of this second poem, which surrounds the first by the flights of fancy found again in his *Zitronenfalter im April* (30). He had over-enthusiastically transplanted the flower to his own window-box, whence it was uprooted by a gale. 'I think of it now' he says ruefully 'as only a lovely ghost'. Perhaps this in turn suggested the classical butterfly-symbol of the soul or psyche. On any view this beautiful poem is highly elusive. But this time its essence is concentrated, not diffused; and Wolf finds a perfect musical equivalent. The whole piano part is distilled from one tiny phrase, typified thus in the prelude

and thereafter repeated some twenty times; and this phrase itself is clearly a two-fold repetition of an even simpler germ-theme. Its basic rhythmic and melodic butterfly shape and symmetry remain constant throughout. But it is treated with such subtle variation of pitch and harmony and graced with so beguiling a vocal line, that the repetition passes unnoticed, as the butterfly hovers unseen. The melodic phrases of the voice sway between modest recitative and long flighted lines – soaring smoothly on 'sammt'nen Flügel' (velvet wing), drooping resignedly at 'nie soll er kosten deinen Honigseim' (it shall never taste your honey-dew), circling dazedly in the falling octaves of the last lines. In the postlude this main theme is heard in its original form for the first time since the song began. Having achieved this poised restatement, it unfolds, drifts upwards, and vanishes.

NOTES 1. Wolf had unusual difficulties with his declamation here. In the autograph version the pause comes after 'Blumenkeim' not 'Schmetterling', and lasts much longer ('-keim', on a crotchet, followed by a crotchet rest and a quaver rest). Understandably, the composer seems to have remained long dissatisfied with his treatment of the sense and syntax of Mörike's first two lines; Walter Legge (*Music Review*, August 1941) gives details of Wolf's attempted revision of bars 3–7, which, however, as there printed seems much *less* clear and competent than the published version, which the *Kritische Gesamtausgabe* very reasonably retains. In the circumstances the best solution is perhaps to make a pause after 'Blumenkeim' to show that it is in apposition to 'der Schmetterling'; the hibernating butterfly is itself imagined as a flower-seed. Other revisions from the same source have been incorporated into the *Gesamtausgabe*, as follows, in the piano part unless otherwise stated. Bar 13 begins *p*, bar 14 *f*, bar 15 *p* again. At bar 20 the voice part is marked 'sehr leise'. Bar 21 begins *pp*. Bars 25–7 have *p* ⟨ *mf* ⟩ *p*. Bar 29 begins *pp*.
  2. For the melody at 'nie soll er kosten deinen Honigseim' see 32, note 2.

34 (M 22) Seufzer (*Sighs*)

12 April 1888 (orchestrated 28 May 1889)   E minor   c#'–e''

The fire of Thy love, O Lord! how dearly I longed to tend it and cherish it! I have not tended it and not cherished it, I am dead at heart, I feel the pangs of Hell!

'Slow and sorrowful' is the composer's direction. But there is more than sorrow in the music; there is torment. The Latin verses (see note 1) on which Mörike based his poem express keen regret; his own mood is a heartfelt sigh, while Wolf's is an agonized groan. The prelude has poignant dissonances which must have seemed very startling to contemporary audiences, and have not yet lost their power to compel attention as well as to symbolize anguish. They are followed by a four-bar sequence of chromatically rising octaves leading to the entry of the voice, which laments over a discordant accompaniment. At 'wollt' ich es hegen, wollt' ich es pflegen' (I longed to tend and cherish it) the piano repeats the poignant opening chords of the prelude, already foretelling the failure of faith. At 'hab's nicht geheget', etc (I have not tended it) the piano repeats the prelude's chromatically rising octaves. The song reaches a climax of remorse at 'bin tot im Herzen' etc (I am dead at heart, etc); the postlude, seizing on the final vocal phrase, cries aloud 'O Höllenschmerzen!'.

NOTES 1. In Mörike's poems, the text is prefixed with some Latin couplets, entitled *Crux fidelis* and said to be extracted from the 'Passion Hymn of Fortunatus', which he had found in an eighteenth-century hymnal. The couplets run *Jesu benigne!/A cuius igne/Opto flagrare/Et te amare:/Cur non flagravi?/Cur non amavi/Te, Jesu Christe?/O frigus triste!*, i.e. 'Benign Jesus, from whose fire I wish to burn and to love Thee, why have I not burned, why have I not loved Thee, Jesu Christ? O sad coldness'. Mörike must have felt these sentiments very deeply; he made repeated attempts to translate them, and referred to them copiously in correspondence (e.g. to Karl Mörike, 22 February and to Charlotte Mörike, 25 February 1832). He felt the last line as 'cutting through marrow and bone'; and his final version substitutes hellfire for the original ice of the last line. He further interpolated the Latin text in *Maler Nolten* (with his translation as a footnote) as a duet for Agnes and Henni, 'the powerful verses of a Latin penitential song in E major', which is then followed by the similar *Neue Liebe* (42).

2. The movement of penance in the poem is solidified within the rigid constraints of Wolf's musical framework. The piano part provides a frame for the voice; and the voice part is itself framed by the minims of bars 9–12 and 23–4. At the centre of this design appears the musical equivalent for the central idea of the poem; 'I longed to . . .; I have failed to . . .'. This is extrapolated and announced as the prelude; the voice tells its sad story; the postlude repeats 'the pangs of hell'. Thus Wolf achieves immense weight and emphasis; the penance is performed in the voice, in a piano solo, and again in both together; and these three components are welded together in the iron frame of thirty-one bars thus – A (4) B (4) C (4) A^1 (4) B^1 (6) C^1 (2) C^2 (7), where A + B is the prelude, C^2 the postlude, and the voice runs from C to the end of C^1. This constructional equivalent for a poetic idea, here derived from the syntactical structure of the verses, is a striking anticipation of the style of the Spanish volume, particularly the sacred songs in a penitential vein, e.g. *Mühvoll komm ich und beladen* (143).

3. The lyric suggests the guilt-feelings of a Tannhäuser; its words 'bin tot im Herzen' and the rhyme with 'Schmerzen' (hence the pangs of motif 34, *passim*) could hardly fail to recall, even to a less devout and expert Wagnerian than Wolf, Wolfram's 'Den Tod, den er ihn gab im Herzen', a passage akin to bars 55–8 here. Wolf's orchestral version draws the parallel closer still.

35 (M 23) Auf ein altes Bild (*On an old painting*)

14 April 1888 (orchestrated 1889)   F$^\sharp$ minor   f$^\sharp$'–e$^\sharp$''

In the summery haze of a green landscape, beside cool water, reeds and rushes, see the Christ-child, born without sin, playing freely on the Virgin's lap!

And there growing blissfully in the forest, already green, is the tree of the Cross.

'My last song, which I have just finished' wrote Wolf to Edmund Lang 'is without doubt the crown of all. I am still in the grip of the enchantment of the mood of this song; everything is still shimmering in green all round me.'

Of the six lines of Mörike's simple but profound couplets, five describe the picture. Only in the last two words, 'Kreuzes Stamm' (the tree of the Cross) does the premonition of suffering lend poignancy to the spectator's delight. So in Wolf; we are in the presence of mystery, not of tragedy. The mood remains gentle, serene, unprotesting. With a modal tonality and slow rhythms the melodies of voice and piano move by step in contrary motion, all within a very limited compass. This gives the song an other-worldly quality of timelessness, as Wolf himself suggests – a motionless summery haze within which the vision is concentrated from a whole landscape to one tree. The small quiet phrases of voice and piano lead up to one stab of pain at the last words, where a transient discord is introduced and resolved. Then the postlude relieves the timeless scene; and if the song has made its proper effect there is eternal grief in that eternal summer.

NOTES 1. Mörike was himself something of an artist and a devoted admirer of the old masters: and in *Schlafendes Jesuskind* (37) his poem describes an actual and identifiable painting. It seems reasonable to infer a similar objective inspiration here also. If so, the emphasis on the landscape element might point to a German work, e.g. Dürer's *Madonna and Child* (a suggestion for which I am indebted to Dr John Sunderland of the Courtauld Institute); but of course the profusion of possibilities must militate against specific identification.
2. Schumann's *Auf einer Burg*, Op. 39 no. 7, achieves a similar timeless quality by analogous means. For Wolfian parallels see 32, note 3 and 37, note 2.
3. The harmonic pang at the last words exemplifies motif 34.

36 (M 24) In der Frühe (*Near dawn*)

5 May 1888 (orchestrated 6 May 1890)   D minor/D major   b♭ –g''

No sleep yet cools my eyes; already the day is breaking there at my bedroom window. My troubled mind is still burrowing to and fro among its doubts, and creates night phantoms. Frighten and torment yourself no longer, my soul! Rejoice! Already, round about, the morning bells are awake.

The quietude and humility of this setting, as well as its position in the volume, suggest that the composer is interpreting the poem, no doubt rightly, as religious in its inspiration. The heavy obsessive chords that fill the first part of the song with sombre tension from the first bar are the very music of insomnia, to which Wolf too was a martyr. This framework is gradually modified to a changing picture of a wakefulness first resented, then accepted and finally welcomed. Over a persistent throbbing rhythm deep in the left hand the repeated ostinato figures (themselves so low that the right hand is written in the bass clef)

make a vivid image of a mind spasmodically and painfully clenching around its worries, unable to let go and relax except when momentarily distracted by the sunrise (at 'dort gehet schon der Tag herfür' etc). Then the piano abandons its chromatics, and steadier rhythms and harmonies allow a little light to filter through. The vocal phrases slowly gain in freedom and confidence. A return of the first themes darkens the mood at the thought of the 'Nachtgespenster' (night phantoms). Then at 'Ängste, quäle dich nicht länger' (Frighten and torment yourself no longer) the key changes, the harmonies lighten, and the motif of sleeplessness quoted above begins to chime comfortingly like a matin bell, in a new form

which is taken up through successively brighter major tonalities from E, G and B♭ to D. All the while the voice sings its exultant reassurance, with sustained high notes welcoming the morning, as light comes welling into words and music, bringing the longed-for peace of mind at last.

NOTES 1. The pervading bass rhythm ♪♩ ♪ is often used as an accompaniment figure in songs about the surrender of the self in worship (motif 1); its persistent repetition anticipates the obsessive rhythm of a later song of insomnia, *Alle gingen, Herz, zur Ruh* (167).

2. The culminating chain of mediant modulations (motif 24) is typically associated with the idea of mounting excitement or aspiration, especially in contexts of increasing intensity of light; cf. also *Ganymed* (135) or *Jägerlied* (16). It may not be coincidence that the latter was written on the same day, 22 February 1888, as Wolf's letter quoted in the commentary to 14 above, which says that the thought of the future 'quält und ängstigt mich' (torments and frightens me), with a clear echo of Mörike's text here. (The form 'Angst'ge' actually appears in the first and the Peters edition; it should be corrected to Mörike's archaic 'Ängste'.) Perhaps *In der Frühe* was also in Wolf's mind then; its text, like that of 14, 15 and 16, appears early in Mörike's *Gedichte*.

4. Cf. Reger (no opus number).

37 (M 25) Schlafendes Jesuskind (*Sleeping Christ-child*)

6 October 1888 (orchestrated 1890)   F major $c^{\#\,\prime}-a^{b\,\prime\prime}$

Son of the Virgin, child of Heaven, lying on the floor asleep on the wood of suffering that the pious painter has placed – a meaningful allusion – under your light dreams.

You flower; even in the bud, darkling and sheathed, still the glory of God the Father! Oh, who could see, behind this brow, these dark lashes, what softly-changing pictures are being painted!

[Son of the Virgin, child of Heaven.]

Our understanding of the 'Holz der Schmerzen' (wood of suffering) is helped by a similar descriptive passage, perhaps among the sources of Mörike's inspiration, in Goethe's *Wilhelm Meisters Wanderjahre* (. . . Years of Travel), Chapter II:

> . . . a wondrously beautiful picture. We see a wide variety of timber-work, which is about to be assembled, and by chance two of the pieces form a cross. The child has fallen asleep on the cross. The mother sits nearby and looks at him lovingly, the foster-father stops work so as not to disturb his sleep.

The music, like the poem, meditates on a given theme; each enriches and illumines the other. 'Very sustained and solemn' is the composer's direction for a meditative prelude that creates the mood of rapt reverence whence the vocal line proceeds. The piano part gradually changes from pious chorale to sequences in a lower register as the imagined gaze goes down to a sleeping child; and this vision is subtly rendered still more vivid by such quiet touches as a full high sustained chord for 'Träumen' (dreams). Then the music itself becomes the painting. The piano interlude after 'unterlegte' is placed under the vocal line, continuing and completing it without a break, just as carefully as the 'wood of suffering' has been placed by the painter under the dreaming head. There follows a slow transition from tenderness to hidden strength, 'Blume' to 'Herrlichkeit', when the budding flower is perceived as hidden glory. The same music is subtly varied and decorated to suggest the delicate interplay of images in the child's dreams. The last vocal phrase 'in sanftem Wechsel malen!' ends on a slight rising inflection as if reluctant to leave its contemplation. The hymnlike prelude is then repeated, followed by the opening words and accompaniment. Here Wolf asks for the words 'Sohn der Jungfrau, Himmelskind!' to be sung in the softest of breaths, and 'wie in tiefes Sinnen verloren', as if lost in deep musing, an inward singing of heart and mind.

NOTES 1. This final verbal repetition is Wolf's, not Mörike's.

2. In both source and song-book the poem is laconically headed 'Gemalt von Franc. Albani'. We know from a letter to Wilhelm Hartlaub (23 March 1862) enclosing a copy of the poem, that Mörike had seen the picture he describes, by Francesco Albani (1578–1660), reproduced in the journal *Freya* with the caption 'The child Jesus in an agreeably shady spot in the open air asleep on a small and as it were decorative cross'.

3. At 'eingeschlafen' in Wolf's setting appears exactly the same poignant harmony (motif 34) as in *Auf ein altes Bild* (35), at the final word 'Stamm'; perhaps a deliberate cross-reference. Similarly the contemplative minim movement quickening to crotchets and quavers in response to an awakening poetic imagery is akin to *Auf eine Christblume I* (32).

4. The piano part at bar 7 also recurs in *Wo find ich Trost* (43, bar 7) dated the same day, and in the earlier Heine song *Wo wird einst* (236, bar 3), though with no very clear thematic significance. The piano bar here marked 'sehr ausdrucksvoll' before the words 'Blume du' (bar 13, and again at 16) however has a possibly thematic parallel in *Im Frühling* (25, bars 1–2, 23–4); the opening flower is a shared image. The rising semitones in the piano here at bars 19–20 are used elsewhere in similar reverential moods (see 32, note 4).

38 (M 26) Karwoche (*Holy Week*)

8 October 1888 (orchestrated 29 May 1889)   A♭ major   b–a♭ ''

O week, witness of holy suffering! You are so earnestly in accord with this springtime bliss; in the renewed ray of the sun you spread the shadow of the Cross over the bright earth, and silently you let down your veils. Meanwhile the spring is allowed to go on burgeoning, the violet smells sweet under trees in blossom, and all the birds sing songs of jubilation.

Oh be silent, you birds on the green meadows! All around muffled bell notes are tolling, angels are singing soft dirges; be silent, you birds high in the blue skies! You violets shall adorn no maiden curls today. My pious child has plucked you for a dark garland, you must journey with her to the church of the Virgin, there you shall wither on the Lord's altar.

Oh there, dazed with mourning melodies and sweetly overcome by the heavy fragrance of incense she seeks the Bridegroom in the vaults of death; and love, and springtime, all is lost for ever.

The poem (like those of *An die Geliebte*, 44, and *Lebe wohl*, 48) was inspired by Luise Rau, from whom Mörike was later to part after a broken-hearted four-year engagement. She was the daughter of the vicar in a parish where Mörike served as curate; but these verses hint at doctrinal dissensions, even at resentment of religion itself. Their blend of spiritual mood and heady sensuality in imagery and verbal melody seems to have put Wolf in mind of the piano music of Chopin or Liszt, while the title and topic are clearly reminiscent of Wagner. The total effect of the song is thus somewhat indistinct and indirect. The composer's own voice can still be heard in the series of intimate equivalents for the poet's thought, sometimes emotive, as in the sweet and sad first pages, and sometimes pictorial, as in the high swooping and floating runs and trills of the song-bird interlude after 'Jubellieder' (songs of jubilation). In particular the tender vocal entry at 'Der Frühling' (The spring) is a memorable moment. But perhaps the work does not quite cohere, despite its sensuous appeal. The first page reappears as the last in a literal repetition of the piano part which owes more to formal musical contrivance than to any aptness of reference to the poem.

NOTES 1. Some Peters editions have F natural at the first piano left-hand crotchet in the second bar from the end: this needs correction to F♯, tied from the previous bar (as in bars 15–16). The *Kritische Gesamtausgabe* changes the note for 'die' after 'Glockenklänge', bar 33, from A♭ to E♭, following the autograph; but the first edition's A♭ seems permissible or even preferable in its context of repeated notes.

2. The trilling birds are highly Lisztian, bars 29–37; the sighing chromatic quavers of plucked and withering violets at 'zart und ausdrucksvoll', bars 39–45, are highly Chopinesque, like the very deliberate modulation back to the home tonic and reprise at Tempo I. The Good Friday (Karfreitag) mood of *Parsifal* and the heady atmosphere of *Tristan* also impregnate the musical style.

3. In the result, there is little room for Wolf's own typical equivalence. But the worshipping rhythm of motif 1 in the opening bars is characteristic enough; and see also 191, note 3.

39 (M 27) Zum neuen Jahr – Kirchengesang (*To the new year – a hymn*)

5 October 1888   A major   d'–b''

Like a cherub softly and secretly treading on the earth with rosy feet, so the morning neared. Sing in jubilation, all ye faithful, a holy welcome [a holy welcome.] You, my heart, sing in jubilation too!

May this new year begin in Him who moves moons and suns on blue canopies of sky. Thou, Father, counsel, guide and lead us! Lord, into Thy hands be laid beginning and end and all things [all things]!

Mörike wrote these verses to the tune of 'Wie dort auf den Auen' (As there on the meadows) from Salieri's opera *Axur, Re d'Ormus* (1787); perhaps that source suggested to him the baroque décor of rosy cherubs and blue skies. Much of the same feeling-tone animates the light colours and textures of Wolf's music. The vocal line has an operatic compass and tessitura. The decorative frieze of consecutive thirds high in the piano at the beginning and end of the song has been compared to 'cherubs blowing silver trumpets'. More prosaically, a carillon of bells heralding the new year may have been the notion in mind. On any interpretation the music is admirably designed to match the jubilation of the poem. The thematic material is all drawn from the same source. The delightful vocal melody that steps in time to Mörike's metre (much as in *Der Gärtner*, 29, with similar ideas of dancing feet) is later transferred to the piano part and assumes a solemn expression in response to new hymn-like melodies and sentiments over a gently syncopated bass.

Like other Mörike songs, whether secular as in *Der Gärtner* or religious as in *Neue Liebe* (42), this setting arguably leaves part of the poem's deeper content unexplored. But performers may safely rely on that aspect of the verses which is most clearly and effectively preserved in the music; the concluding section in particular, where voice and piano stream out together in a full flood of joy ('überströmend' is the composer's direction), can be overwhelming in its appeal.

NOTES 1. The repetitions are Wolf's, not Mörike's.
2. Consecutive thirds have been noted (motif 16) as expressive of companionship. Here they are primarily decorative and allusive rather than motivic; a similar use of thirds and sixths is found in *Sankt Nepomuks Vorabend* (105). But they also serve expressive ends; thus the excited jubilation of the interlude here after 'jauchze du mit!' can be compared with the piano postlude of *Erstes Liebeslied eines Mädchens* (54). Again, the pattern of thirds and sixths can convey a musing and reverential mood (at 'in Ihm') in a way interestingly evocative of the first movement's second subject in Schubert's String Quintet in C, D956. The syncopated bass rhythm here is typical of a worshipping mood (motif 1).

40 (M 28) Gebet (*Prayer*)

13 March 1888 (orchestrated 4 September 1890)   E major   d#'–e''

Lord! send what Thou wilt, pleasure or pain; I am content that both flow from Thy hands. Yet I pray Thee not to overwhelm me with either joys or pains. For midway [for midway] lies blessed moderation.

The concept of the golden mean is classical rather than Christian; but both traditions are strong and vital in Mörike. As in *Verborgenheit* (24), also composed on Wolf's twenty-eighth birthday, this setting may well contain subjective elements. With a temperament even more cyclic than Mörike's, bordering on the manic-depressive, Wolf had good reason to dread being overwhelmed by either joy or sorrow. But prayer would hardly have come naturally to his own sceptical mind, and the song perhaps suffers from having its piety instilled into the music by means of a four-part and rather four-square hymn-tune, imparting a faint air of religiosity. The mood of quietude and humility is effective and not unpersuasive. Nevertheless it is only when the poem stops praying and adds its own personal meditation that Wolf evinces a corresponding sense of freedom and sympathy, confirming that he was less moved by the hymn-like qualities of the verses than by their plea for joys and sorrows in moderation. His own life would have been profoundly alleviated by such a disposition of fortune. So as the prayer ends the two hands separate and the piano part is free to play its own independent melodies entwining tenderly among the vocal lines, which have themselves also been rendered more flexible to enhance still further the feeling of release from constraint. Finally however prayerfulness prevails; the piano melody hushes, soars like a violin obbligato, and in the postlude slowly falls again into a long, hushed and heartfelt Amen.

NOTES 1. The blessing of the golden mean, or 'aurea mediocritas', finds its most famous classical expression in Horace's *Odes*, Book II, 10 – the next after the ode quoted by Mörike as an epigraph to his *An eine Aeolsharfe* (see 23, note 2) and no doubt well known to him. It is this idea of the balanced mid-point that Wolf finds especially significant and moving; the repetition of 'Doch in der Mitten' is his, not Mörike's. Perhaps this slightly disturbs the balance of the poem, the famous and untranslatable final phrase of which, 'holdes Bescheiden', connotes clemency in the assignment of our joys and sorrows as well as equality in their distribution.

2. Appealing though the concluding passage is, one feels that Wolf at a later stage of his development would not have countenanced such transparent expressive techniques as the violin-like cantilena of the piano melody (which in the orchestral version is in fact scored for solo violin) with its Wagnerian echoes, e.g. in the Act II love-duet of *Tristan und Isolde*. In the Italian Songbook, devices such as these are refined to a new essence of the song-writer's art, e.g. throughout the masterly *Wenn du mich mit den Augen streifst* (224).

3. There is an interesting thematic kinship between this song and *Fussreise* (22), written soon after, which is also a prayer with non-religious aspects that caught Wolf's fancy. The main similarity lies in indefinable feeling-tone; but there are identifiable parallels in the harmony (compare bars 6–8 here with 24–6 there) and in one passage a shared vocal line ('wollest mit Freuden und wollest mit Leiden' echoes 'also bist du nicht so schlimm, o alter Adam').

4. Similarly, the *Wanderers Nachtlied* (11) of 1887 is almost a study for *Gebet*. The opening rhythm and harmonies (note motif 21 in both) and the treatment of the final section are closely akin. Again the two poems have much in common, in their prayerful invocations; a close comparison of texts and music illuminates Wolf's rapidly developing mastery.

5. Cf. Bruch, Op. 60 no. 4; Schoeck, Op. 62 no. 33; Distler, Op. 19 (two settings, SA and SSA).

41 (M 29) An den Schlaf (*To Sleep*)

4 October 1888 (orchestrated 4 September 1890)

A♭ major/E major   f♯'–f♯''

Sleep! sweet Sleep! Although nothing is so like unto Death as you are, yet I bid you welcome to this couch!

For thus without life how sweet it is to live; so far from dying, oh, how easy it is to die!

Like *Seufzer* (34) the poem is a free rendering of Latin verses. Underlying its play on words there are deeper levels of unrest, even despair; but Wolf, the martyr to insomnia, treats the poem mainly as a heartfelt and successful appeal to Sleep for sleep, a counterpart to *In der Frühe* (36). A slow and intense piano prelude creates a dreaming mood which is prolonged and echoed in the piano part as the voice enters with its quiet invocation 'Schlaf! süsser Schlaf!'. The music concentrates throughout on announcing and then resolving small-scale harmonic tensions, like little rehearsals for sleep. The piano's repeated motif suggests a half-heard hypnotic voice saying 'Sleep' at regular intervals, so that this idea is subliminally imprinted on the listener, at 'Tod wie du nichts gleicht' (nothing is so like to Death as you), and 'willkommen heiss ich dich', again at 'ohne Leben so, wie lieblich' and once again at 'so weit vom Sterben'. By this time the music has reached the new key of E major, where it remains throughout the slow final relaxation of the postlude, without returning to the original tonality – as if sleep had indeed intervened.

NOTES 1. Poem and song both reproduce the original Latin text, attributed to Meibom, viz.,

> *Somne levis! Quamquam certissima mortis imago,*
> *Consortem cupio te tamen esse tori.*
> *Alma quies, optata, veni! Nam sic sine vita*
> *Vivere, quam suave est, sic sine morte mori!*

'Light sleep! Although you are the most faithful picture of death, I nevertheless invite you as bedfellow to my couch. Gracious quietness, longed-for, oh come! For how sweet it is thus to live without life, thus without death to die!'

2. The new key is that of the flattened sixth above the tonic A♭, i.e. F♭ major, here notated as E major. That note has a lullaby significance in the early *Wiegenlied im Winter* (5) and is associated with the hypnotic effect of mourning melodies in *Karwoche* (38). Here the solemn and somnolent significance is incorporated into the harmonic structure. Both interval and chord are also a feature of some of the A♭ major Italian songs in a similarly somnolent mood, e.g. *Und willst du deinen Liebsten sterben sehen* (203): motif 37.

3. Note the striking parallels between the last eleven bars here and the last eight of *Gebet*. The main difference is that the sixth of the new key of E major in this

108

song is still being flattened, to C natural. The mood of invocation and intercession is common to both songs.

4. Not surprisingly, there is even closer affinity here with the *Liebestod* from *Tristan und Isolde*; the last six bars of vocal line recall Isolde's appeal 'ewig zu fliehn', i.e. to shun the daytime and seek the night.

42 (M 30) Neue Liebe (*New love*)

4 October 1888 (orchestrated 5 September 1890)   B♭ major   c'–a♭''

Can two people ever belong wholly to each other, as they would wish, here on earth? In the long night I thought this over to myself, and had to say: no! So I can belong to no one here on earth, and no one can be mine? From the darkness a flame of joy flashes up bright within me: should I not be able to be with God, just as I would wish, mine and Thine? What would keep me from being so today? A sweet terror pervades my frame. I marvel that it should have ever seemed to me a marvel to have God Himself for my own here on earth!

Mörike's poem is all fiery revelation and devotional message; the full force of his inspiration goes into proclaiming the good news. But our enjoyment is rather of the music as such than of that perfect union between music and poetry which characterizes Wolf's art at its highest and most representative. The magnificent song sounds secular rather than sacred in its inspiration, operatic rather than lyric in its expression. The prelude asks the question, and then withdraws, leaving the voice in effect alone to sing its recital of loneliness and isolation. But the accompaniment offers its sympathetic understanding, in long low chords for the deep thought 'in langer Nacht' (in the long night). Then the loud-soft dominant and minor tonic harmonies with their typical question-and-answer pattern add further inflexions to the sung words at 'musste sagen: nein!', with an effect of 'had to say (what?) – No (alas!)'. At 'so kann ich niemands heissen' etc (So I can belong to no one?) the vocal line is heard with a quite separate melody developed from the pessimistic inflexions of the prelude; the two co-exist, but do not belong together. At 'Aus Finsternissen' (From the darkness), voice and piano both fall, only to rise again in pitch and tone and intensity before shining out in full splendour at 'Freudenschein' (flame of joy), in the same tonality as the earlier 'night' chord but in a much higher register, as if to suggest that the triumphant answer was already hidden there and needed only to be located and brought to light. Now the uncertain rhythms and drooping themes heard in the piano thus far begin to revive and assert themselves more strongly, with a rising turn of phrase. But the song itself arguably begins to decline

109

from this point. The great chords and rolling tremolandi seem more like a passionate Wagnerian love-duet than a mystic revelation of union with God. In its own terms however the music remains admirably impressive. In particular the way in which the conclusion of the song is made to relive a moment of great joy, in a sweeping crescendo from the *ppp* of 'Ein süsses Schrecken' (a sweet terror) to the *fff* of 'Gott selbst', with the long final vocal phrase falling through an octave and a half in pitch and a correspondingly wide dynamic range until it merges into the solemn and majestic postlude, is wholly compelling.

NOTES 1. The poem was included in *Maler Nolten*, though (and this also applies to the next two songs, *Wo find ich Trost?* and *An die Geliebte*, as well as to *Karwoche*, 38) not in any context nor with any comments that seem likely to have given any help or inspiration to the composer.

2. The thematic affinities between this song and the next two (compare e.g. the main theme here with the prelude of 43 and the darkness-to-light tremolando progression with that of 44) may imply that Wolf's interpretation of this poem had contained subjective and secular elements. Similarly the music of the last page here is akin to his human love-motif 13, while the virile march-rhythms of the postlude sound almost aggressively triumphant.

3. On the other hand Mörike's careful and significant threefold underlining by repetition of 'auf der Erde', the heart of the religious mystery, remains without any specific musical equivalence; while the awakening six-four climax (motif 36) with added vocal sixth and a long melodic line kneeling down into a final Amen cadence is perhaps too clearly indebted to the end of *Gebet* (40). The special awareness implicit in motif 36 was already heard at 'werde?', where the questioning dominant sevenths, themselves anticipated in the persistent inflexions of 'sein?', 'mein?' and 'Dein?', are motif 32.

43 (M 31) Wo find ich Trost? (*Where shall I find solace?*)

6 October 1888 (orchestrated 6 September 1890) C minor d'–a♭''

I know a love that is true, and has been faithful ever since I first found it; with deep sighing ever renewed it has, always forgivingly, espoused my cause. He it was who with heavenly forbearance drank the bitter, bitter drops of death, hung on the cross and atoned for my sins until they sank in a sea of mercy. And why is it that I am now cast down and writhe in torment on the ground? I ask 'Watchman, what of the night?' and 'What saves me from death and sin?'.

Wicked heart! yes, only confess it, you have again harboured evil pleasure; the traces of pious love, of pious faith, have vanished, alas, long ago. Yes, this is why I am cast down and writhe in torment on the ground. Watchman, watchman, what of the night? What saves me from death and sin?

Once again the music is by no means flawless as a setting of words. But dramatically this is a work of immense power. The basic design is simple and strophic, like the insistently repetitive pattern of the poem. After a short prelude full of repentant groans and an introductory verse set to a tender and worshipping strain, the story of the Passion is told. Here the stern chords and ominous rising octaves in the piano already seem to anticipate the sense of guilt and unworthiness later described; the sinful soul is judged and condemned. Yet in an expressive interlude we hear the pleading of that ever-faithful love, and the piano continues to sing the opening words 'Eine Liebe kenn ich, die ist treu' until the voice reaches its downcast state of writhing on the ground, at 'am Boden winde'. Then the expression in the piano part also becomes contorted, and that moment of torment is swept away into insignificance by a huge despairing cry – 'Hüter, ist die Nacht bald hin?' (Watchman, will the night soon be over?') – set to widespread chords interspersed with ringing repeated octaves; the knocking on the door, the summons itself. The voice reiterates its confession of unworthiness, unreadiness; the piano part again seems to pronounce the death sentence. But then the pleading voice of the ever-faithful counsel for the defence is again heard. Perhaps there is still time? 'Watchman, what of the night?', and again the despairing cry 'What saves me?' Nothing; no salvation, cries the clamorous music, even as the question is asked. The only answer is the inexorable summons, clarion at first, but in the postlude dying away, returning in a grinding dissonance, then fading into inaudibility.

NOTES 1. Some of Mörike's best sermons were preached in his poems. Here, as in *Nimmersatte Liebe*, he assumes knowledge of Biblical texts; the watchman is from Isaiah XXI, 11, seen here as a herald to the day of judgement.

2. Wolf's mastery of musical equivalence is more apparent in themes of human than of divine love, at least in 1888. Only two years later he was emotionally capable of writing the profound music of contrition (e.g. in the Spanish sacred songs) which is here at best subordinated to dramatic effect and hence to the Wagnerian influence, which is especially apparent in the orchestral version. The repeated sustained octaves and rising phrases from bar 12 onwards recall the music of Tannhäuser as unworthy pilgrim in Act III scene 3; the rising phrases also have something of the repentant Parsifal in Act II.

3. This song has some affinity with *An die Geliebte* (44) and *Lebe wohl* (48), where similar material (e.g. the first bar of piano interlude in all three) is put to more compelling use. For one possibly coincidental resemblance to the piano part here at 'war getreu' etc see 37, note 4; for another, cf. bars 1 and 5 here with *Der Tambour* (17) at '(Franz)ösch herein'.

4. At 'hing am Kreuz' etc in both voice and piano appears the mystery of motif 19.

44 (M 32) An die Geliebte (*To the beloved*)

11 October 1888   E♭ major   e♭ ¹–a♭ ¹¹

When I, deeply stilled by the sight of you, take my mute delight in your saintly goodness, then truly I hear the soft breathing of the angel that dwells concealed within you.

And an amazed, a questioning, smile springs to my lips – has a dream perhaps deluded me that here and now, in you, to my eternal joy my boldest, my only wish is being fulfilled?

Then my mind plunges from depth to depths; from out the dark distance of Godhead I hear the springs of fate running in melody. Dazed, I turn my gaze on high, up to Heaven.

There all the stars are smiling. I kneel to listen to their song of light.

Mörike's sonnet, addressed to Luise Rau, was later included (rather to her distress) in his novel *Maler Nolten*, together with four other such sonnets – perhaps more as a way of bringing his poetic work to public attention than as an integral part of his prose romance. But this poem in particular shows his typical mastery not only in intensity of verbal expression but in strength of formal construction. The emotion is gradually heightened first from contemplation to tenderness within the human world and then from vision to transfiguration within the divine world, each successive step coinciding with a symmetrical division of the sonnet-pattern (two quatrains within the octave, two three-line groups within the sestet). To this challenge Wolf responds superbly. There is great power latent within the quiet simple rhythms of the bass octaves and right-hand chords which fill the music with an absolute assurance of devotion. Such strong support enables the voice to linger out its long expressive melodic line by dwelling on the worshipping words 'stumm' (mute), 'heil' gen' (saintly), 'Engel' (angel), ignoring or even contradicting the bar lines without ever troubling the calm surface of the musical flow.

This unbroken serenity is maintained by the deep bass octaves, which continue in an expressive piano interlude. But they cease when the voice resumes at 'Und ein erstaunt, ein fragend Lächeln' (And an amazed, a questioning smile), because the assurance is no longer being asserted. There is less certainty in the music, and thus an even greater tenderness, which is further enhanced by a typically Wolfian touch at 'Traum' (dream). The note is high and soft, and specially marked 'zart' (tender); the composer wishes to say that it is really no remote dream but the tenderest and dearest of realities. At 'Von Tiefe dann zu Tiefen' (from depth to depths) the piano plunges down with a new tremolando figuration, then rises again as eyes are raised heavenwards. This treatment of words is perhaps over-dramatic; but if this is a defect it is richly compensated by what now follows. Soft repeated chords shine out in the piano treble, in one of the most clear and vivid of all Wolf's musical metaphors. High, distant, clustered, gently pulsating: 'Da lächeln alle Sterne' (There all the stars are smiling). The voice finds a quiet climactic note and bows down from it in the long final falling phrase 'ich kniee, ihrem Lichtgesang zu lauschen'. In the postlude the soft treble chords shine out brighter than ever, then fade and cease.

NOTES 1. In some Peters editions the last quaver chord in bar 5 lacks a natural before the G, and the note on 'mein' in bar 19 needs correcting to A natural; analogously in transposed versions.

2. As in *Der Genesene an die Hoffnung* (13, note 7) the music evolves continuously. But the song is perhaps not quite so convincing in its formal structure as the poem. Just as in the *Peregrina* songs (45–6) and *Gebet* (40) the individual felicities foreshadow passages of exquisite refinement in later songs. Compare, for example, this song at 'dass nun in dir' etc with the whole of *Wenn du mich mit den Augen streifst* (224) or from 'da lächeln alle Sterne' with the corresponding close of *Gesegnet sei* (190) on a similar verbal theme.

3. For affinities with other Mörike songs see 42, note 2 and 43, note 3. The melodic descent from a high note into a postlude with plagal or related cadence is shared with *Gebet* (40), *An den Schlaf* (41) as well as *Neue Liebe* (42).

4. The pervading rhythm ♪ ♩ ♪ of the first part of the song is the self-surrendering motif 1. For the star-music, see motif 25. No doubt the vocal melody and high accompaniment of the last page were influenced by the bright sound and lifted gaze in *Tannhäuser* Act III, for the dawn carillon and jubilation after the vigil. But the specific light effects of high staccato chords may well be more a reflection of Loewe, e.g. in *Der Schatzgräber*, Op. 59 no. 3, at the words 'und ich sah ein Licht von weitem'. The same idea is also frequently observable in Schubert and earlier sources (notably Haydn, *The Creation*). The serene bass notes are motif 39.

5. The beauty of a face, especially of eyes, was one to which Wolf's musical response was invariably sensitive and profound. From 1888 to the last song of all (*Fühlt meine Seele*, 245) in 1897, any poem, or any phrase in a poem, that speaks of such beauty elicits a music so manifestly heartfelt as to suggest some overwhelming personal emotion. We are told that Wolf's mistress Melanie Köchert was 'an extremely handsome woman with a high clear brow and the most wonderful liquid brown eyes' (Frank Walker, op. cit.). Perhaps those features influenced Wolf's choice of poem in the next song, *Peregrina I*.

45 (M 33) Peregrina I: aus Maler Nolten

28 April 1888   E♭ major   c♭'–g♭''

The mirror of these faithful brown eyes is like a reflected gleam of inward gold; it seems to be drawn up from deep within your breast, where such gold loves to thrive in hallowed grief. Into this night of your gaze, unknowing child, you yourself invited me to plunge. You want me to consume us both boldly in fire, smiling you offer me death in the chalice of sin.

46 (M 34) Peregrina II: aus Maler Nolten

30 April 1888   G♭ major   d♭'–a♭''

Why, my love, do I now suddenly think of you with a thousand tears, and can find no fulfilment, and long to yearn my heart out to the farthest horizons?

Oh, yesterday in the brightly-lit children's room, amid the gleaming of festive candles, where I had lost myself among noise and mirth, you entered, image of torment made beautiful by compassion; it was your phantom, it joined us at the feast, we sat sundered in mutely suppressed grief; at last I broke out into loud sobs, and hand in hand we left the house.

The two poems are the first and fourth of a series of five. Like many of the others in this songbook, they were included in Mörike's novel *Maler Nolten*, which was published in 1832. But when his collected poems appeared, only the Peregrina cycle had their previous publication acknowledged, as if they stood in need of some further elucidation, which their context in the novel could supply. Wolf scrupulously retained the sub-title 'aus Maler Nolten' and indeed awarded it to each song separately; he too was no doubt aware of the literary background and may well have thought it relevant to his settings, the texts of which are far from self-explanatory.

Maler Nolten is a long discursive quasi-autobiographical work owing much to Goethe's *Wilhelm Meister*, the interspersed lyrics of which were also set by Wolf (86–95). It germinated from Mörike's youthful infatuation with a vagrant girl, Maria Meyer, of great beauty and temperamental instability. She had an incurably wayward and roving disposition in every sense; but a nineteen-year-old poet could discern inward sanity and saintliness. Hence his name for her, 'Peregrina', connoting sacred pilgrimage as well as worldly wandering. Hence too the recurring imagery of passion and virtue together; fire and gold, and their shared shining. This elemental character, no doubt further enriched by a study of the analogous figure of Mignon in *Wilhelm Meister*, was transmuted into the strange crazed gypsy Elisabeth who contrives to haunt the pages of Mörike's novel, though her actual appearances are infrequent, just as the brief vision of Maria Meyer coloured his life and art for many years. He is explicit on this point, in letters to his friend Friedrich Vischer, e.g. on 23 May 1832; the fate of his artist-hero Nolten is 'linked to the love of his early youth, the enigmatic Elisabeth, even beyond the grave'.

In every context however the five poems retain their air of self-contained privacy. Wolf takes the first and fourth and treats them almost as consecutive diary entries, distilling their secretive essence into the linking phrases that form the postlude to the first song and are continually heard in various guises throughout the second. Deep within innocence dwelt passion; thence sprang irreconcilable conflicts and eventual parting; the manifest meaning of the verses becomes the latent metaphor of Wolf's music. He begins the first song with hardly a preamble; the piano part is impatient to begin painting its picture of a solemn yet bright thought emerging from depths to heights, in conformity with the words. In this striking but unobtrusive musical image, the right hand rises in slow fourths through more than three full octaves, anticipating the words 'tief aus dem Busen scheint er's anzusaugen' (it seems to be drawn up from deep within your breast). Deep within this musical Artesian well the voice declaims the poem, lingering on such significant syllables as 'Gold', 'Wi-(derschein)', 'heil-(gen)'; gold, reflection, hallowed. To introduce that last idea of the darkly sad source of bright gold, the piano chords ascend to their zenith, and fall to a low poignant discord; then they rise again and take on a mysterious chromatic colouring at the mention of night, only to fall two octaves suddenly, on hearing the word 'tauchen' (plunge). Now the music expands into new expressive melodies in insistent quickening rhythms to match the passionate outburst of excitement and apprehension in the voice part; the postlude is eloquent of great love.

The second song takes this love motif as prelude, now verging towards the minor; its rhythm faltering, its melody hesitant, all tenderness and regret. Again the vocal line declaims through piano variations on this theme, now developed and strengthened to match a passionate avowal, now extended and made rarefied and tenuous as the moments of remembered vision are relived. The tonality brightens for candleshine, with a hint of flicker in soft staccato crotchets which also serve to introduce the phantom visitation at 'tratst du' (you entered). After the

115

heartbrokenly hesitant final phrase 'Hand in Hand verliessen wir das Haus' the postlude is left singing its sad song as the vision fades.

NOTES 1. In 46 the third lower crotchet in the right hand of bar 21 is wrongly given in some older Peters editions as C natural (A♯ in the transposed version); it should be C♭ (A natural). The *Kritische Gesamtausgabe* makes this correction. It also amends the usual A, A, G♯, A, at the lower right-hand voice in bar 17 to A, G♯, G♯, A, on the evidence of both autograph and first edition. Here however there seems to be a good case (by analogy with bars 19, 21 and 23) for preserving the Peters reading of A on the second crotchet.

2. In 45, note an analogue of the poignant discord, motif 34, in *Auf ein altes Bild* and *Schlafendes Jesuskind* (see 37, note 2), again as holiness is linked with suffering ('in heil 'gem Gram'). At the following 'In diese Nacht' there is the mystery of motif 19. There is a hint of motif 11 in the voice part at 'Willst, ich soll kecklich' etc. In 46, a brief tonal excursion lights up the 'hellen Kindersaal'; the music is in the relative major of G♭ minor, i.e. B♭♭ major, notated in the three sharps which Wolf elsewhere associates with brightness. In the same passage, the childlike offbeats of motif 2 appear for the first time at the mention of children. Here the verbal accentuation, elsewhere so sensitive, seems to have gone astray ('*in*' on a strong downbeat) suggesting that the piano part was the primary conception in this song and no doubt both. They are deliberately linked by the love-motif 13, in the postlude to 45 and in 46 *passim*, with some beautifully subtle developments, e.g. the transformation of the piano part of 'ach gestern', with its flickering brightness of lit candles in the children's room (motif 25) with the same music at 'es war dein Geist', where a new voice has been added in the upper notes of the left hand to mark the new arrival.

3. These two songs mark a significant stage in Wolf's development. Their thematic material is treated in a style that is highly wrought, perhaps overwrought, in its correspondence with the inward obscurities and tensions of Mörike's poems. For the far simpler and more direct verses of the Italian Songbook, Wolf was to find correspondingly more direct and perhaps more convincing and effective techniques. But whatever view one takes of the success of these two songs, they were certainly deeply felt by the composer (who was likely to have been especially inspired by the faithful brightness of brown eyes; see 44, note 5), and they open up a new wellspring of emotive equivalence which irrigates the later songs. For instance, 45 lends its rhythmic structure to *Der Mond hat eine schwere Klag erhoben* (193, note 4) and its melody at 'tief aus dem Busen scheint er's anzusaugen' to the parallel verbal phrase 'am liebsten grüb ich es tief aus der Erden' in *Was für ein Lied* (209). Again, 46 lends its love theme (motif 13) and the mood of passionate yearning thus induced, to the last song *Fühlt meine Seele* (245); while the rhythm c ♩ ♫ ♪♪♪♩ heard at bars 26 and 28, which though simple is rare in Wolf, assumes great importance in similar contexts in the Italian songs (see 224, note 4).

47 (M 35) Frage und Antwort (*Question and Answer*)

29 March 1888   A♭ major   d'−a♭'''

Do you ask me, whence this uneasy love came into my heart, and why I did not take out its bitter thorn long ago? Tell me why the wind should move its wings with phantom swiftness, and whence the sweet spring draws its hidden waters?

Try to halt a wind in its tracks, at full speed; take a magic wand and conjure the sweet springs to be still!

The poem has three quatrains, one to each sentence above. The first verse quotes a real question. The second and third, rhetorical questions, constitute the answer. But it is verses one and two, not two and three, that Wolf takes together and treats similarly; the resulting slight confusion of thought and expression makes special demands on the performer. As in *Nimmersatte Liebe*, the prelude, with its wistful chromatics, seems to hover on the verge of articulate speech, as if murmuring some such phrase as 'wo kam die Liebe her?' in summary anticipation of the opening question. The voice has an unusually wide-ranging melody, poised over a harmonically shifting accompaniment with an occasional discordant pang (e.g. at 'Herzen') for the sharp thorn in the heart. This scheme is repeated, perhaps less appropriately, in the second verse; and the piano then repeats the perplexed questioning of the prelude. But the musical answer when it at last arrives proves to have been worth waiting for, and the more effective for having been delayed. The vocal melody streams out broad and free, in a telling image of the eternal and irresistible blowing and flowing of all elemental forces. In doing so it overrides the natural stresses of Mörike's fine phrases, and yet enhances them and makes them even more memorable. Here the piano quits its evasive chromatics and substitutes direct and affirmatory chords in a higher register and a new and more dynamic rhythm, together with added bass semibreves for extra assurance; the two hands together depict further perspectives of swift stratospheric winds, slow subterranean streams. The altered chords, as the voice floats down from a soft high A♭ at 'Zaubergerte' (magic wand), give the last line a lingering sweetness. The postlude sings the answer again, in a quiet and contented close.

NOTES 1. Both question and answer are about the nature of love. Most of the piano part has the worshipping rhythm of motif 1; the melody of the final answer and of the postlude is associated elsewhere with the idea of adoration (motif 11). This theme pervades the Italian song *Und willst du deinen Liebsten sterben sehen* (203), also echoed in its postlude; a comparison is instructive.

2. But there is a much closer comparison with *Nimmersatte Liebe* (21). The same concept of love as an irresistible elemental force underlies both poems; or so

117

Wolf seems to have felt. There are evident affinities of mood, e.g. in the parlando preludes, as well as specific parallels, e.g. at 'tust ihr nie zu Willen' in 21 and 'Zaubergerte du die süssen...' here. There is the same harmonic progression, in the same key of A♭ major, with almost the same vocal melody.

3. But this song is of course more worshipful in mood, as evidenced not only by motif 1 *passim* but also by the poignant discord of motif 34 (see 37, note 3), at 'Herzen', a presentiment of the bitter thorn; further, the prelude rhythm and the slow descent from a tonic six-four with added sixth are alike reminiscent of *Gebet* (40) and *Neue Liebe* (42, note 2).

4. Note also the serene bass notes of motif 39 on the last page and the intense questioning of motif 32 in the piano prelude and interlude as well as at the vocal question marks.

5. Cf. Distler, Op. 19 (two settings, SATB and TB).

48 (M 36) Lebe wohl (*Farewell*)

31 March 1888   G♭ major   d♭'–a♭''

'*Farewell!*' *You do not feel what it means, this word of suffering; with a hopeful countenance you said it, and a light heart. Farewell! Oh I have pronounced it to myself a thousand times, and in endless anguish broken my heart in saying it.*

The setting shares Mörike's own premonition of suffering and loss in parting from his fiancée of four years, Luise Rau (also hymned in *Karwoche*, 38, and *An die Geliebte*, 44). All the grief, in music as in words, wells and spills from the first simple phrase. Wolf's mourning semitones, falling in farewell, pervade the highly wrought piano part and fill it with the sad sound and sense of 'Lebe wohl!'. The voice has passionate recitative rounded and moulded to the meaning of the text; this wealth of sad rich melody culminates in a crying climax at 'nimmersatte Qual' (endless anguish) which can be unforgettable.

NOTES 1. The descending chromatics matched to the words 'lebe wohl' are used in later songs, particularly in the Goethe and Spanish volumes, as a musical expression of grief or deprivation. The resolving minor ninth dissonance of motif 34 is heard at e.g. 'Du fühlest *nicht*'. In the postlude the 'lebe wohl' theme becomes part of a configuration which characterizes Wolf's love-music (motif 13) here heard for the first time in this form, which permeates e.g. *Peregrina II* (46), dated a month later. The dominant ending is also expressive (motif 31).

2. This conjunction of motifs of loss, pain and love and tension woven within a close (usually four-part) frame, yields material of an exceptionally lush Wagnerian texture, though apparently without any specific verbal or musical reminiscence.

3. Cf. Distler, Op. 19 (two settings, SAA and TTB).

49 (M 37) Heimweh (*Longing for home*)

1 April 1888   F major   c♭–f''

The world changes with each step that I take further away from my dearest love; my heart is reluctant to go on.

Here the sun shines coldly into the countryside; here everything seems unfamiliar, even the flowers by the brook! Everything has so foreign a look, so false a face.

True, the stream murmurs and says 'Poor lad, walk my way, you can see forget-me-nots here too'. Yes, they are fair in every place; but not like there. Onward, ever onward! My eyes fill with tears.

Mörike seems here to be strongly influenced by Wilhelm Müller, whose poems were published in volume form a year before his own and whose verse he may well have read in journals and magazines, or perhaps heard in Schubert's settings of *Die schöne Müllerin* and *Winterreise*. This poem seems already full of Schubertian sentiment in its evocation of mood and scene. The forget-me-nots; the walk beside the murmuring (and talking) brook; the personified heart; the cold sunlight; the reluctant and tearful journey away from the loved one into alien territory; all these sound like deliberate homage to an earlier romantic style. So does Wolf's music, which in its very different way rivals the achievement of Schubert at its most masterly.

After one bar of prelude the sad slow piano chords and resigned vocal line move together downhill and away, like a long and lingering farewell. At 'weiter' (further), sustained in the vocal line to show how far-reaching the separation feels, both voice and piano rise, in the minor, as if to suggest one last wistful look back; then they move down and away again with lagging steps. With this reluctant departure goes a heavy load of unrequited love. We are made to feel that the melodies are being pressed downwards, the tonality flattened, from major to minor. The harmonies are warmer at 'Mein Herz' (my heart) etc with a memorable melody which again rises hopefully, seeking to escape and return, but then falling into line once more as it is forced to go on; much against its will, as the following piano interlude explains. As that melody in turn lapses into glum acquiescence, the voice sings 'Hier scheint die Sonne kalt' (here the sun shines coldly) etc. The piano echoes this, and the following phrases about the alien look of the world, with strange and unfamiliar harmonies. The first themes resume, with the brook murmuring its attempted consolation in a confidential aside of left-hand trills which break off abruptly to show that the comforting thoughts are to be rejected, at 'aber nicht wie dort' (but not like there). Now the journeying rhythm and melodies pass through a nostalgic reverie of key-change, remembering a land of lost content seen shining in the ever-higher initial chords of the falling right-hand motifs which rejoin the original key with an overwhelming effect of finally bowing to fate at the last phrase, 'Die Augen gehen mir über!'. The grieving postlude continues its lone journey.

NOTES 1. Both the style and the content of the poem must have evoked the spirit of Schubert, both in general terms such as the piano's echoing of the voice and the flowing stream of water-music, and in particular comparisons e.g. of the falling farewell melody with that of *Gute Nacht* from *Winterreise*. Wolf's music thus sets Mörike and Schubert together, much as *Das verlassene Mägdlein* (19) sets Mörike and Schumann, and *Lebe wohl* (48) Mörike and Wagner. The expressive vocabulary of the Lied is thereby much enriched.

2. The formal construction of this song will repay careful study. The general ABA form is evident enough; but the unobtrusive bar-by-bar identity between 1–16 and 35–50, in conjunction with the varied melodic line, offers an object-lesson in sophisticated craftsmanship.

3. The deprivation effect of motif 22 resounds throughout.

50 (M 38) Lied vom Winde (*Song of the wind*)

29 February 1888   F# minor   c'–g''

Soaring wind, roaring wind, there and here! [*soaring wind, roaring wind*] *tell me where your homeland is!*

'*Child, we travel for many a long year through the wide world, and we too want to ask this, and track down the answer, from the mountains, the seas, the resounding hosts of heaven. They never know* [*they never know, they never know*]. *If you are wiser than they, you can tell us. Off, away! Don't delay us! Others follow, our brothers; ask again of them.*'

Stop! Steady on! Wait just a moment! Say, where is the homeland of love, its beginning, its end?

'*Who could name it? Teasing child, love is like the winds, swift and alive, never at rest, it is eternal but not always constant. Off, away! Don't delay us! Away over stubble and woods and meadows. If I see your sweetheart, I'll blow a kiss. Child, adieu* [*adieu, adieu*].'

Here the pictorialism runs riot. With a gust of chromatics the winds come whirling on stage in the first bar. Their evasive reply to the child's first question is whispered confidentially through murmuring tremolandi. Then the winds and their chromatic scales rush off again in unabated vigour. Another pause for breath and advice; then another evasion and departure, this time a final flight that goes zephyring up into thin air in the postlude.

This school-of-velocity étude with vocal obbligato, though always very effective in its way given the necessary virtuoso performance, seems at first wholly alien to Wolf's own usual tact and subtlety, as well as to Mörike's. For once there are few melodic felicities in the vocal line; the text seems arbitrarily and rather pointlessly repeated; worst of all, Mörike's gentle and intimate tones sound overblown and even mistranslated. Wolf captures the poetic image brilliantly, but arguably misses, for once, its true inward source of illumination.

His setting can however be explained and justified. As he very probably knew, the poem appears in Mörike's novel *Maler Nolten* in a context to which the wild and whirling music is clearly appropriate. The words are no longer an amused colloquy, but a monologue put into the mouth of the heroine Agnes in her madness. She has climbed to the top of a 'small bare conical hill that rose above the little forest. "The wind is blowing there! I must sing the wind song" she cried, hurrying on ahead. There she stood on high, and she sang, in a free style, the following verses, changing her voice very cleverly each time to render the question and answer and at the same time gesticulating spiritedly'. In this context the latent erotic and daemonic sense of the poem is made musically explicit, as in *Erstes Liebeslied eines Mädchens* (54).

NOTES 1. According to Walter Legge (*Music Review*, August 1941) Wolf amended his copy of the first edition at bars 86–7 ('Kindlein, ade') to include slurs from the left-hand E and C♯ to the A and F♯ respectively; so in the *Gesamtausgabe*.

2. The main source of the 1888 Mörike settings was no doubt, as has generally been assumed, a volume of the *Gedichte*, and presumably the sixth edition of 1876 which Wolf owned. But extensive verbal repetition and overtly dramatic treatment typify the earlier rather than the later Wolfian style; if they also suggest a non-lyrical source, then this song (like *Er ist's*, 18) may have been inspired by a prior reading of *Maler Nolten*. The eerie power of the mad scene could readily explain the Wagnerian analogues and overtones – chromatics and tremolandi as in the winds of the *Flying Dutchman*, arpeggio melodies as in the *Ride of the Valkyries* (perhaps spurred by the words 'des Himmels klingenden Heeren').

3. Another Mörikean comparison between winds and love is found in *Begegnung* (20), where the words are far more outspoken and the music far less.

4. The postlude here disappears into thin air like those of *Nixe Binsefuss* (57) and *Der Rattenfänger* (96).

5. Cf. Distler, Op. 19 (SSA).

51 (M 39) Denk' es, o Seele! (*Think on this, my soul*)

10 March 1888 (orchestrated 4 May 1891)   D minor   b#–d''

A fir sapling is growing green, who knows where, in the forest; a rosebush, who can say in what garden? They are already appointed – think on this, my soul – to root and grow on your grave.

Two black colts graze in the meadow, they come trotting cheerfully home to the town. They will tread, slow step by step, with your dead body – perhaps, perhaps even before they cast the shoes that I now see shining on their hooves.

Mörike's short story *Mozart on the way to Prague* has been described as the loveliest and brightest in all literature. It recounts an imagined incident. During a halt in his coach journey the composer strays into the grounds of a great house, is recognized after some misadventures as the famous Kapellmeister from Vienna, and is persuaded to stay and make music for a wedding celebration. After his departure the bride, while rearranging the music, chances to pick up an old songbook from which falls a single page containing a 'Bohemian folk-song'. Its imagined words, given in Mörike's poem, end the story. We are told that the young woman was still under the spell of Mozart's music; that she closed and locked the instrument he had played, so that no other hand should touch it again; and that as she read the words she wept, sensing that Mozart had not long to live. So bright a genius, she feared, must soon be consumed in its own fire.

Wolf, too, thinks of Mozart; or so his unexpectedly transpicuous textures and thematic contrasts suggest. The setting is delicately lyric and sombrely dramatic by turns, in the D minor of *Don Giovanni*, the ominous climax of which pervades the closing pages of Mörike's tale and may also have contributed to the motive force of Wolf's drama and conflict, which seem to go beyond the restrained and resigned sadness of the poem. In the piano prelude we hear first a passing bell and then a light sigh. Each is repeated, the latter slightly higher to increase the tension. The voice enters to a new baroque pastoral 6/8 strain for the woodland scene; this lightly-scored music is also repeated slightly higher. A long pause; then the tolling bass octaves reappear, this time lower than before and with ominous insistence, at 'Sie sind erlesen schon' (They are already appointed); harmony and texture darken and deepen. The piano part resumes its sighing and tolling (now in that order) until the opening vocal recitative tones are set cantering at 'Zwei schwarze Rösslein' (Two black colts). Then their rhythms are suddenly harnessed to the hearse and are felt taking the strain at the held-back change to 2/4; 'sie werden schrittweis gehn' (they will go step by step). The voice declaims, the measured tread of the cortège in the accompaniment gradually gathers strength and attains an irresistible forward impulse. The piano chords burst into fortissimo tremolandi, then hush into awe-struck silence. A postlude has the last word, with the sorrowful flow of the prelude transformed rhythmically into a wistful funeral march which in turn dies away in the distance.

NOTES 1. The *Kritische Gesamtausgabe* prefers the autograph reading of B♭, not A, at the lowest note of the last right-hand quaver chord in bar 47, on the ground that this follows the middle voice of the left hand; but a lower pedal A may equally have been the intention (as in bars 46, 49 and 50); see note 3. The pedal marks at bars 55 and 57 surely apply only to those bars, and not (as sometimes interpreted) to the whole postlude.

2. According to the 1926 edition of Paul Müller, who knew Wolf well, an 'etwas bewegter' should begin at bar 33, which seems entirely plausible; so in the *Gesamtausgabe*.

3. In *Mozart auf der Reise nach Prag* Mörike makes great play with the churchyard scene in *Don Giovanni*, and cites the statue's four- and five-bar phrases beginning 'Di rider finirai', which he defines (disputably) as being in D minor. Wolf's cortège at bars 43ff may also be compared with the dragging and effortful tread of the undeniably D-minor statue-music in Mozart's overture and finale, where also the dominant A is strongly stressed.

4. In the same section this song also evinces resemblances to *Heimweh* (49), dated some three weeks later. The 2/4 rhythm common to both is in each case related to a Schubert song from *Winterreise*; in *Heimweh* to *Gute Nacht* (journeys away from the loved one) and here to *Der Wegweiser* (journeys towards the grave).

5. The 6/8 hoofbeat rhythm recalls *Der Soldat I* (70) of the previous year, and (even more clearly) *Der Gärtner* (29) dated only three days earlier than this song. Cf. also *Auf einer Wanderung* (27, note 3), begun on the next day.

6. Cf. Franz, Op. 27 no. 6; Pfitzner, Op. 30 no. 3; Distler, Op. 19 (SATB).

52 (M 40) Der Jäger (*The huntsman*)

23 February 1888   G minor   c'–g''

Three days of rain, on and on, no sunshine now; for three days, no kind word from my love's lips! She's sulky with me and I with her, that's how she wanted it; but the bickering and bitterness are gnawing me here at my heart.

Welcome then, huntsman's delight, thunderstorm and rain! The ardent breast securely buttoned up, I plunge exultantly out to meet you! Now I expect she'll be sitting at home laughing and joking with her brothers and sisters; I hear the old leaves whisper in the dark forest. Now perhaps she'll be sitting and weeping aloud for sorrow, in her own little room; I feel at

home here hidden in the darkness, like a deer. Not a stag or roe anywhere!
A shot, to pass the time! The healthy crack and echo refresh the marrow in
my bones.

But as the thunder now dies away in the valleys around, a sudden
sorrow overcomes me, my heart sinks right down.

She's sulky with me and I with her, that's how she wanted it; but the
bickering and bitterness are biting me here at my heart. So away to my
love's house to clasp her round the waist! 'Wring out my wet curls and
kiss me and take me back again!'

Wolf was highly indignant when (as he told his mother, in a letter of 19
April 1890) a critic praised this song for its freshness of feeling but
incautiously referred to it as a 'Liedchen', or ditty. The affronted
composer complained that one might just as well call *Tristan und Isolde* a
comic operetta. Certainly the song is extended, even diffuse, in
construction; but one has a certain sympathy with the critic. There is a
homeliness about the poem, and in some respects its setting, that goes far
to justifying the term 'Liedchen'.

Mörike's highly articulate verses are deliberate in their portrayal of
naiveté, with dialect touches; the simple sentiments are cleverly linked in a
chain of unreflecting and intuitive reactions. Sunshine reminds the singer
of his love's smiles and favour; but her frowns are like thunder. Her quiet
domestic talk recalls the whisper of leaves; her bedroom suggests a
sleeping deer, the huntsman's prey. No wonder the shot sparks off the
thought of reconciliation; as so often in Mörike, the reverberations are
erotic. Here as elsewhere, his rustic wooing scenes may well derive from
his soft-hearted but sharp-eyed curacy among a country congregation.

Wolf has the same ideas. The restless rhythm announced by the left
hand and emphasized by punctuating chords often makes a somewhat
harsh comment on the situation; but the opening melody is simplicity
itself, almost a folk-song strain. Thus the music blends ostensible
roughness with underlying tenderness in the same proportions as the
poem and its central character, with an added rhythmic drive that gives
fresh impulse to the succession of linked ideas. The figurations become
more boisterous and less surly at the energetic welcome to the
thunderstorm at 'Willkommen denn' etc. Thereafter the original left-hand
motif returns with its asperities much softened at the thought of the loved
one happy at home; 'Nun sitzt sie wohl daheim' etc. After the mention of
the whispering leaves in the forest ('Blätter flüstern') the motif briefly
resumes its former harshness, as if sharply reminded of the huntsman's
plight; no intimate whispering for him. But then the music suddenly
relents and softens more than ever before, at 'Nun sitzt sie wohl und

weinet' (Now perhaps she'll be sitting and weeping), only to resume its grumbling at the complaint about being hidden in darkness ('in Finsternis geborgen').

The song, admirable so far, now strikes a comparatively bad patch, in which operatic conventions supervene. In other settings, such as the two previous songs, an analogous treatment can be justified by reference to the quasi-dramatic context in which Mörike incorporated the poem in a novel or story; but these verses, though included in *Maler Nolten*, are in no way integrated with the narrative. It is only in Wolf's setting that (at the sixth quatrain, beginning 'Kein Hirsch', no stag) the central figure steps out of his solitary mood and on to a stage. The unquiet lover alone in the night reverts to the stock character of the professional huntsman. The result is disturbing in the poem, and jarring in the song. In the piano part, a gun fires and an attempt at manly sentiment misfires; at the mention of thunder the harmonies are set shaking and pealing in a way just right for a Weber opera but not wholly convincing in this Wolf song. However, the balance is somewhat redressed by the reappearance of the original theme in voice and piano for Mörike's almost literal repetition of his second verse; and the song, suddenly fitted out with new if still homespun material, to suit the sudden new inspiration of directly patching up the quarrel, dashes off to a racy conclusion with a spirited postlude designed to come stumbling and grabbing clumsily in with a boisterous shout of 'here I am!'.

NOTES 1. There is a certain roughness about some of the details. Thus Mörike's very deliberate change from 'nagt' to 'frisst', when the second quatrain reappears as the eighth (showing that the dull ache has by then become a sharp pang), is not acknowledged by any corresponding musical intensification. Similarly the prolonged 'durch' in the recitative passage beginning 'Doch wie der Donner' seems to have acquired more weight than either the stress or the sense can readily justify.

2. The piano left hand throughout typifies unrest, motif 5; the piano at 'Gesunder Knall' has the manly motif 6, cf. *Der Freund* (66); at 'Regen' and 'entgegen' appears the F# major tonality associated with such words as the intervening 'Lust' and 'jauchzend' (motif 40). Other equivalents less obvious and more engaging than the gun and the thunder are the accented chords for the vigorous towelling and drying of soaked hair following the frankly two-handed clutch round the bodice; all this maladroit reconciliation takes on the roughness of motif 27.

3. The latent erotic content suggests that Wolf had strong if unwitting reason for his own comparison with *Tristan und Isolde*. There are occasional overtones here of the 'sick Tristan' motif of e.g. Act I Scene 2, which also speaks of pain, quarrels and reconciliation.

53 (M 41) Rat einer Alten (*An old woman's advice*)

22 March 1888   E minor   d#'–g''

'*I've been young, so I can put a word in, and grown old, so my word carries some weight.*

Sweet ripe berries hang on the bush; neighbour, a fence round the garden won't help; blithe birds know the way.

But you take a tip from me, my girl; make sure you hold your young man with love and respect!

With those two threads twined into one you can draw him along after you with your little finger.

Be frank at heart, yet know when to keep quiet, up with the sun and to work with a will, sound limbs, clean linen, these make a woman and a wife of real worth.

I've been young, so I can put a word in, and grown old, so my word carries some weight.'

Again we are given affectionate observation from the curate Mörike, moving unobtrusively among his parishioners; the scene by the garden fence with all its homely wisdom and racy talk comes to vivid and vigorous life. Even the non-speaking roles are deftly delineated; through the gaps in the sentences we catch a clear glimpse of the head-scratching father, proud but solicitous, and the blushing and gauche proprietress of the ripe berries. But the worldly-wise old lady dominates the words and the music. Her portrait is naturally painted with a broad and rather stiff brush. In particular the verbal accentuation lacks Wolf's usual sensitivity, and there is a touch of the conventional about accompaniment and melody alike. The composer himself later confessed dissatisfaction with this setting, almost alone in the Mörike volume.

Yet the portrait is irresistibly lifelike in its forthright vitality and forcefulness; and this exact match for the poem is also graced with a persuasive melodic lilt well designed to win affections as well as arguments. The song begins and ends uncompromisingly enough, with clipped didactic rhythms and an emphatic off-beat accent, all wagging forefinger and thumped walking-stick. But in the meantime it is as if the old woman's memories have mollified her recitative into melody. The grace-notes that cackled through the first incisive phrases, to suggest laying down the law, begin to chirrup cheerfully and decoratively for the metaphor of the birds and berries, at 'schön reife Beeren'. They remain didactic but half-affectionate and teasing in warmer major harmonies at the direct address to the girl herself, at 'Aber mein Dirnchen' etc. Here there are further characteristically Wolfian touches of detail. Thus the voice briefly links a pair of auxiliary grace-notes to a sustained tone at 'gedrehet', as the two threads are twisted into one, and then tactfully holds its peace for a moment by slowing down at 'schweigen', to show that it too knows when to leave its thoughts unvoiced. Finally the first strain reappears and the clinching chords round off the song.

NOTE. Acciaccaturas are used by Wolf to indicate didacticism, criticism, or teasing or mocking laughter (motif 4; cf. also *Cophtisches Lied I*, 99). As all of these occur in this song, it is not surprising that the device is found here, if anything, too often. Much the same applies to the accented chords, which are one aspect of motif 27.

54 (M 42) Erstes Liebeslied eines Mädchens (*A girl's first love-song*)

20 March 1888   A major $e^{b\,'}-a^{b\,''}$

What's in the net? Just look! But I'm frightened: is it a sweet eel I can feel, or a snake? Love is a blind fisher-girl; tell your child what she has caught.

Already it's whipping in my hands, oh misery and joy! by nestling and wriggling it slithers to my breast.

I marvel as it bites its bold way through my skin and shoots down to my heart! o love, I'm scared! What can I do? The horrible thing is snapping inside, coiling into a ring! I must have poison; here it's sliding around, blissfully burrowing, it will slay me yet.

'Today' wrote Wolf to Edmund Lang 'I have produced my masterpiece. *Erstes Liebeslied eines Mädchens*' (the twenty-second song in the Mörike volume, in order of composition) 'is by far the best work I have yet achieved. By the side of this song, all the rest is child's play. The music is so strikingly characteristic and at the same time of an intensity that would lacerate the nervous system of a block of marble.' Other songs even finer were to follow; but Wolf's own description of this one is hardly exaggerated. The poem, with its short-breathed lines full of panting cries and questions, and its manifestly erotic imagery, could readily become the subject of much Freudian commentary. Wolf himself must have thought it rather daring, even sixty years after it was first written. He had described it, and his own music, as 'crazed' in the letter quoted above; and in later correspondence* he writes 'Even Mörike, that darling of the Graces, – to what excesses does he not permit himself to be tempted by his Muse when she turns her gaze towards the daemonic side of reality. The *Erstes Liebeslied eines Mädchens* is a striking example'. What still seems

---

* to Emil Kauffman, 5 June 1890

remarkable in retrospect is its poetic fusion of innocence with passion into one single obsession.

Wolf's musical equivalent is a piano part with an eightfold repetition of a sixteen-bar theme which is itself repetitive. The essential innocence is suggested by this basic simplicity of structure and by naive snatches of melody throughout, like the crazed Ophelia. The passion is reflected in the texture of the music as well as its fiery speed. Thus the brief recurrent right-hand theme is always preceded by a quaver or two quavers' rest, like a sharp gasp; the syncopations of the vocal line sound like a fighting for breath. The explosive incandescence of the mixture is brought out by the brightening key-changes that carry the theme round in an octave circle during the course of the song, and by the regular flare of sustained high notes, coinciding with those key words that Mörike also highlights, by rhyme and placement: e.g. 'Schlange' (snake), 'Lust' (joy), 'Ring' etc. The central symbol of the cause of all this tumult has been implanted deep inside the music, where it assumes a Protean variety of shapes. The main piano themes are high-arched or slightly curved, and are linked together in long spirals of melody which are taken round in a cycle of key-change. In addition, the triple sforzandi chords that graphically describe a ring are used as further illustration at regular four- or eight-bar intervals; their first appearance coincides with the words 'Schon schnellt mir's in Händen' (It's whipping in my hands). Finally the postlude generates its own frantic lithe circular movement which is mercifully cut off by a final fortissimo chord.

NOTES 1. Two other typically Wolfian motifs are present in an adolescent stage of development: the love music of e.g. the first piano bars, motif 13, and the brightening mediant key-changes of motif 24. For a later quieter aftermath of the jubilation of the postlude, see 39, note 2.

2. The twenty-four year old Mörike sent this poem as a highly original wedding gift to his boyhood friend Friedrich Kauffmann (letter of 7 July 1828); the Emil Kauffmann to whom Wolf wrote about Mörike as quoted above was the son of that marriage.

3. Cf. Distler, Op. 19 (SSAA).

55 (M 43) Lied eines Verliebten (*A lover's song*)

14 March 1888   B minor   c#–e''

In the dark hours, oh, long before dawn, my heart wakes me to think of you, though healthy youth would wish to sleep. My eyes are still bright at midnight, brighter than early matin bells; when would you ever have thought of me, even by day? If I were a fisherman I'd get up, carry my net down to the river, take the fish to market with a glad heart. In the mill at first light the miller's lad is bustling about; all the machinery is clattering. Such busy activity would be just right for me! Alas! But I, poor wretch, must lie idly grieving on my bed, thinking of an unbiddable little girl.

Mörike's poem begins:

> In aller Früh, ach, lang vor Tag,
> Weckt mich mein Herz, an dich zu denken...

This is the only direct mention of the love that inspires the verses; but these few words are heard underlying each of the lines that follow, and setting their tone. So with Wolf. The unforgettable melody of his eight-bar prelude sings a left-hand love-song, as it were below the surface of awareness, accompanied by the sleepless throb of off-beat right-hand chords. The successive phrases of unrest and tenderness are linked together in a long upward spiral of melody that traverses two octaves before arriving at a momentary point of repose, only to begin again as the voice enters and to continue thereafter in a powerful evocation of separate lives and loves, as the two independent melodies go their own ways in different directions. The downward-tending vocal counterpoint is subtly framed to the inflexion of the words. It rises questioningly at 'mein gedacht?' (thought of me). It takes another upward turn for the activity of the fisher and the miller, and again at the end of the song. Meanwhile the piano melodies, though subtly varied, persist in essentially the same shape and scope as in the prelude; and these two interweaving strands, vocal and instrumental, now dividing, now joining, give new life and meaning to each other and to the words. As ever, Wolf highlights certain moments and thoughts. He has a C♯-major triad for the brightness of matin bells (at 'Morgenglocken') and a brisk staccato for the further work 'in der Mühle', with an effortful accent for the hard-working 'Müllerknecht' (miller's lad). Subtly, the piano postlude echoes the prelude, only to break off suddenly and unexpectedly, as if to deny the solace of the theme. These details in no way disturb the perfect organization of this song, which with its twin streams of clear fresh melody is among the enduring delights of the Mörike songbook.

NOTES 1. The reiterated eight-bar pattern and its variants are worth studying. The structure is so strongly symmetrical as to make the intercalated bar 41 sound somewhat contrived as a pivotal point for return to the home key with the last verse. The occasionally dubious accentuation (e.g. 'zum Verkauf') offers further pointers to the primacy of the piano part.

2. In the autograph, the song originally began at its present bar 9; the extrapolation of its first eight bars of accompaniment for separate use as a piano prelude was an inspired afterthought. It is clear from later songs that these

preluding melodies meant much to Wolf. Thus their shape and feeling-tone at e.g. bars 1, 3, 5, are heard again in later love-songs (122, 164) and at e.g. bars 2, 4 and 7 have the 'unrest' idea of motif 5. The abruptly questioning dominant ending (motif 31), recalling the interrogatory tone of 'mein gedacht?' anticipates the bittersweet mood in some of the Spanish songs (e.g. 171, 175).

3. Cf. Distler, Op. 19 (TTBB).

56 (M 44) Der Feuerreiter (*The fire-rider*)

10 October 1888 (arranged for chorus and orchestra October-November 1892)   B minor   c'–g''

Don't you see – there at the little window – the red cap again? There must be something weird afoot, for he's pacing up and down.

And suddenly what thronging crowds by the bridge, off down to the meadow! Hark! the fire-bell is shrilling: behind the hill, behind the hill, the mill's on fire!

Look! There he comes at a frantic gallop sheer through the gate, the fire-rider, on his skinny-ribbed mount, as if on a fire-ladder. Cross-country! Through thick smoke and heat-haze he races, and arrives! In the distance the bell peals on and on – behind the hill, behind the hill, the mill's on fire!

You who had so often scented fire from miles away, and with a splinter of the True Cross blasphemously conjured the blaze – look out! – from the rafters the Devil is grinning at you amid the flames of hell. God have mercy on your soul!

Behind the hill, behind the hill, he's running wild in the mill!

It took less than an hour for the mill to burst in ruins. But the rash rider was never again seen from that hour.

People and carriages in a throng return home out of all that horror. The bell too rings itself out – behind the hill, behind the hill ... fire!

Some time later the miller found a skeleton with a cap on seated bolt upright against the cellar wall on the bones of a mare. Fire-rider, how chill you ride in your grave! Hush! It's all flaking away in ash.

Rest, rest in peace, down there in the mill.

Mörike was adept in the poetry of magic and dream. This ballad is all black magic and nightmare. It is remarkable alike for its vividness and its obscurity, like the strange fire-lit scenes it describes. The origins of the poem have been traced back to various local beliefs and legends. These have antiquarian interest; but in an important sense it is Mörike's own perfervid creative imagination that has given legendary force to this bizarre narrative by making it seem so true and so compelling. Some of the personal and literary background may nevertheless be worth recalling; Wolf too may have been aware of it and perhaps influenced by it. An early version of the poem was included by Mörike in his novel *Maler Nolten*. After a fancy-dress ball a group of artists meet and chat. The painter hero is present, together with an actor friend. The talk turns on strange characters; a fire-rider is mentioned. The actor tells a local legend dating from the Thirty Years' War, of an army officer known as the 'Mad Captain', an eccentric recluse who was never seen on the streets save when a fire had broken out somewhere. Then he could always scent it, and 'he would be seen at his little window, wearing a red cap, pale as death, and pacing uneasily up and down. Immediately after the first fire alarm, and indeed quite often even earlier, and before it was generally known where the fire was, he came galloping madly out of the stable below on a bony nag and chased off at top speed to what was infallibly the right scene of the tragedy' – perhaps with the implication that the fire-rider was also a fire-raiser. Finally the actor agrees to sing the ballad. We are told that the relation of voice to accompanying instrument was, in accordance with the strange subject of the song, more of a shrill and nervous monotone than an actual melody, and that the declamation was brought to its most complete expression only by a restrained play of gestures and features.

There are two other relevant points. First there is a tradition that the opening lines of the poem were inspired by seeing the mad poet Hölderlin, whom Mörike greatly venerated and sometimes compassionately visited, run crazily up and down past the window of his cell wearing a white night-cap. Secondly, another friend of Mörike's was the poet Justinus Kerner (also set by Wolf, cf. no. 12), who was obsessed with the occult, and whose periodical *Magikon*, 1840–53, contained details of fire-riders, fire-sensers, and so on. We also learn from Friedrich Eckstein that Wolf would not rest until he had mastered the background detail and studied the relevant issues of *Magikon*, where Mörike too had found the inspiration of the idea in his third verse, about mastering fires by the use of black magic and the inevitable penalty to be paid. Thus the imagination of both poet and composer was fired and fused from the same sources into music and verse of nerve-flaying intensity; and the song rivets attention and compels acceptance with a force that all but outmatches the poem. It is formidably difficult for both performers; but a fully-achieved version will include some of the most impressive and memorable moments in music. Very literally, it must be heard to be believed. It does not seek popularity or inspire affection; no normal human emotion is involved in this extraordinary gallimaufry of fire, crowds, bells, hoofbeats, madness and annihilation.

It begins with generalized feelings and crowd scenes – alarms and excursions. The initial impulse is therefore mainly rhythmic and dynamic. The drumming octaves in the piano part mutter apprehensively, a shiver of excitement and fear. The voice breaks in with an agitated whisper – 'Sehet ihr am Fensterlein dort die rote Mütze wieder?' Tension mounts as the right-hand piano figure rises gradually through more than two octaves and finally comes bursting out at the top of a new piano theme crowded with thronging rhythms, at 'Und auf einmal welch Gewühle' (and suddenly what thronging crowds). To this in turn is now added, high in the treble, a persistent ringing note, at 'Horch! das Feuerglöcklein gellt'. This is the fire alarm bell, which breaks out into insistent ringing tremolandos as voice and piano come storming up to the frantic cries of 'hinterm Berg' etc (behind the hill); the mill's on fire. The excitement and drama of the voice part derive from the masterly organization of the music as a whole. In the twenty-six bars of piano part heard so far, a group of themes, each adapted superbly to its graphic and motivic purpose – excitement, crowds, alarm bell – has been fused into one single impulse that climbs in a great uninterrupted sweep over three octaves in pitch and from pp to fff in volume, and in texture from swift running notes to thick powerful chords. All this prodigious panoramic vision of movement stretching from the foreground street and window through the surrounding countryside over the bridge and into the meadow, and finally to the distant glow and alarm over the hill, serves essentially just to set the scene on which the Fire-rider himself now appears. Great octaves run raving down the bass surmounted by rising figures in the treble that cut and crack like a whiplash – 'Schaut! da sprengt er wütend' etc (Look! There he comes at a frantic gallop). In contrast to the first descriptive group of generalized themes, these bold motifs typify one single individual. They are melodic and extended, and thus stand out from the music as if in an extra dimension. The thronging crowd rhythms recur at 'Querfeldein!' (cross-country), with the Fire-rider's music riding sheer through and over them. Again the bell notes ring out, and voice and piano reach another frenzied climax at 'hinterm Berg' etc (behind the mill).

Now the tension relaxes somewhat in a ballad-like strain with a broad vocal melody and orthodox accompaniment. But not for long. The harmonies become contorted, the repeated quavers ominously insistent. The voice recounts the horror in the mill and chants 'Gnade Gott der Seele dein!'. This leads to the true dynamic climax of the song, where fresh power previously held in reserve is suddenly unleashed. With a tumult of jagged chords in dotted rhythm the Fire-rider's theme is sent jerking and tearing in unbridled and terrifying violence 'running wild in the mill' (hinterm Berg, rast er in der Mühle). In the interlude these chords resolve into octaves that plunge down from the heights of the keyboard to the depths. Now the right hand takes over the insistent dotted rhythm as in the left hand the Fire-rider's theme broadens out and hushes for the re-entry of the voice at 'Keine Stunde hielt es an' (It took less than an hour). There is a sudden brief outburst from the piano as the mill collapses in ruins (after 'borst in Trümmer'). Then the voice drops suddenly to its lowest register and intones the fate of the rash rider, who was never seen again from that hour. Under pianissimo chords his theme duly disappears and is never heard again. Instead the thronging crowd motifs resume, now taking a downward turn for the return home, after 'Volk und Wagen' (people and carriages). After the repeated 'hinterm Berg' at this point in the poem, the rest of the refrain is reduced to one word 'brennt's' (fire). Thus Mörike depicts the noise and excitement dying away. Wolf reproduces this idea in a brilliantly conceived piano interlude. The repeated bell notes in the treble break off, resume at irregular intervals, and fade, while the bass chords have a stammering and confused version of the refrain 'hinterm Berg', all with a total musical effect of vague disjointed speech – 'The mill ... burning ... fire ...'

After a long pause, the folk-ballad accompaniment resumes, somewhat more leisurely in its rhythm, with a warmer melody. All this was long ago, it seems to say, reassuringly; all forgotten, if indeed it ever happened. But suddenly the warmth dies out of the music, a great chill strikes into it and from it. The anguished harmonies that told of the encounter in the mill reappear, softly and haltingly, to describe its aftermath. Groups of quiet, detached, strange, widely spaced chords are heard interspersed by eerie whispers from the voice. The compelling music of the warlock, the ride, the fire – all this life and movement is destroyed and turned to dust and nothingness; cold bones under drifting ash. Now the voice intones its final requiescat through the tolling of the accompaniment, now lowered in pitch, slowed down in rhythm, and thus transformed from a local fire alarm into the universal *memento mori* of a funeral passing-bell. 'Ruhe wohl, ruhe wohl, drunten in der Mühle'.

NOTES 1. The autograph shows signs of great haste, perhaps because the notes were cast on to paper still ablaze with inspiration, as with Schubert and *Erlkönig*. Yet there are no serious textual problems, despite the immense complexity of the score. On the contrary, the song impresses by its subtle and perfect organization, which repays detailed study. Among points worth especial notice are: (a) the excited crowding rhythms in bars 15–18, traversed by the Fire-rider music in 35–8 and set running or driving home again in 84–7; (b) the transitions of the Fire-rider theme itself from its first arrival on the scene at bar 27, through its use in diminution at 63 and its final disappearance after 83; (c) the harmonic identity, and rhythmic variety for dramatic effect, of bars 47–62 as compared with 103–20.

2. The mysterious harmony of motif 19 greets the diabolical apparition at bars

133

55—6 and reappears at 111–12, marked 'geheimnisvoll'; the manly dotted rhythm of motif 6, indicative of boldness, is ubiquitous.

3. For what may be a deliberate reference to this song in the Goethe songbook, with the common theme of 'ash', see 132, note 3; for a possibly less intentional affinity of crowd-motif, see 123, note 5.

4. So intensely dramatic a portrayal of character, narrative and scene could hardly fail to have some Wagnerian resonances. Thus the simultaneous disappearance of the Fire-rider and his motif, note 1 (b) above, is a highly Wagnerian device. More specifically, the opening theme described above as a shiver of fear assumes forms analogous to those at 'Ist dies das Fürchten?' in *Siegfried*, Act III, while the piano's cataclysmic outburst after 'Seele dein' recalls the orchestral rendering of shipwreck after 'zerschlag' es dies trotziges Schiff' etc in *Tristan*, Act I scene 1.

5. The orchestral version has some interesting and effective new material, e.g. the Valkyrie hoofbeat rhythm on bassoons and lower strings as the Fire-rider gallops off; but the extra complexity of even more added detail takes the edge off the necessary fiery pace in practical performance.

57 (M 45) Nixe Binsefuss (*The Nixie Reedfoot*)

13 May 1888   A minor   e'–g''

The water-elf's daughter is dancing on the ice in the light of the full moon; boldly she comes singing and laughing right past the fisherman's house.

'I'm the maiden Reedfoot, and I must look after my fish. My fish are in a tank, having a cold Lent; the tank is made of Bohemian glass, so that I can count them at every opportunity.

Do you hear, you fisher brat, you old wretch, can't you understand that it's winter? Just you come anywhere near me with your nets and I'll tear them to shreds for you.

But your little maid is pious and good, her sweetheart a fine young huntsman. So as a wedding-bouquet I'll hang a wreath of reeds at the front door, and a pike made of heavy silver, inherited from King Arthur. This masterpiece by a dwarf goldsmith brings its owner the best of luck. Every year it sheds its scales, worth five hundred groschen in cash.

Farewell my child! farewell for today! The morning cock is crowing in the village.'

Water-sprites were never really acclimatized in English-speaking mythology; so that the ontological status of the singing Nixe and her father the Wassermann would be far from clear even without the further obfuscation of Mörike's exuberant invention. But she is certainly not a 'mermaid', as the Peters translator has it; rather a 'nixie' or female water-elf. 'Reedfoot' or 'Bulrushfoot' is the poet's notion of the appropriate name for such a being, meaning perhaps that she lives at the foot of the water-reeds. The poem is full of such fantasies; thus the Bohemian glass no doubt means the ice on the frozen river, serving as the glass of an observation tank. But the music is the most illuminating commentary on the poetic obscurities. As in *Elfenlied* (28) a slight theme and slender treatment are made memorable by the sheer brilliant perfection of Wolf's evocative musicianship. Wearing only a wisp or two of chromatics the nixie drifts diaphanously on to the scene in the piano prelude. The poetic interpretation may be unclear, but at least we can hear exactly how the composer envisaged her. The voice then enters with an ingratiating melody, and the piano abandons its chromatics in favour of an accompaniment figure which is a study in transparency. Staccato bare fifths and bare octaves are heard in the treble left hand, and the same motifs are set delicately dancing in the right. Even the look of the music on the printed page conveys a vivid impression of lightness and airiness. After the last syllable of 'vorbei' (past) has been prolonged over four bars, to project a picture of the nixie moving fearlessly right past the human habitation, the gauze and gossamer chromatic runs resume, only to stop and stand in air as the song within the song begins: 'Ich bin die Nixe Binsefuss'. Under the light repeated treble chords the sharply-accented grace notes and flashing scale-passages hint at anger. An icy breeze sweeps into the upper register of the piano at the wintry threat to the nets. But the dainty accompaniment is momentarily more mellow at the thought of the young girl ('Dein Mägdlein') and tender for the promised wedding gift ('Drum häng ich ihr' etc). Then it becomes sharp and fey once more. In a piano interlude the dancing accompaniment figures gradually fade and are metamorphosed into a minatory cock-crow, the traditional signal for the disappearance of all apparitions. Wolf finds time for further character-sketching during the very long pause he imposes on the cock-crow chord; his bold and spirited nixie is thereby depicted as being disposed to defy the summons and stand her ground. But even she must capitulate. The drifting gauze of the original themes returns, covering but not hiding the bare fifths and octaves. With the last words, the final reluctant acknowledgement – 'Der Morgenhahn im Dorfe schreit' – the chromatics reappear, flit up the keyboard and vanish, leaving the ice empty in the cold light of dawn.

NOTES 1. The nixie here seems much more elfin than her cousins in Mörike's Seven-Nixie-Chorus, a poem in the same genre. Similarly his Wassermann is only very distantly related to Eichendorff's, who makes a brief appearance in *Seemanns Abschied* (82).

2. It sounds as though Wolf has imagined the nixie-figure here as tiny (minor seconds, motif 3) and diaphanously clad (bare fifths and octaves, motif 35); in turn perhaps a more conventional concept than Mörike's. For a possible Goethe

parallel, see 111, note 3. For another use of bare octaves in a verbal context of transparency see *O wär dein Haus durchsichtig* (226); for a possible influence see 59, note 3. The tetchily-accented left hand crotchets are motif 27.

58 (M 46) Gesang Weylas (*Weyla's song*)

9 October 1888 (orchestrated 21 February 1890)   D♭ major   d♭'–f''

You are Orplid, my land! that shines afar. Your sunlit shores send up sea-mists that moisten the cheeks of the gods. Ancient waters rise renewed about your waist, child! The kings who wait upon you bow down before your divinity.

In Mörike's mythology the dream island Orplid, under the special protection of the goddess Weyla, was her home and the source of her magic power; a land so charged with divinity as to purify and invigorate its surrounding waters, and to command the vassalage and worship of kings. This island is the scene of the shadow-play *Der letzte König von Orplid*, which Mörike inserted in his novel *Maler Nolten* and which contains (together with some lyrics not set by Wolf) the text of *Die Geister am Mummelsee* (59). The present poem was written five years later; the magic kingdom exerted a durable sway over Mörike's mind. In Wolf's treatment too the lyric style is incantatory, almost religious. We are privileged to attend a mystic ceremony as it takes place in the poet's imaginary world.

The song begins with four hushed repeated arpeggio chords in solemn equal measure. These establish the mood and rhythm of ritual harp-music, which sounds throughout the piano part. Here Wolf provides extra dramatization of his own; as we know from his friend Emil Kauffmann, he imagined the goddess Weyla sitting on a reef in the moonlight and playing on the harp. As she begins to intone her invocation to her beloved and protected island, the atmosphere of witchery is complete. The music becomes more obscure and tense as mists and mystery cloud the rhythm and harmony. The voice part has thus far lingered on the same note, in monody and prolongation; the sustained notes on 'Land' and 'fern' tell us how strangely remote that island is. The widest intervals are the falling fourths that identify the next words 'leuchtet' (shines) and 'Nebel' (mist). Then there is a sudden leap of a seventh at 'steigen' (rise) and another at 'Kind' (child), when the piano repeats the melody of 'Wasser steigen'; here the swelling and fading arpeggios take on the further significance of the deep sea. Then the harmonies clear from chromatic to diatonic, the mists disperse, and the plain accompanying harp-chords resume. In a graphic final phrase the voice for the third time lifts a seventh, this time a major seventh, to shine out royally on a high F at 'Könige' (kings); then it bows down, just as they do, leaving the solemn harp-notes to die away as the song ends.

NOTES 1. The arpeggios (motif 28) with their changing harmonies have something in common with Schubert's resounding seascape of space and depth in *Meeresstille*. The transitions away from and back to the tonic (I-Ic, bars 5–8) or the tonic seventh (I⁷– I⁷c, bars 10–11) via unrelated tonalities are akin to the mystery motif 19.

2. The orchestral version is given further eloquence by added voices in horn and clarinet.

3. Unless the top note on 'Könige' is restricted to the *f* marked, the dynamic balance is marred, and so is the meaning; not the majesty of the kings, but their subservience, is the point being stressed.

59 (M 47) Die Geister am Mummelsee (*The ghosts of the lake*)

18 May 1888   C♯ minor   a♯–g♯''

What is that coming down the mountainside in the dead of midnight, so splendid with torches? People on their way to a dance, perhaps, or a feast? The singing sounds so blithe. Oh no! Then tell me, what can it be? What you see is a funeral cortège, and what you hear are laments. It is grief for the king, the wizard; they are carrying him back home. Alas! It must be the ghosts of the lake! They glide down into the Mummelsee valley, they have already set foot on the water, they move along without ever wetting their feet, they are droning soft prayers; oh see! the shining woman by the coffin! Now the lake opens its green-sparkling door, look out, now here they come down in a cascade, a living stairway, and down below the songs are already humming. Do you hear? They are singing him to rest there below [they are singing him to rest there below]. How lovely the waters are as they burn and glow, they play in greening fire. The mists ghost away on the shore, the lake swells into a sea. Hush now! is that not something moving there? There's a quivering in the middle, oh heaven help me! now they are coming again, they are coming, the wind swells in the reeds, the dry sedge whistles – now quick, take to your heels! Run! Already they scent me, they grasp me [they scent me, they grasp me, they scent me, they grasp me].

This dream poem from Mörike's fantasy world appears in his novel *Maler Nolten* as a colloquy for two fairy children in a shadow-play. Their vision prophesies the end of the sombre wizard Ulmon, ancient heathen

137

conqueror of the magic island Orplid. Supported by his people, a race of heroes, Ulmon claimed equality with the most high gods, who promptly exterminated the populace by plague and condemned the king to reign alone for a thousand years of mortality. He overhears this dialogue and dreams that he is lying in a crystal coffin, smiled over by his long dead wife (the 'shining woman'); and he is grateful to the merciful god who has revealed the approaching end in this shadow-play and in these lines. This seventh scene of *The last king of Orplid* is prefixed by a stage direction that fixes the action firmly in Mörike's native Swabia; 'Night. Moonshine. Wooded valley. Mummelsee' (the name of a dark and sinister tarn in the Black Forest). In the background a great funeral procession of hovering wraiths comes winding down the mountainside. In the foreground, on a hill, the king, looking fixedly at the cortège. On the other side, below, not noticing the king, two fairy-children.'

An effective musical treatment can hardly avoid setting the ballad in a human context, as Schubert did in *Erlkönig*. Here both the menace and the action are removed several stages further into the world of the imagination. Nevertheless the fine tunes, the opportunities for dramatic effect and the brilliant musical illustrations, all held so firmly within the rigid frame of a sombre death-march, make this song a certain success for the virtuoso singer and pianist. The prelude begins as a ceremonial cortège with eerie open fifths low in the left hand like muffled drums and rumbling carriage wheels. As the voice enters with its fine tune the piano adds faint hints of spectral trumpets, the horns of Elfland, with an added sparkle of staccato for the torches (at 'Fackeln'). So the procession marches along until at 'Sie schweben hinunter' (they glide down) the right hand hovers in high tremolandos while the voice and left hand interchange new horn and trumpet motifs. The bass counter-melody has what sounds like a new rhythm, but is in fact derived from and intended to echo the first bars, to remind us of the sound and sense of the first words 'Vom Berge was kommt dort um Mitternacht spät?'. This heavily accented version reinforces the feeling of growing menace and eeriness. At 'Jetzt öffnet der See' (now the lake opens) the left hand sketches a divided wave-motion; then the living stairway ('lebende Treppe'), the cavernous droning ('summen die Lieder') and the requiescat ('singen ihn unten zur Ruh') are all graphically presented. Now Mörike fills his outlines with brighter colours, as the waters burn and glow in green fire. Wolf responds with dazzling right-hand virtuosity, while the left hand asks as before, with even greater insistence, what are these strange figures coming down from the mountainside? With sustained pictorial invention the music illustrates the ghosting mists ('es geisten die Nebel'), the swelling waters ('zum Meere' etc), the apprehensive question, the sudden reappearance of the phantoms, the great wind of their arrival, the hopeless attempt at flight. Finally the repeated last words of the poem, 'sie wittern, sie haschen mich schon', become last words in another more sinister sense. The whole brilliantly depicted scene has become a landscape without figures.

NOTES 1. The textual repetitions are Wolf's, not Mörike's.

2. The music teems with lively allusion, from the general C♯ minor tonality of night and dreams and the fearfully questioning dominant sevenths in bar 5 (motif 32) to such fine details as the spotlighting staccato at 'Fackeln' (motif 25), the mysterious progression at 'Totengeleit' (motif 19) and the emptiness of the first and final chords (motif 35). Note in particular the resemblance between the postlude here and the final section of *Abschied*; this is the music of precipitate departure, whether serious or comic.

3. The ballad-writing of Carl Loewe (1796–1869), whose work Wolf greatly admired, exerts a perceptible influence on this song as in others (e.g. 57) in the Mörike volume, especially in the use of the piano's upper register for brilliant and fanciful effects in ballads of the supernatural.

4. Loewe is also a forerunner of Wagner, another spirit haunting some of Wolf's eeriest passages here. Perhaps Wagner himself was familiar with Mörike; their creative imaginations had much in common. At any rate the first scene of *Parsifal* echoes the words 'sie bringen ihn ... getragen. Oh weh!' and its last scene has the 'Totengeleit' of Titurel's funeral procession. Wolf's solemn march-themes, though not directly derivative, are surely linked with this chain of association. There is a more direct comparison between the bass motif at bar 13 and the theme of the Flying Dutchman, which the picture of haunted waters may well have conjured up in Wolf's mind.

60 (M 48) Storchenbotschaft (*Message by stork*)

27 March 1888   G minor/B♭ major   c′–b♭″

The shepherd's house, and it stands on two wheels, stands high on the moorland, early and late; and there are many who'd be glad of such a night's lodging. A shepherd wouldn't change his bed with the king. And if anything strange should happen at night, he says his few words of prayer and settles down to sleep; let ghosts or witches or such airy wights knock as they please, he won't answer.

But once it really went too far; the shutter bangs, the dog whines; so our shepherd lifts the latch and what should he see but – two storks, male and mate. This happy pair bows elegantly; they would like to say something, if only they could. 'What are these varmints after? who ever heard the like? But it must be good news they're bringing me.

I suppose you come from back home on the Rhine? Bitten my girl on the leg, I dare say? Now the baby will be crying, the mother even more,

139

*wishing her best beloved were with her? And wanting the christening
presents ordered as well: a lamb, a sausage, a purse full of money? Well,
just say I'll be back in two or three days, and give my baby a kiss for me,
and stir his pap for him. But wait a minute – why are there two of you? It
can't be – no – surely not – not twins?' Then the storks flap and clatter in
the cheeriest of tones; they nod, and curtsey, and fly off.*

A shepherd's bagpipe tune, complete with drone and bass and
unsophisticated dissonance, is announced by the piano; the voice joins in
with a yodelling strain. This theme is sung through the first verse, with a
sturdy pastoral swing. Then the variations begin. The voice repeats the
air, but now the piano part is embellished with odd moanings and
flutterings for ghosts and witches, together with a left-hand knocking (at
'klopfen') which makes the music slow down briefly to reflect for a
moment before deciding not to answer and resuming *a tempo*. In the third
verse the piano's further shutter-banging variation is frankly agitated and
apprehensive. Then the latch ('Riegel') is lifted with an audible rasp, and
the accompaniment looks slowly out in lingering stupefaction, with an
unexpected chord: all in less than half a bar.

The shepherd's tune reappears in the voice, with further surprised
harmonies, and then in voice and piano together with an absurd yodelling
effect as the storks make their bow ('ein schön Kompliment'). This is
followed by a lively cross-examination in which the words, the bagpipe
tune and the storks' nodding-and-bowing motif combine hilariously in a
musical pantomime as enjoyable as it is inventive and effective. 'You've
come from the Rhine?' – pause for thought, then big octave nods of joint
acquiescence. 'Bitten my girl in the leg?' (gebissen ins Bein, as the German
idiom has it) – redoubled beaky nods of vigorous agreement. 'I expect she
wishes I were with her?' (den Herzallerliebsten sich her) – great
excitement – 'arranging the christening presents' (die Taufe) – more nods
– 'a purseful of money' (Geld) – emphatic nods. Voice and piano come
pounding up together in happy anticipation at 'just say I'll be back in two
or three days' (zwei Tag' oder drei). But then both drop back in awful
suspicion. A hesitant inquiry – 'why are there *two* of you?'; ominously
encouraging nods. The voice falters and stammers, reluctant to

pronounce the dread word 'Zwillinge' (twins). The following tableau is spectacular. The storks' confirmatory octaves climb up with a great clattering of beaks and flapping of wings, and, to the accompaniment of the blithest of waltz tunes and a brilliant top note from the voice, fly off, wellnigh falling out of the sky with laughing.

NOTES 1. In some Peters editions the text at bar 4 needs correction from 'sein' to 'so'n' (i.e. 'so ein'). The diction is deliberately vernacular (e.g. 'spat' for 'spät'), and Wolf invents a correspondingly bucolic style; the music is as it were written in dialect throughout, with a slight roughness like the shepherd's out-of-tune bagpipes. In addition the accompaniment, like Mörike's diction and metre, no doubt envisaged the clacking beak and flapping wings of the Klapperstorch, a familiar visitor in Germany and Austria.

2. The main theme throughout has the 'singing' of motif 10. At 'da stehen zwei Störche' is the mysterious motif 19; at the piano solo before the address to the storks at 'Doch halt' is the uneasy motif 5; the rasp of the lifted latch anticipates St Peter's cobbling in *Wie glänzt der helle Mond* (186).

3. The rattling at 'zu bunt' etc recalls the rattling under the bed in Loewe's *Hochzeitslied*.

4. Cf. Distler, Op. 19 (SATB).

61 (M 49) Zur Warnung (*By way of warning*)

25 February 1888   A minor   b–e''

Once, after a convivial night, I woke next morning feeling very strange. Thirst, together with hydrophobia, irregular pulse, and a sentimentally emotional, yes, almost poetic mood in which I asked my Muse for a lyric. She, with feigned pathos, made fun of me by presenting me with this odious doggerel:

> *A nightingale calls*
> *By the waterfalls;*
> *Another bird does the same,*
> *Wryneck is its name,*
> *John Jacob Wryneck its full name;*
> *Performing a dance*
> *Among the plants*
> *By the aforesaid waterfalls.*

So it went on. I grew more and more alarmed.

Then I jumped up; more wine! That proved to be my salvation. Mark this well, ye lachrymose versifiers — you'll never summon the gods with a hangover.

This song is an extreme example of a very intimate art, relying greatly on interpretation and assuming foreknowledge and sympathy on the part of the listener. No doubt it was the work that Wolf had in mind when he wrote to Marie Lang on the same day:

> Today two new Mörike songs have occurred to me, one of which sounds so horribly strange that I feel quite afraid of it. God help the poor people who will hear it one day.

It sounds bizarre because of its fidelity to the text; it is the musical equivalent of Mörike's mocking and self-depreciating humour. Bathos is taken seriously; the sick sluggish themes interspersed with neurasthenic twinges are deployed with the solemnity of a late Beethoven quartet. In the result, the first section, with its crawling and croaking figurations in piano and hoarse hollow interjections from the voice, is unique in Wolf. Normality creeps in at 'Ja, ich bat die Muse um ein Lied' (I asked my muse for a lyric), though even here the word 'Lied' is bleated rather than sung. Mocking acciaccaturas lead into the delightful middle section where the would-be poet delivers himself of his masterpiece. But Mörike's parody is uncharacteristically heavy-handed; it seems that he could take a relaxed view of hangovers, but not of bad verses. Wolf has no such inhibitions; his rendering of the shrill exaggeration of the poetaster is as adroit and apt as anything he ever wrote in this genre. The voice is allotted a banal melody, with a wrong stress on 'und', a wry wrong note at 'Wendehals' (wryneck), and a clumsy insistence on the tonic keynote. In the piano, the lightly-flicked fifths tinkle trivially over a rigid and empty accompaniment, all in single notes. The image of the feeble poet striking his tiny and tinny lyre is irresistibly vivid. This texture is subtly blended into what follows; 'So ging es fort' (so it went on), just as the poem says; as the voice proclaims its alarm and distress ('mir wurde immer bänger') the left hand fails to shake itself free of the doggerel themes. Finally the accompaniment trills happily and leaps up with alacrity at the thought of more wine, and is mock-pompous, mock-maudlin and mock-didactic by turns in the closing bars, ending with a burlesque mock-Handelian recitative.

NOTES 1. Augmented fifths are used for bathos, e.g. in the piano prelude (motif 23); the acciaccaturas illustrating the Muse's mockery are motif 4. The hint of self-parody in the passage marked 'Pompös' on the last page drives from motif 6, often used by Wolf in contexts suggesting manly endeavour. It also occurs quasi-parodistically in *Der Jäger* (52), written only two days earlier. In many of the Eichendorff songs (e.g. 66) this motif is used in all earnestness. The semiquaver figures in bars 3, 6–8 and 10 are part of the evidence for the suggestion that sliding chromatics mean 'deception' to Wolf (motif 20). The final Handel burlesque is again put to effective use in *Spottlied* (89).

2. For an early anticipation of the recitative effect here see *Mausfallen-Sprüchlein* (6), note 1.

3. The 'masterpiece' middle section, with its designedly vacuous fourths and fifths (motif 35), makes what is no doubt a deliberate allusion to the falling fifths in the first movement of Beethoven's Ninth Symphony. Similarly the resemblance in the same section to the motif of Beckmesser's cudgelling (*Die Meistersinger von Nürberg*, finale to Act II), here lightly administered by the left hand, may well be equally intentional. If so, Wolf's prelude may be designed to recall Beckmesser's lame Merker-motif as it comes limping into Act III, scene 3. The cadence at 'Ihr tränenreichen Sänger' has apt echoes of *Tannhäuser*.

4. 'Wendehals' seems to need a word of explanation; is it possible that Mörike, who knew some English, intended his 'wryneck' as a covert allusion to the banal minor poet Reinick?

62 (M 50) Auftrag (*A commission*)

25 February 1888   F major   f'–f#''

In a poetic epistle a desperate fellow wrote thus: 'Dear cousin! Cousin Christel! Why ever don't you write? You must know that hearts touched by the breath of love are in no way to be trifled with, and a poet's least of all. For I am one of that crew, whose brains are constantly active; and if I'm only half a poet, at least I'm half mad.

Cupid has pledged you to me, and you already know your reward, and the lips that keep you informed won't go unrewarded either.

So just you contrive to pass by at the right time when your sweetheart is looking out of her window, and cajole from her lips every word that my sweetheart confided to her. Then write me a letter of half-a-dozen closely-written sides all about my girl, and enclose a treatise of advice on what move I should make next [what move I should make next].'

The verses are offered as a piece of light-hearted entertainment for a casual moment. Wolf's sub-title 'Couplet' suggests that he has a French operetta style in mind; his setting matches and even outdoes the young Mörike in ebullience and élan. The result is a slight song disproportionately full of charm and appeal. A breathlessly excited prelude shouts out for help, with repeated accents and some startling dissonances. The bouncy little tunes and rhythms are artfully varied from verse to verse in a vein reminiscent of Schubert's *Die Taubenpost* on a similar theme; the piano echoes the voice part in a manner wholly Schubertian. Just as characteristically Wolfian are the subtle inflexions of detail, such as the way in which the dissatisfied and empty-sounding harmony after 'Warum schreibt Er aber nicht' (Why ever don't you write) and 'Nur vollends ein Poet' (least of all a poet), stands for the idea of waiting impatiently for an answer. This is heard again after 'das mein Schätzchen ihr vertraut' where the feeling is once again that of exasperated and frustrated expectation; but elsewhere the corresponding chord is full and sweet, especially at the mention of the lips' reward ('geht dabei auch leer nicht aus'). After the repeated last line the postlude recalls the prelude's impatient cries for help and goes dashing off excitedly in all directions.

NOTES 1. The repetition is Wolf's, not Mörike's. The poem parodistically uses the 'Er' form, an archaic mode of address to an inferior; similarly the diction is deliberately high-flown.

2. The final phrase of the postlude has the typical phrase lifting up to the tonic that is the Wolfian prototype of irrepressible ebullience, motif 7; the empty fifths at 'Poet' etc are one aspect of motif 35; the insistent accents of prelude and postlude clamour for attention in the manner of motif 27.

63 (M 51) Bei einer Trauung (*At a wedding*)

1 March 1888   F minor   d'–f''

In the exclusive presence of exclusive people, two of them are being united in holy matrimony. The organ is all vox angelica, but there won't be much joy in heaven, I'm sure. Just look; she's weeping piteously, he's grimacing horribly; for the obvious if unfortunate fact is that it's not a love match at all.

This is again a trifle, but by no means ineffective or negligible. Wolf solemnly points up Mörike's social criticism by providing music suitable for so unusually serious a marriage ceremony – namely a funeral march. The dull, plodding organ accompaniment, so vividly evocative of reluctance to reach the altar, is interspersed with wry commentary from both voice and piano; the Lied repertory has no more telling or original example of irony expressed as sonority. It is hardly programme music in any ordinary sense; it is perhaps more akin to epigram or even journalism – a musical rendering of some such headline as 'No Love Lost At Society Wedding'.

NOTES 1. The augmented fifth is so authentically Wolfian for pathos (motif 23) that its derisively bathetic use here seems almost self-parody.

2. The drily critical snickering of the persistent little right-hand accompaniment figure ♫ is related to motif 4.

64 (M 52) Selbstgeständnis (*Personal confession*)

17 March 1888   F major   c'–f''

*I am the only child of my mother, and because the others failed to appear
– how do I know how many, say six or seven – everything had to centre on
me.*

*I had to eat up, all on my own, enough love, loyalty and kindness for a
whole half-dozen. I shall never forget it as long as I live. But I dare say it
would also have done me good if I'd been whacked for six as well.*

A pleasantly homely and humorous song, well in keeping with the words.
A jauntily cheerful prelude leads into an agreeable vocal melody with an
orthodox domestic accompaniment, like happy hymns round the home
harmonium. The melody at 'ist eben alles an mir' (everything had to
centre on me) is extrapolated and repeated for mock-serious emphasis
over a chromatically climbing chordal bass line – a powerful image of
warm emotion uncomfortably concentrating and converging on one
individual, like a burning-glass. To point the moral in the final postlude
after that same phrase has been used to end the song at 'Schläg' für Sechse'
(whacked for six) it recurs again and again in the accompaniment. But this
time it is equipped with whip-like runs to the top note, and the effect is
striking.

NOTES 1. For the diverging melodic lines in the postlude, see motif 14.
2. At 'ich hab' müssen die Liebe' etc, the vocal line corresponds, for no very
obvious reason, with a melody found in *Fussreise* (22) and *Gebet* (40).
3. The resemblance between the melody at 'ich will's mein Lebtag nicht
vergessen' and Hans Sachs's description of the unforgettable masters of old, at
'Von Lebensmüh bedrängte' (*Die Meistersinger von Nürnberg*, Act III, scene 2), is
no doubt also coincidental.

65 (M 53) Abschied (*A valediction*)

8 March 1888   C minor/B♭ major   d'–b♭''

*A gentleman walks into my room one evening without knocking first. 'I
have the honour to be your critic!'*

*He instantly takes the lamp in his hand, surveys my shadow on the wall
for a long time, from all angles: 'Now, my dear young man, will you be so
good as to look at your nose from the side? You concede that that's an
excrescence.' That? Good heavens – you're right! Bless my soul, I never
thought, not in all my born days, that I bore such a world-size nose in my
face!*

The man made various other comments; for the life of me I can't remember them now. Perhaps he expected me to make a full confession. Finally he got up; I held the light for him. When we are at the head of the stairs, I give him, in the best of good spirits, a little kick from behind on his backside. Goodness gracious, what a stumbling and a rumbling and a tumbling! I've never seen the like, no, never in all my born days have I seen a man go downstairs quite so fast!

There is, as Mörike points out, a kind of intrusive and impertinent criticism of contemporary art; as common in our own day as in his, and as unwarrantable. Like the visitor in the poem, it enters the artist's own domain, uninvited and unannounced; it examines the shadows, not the substance, of his features, not their true expression; it does so in the borrowed light of his inspiration, but from a quite different standpoint, manoeuvred to the critic's own advantage; it magnifies trivial and irrelevant detail; it is personally offensive, and would not shrink from scandal-mongering given half a chance. The gentle Mörike confined his protest to this one good-humoured poem; but he chose it to stand at the end of his collected verse, as a mild reproof to certain reviewers. Wolf on the other hand had been a critic, and often a remarkably trenchant one. Interestingly, he introduced an unacknowledged reference to this poem into one of his reviews*; the subject was clearly much on his mind, both as victim and as tormentor. His ferocious savaging of Brahms shows that he was not above employing the tactics here deprecated by Mörike; his counter-attacks when his own work was in question show that he was not averse from replying in kind. Much of the simple pleasure of retaliation is packed into the ebullient music of this song. So too are the delights of invective, which Wolf also knew at first hand. His setting thus directly commands both the viewpoints described; hence its depth of perception and perspective, and its immediacy of feeling and communication. Both its title and its content made it an obvious choice for the last word in his book of lyrics, as in Mörike's.

The music, like the encounter described, begins brusquely, without a proper introduction. Voice and piano in unison share an angular carping theme deliberately so framed as to be apparently incisive but in fact insipid – and devious – like critics, the music suggests.

* 18 April 1886

146

As the voice explains 'Ich habe die Ehr', Ihr Rezensent zu sein' (I have the honour to be your critic) the piano has a rapping figure of two accented chords, four times repeated, in a highly peremptory tone. Then the left hand flings itself down, presumably into the best armchair. No doubt Wolf noticed that the critic must have taken a seat at some stage (since he later stands up to go) and notionally suited the action to the note; the poem offers no word on the subject. The left hand now settles down on its bottom C, making itself comfortable, in no hurry for a minim or two. Then it rises waveringly, as the lamp is lifted in imagination; and then the critical crotchets resume. As the comments become more personal and pressing, the angular theme is heard at double the first tempo (in quavers) and this figuration completely dominates the music until at 'gewiss' (you're right) the victim has to admit the Cyranesque enormity of his nose, which the accompaniment taps and fingers in surprise at 'Ei Hasen!' (Bless my soul). He duly broods on this fatal defect, to a mock-epic theme of world-shaking grandeur and an illustration of heroic proportions – three octaves thick and well over three minims long. This is followed by a new variant of the peremptory motif in the piano part, which is spun out and made to drone on boringly at 'Der Mann sprach noch Verschied'nes' (The man made various other comments). Now the piano evinces little starts of excitement; a mischievous idea is beginning to bubble to the surface, inspired by the sight of the critic rising from his chair. ('Zuletzt stand er auf'). The angular carping theme takes its leave, now rhythmically altered so as to appear mellow, ingenuous and unsuspecting, until we reach the touching little scene at the top of the stairs. After 'ganz froh gesinnt' (in the best of good spirits) the piano begins to cackle gleefully, reflecting that the boot is now about to be on the other foot. A not-so-gentle kick is instantly followed by a gleeful hammering of broken octaves as the critic and his theme and his opinions are despatched downstairs. That done, and the parting guest duly speeded, the music can at last relax. Its instant response is to become simple and diatonic, and break into a lilting Viennese waltz for voice and piano, at 'Dergleichen hab ich nie gesehen' (I've never seen the like). In the postlude, the hilarious waltz theme, now in quick time, laughs and exults with a bewitching gaiety which suggests that Wolf could have made a fortune as a composer of salon music or operetta; a finale as delightful as it is unpredictable.

NOTES 1. The 'critical' theme in unison and octaves is made of motifs 4 plus 30; it is also cognate with Siegfried's anger with Mime in Act I. Analogously angular themes were used by Schumann for moods of distress or discontent. The related 'peremptory' motifs 4 plus 27 serve similar purposes in e.g. *Rat einer Alten* (53) and *Cophtisches Lied I* (99) for both admonition and amusement; here it turns to laughter in the last page, after 'froh gesinnt'. Its extended use at 'Der Mann sprach' is interestingly akin to the piano part at 'Gevattern stehn und schnattern' of *Der Schreckenberger* (74) written in the same year; 'tiresome chatter' is the underlying idea of each. The off-beat crotchet rhythm at bars 11–13 may perhaps be an image of wavering light, related to motif 2; the moment of impact is the same diminished seventh chord, motif 33, as in *Elfenlied* (28).

2. The rasping interjections after 'beichten' recall the critical motif of Beckmesser in *Die Meistersinger von Nürnberg*.

III. The Eichendorff songs

Joseph Freiherr von Eichendorff (1788–1857) appears in anthologies as a poet of blameless rusticity (as implied even by his name, literally 'Oakenthorpe') whose theme is nature and whose medium is folksong. His nature poetry had already been masterfully set by Schumann in 1840, notably in the *Liederkreis*, Op. 39; and it was Wolf's settled policy not to compose lyrics which had in his judgement already been definitively set by his great predecessors. So when in the autumn of 1888 he turned from Mörike to Eichendorff as the source of a new songbook, it was in conscious quest of new ideas. Eichendorff had earlier proved a fertile source of inspiration. The transition itself was easy and natural, for the two poets had much in common; thus the Mörike lyric *Der Gärtner* (see no. 29 above, note 2) is clearly indebted to Eichendorff. Mörike had also taken over and extended the older poet's genre of humorous character-sketch, for example in *Der Tambour*, whose sprightly metrical drum-beat signalled the onset of Wolf's first sustained inspiration, in 1888. It was not surprising therefore that Wolf should deliberately have gone prospecting for similar fertilizing sources when the Mörike springs began to run dry. Indeed, he later says as much in a letter of 12 March 1891 to Humperdinck:

> In accordance with the current trends to greater realism in art, the romantic element almost entirely abdicates in favour of [Eichendorff's] comparatively unknown humorously and robustly sensual side, to which the composer has deliberately turned for certain select traits. Examples: *Schreckenberger, Glücksritter, Unfall, Scholar, Soldat I, Seemanns Abschied*.

Wolf might also have cited his delectable *Die Kleine*, so 'robustly sensual' that he had felt constrained to omit it from his published Eichendorff songs. Like another of the examples he cites (*Soldat I*) it had already been written in March 1887; so the development was not a new one in 1888. It corresponds to the innate realist strain which complemented the romantic in Wolf's own creative temperament, and

149

hence also in his expressive musical vocabulary and its application to the poets and poems he chose. Like Mörike and Goethe, Eichendorff offered a wholly palatable and assimilable blend of human nature in character-studies and external nature in mood- and scene-painting. But the Eichendorffian savour though far from insipid was less rich than theirs. He evinces little of their scholarly learning or their wide-ranging spiritual inquiry, and correspondingly little of their classical or free verse-forms. Instead, his unshakable Catholic faith orders all his works and thoughts within a structured hierarchy of mother church and fatherland. The wandering students, strolling players, soubrette heroines and soldiers of fortune, no less than the shifting cloudscapes and the revolving seasons, are all held securely in God's cherishing hands.

These feelings have their technical poetic equivalents. The vague rhythms and dreamy assonances of the lyrics, like the alertly marching or trotting metrical feet of the freebooter or cavalier songs, are all firmly fixed within the formal strophic framework of German traditional verse, whether church hymn or popular song; and such patterns are in turn well adapted for direct conversion into the musical lyric mode. There may also have been an ancillary dramatic aspect latent in the poems. Eichendorff loved to scatter verses throughout his prolific prose narratives, with which Wolf was naturally familiar both as favourite reading and as candidates for a suitable opera libretto. It is thus arguably relevant to provide some contextual details for those poems which also appear in the *Novellen* (as in the notes to songs 68, 74, 77, 78, 82 and 85 below). But in composing his settings Wolf seems to have used only that volume of the collected works which contains the poems as such.* His typical concern was to express the poetic content, including any inherent elements of drama and scene, character and gesture, solely through the medium of voice and keyboard.

In this connection it is worth recalling his letter of 7 March 1894 to his friend Emil Kauffmann, which illustrates Wolf's critical acumen as well as his aesthetic attitude:

At your instigation I have recently re-read the Eichendorff narrative *Das Schloss Dürande* [in quest of an opera libretto]... But the characteristic clair-obscur of the Eichendorffian mood is still not in keeping with the hectic arc-light of the stage. I would call his narratives written landscapes, where the figures that have been painted into them play only a quite secondary role, somewhat that which painters call accessories. But on the stage it's quite the other way round; the scene is

---

* *Gesammelte Werke*, 1864, Vol.1, a source not collated by the *Gesamtausgabe* editor, whose textual commentary is in consequence dubious

the accessory and the personages must occupy the foreground, and indeed with all possible distinctness. Just examine Eichendorff's characters and you'll see that apart from the costume and a little colour there's nothing specific about them, nor is there any trace of drawing and psychological perspective. They are only vague shadowy outlines, without features or personality; they suddenly appear, like dream phantoms – we know not whence, and then evaporate, we know not whither. They go past like clouds in the sky, or, to use another Eichendorffian simile, like silent dreams, assuming now one form or shape and now another. All this may be very beautiful and highly poetic, and occupy the imagination pleasingly, but it won't do on the stage.

In the concert hall however it will do admirably; there the imagination is instantly engaged and captivated. Some of Wolf's landscape settings (e.g. *Nachtzauber* or *Verschwiegene Liebe*) rank beside Schumann's in the latter's own genre of nature nocturne. But only a few of the poems in this songbook are thus typical, and none is a well-known anthology piece. Instead we are given, in Wolf's own acknowledged depiction and arrangement, a portrait-gallery of sailors, students and minstrels, gypsy girls and forest sprites, in verses of exhilarating zest and freshness framed, rounded and coloured by the added dimensions of music. Admittedly some of the songs are youthful efforts thrown in as make-weights; and even among those dated 1888 there are a few that suggest earlier work revised by the mature craftsman. Nevertheless the Eichendorff songbook is valuable not only as an introduction to the lighter side of Wolf's genius but also in its own right. The music often hits off perfectly the swagger or the sentiment of the verses; at the same time it can provide a convincing match for Eichendorff's essential seriousness of thought and outlook. It contains many attractive songs of the highest quality, and, in *Das Ständchen*, at least one acknowledged masterpiece.

66 (E 1) Der Freund (*The friend*)

26 September 1888   E major $c^{\#\,\prime}$–$f^{\#\,\prime\prime}$

Whoever sleeps on the waves, a softly cradled child, knows not the depths of life, being blinded by sweet dreaming. But whoever is called by tempests to wild dance and revel, and is left high on the dark seaways by the deceitful world – he learns to bear himself bravely and to steer safely, through night and reefs with a staunch and earnest heart. He is a man of

151

true grain, tested in joy and grief; he believes in God and the stars, and he
shall be my helmsman.

Ernest Newman and Frank Walker, two devoted Wolfians, have
stigmatized this song as 'Wolf at his worst'. No doubt the manly
sentiment is exaggerated in the music as in the poem; while the song's
place at the head of the Eichendorff volume, and perhaps some of its
musical rhetoric also, may have derived too palpably from the composer's
wish to pay personal tribute to his own trusted friends such as Friedrich
Eckstein, who once again helped to defray publication costs, and the
brothers Joseph and Friedrich Schalk, to whom the Eichendorff volume
was dedicated. But even at his worst Wolf would repay attention. Here the
reward is the delightful melody of the first verse set to a gently rocking
accompaniment evocative of a quietly moving sea at night. It is clear that
Wolf was taken by the first two lines of the poem:

> Wer auf den Wogen schliefe,
> Ein sanftgewiegtes Kind,

One suspects that he set them lovingly, as if in process of reading them and
instinctively responding with a lullaby strain, only to discover later that
the idea of childlike sleeping at sea is one of which the poet strongly
disapproves. This opening melodic mood is therefore hurriedly
repudiated, as the text requires, in a series of grand gestures and
protestations; and these though overly histrionic are exhilarating to hear
if not performed too dramatically.

NOTES 1. The change from Eichendorff's 'vom echten' to 'von echtem' (Kerne)
seems to be Wolf's, perhaps by oversight; if so the original words might be
restored, even though the difference in meaning is slight. In his second edition
(1898) Wolf changed the left-hand rhythm in the second halves of bars 11 and 15
to a minim from the insistent crotchet-dotted quaver-semiquaver rhythm that
characterizes the first half of those bars and the whole of 13. In bar 15 the text was
further amended to

The *Kritische Gesamtausgabe* retains these changes; but in view of Wolf's mental
state in 1898 it seems permissible to prefer the original printed text, as in the
present Peters edition.

2. As in *Biterolf* (9), the composer is attracted by the tender aspects of the poem,
and catches them to perfection; but in each case, the poets would have us believe,
they are the 'wrong' aspects, to the detriment of the setting. Here Wolf's

instinctive excursion into his blissful key of F$^\sharp$ major (motif 40) seems to confirm that his real sympathies lie with the cradled child.

3. Three other characteristic motifs are present: (a) the off-beat accompaniment of the opening bars, elsewhere associated with the idea of childlike submissiveness (motif 2); (b) the left hand's rocking quavers in the opening bars evocative of night and sleep (motif 18); (c) the rising bass octaves (bars 12, 14, 16, 27–30) often used in conjunction with ubiquitous dotted rhythms, in contexts connoting manly vigour (motif 6). This last idea in particular sounds overworked here; and all three were put to more refined use in greater songs, e.g. (a) in *An die Türen* (87), (b) in *Um Mitternacht* (31), and (c) in *Prometheus* (134).

4. The two preceding notes in conjunction might suggest that this song, like other Eichendorff settings ascribed to 1888, dates in conception from 1887 or earlier.

5. The younger Wolf was strongly influenced by Schumann, whose *Mein altes Ross*, Op. 127 no. 4, at bar 31ff., has a predecessor of Wolf's manly motif 6 which may be compared with bars 27–30 here.

67 (E 2) Der Musikant (*The musician*)

22 September 1888   A major   d$^{\sharp\prime}$–e$''$

I love to wander through life, and to live as best I can. Even if I wanted to take pains, it just wouldn't suit me.

I know beautiful old songs; in the cold, barefoot, I strike my strings in the street, and know not where I'll rest at night!

Many a fair one makes eyes, it's true, and thinks I would please her well if only I'd settle down and weren't such a poor vagabond.

May God scrape up a husband for you, and provide you with a good house and home! If we two were together, my singing might die away.

There could hardly be a better introduction to Wolf's work than this delightful song. Nothing about it is exacting, for performers or listeners; it perfectly epitomizes the undemanding affability of Eichendorff's typically vagrant hero, who like the music exists only to stroll and sing. It is not solely a matter of charm; the deployment of musical material is eloquent of the master craftsman. From an unsubtle little tune or two, and an uncompromisingly square rhythm ($\frac{2}{4}$ ♪♪ ♩) that persists with hardly a change in the piano part, Wolf has fashioned a brilliantly lifelike sketch of the wandering minstrel. Some of this transmutation is effected by deft touches of conscious musicianship, such as the arpeggios of the prelude which reappear briefly at the later mention of lute-songs, at 'draussen in die Saiten reiss' ich' (I strike my strings in the street), and the sadly flattened sixth, again in the piano, that adds a brief but telling touch of mock-pathos to the girl's imagined pity for a poor vagabond, at 'so ein armer Lump'. But much of it lies in the deeper re-creative power of the

153

great song-writer, for example in the new piano interlude after 'weiss nicht, wo ich abends ruh' (know not where I'll rest at night). These same four bars in isolation would hardly be so memorable; yet in their context they convey a whole essence of easy-going good humour together with a lingering wistfulness underlying poem and song together. The musical figure too is made to smile, sigh, shrug and pass on.

NOTES 1. Perhaps this vivid picture was drawn from the life, in a self-portrait. Eichendorff's poem here might well have been sung by his good-for-nothing musician hero in *Aus dem Leben eines Taugenichts* (also evoked by the phrase 'wenn ich nur was wollte taugen'), a work which surely had special significance for Wolf; cf. E. Sams: 'Literary Sources of Hugo Wolf's String Quartets', *Musical Newsletter* iv (1974), 3.

2. The vocal melody is of the kind elsewhere associated by Wolf with the idea of singing (motif 10); its occasionally casual accentuation (e.g. *'in der Kälte'*) suggests that this walking rhythm was the primary inspiration on which the singing melody was superimposed, just as the poem itself starts with a stroll and proceeds to sing.

68 (E 3) Verschwiegene Liebe (*Silent love*)

31 August 1888   G minor $c^{\#'}-f^{\#''}$

Over the treetops and the standing corn, away into the brightness – who can guess their secrets, who could overtake them? – thoughts go floating; the night is silent, thoughts fly free. If only she could guess who has thought of her amid the rustling of the groves when no one else is awake but the flying clouds; my love is as silent and beautiful as the night.

The poem is typically Eichendorffian in its dreamy identification of feelings with natural scenes. Wolf's response was heartfelt and, according to tradition, instantaneous; this song was said (by Friedrich Eckstein, with whom he was staying at the time) to have been written down in one sudden flash of inspiration immediately following a reading of the verses. This might seem an unlikely procedure for a composer whose normal practice was to work at the keyboard, who had been familiar with the lyrics of Eichendorff since boyhood, and who had already sketched a quite different setting of this same poem. But the song, like the verses, is so clearly natural in its feeling, so limpidly easy in its flow, that the story is understandable and even persuasive. The felicity with which the poet's picture is redrawn in floating melodies and lulling rhythms, and painted with all the dark and bright of the harmonic palette, makes of this brief nocturne for voice and piano a memorable and moving experience. Three bars of prelude set the scene. The right hand has single notes that sway and drift upward; the left hand, also in the treble, has a tender expressive melody. The musical imagery thus already hints at, and no doubt derives from, the idea of a continuing love-song over which thoughts and clouds fly free into the sunset. The voice then sings a variant of the piano song just heard; the swaying rhythm shifts imperceptibly into slightly fuller chords and more recondite harmonies at the parenthetical questions – 'wer mag sie erraten' (who can guess their secrets) etc – which are as it were enclosed in a bracket of modulation. In the new warmer tonality thus established, over the continuing background of the piano's lullaby murmurings, now in a lower register, broad melodies come welling up in the voice part as the harmony moves through poignant dissonance at 'verschwiegen' (silent) to a new unclouded brightness at the word 'frei' (free). This is sustained as the accompaniment rises to regain the higher register with which the song began, and in which the music is now repeated for the second verse. Finally the last word 'Nacht' is lovingly prolonged still further while the postlude meditates on those harmonies which have become associated with the words 'free' and 'silent', creating another vividly meaningful image-cluster which gradually fades as the poignant discords are lingeringly resolved.

NOTES 1. Some Peters editions, following the first, wrongly omit the accidental (E natural, in the original key of G minor) at the first and third quavers of bar 3. The *Kritische Gesamtausgabe* suggests that Wolf changed the text (at bar 17) from Eichendorff's original 'als Wolken' to 'als die Wolken'; but it seems more likely that Wolf was using one of the editions of the *Gedichte* which contain that latter reading. This also occurs in the text of the lyric as incorporated into Eichendorff's verse narrative *Robert und Guiscard* (1855), where it is introduced thus:

Already all were asleep, garden, castle and breezes; only Guiscard and the nightingales were awake. He stood at the open window, the night breathed the scent of lilac upward in the moonlight; then he thought he heard footsteps – at this hour Marie was wont to rove – and he sang from the depths of his heart!

2. The typical rocking rhythm of Wolf's night-music (motif 18) is heard from the first bar, most conspicuously at e.g. bars 6–8 etc. No doubt the rhythmic framework, into which the verse is occasionally forced against its natural accentual tendencies (e.g. 'in den Glanz hinein'), was the original inspiration. This motivic rhythm, together with the strophic form and the occasional semitonal clashes, is shared with *Um Mitternacht* (31). The night-music is as it were passed through the harmonic prism of the motif associated by Wolf with the idea of mystery (motif 19). The horn-passages suddenly released by the word 'frei' (bar 12) are a clear example of the release of motif 8 and its open-air connotations. The empty fifths, all on the dominant (second half of bars 1, 2, 4, 5 etc), give an air of exceptional clarity to the evening scene (motif 35). The harmonic pattern is worth noting, with its central focus on Wolf's blissful tonality of F♯ major (motif 40) and its final questioning suspense on a chord which (despite its notation as the tonic of a new key, D major) is heard as the dominant of the initial G minor (motif 31). The questioning becomes still more intense at the dominant sevenths of 'wer holte sie ein?' (motif 32).

69 (E 4) Das Ständchen (*The serenade*)

28 September 1888   D major $c^{\#\prime}-g^{b\prime\prime}$

Over the rooftops between pale clouds the moon shines out; there on the street a student is singing at his beloved's door. And the springs plash again through the silent solitude, and the wood rustles down from the hillside, just as in the lovely times of long ago. So in my young days on many a summer night I have played the lute here, and composed many a glad song.

But from the quiet threshold they carried my love to rest. Pray you, my blithe friend, sing, just sing on and on [just sing on and on].

By general consensus, this is the outstanding masterpiece of the Eichendorff volume. But it calls for sensitive performance and sympathetic hearing if its excellence is to be fully savoured. Thus even the eight bars of piano prelude may sound rather odd at first hearing. Yet given the situation latent in the poem – walking at night in well-remembered places, hearing the sound of a serenade, being reminded thereby of past singing and old sorrows, trying out mentally the accords of a half-forgotten instrument, elatedly finding one's touch again, sketching a simple accompaniment figure – the prelude is a miniature masterpiece of depiction in its own right, a musical equivalent of the mingled emotions which the 'I' of the poem may be supposed to have felt even before his own lyric meditation begins. Similarly in what follows Wolf continues to weave his music imaginatively around the pattern of the words and their meaning, adding new significance of his own. Thus the singer seems to be imagined and presented as an old man; the matching texture and pulse of the song are alike tenuous. The piano part is itself a lute song with thin strands of melody or repeated pizzicato in the right hand accompanied by a continuous figure of single notes in the left. Through this background the vocal melodies go wandering, as wistfully and elusively as the memories they portray, with accents straying vaguely among the barlines. The result is a superlative evocation of the sad echo of a remembered song from long ago mingling with a present serenade, the entire scene glimpsed through shifting moonlight. The end is especially effective. It is as if the present serenader has heard the affectionate and sympathetic voice of his visitant from the past, bidding him sing on; 'singe, sing' nur immer zu!'. The music responds accordingly, in livelier rhythms and with only a hint of hidden sadness. There, with a few final chords, the song ends, as if the older singer had now faded back again into the past, with the thought that in time to come it will be his young successor's turn to have his own sad memories reawoken by the sound of music at night. The essence of a whole century of German romantic poetry and its aftermath, from *Des Knaben Wunderhorn* to A. E. Housman, is caught and held here.

NOTES 1. The repetitions are Wolf's. Eichendorff has 'scheint', not 'schaut', at bar 13: Wolf would surely have wished the correct text to be sung.

2. The piano solo was clearly the basic inspiration; the consequent need to adjust the vocal line partly accounts for the latter's flexibility which in turn becomes an expressive device. But some odd features remain, e.g. the whole minim allotted to the second syllable of 'schlagen', and the placing of the last syllable of 'fröhlicher' on a strong down beat. Both voice and piano need to feel free of the more obvious constraints of the bar-line throughout the song.

3. Interspersed in the text is the idea of 'singing', motif 10, in the lifting sixths of the accompaniment *passim* plus the lifting and dipping sixths of the right-hand melody (bars 12–13 etc). The mediant modulations from D to F♯ to B♭ back to D may suggest that Wolf is thinking in terms of the poem's changing effects of light, whether literally (moonlight from pale clouds) or metaphorically (memories becoming clearer) or both. This impression is further enhanced by the repeated staccato notes, which may here as in other contexts (motif 26) suggest intermittent nuances of colour or light as well as the more evident notion of lute-music. This would conform with the pattern of the poem, where each successive verse has its own underlying idea; first the sight of the moon, next the sound of the forest, and then the memory of a serenade, which finally becomes a symbol of continuing life. It will not be mere coincidence that Wolf reaches his elated tonality of F♯ major (motif 40) for the moments of deepest contentment. The narrative-reflective harmony of motif 21 at bars 9–11, 15–17, 21–3 etc is an indicator that the piano part is 'about' a remembered serenade from the past.

70 (E 5) Der Soldat I (*The soldier I*)

7 March 1887   C major   e'–f''

My horse may not be well-groomed but he's very knowing; he can find our way in the dark to a certain château quickly enough. The château may not be sumptuous, but there's a girl who comes out of the gate into the garden every night in a friendly way. And although the little love may not be the most beautiful in the world, there's no girl I like better [none I like better, none I like better]. And if she talks of courting, I'll mount my steed; I'll stay in the open, and she in the château [and she in the château, and she in the château].

This earlier work has all the dexterity of the 1888 Eichendorff songs in similar mood. Wolf is audibly much taken by the topic of loving and leaving, as in *Der Musikant* (67) with its walking themes that go strolling by. Here the chosen image is the knowing horse who can find his way in the dark, but is as little attracted as his master by the notion of quitting the

157

great outdoors for a stable way of life. He appears only in the first and last verses of the poem; but in the song the hoof-beat rhythms are heard from the prelude onwards, in a bouncing jog-trot amusingly eloquent of the cavalier temperament and philosophy of the singer. Even his syntax is brilliantly reflected in the music. Although *this*, nevertheless *that*, says each of the first three verses in mounting sequence; the voice begins a tone higher each time, and always returns to an emphatic close in an unexpected key after a thoughtful harmonic excursion. In the third verse the melodies take on a lilting and tender tone, leading into the twice repeated 'die mir besser gefällt' (none I like better), and finally develop an extra jauntiness at the last words (also twice repeated) 'und sie auf dem Schloss'. Just as in *Der Musikant* there is deep inventiveness as well as surface charm. Note, for example, the way in which the piano's melodies are sustained and carried along by the recurrent rhythms, in a graphic image of rider and steed; and how those melodies, announced in the prelude, are teased apart into separate strands shared between voice and piano in an equally lively evocation of tuneful snatches of carefree song. Note also how decisively, in the postlude, Wolf returns to the home tonic of C major for the final declaration of independence and freedom, the keynote of the lyric, as the little decisive tune that has ended the vocal line in each verse canters briskly off into the distance.

NOTES 1. The textual repetitions are Wolf's, not Eichendorff's. Some Peters editions have the garbled reading 'allmächtig' for 'allnächtig' in bar 39; all editions would be clearer with a second tied A$^\sharp$ on the word 'Welt' at bar 52.

2. The harmony and texture and their relation to sense and syntax are worth close study. In each of the first two verses a long tonic pedal finally resolves on a mediant, via a mid-point pivot on VII treated as dominant, and then begins again a tone higher, as successive conditional clauses modulate on to a new idea. In the second verse the mediant turns out to be major, and in Wolf's favourite ebullient tonality of F$^\sharp$ major (motif 40). This second verse is lighter in a higher register, as the topic turns from steed to sweetheart. The third is higher still, with increased harmonic variety including a return to the chord of F$^\sharp$ major at 'die Kleine'. The last runs the gamut of contrasting registers, first reverting to its original pitch at 'und spricht sie vom Freien' and then lifting to a lively treble melody, thus pointing both the pun ('Freien' means both courtship and the open air) and the contrast between constraint and freedom.

3. The delectable dance-music at 'die mir besser gefällt' etc is a striking anticipation of a passage (bars 425–50 etc) in the *Italian Serenade* for string quartet written only two months later.

4. The abounding acciaccaturas (motif 4) are a Wolfian coinage for a laughter not wholly innocent of *Schadenfreude* or even malice; note how the grace notes in the last verse are introduced for the first time into the left-hand hoof-beats and specially accented (after the first 'auf dem Schloss') in a sprightly pantomime that kicks up its heels before trotting cheerfully off.

71 (E 6) Der Soldat II (*The soldier II*)

14 December 1886   C minor $e^{b\,\prime} - a^{b\,\prime\prime}$

You must venture and capture with all speed, already I hear footsteps coming behind us through the night, quick, leap on to my steed with me, and kiss me in our flight, my wild lovely girl; hurry, for Death is a swift fellow [hurry, for Death is a swift fellow, hurry, hurry, hurry, for Death is a swift fellow].

This song is youthful, naively eager, solemnly excited – in striking contrast to the more relaxed, worldly and ironical humour of its counterpart. The difference is perhaps more attributable to Wolf's own personal temperament and development than to any special stylistic contrast between the two lyrics. As before, the hoof-beat rhythm is established at the outset; again it functions as a continuous symbol, this time of precipitate flight. But this arguably distorts the sense of the poem, which is about doing and daring while there is still time. The first page translates those sentiments directly into a cavalry charge for voice and piano, all hoof-beats and rallying-cry. But then after the moment of mounting excitement death is imagined by the composer more as a threat of annihilation than a spur to action; hence the transition to bleak octaves drumming in pursuit, and the repeated exhortations, 'Geschwind, denn der Tod ist ein rascher Gesell', dying away at the end to an ominous whisper, almost overtaken by death in mid-career. On any interpretation, such a treatment seems immature; at a later stage in Wolf's development he would hardly have countenanced this operatic convention in a solo song.

NOTES 1. The poem is the second of a pair of related lyrics under the generic heading *Der Soldat*. The repetitions are Wolf's, not Eichendorff's; and they arguably detract from rather than enhance the text. Thus the rhyming fifth line of a six-line stanza is suddenly compressed by the poet into the one word 'Geschwind!' with a striking effect of urgency which is atypically lost, not to say spoiled, in the musical treatment.

2. The rising piano octaves in the left hand at 'erbeuten' and 'schreiten' are no doubt expressive of the imagined footsteps in pursuit; but they also serve as the manly militancy of motif 6. They rise to the tonic in the right hand in the élan of motif 7, and the excitement of F♯ (here notated as G♭) major, motif 40. But their nerve seems to fail in the last page of headlong flight. Loss of control is further hinted at in the treble outburst, four bars from the end, of what sounds like hysterical laughter, motif 4; cf. 'Er aber lacht' in *Unfall* (80). The idea of being overtaken by death (cf. the end of *Die Geister am Mummelsee*, 59) is perhaps implied by the overlapping canonic imitations in the last three bars.

3. The hammering hoof-beats recall Wagner's 'Nibelungen' motif, e.g. in *Siegfried*, Act I.

4. Cf. Cornelius, Op. 12 no. 2 for double male chorus.

72 (E 7) Die Zigeunerin (*The gypsy girl*)

19 March 1887   A minor   c'–a''

At the crossroads, there I lurk and listen when the stars and the camp fires are burnt out; and where the first dog barks in the distance, that's the direction my lover will come from [la la la, etc].

    'And as day dawned, I saw a cat slinking through the coppice, I fired and peppered her nut-brown skin, how high she jumped! [how high she jumped, ha ha ha etc].'

    It's a pity about the skin; but you won't catch me. My sweetheart must be like the others, swarthy and mustachio'd in the Hungarian style, with a blithe heart for the wandering life, [la la la etc].

The poem begins well with its lyric version of a peasant or gypsy superstition; but its three sections do not cohere closely enough for a singable lyric without the highest interpretative skills from both performers. The general point of the allegorical duologue is clear enough, and is somewhat further clarified by the context in which these verses are incorporated into Eichendorff's Novelle *Dichter und ihre Gesellen*. The actress Kordelchen entertains the company by playing her tambourine, performing a gypsy dance and singing the first verse above. The hero Fortunat chimes in with the second verse; and the actress resumes and concludes with the third. She is said to resemble a cat, as the poem implies. In order to express these diffuse ideas, Wolf is forced not only to repeat words but to invent them. The music aims at, and excitingly achieves, a bravura effectiveness, with flouncing gestures and warm gypsy melodies in the first and last verses and in the second brilliant piano writing, complete with slinking cat-figures that sneak in unobtrusively long before they are mentioned (at 'sah ich eine Katze sich schlingen'), rifle-shots (after 'ich schoss ihr'), increasingly wide leaps ('wie tat die weit überspringen') from two tenths to two twelfths, and outbursts of sardonic laughter. But the last laugh is the cat's: her motif's continuance into the beginning of the third verse ('Schad' nur ums Pelzlein') amusingly shows that she has saved her skin and remained unscathed. To reinforce the point, the original themes now have echoes in a higher register, and the song ends with a triumphant vocal flourish and a two-handed high-jump.

NOTES 1. Textual variants show that Wolf's source was the poem, not the short story, though he may well have known the latter also. He omits ''s ist' before 'schad'', repeats one phrase, and invents ha has and la las galore. These, and the ad lib marking that accompanies the final chromatic downrush of the vocal line, are among Wolf's rare concessions to the display of vocal technique as such. They also add a gypsy touch. Other examples of such vocal colour are the diminished intervals (C–G♯), the grace notes, the cadence at 'andern', the semiquaver snap of bar 38, and the syncopations of bars 41–2.

2. As in *Unfall* (80), pressing the trigger brings about the release of motif 8 (last four semiquavers, right hand, of bars 23–7, repeating the melody of the words 'ich schoss ihr' etc). At 'ein fröhliches Herze zum Wandern' appears the cadence of Wolf's contented open-air melodic line, motif 9. But if the choice of key and the continuous keyboard acciaccaturas of sardonic laughter, motif 4, are any guide, the general mood is not one of contentment. On the contrary, the tensions and colouring of the music suggest the wry passion of the Spanish songs.

73 (E 8) Nachtzauber (*Night magic*)

24 May 1887 F♯ major c♯'–f♯''

Do you not hear the distant springs flowing between rocks and flowers down to the silent forest lakes where the marble statues stand in the lovely solitude?

Softly from the mountains, awaking the ancient songs, the wondrous night descends, and the valleys shine again, as you have often imagined in dreams [as you have often imagined in dreams].

Do you know the flower burgeoning in the moonlit valley? From the half-closed bud, young limbs come blossoming, white arms, red lips; and the nightingales sing, and all around begins a lamentation, oh, wounded to death with love, for the vanished beautiful days; come, oh come, to the silent valley! [Come, come].

The poem is typically Eichendorffian in its tone and topic. It has a hypnotic effect that lulls the mind into an uncritical acceptance of its rather obscure Romantic paraphernalia. Such mood-music inspired masterpieces from Schumann, and it also exercised a profound influence on other German poets, notably Mörike. Here it translates readily enough into Wolfian terms. His harmonies exactly match the poem's richly confused texture of thought, his melodies and rhythms catch to perfection the trance-like imagery and lulling movement of the verses. 'Softly flowing' is the composer's revealing direction; the nocturnal springs provide the motive power of the prelude with its murmuring right-hand cross-rhythms and lullaby left-hand melody. The latter flows lower as the voice enters, and lower still as the springs find the deeper levels of the lakes ('Waldesseen'), and lowest of all for the loneliness ('Einsamkeit') of the deep valleys ('Gründe'). In between those two ideas the night slowly wells up unnoticed in the left hand. The long-flighted melodies, at times more characteristic of Brahms than of Wolf, find time for special facilities of declamation; thus the motionless forest lakes ('nach den stillen

161

Waldesseen') offer the unbroken surface of a low monotone, while the appearance of night ('steigt') and dream ('Traum') is greeted with high floating notes. The vocal lines are constantly inflected to suit the second verse also; in particular the long plunge down to the silent valley at the first words of 'komm zum stillen Grund', is impressively graphic. But the piano part remains largely unchanged save for its meaningful reprise, after 'versunk'nen schönen Tagen' (vanished beautiful days), of the first verse's dream-melody ('wie du's oft im Traum gedacht'). So all this reiterated richness and sweetness may tend to cloy, without the most sensitive and varied of interpretations. The music sounds inspired mainly by (and the poem mainly in) the first verse. But the final appeal, in which the voice is sustained while the opening melody is set floating up the keyboard and away in a last sigh, remains most memorable and compelling.

NOTES 1. The textual repetitions are Wolf's, not Eichendorff's.

2. Some Peters editions lack a natural on the upper note of the last left-hand quaver of bar 26 (at 'du's') and again on the word 'junge'. The repetition shows that in bar 55 (at 'Tagen') the first right-hand B needs a sharp and the second E a natural, as in bar 26; and that in bar 58 ('stillen') the right-hand A needs a natural, as in bar 29. The Peters lower voice edition, in some older versions, needs a flat before the B at the penultimate 'komm!' (bar 60). On all these points the *Kritische Gesamtausgabe* offers much-needed corrections.

3. Only a year separates this song from the even more masterly Mörike *Um Mitternacht*, a strophic song, closely related in poetic mood and vocabulary and hence also in their musical equivalents (motif 18 *passim* in both).

4. At 'steigt die wunderbare Nacht' is the open-air contentment of motif 9. The association of joy with F♯ major (motif 40) may well be relevant here; but the tonality is so lavishly enriched by chromatic variety that it is clearly heard only in the blissful postlude. The melody at 'zwischen Stein und Blumen weit' anticipates 'tust ihr nie zu willen' in *Nimmersatte Liebe* (21).

74 (E 9) Der Schreckenberger (*The dare-devil*)

14 September 1888   G major   d'–f''

Here's to the health of my lady! A weathervane is her device, Fortune is her name, and the camp is her billet. And if she turns away I won't care, for life in the outside world, without cavalrymen, is so dull. Instead of the flash of powder and the rattle of muskets, old wiseacres peer out of every mean house and prattle all pleasure out of life. Fortune weeps with vexation, trickling pearl on pearl. 'Where is my dare-devil? He was a real man!'

She offers me her arm, Fame sounds the advance; so we go up together into the Temple of Immortality.

'Schreckenberger' combines the ideas of dare-devilry and knight-errantry. The song begins without preamble in a burst of panache. Swift scale passages flash out like drawn swords as the toast to Fortune is proposed, with a veering piano tremolando variant briefly intervening as an expressive device at 'Windfahn'' (weathervane). The music falls into a more reflective mood at 'Und wendet sie sich weiter' (and if she turns away); the piano's carefree strumming accompaniment is briefly varied at 'Gevattern' to illustrate the dull prattling of boring old wiseacres. The strumming resumes with a new and delightful vocal melody at 'Fortuna weint' (Fortune weeps), which gradually broadens into a swashbuckling climax in the piano interlude after 'Das war ein andrer Kerl!' (He was a real man!). The voice resumes with quiet confidence at 'Sie tut den Arm mir reichen' (She offers me her arm), only to build up to an even more resounding climax of mock-heroics at the extended accentuated melodic curve on the last word, 'Unsterblichkeit'. Then the postlude thunders out its processional March to the Temple of Immortality, half earnest, half parody, and wholly effective.

NOTES 1. The *Kritische Gesamtausgabe* suggests that Wolf read 'tut' for 'tat' (bar 36); but the obvious riposte is that he was using a text containing the former reading, e.g. not only certain editions of the poems but also the historical Novelle *Die Glücksritter* (Soldiers of Fortune). There Schreckenberger is the name of the character who appears in Chapter V, *Fortunas Schildknappen* (Fortune's shield-bearers), as a typical soldier of fortune. He sings this song after a swig from his campaign flask. At the end his comrades wave their hats in a similar mock-heroic vein, and cry 'three cheers for the highborn happy pair, long live our lord of the temple of immortality!', while a bagpiper drones a further fanfare. Perhaps this drone inspired the repeated left-hand chords of the postlude.

2. The vocal line at 'Fortuna weint vor Ärger' etc is closely akin to Wolf's singing motif 10, while the piano has the narrative harmony of motif 21. Both recur as the opening of *Cophtisches Lied I* (99), dated some three months later. At 'Gevattern sehn und schnattern' is a prattling version of motif 4; an echo of *Abschied* (65, note 1).

3. The most striking general feature here is the prodigal invention of new material within a short song, usually characteristic of Wolf when beginning a new creative outburst after a period of infertility; this was in fact the first of the Eichendorff songs to be newly composed in September 1888. Wolf soon began to economize; the final processional march theme recurs in the next song, two days later, giving musical as well as verbal unity to the pair.

75 (E 10) Der Glücksritter (*The soldier of fortune*)

16 September 1888   C major   c'–f#''

When Fortune is coy, I leave her alone. I sing loudly and drink deeply, and Fortune cheers up too, and sits down at my side.

But I stay standoffish: 'Hi, another drink!', turn my back on her, drink the health of other girls – that makes her very cross.

And soon she comes gently close to me: 'Any more of them?'

'As you see, three whole quarts, and all malt beer! But that's no trouble at all.'

Then she smiles slyly: 'You're a real man!', summons the waiter, calls for wine, drinks my health and pours my glass – real bouquet and sparkle.

She pays for the wine, and the beer; and I, my good humour restored, squire her out of the inn on my arm, like a cavalier. Everyone doffs his hat.

The Austrian Schubert and Wolf seem to have had a penchant and a gift for military march themes, written in a style quite foreign to the German Schumann or Brahms. The streets of nineteenth-century Vienna must have resounded to the strains of high-quality band-music which was intuitively absorbed and recreated by its indigenous composers. Each reacted in a typical way. The military music of Schubert is sweetly solemn and round-eyed, as if he had been held up to watch the soldiers go by. The more worldly Wolf however was already a young man before he came to live in Vienna; he always fashions bright little marches of great brilliance and verve, with more than a hint of ironical humour and parody. Just such a march forms the piano part of this song, to match the laconic colloquial swagger of the words. First of all voice and piano offer a joint unison prelude, in which Fortune trips and trills coquettishly off-stage. Then independence is declared, followed by a cheeky toy trumpet flourish after 'lass ich sie in Ruh'' (I leave her alone). At 'singe recht' (I sing loudly) the march comes stepping out, discreetly at first, but soon bursting irrepressibly into a further solo flourish as soon as the voice part is temporarily silent. The poetic form is perfectly framed by Wolf's schema. In each verse the march is ushered in by voice and piano together; in the first two and the last two by fanfares, and in the middle verse, at 'Und bald rückt sie sacht zu mir' (And soon she comes gently close to me) by an amusingly contrasting tender variant with conciliatory flutes instead of brash trumpets suggested in the piano part. In each verse the march itself undergoes slight but telling changes of harmony and texture, as Wolf adapts his basic theme to suit the mood and meaning of the words, for example in the fizzing and popping at 'echte Blum' und Perl' (real bouquet and sparkle). In the piano postlude it goes strutting off triumphantly into the distance, recalling for the purpose a variation on the processional exeunt theme of the preceding companion piece, and culminating in a loud boastful comment from the heroic squire of Dame Fortune.

NOTES 1. The title is also that of Eichendorff's *Novelle* in which the preceding poem (though not this one) appears; the thematic connection seems entirely justified. Wolf's text here fails to make clear how the imaginary dialogue is allocated in the poem, viz. Fortuna: Hast du deren mehr?/Glücksritter: Wie Sie sehn. Fortuna: Drei Kannen schier,/und das lauter Klebebier! Glücksritter: 'S wird mir gar nicht schwer. Skilled interpretation could, and should, rectify the unfortunate omission of Fortuna's inverted commas.

2. The bluff beginning in octaves and unison is motif 30; the rising scale passage at the end of the march and of the piano postlude is an equivalent for élan (motif 7). Many other songs have similarly engaging march-tunes. In *Ihr jungen Leute* (202) bars 20 and 22 recall the piano part here at 'echte Blum' und Perl' in such a way as to suggest that this (apart from its expressive sense in the latter passage) was an actual drum-fife-and-cymbal effect that Wolf had heard in performance. Similarly the sustained crotchets of the descending tenor part in the postlude here sound like an affectionate and authentic reminiscence of the brass-band arranger's descant.

76 (E 11) Lieber Alles (*All three*)

29 September 1888   G major   d'–g''

Soldiering is dangerous, studying is very onerous, writing poetry is sweet and pretty, but the poet is a figure of fun in these barbarous times. I had best ride out, a good sword at my side, the lute in my right hand, and a student's heart for a good fight. 'Life is an untamed steed, its hoofs strike sparks; who honestly dares can tame it, and where it treads it resounds.

A pleasant genre piece in which much depends on the handling of the vocal line. The poem, though agreeable, is too slight to warrant any special dramatic or expressive treatment. The piano part helps, as ever, with illustration of the mood; but the words seem not to have made any very profound impression on the composer. The musical responses are rechauffés from the Wolfian stockpot; and the song as a whole does not figure among Wolf's outstanding successes, despite its melodic appeal and occasional touches of true quality (in the prelude for example with its incisive character-sketch of a fiery, effortful and yearning approach to life – soldier, scholar and poet, like Hamlet, all three in as many bars).

NOTES 1. The *Kritische Gesamtausgabe* suggests that the B♭ of the autograph in the upper voice, left hand, third and sixth quavers of bar 17, was inadvertently omitted in the first and second editions; and the accidental is accordingly restored. There is some motivic support for this reading; see note 2. The last two rather colourless bars were substituted by Wolf in 1898 for the more flamboyant cadence of his first edition,

which still seems rather more effective and might perhaps (in view of the composer's mental state at the later time) now be restored. The second edition amendment was also followed by Peters, where however an arpeggio needs to be restored in the left hand at the third chord of the penultimate bar.

2. The acciaccaturas of motif 4 are decorative at 'zierlich', but motivic at 'possierlich', bar 17, for the figure of fun. The motif commonly falls or rises in semitones; hence B♭ seems a better reading than B in that context, see note 1 above. There is a wild upward left-hand leap at 'wilden'; the liberation of motif 8 after 'Zeiten', for riding out into the world; the narrative idea of motif 21 at those words; the manly octaves of motif 6 for the sword-bearing quest at 'Rechten' and later. Each occurs in one of its most obvious and least sophisticated forms; and their successive juxtaposition in this short song seems to indicate that Wolf's inspiration is showing signs of temporary abatement.

77 (E 12) Heimweh (*Longing for home*)

29 September 1888   E♭ major   d'–a♭''

Whoever wants to travel in foreign lands should go along with his loved one; for there people laugh and allow the stranger to stand alone.

What do you know, dark tree-tops, of the old, dear days? Oh, my homeland behind the mountains, how far away from here it lies.

My greatest joy is to watch the stars, they shone as I made my way to her; I love to hear the nightingale, which sang at my loved one's door.

The morning, that is my joy! Then I climb in the quiet hour on the highest peak for miles around and greet you, Germany, from the depths of my heart!

This song has a quality found hardly anywhere else in Wolf's work; it verges on tedium. The basic walking rhythm announced in the prelude hardly justifies its use as an unvaried accompaniment figure for nearly fifty bars of moderate 4/4 time. True, much of Wolf's melodic line here is agreeably tuneful; but at the moments when it relies on recitative the repetitious piano part can become irksomely obtrusive. There is typical tenderness in the music at the thought of the distant homeland (with the word 'weit' prolonged and inflected to show just how dishearteningly distant it is), the far-away loved one and the ubiquitous nightingale. But the notion of saluting the fatherland from a handy mountain-top seems to have left the composer, staunch pan-Germanist though he was, largely unmoved. The postlude's patriotism protests too much to be wholly convincing.

NOTES 1. The song might gain from being related to its context in Eichendorff's famous Novelle *Aus dem Leben eines Taugenichts* (Chapter VI). It is there introduced as an old air learned from a travelling apprentice miller and is sung by the hero after a journey to Italy (hence perhaps the dark foliage and the sundering mountains). The imaginary greeting is also related to the narrative; as the song ends, a letter arrives from the loved one far away in the German homeland.

2. In other songs, e.g. *Biterolf* (9) there is arguably the same inadequacy of response, for similar reasons.

3. The persistent rhythm ♪♩ ♪ is a feature of many songs in worshipful mood (motif 1). Note also the mysterious harmonies of motif 19 in the passage marked 'heimlich' (misterioso).

78 (E 13) Der Scholar (*The scholar*)

22 September 1888   A minor   e'–g''

In the pleasantest of weathers all the birds sing; when raindrops rattle on the leaves I can sing like that too, just for myself alone.

For however cruelly the lightning may blaze, I can discern nothing in the wandering life that could hold any terrors for a contented mind. Free from Mammon I will traverse the field of knowledge, thinking deeply, and now and then taking a mouthful of the juice of the grape.

Whenever I tire of studying, then, as the moon softly treads up the sky, I am wont to sing and play serenades before my sweetheart's door.

Unassumingly quiet and modest, this song is nonetheless a masterpiece of its kind. There are grateful and memorable melodies for voice and right hand, and a pensive flow of scholarly quavers throughout the left hand; the whole is blended into a light-hearted character-sketch of extreme deftness and charm. The quavers are staccato in the prelude and throughout the first verse (the first sentence above, down to 'sing ich so für mich allein') and then legato in the second sentence (down to 'ein zufriedenes Gemüt'). These treatments continue to alternate as the changing mood of the poem dictates; staccato for detachment and irony,

167

legato for emotional involvement. There are the usual special felicities, such as the hint of burlesque in the élitist accents at 'auf dem Feld der Wissenschaft' (the field of knowledge), the unexpected changes to the major chord at the end of the last two verses, bidding a warm welcome to wine and love (at '-saft' and 'Tür'), the prolongation of 'müde' to show how tiring study can be, and then the delicious anticipatory serenade from the piano at 'Wann der Mond' etc (as the moon). The postlude summarizes the whole detachment, amusement, and genuine emotion (including a few lute chords by way of final farewell) of this masterly song.

NOTES 1. Eichendorff's title in some editions is *Der Student*, in others *Der wandernde Student*, a characteristic figure in his verse and prose, symbolic of the Romantic conception of life and values. This poem reappears in his Novelle *Dichter und ihre Gesellen* (Chapter VI). The hero Fortunat hears the first two verses sung from a distance by one of a troupe of strolling players, who are caught out in a thunderstorm. The third and fourth verses are sung as they come to a town and find shelter.

2. The right hand's falling fifths recur in the next song, also about a student.

3. The vocal phrase at 'singen alle Vögelein' has the melodic curve associated by Wolf with the idea of singing (motif 10). The semiquavers running blithely upward at the end of the first piano interlude are characteristic (motif 7). The vocal phrase at 'ein zufriedenes Gemüt' is aptly associated with walking and the open air (motif 9). The staccato of detachment is motif 26; the accented vocal crotchets at 'auf dem Feld der Wissenschaft' are motif 27.

79 (E 14) Der verzweifelte Liebhaber (*The despairing lover*)

23 September 1888   G minor   d'–g''

Studying is unprofitable, my coat is out at elbows, my zither won't play, my sweetheart doesn't love me. I wish that the fairest of women were walking in the meadows; I'd be a dragon and carry her off away with me into the blue. I wish I were out questing in armour; with couched lance, I'd chase all the Philistines out of sight. I wish I were now lying in silent and spacious heaven, asking nothing about the world's vanities, just filled with contentment.

An unassuming trifle, pleasant but inconsiderable. The voice begins unaccompanied and continues in recitative style punctuated by piano chords; the parallel phrases of the poem are translated into musical sequences, which are then summarized for further emphasis in one concentrated bar of piano interlude. The ensuing romantic fantasy of the fair damsel walking in the meadows, at 'Ich wollt' im Grün spazierte' etc is treated almost as a parody of Schubert; and much of what follows sounds almost like self-parody by Wolf – the rather gently roaring dragon, the knight-errant's cantering steed and so on. The music, like the poem, is written with tongue in cheek.

NOTES 1. Eichendorff has 'all'' not 'alle' (Philister), and the subjunctives 'säss'' and 'früg' (the latter archaic) instead of 'läg' and 'fragt'; the correct text might now be restored.

2. The song resembles *Lieber alles* (76) in its miniature episodic structure, and also in consisting so largely of thematic material already better deployed elsewhere.

3. The falling fifths of *Der Scholar* (78) reappear here in the opening recitative, perhaps in deliberate cross-reference.

4. The 'mysterious' piano part (motif 19) at 'Ich wollt', ich jagt' finds much apter use in other songs; here it is mainly stereotype.

80 (E 15) Unfall (*Mishap*)

25 September 1888   D minor   d'–g''

One night when I was out for a country walk I met a little boy. He has a gun in his hand, and the saucy imp aims it at me most maliciously. Provoked, I rush at him in a rage; he fires, and I fell flat on my face. Then he laughed in my face at having shot me. The little fellow was Cupid. I was extremely vexed.

Herrick could write charming lyrics in this genre. But Eichendorff's verses are more pedestrian, and Wolf's setting is almost flat-footed; the typical touches of illuminating detail serve mainly to highlight and underline the uninspired content of the verse. The staccato piano movement picks its way cautiously, to suit the idea of walking at night; the moment of meeting (after 'ein Bürschlein traf ich draussen') is defined by sharp chords of confrontation. At 'ich renne' (I rush) the walking left-hand quavers are turned into running semiquavers, complete with agitated treble dissonances that rush up in a rage, at 'in vollem Rasen'. Then the musket is duly presented and discharged, the victim falls, the small assassin chuckles gleefully, the sufferer groans and grumbles. The musical material could hardly be more fitting. But it matches the verse all too closely in its rather homespun quality; and all the many and varied attempts in the piano part to infuse life and character into the song will fall as flat as its hero unless lifted and sustained by inspired performance.

NOTES 1. Some Peters editions omit the flats on the first syllable of 'Gesicht' (G♭) and at the lowest note (E♭) of the first piano chord in that same bar.

2. At 'Bürschlein traf ich *draussen*' – the open-air motif 9. The falling semitones of malicious laughter (motif 4) are clearly heard at 'er aber lacht'; earlier they fell

chord-wise for the intenser malice of 'Grausen', in consecutive octaves and fifths, bars 7–8. At 'drückt das kecke Bürschlein *los*' – the release of motif 8, just as in *Die Zigeunerin* (72, note 4).

3. The running semiquavers at 'ich renne' anticipate a passage in *Philine* (see 93, note 2), also about Cupid; the precipitate left-hand descent at 'auf die Nasen' recalls the critic's abrupt occupancy of an armchair in *Abschied* (65) and anticipates a comparable collapse in *Mein Liebster ist so klein* (201).

4. The song is also a forerunner of two other quasi-humorous disquisitions on the pains of love, again in the Goethe and Italian songbooks respectively, i.e. *Der Schäfer* (107) and *Ich liess mir sagen* (212); a comparison of all three is rewarding.

81 (E 16) Liebesglück (*Love's happiness*)

27 September 1888   E major   d'–g#''

I have a sweetheart that I love with all my heart, she has bright sparkling eyes like two candles, and where her blithe glances light on the meadow, oh how joyously the world shines! As in the darkness of the forest between ravines the valleys suddenly divide into bright sunlight and the streams sparkle and the blossoming wilderness rustles heavenwards, so is my heart! Like looking from a mountain top down into the sea, like a sea-falcon, hovering in the blue, calling back to find where twilit earth has gone to, so immeasurable is true love!

There is great excitement in the lively springing prelude that announces the song's persistent rhythm; and there is enjoyment to be had from the sheer buoyancy of the impulse that drives the music along. The piano part differentiates the subject of each verse. In the first, 'Ich hab ein Liebchen' etc., the chords are light and bright like the words and their theme, broadening at 'wie so lustig!' (how joyously) to indicate a wider view of the world. In the second we hear the piano left hand deep in the bass for the first time; and when this darkness of the forest, 'wie in der Waldnacht', is penetrated by sunlight, like the heart, the words 'so ist mein Herz' are greeted by full high chords of the home key of E major, also for the first time. But now the inventive impetus is spent. In the last verse the accompaniment is rather perfunctory, while the exultantly leaping postlude (and indeed the whole song) sounds far too clamorous and emphatic for Eichendorff's poem. There the continual dactylic rhythm serves as a sustaining pulse of elation and adoration; when hammered out some ninety times by both hands and frequently underlined in the voice part the effect is more numbing than invigorating.

NOTES 1. Eichendorff has 'wenn' in bar 17, not 'wann', which should be corrected.

2. The insistent rhythm takes precedence over natural scansion; hence 'und' and 'wie' on the strong first beats of a 12/8 bar.

3. The joining hands at bars 10 and 11 are akin to the love-motif 13; but the continuous assertive hammering in the style of motif 27 sounds anything but amorous.

4. There is again a comparison with the Mörike volume (see 73, note 3) in the different treatment of related subject-matter; *Jägerlied* (16) has a similar poetic mood, to which Wolf's music is far more sensitively aligned.

82 (E 17) Seemanns Abschied (*Sailor's farewell*)

21 September 1888   F major   c'–a''

Adieu, my dear, you never loved me, I was too lowly for you. One night when you walk in the moonlight you'll hear a sweet music. A mermaid is singing, the night air is balmy, the silent clouds go by. Then think of me and my mermaid wife and find yourself another lover.

Adieu, you troopers and musketeers, we travel on a wild steed that bucks and rears and turns somersaults before many a towering cliff. The merman rises up amid lightning flashes on dark nights, the shark snaps, the gull shrieks, it's a joyous struggle.

Just stretch out your lazy limbs on your bearskin hearth-rugs, you stay-at-homes. God the Father is looking out of his window and sending a second Flood. Sergeants, cavalrymen, musketeers, they'll all have to drown, while we run before a favouring wind straight into Paradise.

The racy poem affords copious opportunities for spirited themes and humorous illustration, and Wolf accepts them all gratefully. The writing is easy and relaxed, full of the boisterousness of the poem and the composer's evident delight in his own music-making. The story goes that Bruckner, when Wolf showed this song to him, exclaimed in astonishment at the very first bar of the prelude – 'Teufel! woher haben Sie *den* Akkord?' (Where the devil did you get *that* chord from?). The whole-tone chord in question

has not wholly lost its power to startle; it makes a rousing introduction to a tall story. The wind shakes the sails in these tremolandi. Soon the waves

171

come pounding up as bass octaves in a good-humoured parody, presenting a Flying Dutchman of comic opera. A broad vocal melody enters at 'Ade, mein Schatz', over a rumbustious capstan-shanty rhythm of alternating chords. The harmonies darken mysteriously for mermaids and moonlight, then brighten again for the sweetheart's final casting off – 'nun such dir einen andern' (find yourself another lover). Here the last syllable of 'andern' falls on the first beat of a bar. But instead of the expected cadence, the prelude figures come bursting out again, as if to remind the singer of more pressing matters claiming his attention. The second verse bristles with comic effects for lightning, sharks and seagulls; the music flashes, snaps and shrieks. At 'Fechten' (struggle) comes an operatic trill to indicate extreme joviality. But then its last syllable again has its tonic cadence cut off by the seascape piano theme. It is as if, while the singer is loyally extolling the grim but exciting struggle of the nautical life, he is suddenly soused in spray. For the third verse the melodies broaden still further. The relentless rhythms abate, and pretend to idle about with the stay-at-homes. The mention of the coming flood is amusingly anticipated at 'Gott Vater aus dem Fenster schaut' (God the Father is looking out of his window). The piano takes the hint, and prepares to steer clear; the left-hand octaves indicate their willingness to start running in good time. The song resumes its original tempo, with the farewell to all land-lubbers, such as sergeants and cavalrymen, at 'Feldwebel, Reiter' etc; and then races along to a striking conclusion. The vocal line sails joyously up and away, and the huge exultation of the postlude sets the theme riding over a renewed heave and swell of bass octaves until it in turn rides triumphantly off to the predicted haven of Heaven.

NOTES 1. The *Kritische Gesamtausgabe* suggests that Wolf changed the text to 'lustig' from Eichendorff's 'lust'ges' in bar 42. But it seems more likely that Wolf's source contained the former reading, which occurs e.g. in the text as interpolated, aptly enough, into the Novelle *Eine Meerfahrt* (cf. 85, note 1), though the context there affords no direct interpretative indications.

2. The mystery of motif 19 is elaborated in bars 9–12, for the moonlight stroll, with the progression from D♭ via D back to D♭, now notated as C♯. In its more usual form it reappears for both the supernatural visitations, at 'ein Meerweib singt' (bars 14–17) and again at 'Der Wassermann' (35–8). The bass octaves of the piano prelude are (apart from their pictorial effect noted above) the manly motif 6. The whole of the final vocal phrase, from 'derweil', with its brief echo (and an effect of 'hear, hear!') in the piano's last two bars, is an analogue of the open-air elation of motif 9. Finally the acciaccaturas added for eerie pictorial effect to illustrate the imagined perils and hazards of the deep belong to motif 4; in this guise they suggest another light-hearted allusion to the music of *The Flying Dutchman*.

3. Wolf's immense enjoyment of his own music-making can be inferred from

the virtuosity with which his harmonic effects are deployed. Among the more subtle felicities is the text-book comedy of the four different ways of resolving the same chord, in bars 5, 6, 9 and 10.

83 (E 18) Erwartung (*Anticipation*)

26 January 1880   E major   c'–g#''

I greet you from the depths of my heart, two eyes bright and clear, two rosebuds on her mouth, shining dress of sunlight! The nightingale laments and weeps, the grove rustles amorously, everything speaks of my dearest, where does she linger so alone? While it was overcast outside I saw many a brighter shine; now it is light and clear, yet I feel as if in darkness. The sun is reluctant to rise, it looks in so sleepily, wishing all day long that night might come again.

Love wings through the sky, goes to meet the beloved far away; off, over mountain and ravine, and she will yet be mine.

This is among the most endearing of Wolf's early songs, full of youthful ardour for his adored Vally Franck, to whom it was inscribed. The music outdoes the poem in its eloquent tenderness, with a piano part in falling thirds making a gentle background for the heartfelt vocal line. Exceptionally, the musical mood is Brahmsian in style, with its sensuous syncopations and broad melody. But the delicate inflections are already wholly Wolfian. In the second quatrain beginning 'Nachtigall klagt und weint' (The nightingale laments and weeps) the alternation of a line of verse with a two-bar piano interlude creates a feeling of tension and expectancy; in the fourth quatrain, from 'Sonne nicht steigen mag' (The sun is reluctant to rise) the same device vividly conveys the idea of the idling and delaying sun longing for nightfall. Meanwhile a brightening touch or two of staccato in the piano at 'Weil's draussen finster war' (While it was overcast outside) illuminates the slightly obscure text. But when presented with a sudden change of mood at the end of the poem the young composer is audibly unprepared and loses his grasp of the song. The last page wrenches the music from shy love to adolescent bragging. The opening themes reappear in voice and piano for a would-be triumphant conclusion; but they are clearly conceived in terms of the initial treatment and are unhappy without it. Dressed in a loud sweeping chordal cloak several sizes too large they look and sound unconvincing. One could wish that Wolf had revised this song before publication at the time of his real mastery of formal construction; his own later dissatisfaction with it, justified or not, is evidenced by its withdrawal from a second edition of the Eichendorff volume.

NOTES 1. The title *Erwartung* seems to be Wolf's own; one can understand his preferring it to Eichendorff's own quasi-humorous superscription *Steckbrief*, i.e. a warrant of arrest. Again the last verse deems to disrupt the mood. The poem was interpolated in the Novelle *Ahnung und Gegenwart*, where it is sung by the hero Graf Friedrich on horseback, and introduced thus:

> The picture of the beautiful Rosa again arose vividly within him, painted and adorned with all the glowing colours of the morning. The sunshine, the gentle breeze and the larks' song wove themselves into the picture, and thus there arose in his happy heart the following ditty, which he sang aloud to himself as he rode on his way.

2. At a later stage Wolf would no doubt have simply matched the new poetic idea with new musical material, just as he does with admirable effect in the comparable *Der Jäger* (52), instead of retailoring the original material just for the form's sake.

3. This song shares with *Biterolf* (9) and others, all mainly early work, an inability to make a convincing change of mood from tenderness to determination.

84 (E 19) Die Nacht (*Night*)

3 February 1880   F# minor   d#'–f#''

Night is like a silent sea. Joy and pain and love-lamenting merge so confusedly together in the gentle pulsing of its waves. Wishes are like the clouds that sail through silent space; who can tell in the gentle air if they are thoughts or dreams?

Though I now close my heart and my lips that so love to lament to the stars, yet in the depths of my heart there remains that gentle pulsing of waves.

The sweetly vague lyric makes an attractive song, clearly prophetic of the coming master. One can understand both why Wolf in his first enthusiasm selected it for inclusion among his maturer work in the Eichendorff volume, and why on reflection he rejected it from a second edition. There is something faintly uneasy and contrived about the way in which the basically simple and suitable melodies are overdressed in somewhat complex harmonies and rhythms, no doubt in a deliberate attempt to match the layers of feeling contained in the lyric, with its cross-references to other Eichendorffian images (nights, thoughts, clouds, breezes, rhetorical questions and love-longings just as in *Verschwiegene Liebe*). The shifts of stress and tonality look more recondite on the printed page than they really are; yet the impression conveyed is one of the conscious use of musical device for purposes and in ways which though effective enough in themselves are not organically related to the poem being set.

NOTES 1. The *Kritische Gesamtausgabe* gives details of textual changes from autograph to first edition, namely the shifting of the fourth crotchet off the beat in bars 1, 5 and 16, which suggest that they were undertaken for the rather prosaic reason of avoiding consecutive fifths. The notation of flats in a sharp key, at bars 12–13, expresses the poetic idea of ambiguity.

2. The perceptible influence of Schumann's *Zwielicht*, Op. 39 no. 10, also an Eichendorff setting, may help to account for the impression of contrivance.

3. This musical mood of night and dreams suggests to the young composer, in the main instrumental and vocal melody, the germ of the rocking movement that later developed into motif 18.

85 (E 20) Waldmädchen (*Forest sprite*)

20 April 1887   G major   e'–g#''

I am a bright fire blazing down from the green crown of the cliff; the sea-wind is my lover and sweeps me off to a joyous whirlwind dance, inconstantly coming and changing, rising wildly, sinking gently, I turn my slender fires; come not near me, I'll burn you up!

Where the wild streams rush and the high palm-trees stand, when the hidden huntsmen listen, many deer tread one by one.

I am a deer, I run through ruins, over the heights, where silently in the snow the last peaks shimmer; follow me not, you'll never catch me.

Now I am a bird in the breezes, soaring over the blue sea, from the cliffs through the clouds, no arrow can fly as far as here. And the meadows, the bend of the cliffs, forest solitude far, far around, are all merged into the waves – I have flown myself away!

Wolf removed this song from a later edition of the Eichendorff volume; one can see why. It was no doubt conceived as a brilliant *tour de force* for voice and piano. But even on that level it is not wholly compelling; vocal melodies and bravura accompaniment alike verge on the banal, and the two set-piece piano interludes, after 'Verbrenn' dich' (burn you up) and 'erjagst mich nimmer' (you'll never catch me) seem absurdly rowdy. Such bluntly programmistic music, often overriding the subtler felicities of the verses, is out of character both for Wolf and the elusively Protean spirit invoked; indeed other composers such as Mendelssohn and Loewe seem to have stood fairy godfather to the main thematic material. But once we accept that Eichendorff's airy fancies have been brought down to earth, there is much to admire in Wolf's added pictorial touches. Thus the long-drawn notes on the last syllables of 'Wirbeltanz' (whirlwind dance), 'einsam gehn' (tread one by one), 'bis hieher' (as far as here) extend an imaginary line of continuous motion and flight over the keyboard's continuing demisemiquavers, while the new piano figurations at 'Bin ein

Reh' (I am a deer) represent a highly ingenious adaptation of the new ideas of skimming and shimmering. Cleverest of all is the way in which the wood-sprite's native essence, distilled in the vocal melody at 'kommt und wechselt' (coming and changing) etc is surprisingly siphoned off into the piano part when that music recurs at 'und die Au'n' (and the meadows) etc, in an unobtrusively deft intensification of the poetic text. Thus the voice is heard as it were disembodied, in a dreamy and disjointed recitative, stripped of its melody and left naked and invisible in thin air, into which the postlude duly vanishes.

NOTES 1. According to the *Kritische Gesamtausgabe*, Wolf changed 'nach' to 'nah' in bar 23; but the latter occurs in some editions, no doubt including the one that Wolf used. All editions however seem to give 'und die Au'n und Felsenbogen', which should arguably be restored. Eichendorff later included the poem in his Novelle *Eine Meerfahrt*, as an additional lyric for his vivacious and mysterious heroine Alma to sing; Wolf's music may perhaps have envisaged this human context.

2. Accompaniment and postlude are illustrative in the manner of Loewe; see 59, note 3. Key, register and progressions recall Mendelssohn's Piano Concerto No. 1 in G, Op. 25; compare e.g. bars 5–6 here with the Concerto's last movement, *molto allegro e vivace* (cf. Wolf's 'Äussert rasch und feurig') where the piano decorates the theme at bars 31 etc. The sustained top notes at 'Wirbeltanz' and 'hieher' are also highly Mendelssohnian.

3. Cf. Schumann, (SSAA), Op. 69 no. 2.

IV. The Goethe songs

Johann Wolfgang von Goethe (1749–1832), poet, dramatist, novelist, painter, critic, scientist, philosopher and statesman, was the greatest and most universal genius of his time. His mind and work dominated two centuries of Europe from the prodigiously influential novel *Werther*, 1774, to the completion in 1832 of the towering drama *Faust*. His poetry has Mörike's qualities of humour, fantasy and beauty of imagery, together with an intellectual vigour, a range of vision, and a depth of understanding, with few parallels in the literature of the world. His poetic genius also irradiated and transformed the history of music, not only by providing ideas, themes and texts for so many overtures, tone-poems, cantatas and operas but above all by projecting the written word so brightly into the musical mind of great composers as to create fused word-tone images and hence a new art-form, the Romantic Lied. From Mozart's *Das Veilchen* and Beethoven's Goethe settings to Schubert's *Gretchen*, *Erlkönig* and a hundred others the process is clear. The poetry of individual emotion and experience, rendered vivid by narrative or dramatic presentation, with strong or elevated feelings expressed in simple words, is translated into musical terms. Goethe himself notoriously approved of the subordination of music to words within the song-form, and carefully cultivated the art and the society of like-minded lesser Lied-composers such as Zelter. But he knew instinctively that a new art was about to be born, and may well have acknowledged his own paternity. In a letter to Zelter*, he noted in general terms that no lyric poem was really complete until it had been set to music. 'But then', he concluded, 'something unique happens. Only then is the poetic inspiration sublimated (or rather fused) into the free and beautiful element of sensory experience. Then we think and feel at the same time, and are enraptured thereby'. This idea of the chemical or physical bonding of two quite different modes of artistic creation is as crucial to the existence and history of the Lied as to its appreciation.

---

* 21 December 1809

It is significant that when Wolf himself came to comment on this composite aspect of his art it was in connection with his Goethe settings and his fear that because of their dual nature they had not been properly apprehended in performance. As he wrote to Melanie Köchert on 12 October 1890, 'On the whole I gained the impression that I had *not* been understood, that my hearers were concerned too closely with the musical and had thus lost sight of what is new and individual in my musico-poetic conception'.

Throughout Wolf's work, that conception is nowhere more difficult to grasp and evaluate than in the Goethe songs. One reason is that despite Goethe's transcendent genius and deserved renown his poetry is so resistant to translation as to be all but inaccessible to English-speaking readers or listeners. This in turn is because the very qualities that make it so sweetly or sharply savoury in its native idiom may often taste insipid for alien tongues. The simple words remain, but their subtle and significant blends are all too easily lost. There are other difficulties. Goethe's verse often seems too intimately connected with his life and thought, and their vast bibliography, to be readily communicable with the immediacy that the song-form requires. Further, Wolf's selection was circumscribed by his own diffidence about setting poems already treated by his great predecessors; and in Goethe songs he had been notably anticipated by Loewe, Schumann and Brahms as well as Mozart, Beethoven and Schubert. For these reasons there is much substance in Frank Walker's assessment that Wolf's Goethe songbook 'seems almost the product of a conscious stiffening of the musician's will and girding of his loins to meet the challenge of the greatest of German poets ... His Goethe volume is not the most immediately attractive of his works; there is here no profuse lyrical outpouring as in the Mörike songbook. The response is intellectual rather than lyrical'.

The force of that response also creates its own Goethean range from sublime grandeur to earthy raciness. Like the poetic style and vocabulary, the music sounds now epic, now colloquial, often both together. It matches Goethe's variety and inventiveness in genre and metre; it echoes the bright ring of his new-minted language and ideas. As in the Mörike volume, the separable musical elements in the poetry are reflected and enhanced in Wolf's setting; not only the special colouring for red-letter words such as 'Blütenherz' in *Frühling übers Jahr* but the 12/8 equivalent for classical hexameters in *Anakreons Grab* and the uncompromising harmonic treatment of the toughly sinewy thinking in *Dank des Paria*.

In this songbook too Wolf strives to serve his poet's cause by presenting his own work in structured groups corresponding to Goethe's own arrangement, like a select anthology. The first ten poems, 86–95, occur as occasional lyrics in the novel *Wilhelm Meisters Lehrjahre* (translated by Carlyle as *Wilhelm Meister's Apprenticeship*). This is especially memorable for the famous lyrics sung by the mysterious Harper and the child Mignon. Neither knows that Mignon is the Harper's child by his own sister. This is the sin that has sent him wandering crazed through the world, far from his native Italy. His songs are heavy with guilt and despair. Mignon's are full of secrecy, grief, and yearning for love and homeland. The sheer magnificence of Goethe's poetry gives all these individual emotions a universal quality that speaks for mankind. Seven of these lyrics (86–8, 90–3) were included by Goethe in a separate section, 'Aus Wilhelm Meister', of the volume of poems (*Gedichte*, c. 1861) that Wolf seems to have used as his main source (see No. 112, note 1). Two others, 94 and 95, began the following group of some thirty ballads. From these Wolf selected four others (96–8, 115), for his songbook. But the *Spottlied* (89) is not found in the *Gedichte* at all. So Wolf's source for the *Wilhelm Meister* poems may have been the novel itself, and some textual background is given in the notes below.

Nos. 117–33 are taken from the *Westöstlicher Divan*. This separate collection of lyrics, the final flowering of a poet in his late sixties, is ostensibly modelled on the work of the Persian poet Hafiz and his carefully-structured stanzas in praise of love and wine. On the same model, it is divided into short books dealing with poetry (*Buch des Sängers, Buch Hafis*) and philosophic wisdom in proverbs and similar reflections (*Buch der Sprüche, Buch der Betrachtungen* etc) as well as love (*Buch der Liebe, Buch Suleika*) and wine (*Das Schenkenbuch*). English readers may catch other ostensibly Oriental echoes, as in Fitzgerald's rendering of Omar Khayyám (e.g. the cup-bearer Saki). But the true home of these poems is early nineteenth-century Germany and their true inspiration as well as their main subject is Goethe's rejuvenating love for Marianne von Willemer. The poet himself appears in the guise of 'Hatem', the lady is 'Suleika', and herself supposedly (though not always on any very clear or convincing grounds) the authoress of some of the poems. Wolf's selection is confined to the topics of loving and drinking and their considerable areas of overlap.

No doubt he felt that he had provided enough profound philosophy in the last three Goethe songs, which form another separate group and were so arranged by the poet in his *Gedichte*. Each is about one aspect of the relationship of man to God. In these settings, Wolf for the first time deliberately and directly challenged comparison with Schubert; and, in the *Wilhelm Meister* songs, with both Schubert and Schumann. It can safely be claimed that he at least equals the former, and wholly transcends the latter. But his choice of Goethe poems would in general have been circumscribed, for the reasons already given; and the other seventeen lyrics selected were mostly taken from those sections containing poems reckoned by Goethe himself to be suitable for singing, namely *Lieder* (103, 107–13) or the convivial songs or *Gesellige Lieder* (99–101, 104), i.e. mainly lovesongs or songs of good life.

Of course no single Goethe selection could possibly be wholly representative of the c. 700 poems in his published *Gedichte*; but Wolf contrives to draw at least one sample from every suitable section except the sonnets. In this sense the songbook is as commensurate with the breadth of Goethe's outlook as with the depth of his thought and feeling – an achievement fully comparable with the *Mörike-Lieder*.

86 (G1) Harfenspieler I (*The Harper I*)

27 October 1888 (orchestrated 2 December 1890)   G minor   B–f′

He who surrenders to loneliness, oh, he is soon alone; others live, others love, and leave him to his pain. Yes! leave me to my torment! And if I can be but just once, truly lonely, then I am not alone. A lover steals softly and eavesdrops – is his loved one alone? So by day and night I am shadowed in my loneliness by pain, in my loneliness by torment.

Oh, when I shall at last lie lonely in my grave, only there will it leave me alone.

In Goethe's novel (Book II, chapter 12) Wilhelm Meister visits the Harper in his lonely room. They speak of solitude, and the old man improvises this song. The words 'Einsamkeit' – 'allein' – 'ein' – 'seiner Pein' – 'einmal' – 'einsam' – 'schleicht' – 'sein' (loneliness, alone, one, his pain, once, steals, to be) toll their long main vowel through the poem like a funeral knell. Yet the feeling of the verses and the song is not so much grief-stricken as pervaded with a gentle melancholy. In this it responds to Wilhelm's preliminary comment to the old man, 'I think you very fortunate that in your loneliness you are able to occupy and entertain yourself so pleasantly and, as you are a stranger everywhere, can find in your own heart the most agreeable company'. The Harper's sung rejoinder gently demurs; though suffused with feeling it is not emotionally demonstrative, and this restraint heightens the effect immeasurably. The setting begins, again in conformity with the scene in the novel ('the old man looked down at the strings, and after playing a soft prelude struck up and sang...'), with a gentle introduction of spread harp-chords, falling like gestures of abnegation. These lingering phrases, subtly varied in voice and piano, are the source of the musical material of the whole first section of the song, down to the tender cadence at 'nicht allein'. Here the melody, harmony and rhythm are modified to match what Wolf hears as a new note of hopefulness. The vocal line, which has preponderantly drooped and languished, and thrice fallen by as much as a seventh at the thoughts of the separated lives and loves of others ('ein jeder lebt, ein jeder liebt') and again at 'recht einsam' (truly lonely), now assumes upward inflexions. We also hear unequivocally major chords, again for the first time. Further, the rhythmic tread is slowed and softened by hesitations and a smoother flow in the voice part, and by triplet quavers in the piano. These latter then take temporary charge of the accompaniment, while the voice is left with its gentle meditations. Here Wolf has found a masterful solution to the problem imposed by Goethe's discursive image of the lover stealing to see if his loved-one is alone. The wistfulness of his first section, the sighing harp-music of the piano part, the tender cadence, specially marked 'zart', at 'nicht allein'; all these have prepared the listener for the notion that grief and pain can cherish and be cherished, with a jealous love on both sides. So in the new graphic depiction at the words 'Es schleicht ein Liebender' (a lover steals) etc there is the required impression of contrast, but also of continuity. There is even fulfilment in the music as voice and piano rise gently but almost triumphantly together to the word 'Pein' (pain) and stoop together to 'Qual' (torment) as if embracing them both in the one gesture. The tender accompaniment figure then leads the voice back to the opening strain. The spread harp-chords resume; the voice dies away in infinite regret, the postlude again in wistful questioning.

NOTES 1. The final dominant cadence is the questioning motif 31. The torment is imagined almost masochistically, as redemptive physical suffering, if the painful presence of motif 34 is any guide (bars 2, 4, and, on 'Pein', 12).
 2. The falling melody of the first five bars, which is also heard in augmentation in bars 6–7, resounds through this and other Harper songs (motif 22).
 3. Some possible corollaries of the interpretation suggested above: the phrase 'bin ich nicht allein' needs some expressive rallentando; the middle section may be taken a shade faster than the main tempo, to clarify its depictive function; the high F on 'Pein', bar 27, may need some restraint.
 4. Cf. Reichardt; Zelter; Schubert, D325 and D478; Schumann, Op. 98a no. 6.

87 (G2) Harfenspieler II (*The Harper II*)
29 October 1888 (orchestrated 4 December 1890)   C minor   c–d'

I will creep to the doors, I will stand silent and humble, Christian hands will give me food and I shall go on my way.
 Everyone will count himself fortunate when my figure appears before him; he will shed a tear, and I know not why he weeps.

In *Wilhelm Meister* (Book V, chapter 14) the unhappy Harper is showing unmistakable signs of insanity; he is becoming a danger to himself and others. He determines to desert Mignon and escape, but is eventually dissuaded by Wilhelm, after 'a strange conversation', deliberately left unrecorded by Goethe in the interest of 'sparing our readers the distress of unconnected ideas and anxiety-feelings'. These were earlier evident in the lyric, which is described as the last strophe of an overheard song; Wilhelm is said to be well placed to understand its meaning of 'comfort for an unhappy man who feels that he is on the borderline of insanity'. Wolf's music expresses the tragedy of an old man crazed with suffering and become docile and uncomprehending, like the last of King Lear. The feeling is perhaps deeper than in the previous song, and for the composer perhaps more personal also. The syphilitic Wolf had good reason to dread madness, a fate which was in fact to overtake him within only eight more years. But again the keynote is restraint, and again the effect is immeasurably heightened thereby. The prelude has an imploring melody over chromatically creeping minor thirds; thus the Harper's figure already appears before us. At the entry of the voice with its docile flow of even crotchets the accompanying chords shift off the beat. The following interlude is the prelude with this new off-beat rhythm incorporated, as if affected by what has just been heard. In the second verse, the first and third beats of each bar are marked by left-hand minims; the music as it were assumes a more solid and stable stance, with added warmth and interest, exactly as the poem does. The postlude returns to the prelude's figuration, dying away brokenly yet peacefully, again in close harmony with the sense of the words. But perhaps the problem imposed by the lyric's shift from beggar to bystander and back again with enhanced perception is not wholly resolved in this song, for all its mastery of musical equivalence.

NOTES 1. This *Harfenspieler*, unlike I and III, offers no arpeggio harp chords. The Wilhelm Meister context quoted above makes no mention of any harp accompaniment; and indeed we are told in the next chapter, which Wolf had no doubt read, that the old man's harp had been burnt in an outbreak of fire in the town.

2. The off-beat rhythm *passim* in a song of childlike submissiveness is a clear example of motif 2; the sorrow of motif 22 also resounds throughout. The incorporation of the voice's first two bars into the accompaniment at bars 9–10 is characteristic of songs of intense inwardness in Wolf (e.g. *Verborgenheit*) as in Schubert (e.g. the last page of *Ganymed* D 544). The final chord though ostensibly a tonic *tierce de Picardie* has at least aspects of the questioning dominant, motif 31; in the second part of the song much of the music centres on F minor.

3. That key may have had associations with *Tristan und Isolde*; cf. the passage at bars 11–15 etc of Act III scene 1 later related to Kurwenal's 'erschien zuvor die

Ärztin nicht, die einz'ge die uns hilft'; there too the hero is depicted as a broken man, helplessly docile and dependent.

4. Cf. also Zelter; Schubert, D 479; Schumann, Op. 98a no. 8; Mussorgsky; Medtner, Op. 15 no. 2.

88 (G 3) Harfenspieler III (*The Harper III*)

30 October 1888 (orchestrated 4 December 1980)   F minor   c–e'

Who never ate his bread with tears, who never sat through the miserable nights weeping on his bed, he knows you not, you heavenly powers.

You lead us into life, you let the poor wretch become guilty, then you abandon him to torment; for all guilt is avenged here on earth.

This striking song is perhaps the most deeply felt of the three; and, arguably for that reason, perhaps also the least satisfactory. In *Wilhelm Meister* this lyric immediately precedes that of 86 above, in Book II, chapter 13. Wilhelm fancies himself vexed by evil spirits; he hopes that the Harper's music can exorcise them. He visits the old man in his mean garret; already on the landing he hears sweet harping.

> They were heart-moving, mournful tones, accompanied by sad and anxious singing. Wilhelm stole to the door, and as the old man performed a kind of improvisation, in which a few verses, now sung, now declaimed, were constantly repeated, the listener, after attending for a while, could discern some such strains as the following.

The lyric is then cited; and Goethe continues, 'The heartfelt plaintive lament penetrated deep into the hearer's soul. It seems to him as if the old man were often hindered by tears from continuing; then the harp-strings would be heard alone for a time, until the voice joined in again softly, in broken sounds'; with more in the same strain about the effect on the hero's own emotions. Wolf thus has special warranty for treating this song, like the first two, in terms of mixed melody and recitative. His prelude here seems designed to say that III is an express amalgam of I and II; the music combines the falling phrases of desolate loneliness with the creeping movement of crazed submissiveness and abject dependency. As in the previous song, these unifying themes serve as interlude and postlude; the heartbroken harp-strings are heard alone, as in the scene Goethe describes. Already in the first verse the disturbed harmonies sound a quasi-pathological note; in the powerful declamation of the second, reinforced by huge harp-chords, restraint is thrown aside. The final *fff* outburst at 'denn alle Schuld rächt sich auf Erden' has few parallels in

Wolf's song-writing. No sooner is it over than the postlude, now intensified by insistent repetitions, is heard to despair and die.

NOTES 1. Goethe's Harper is sexually guilt-stricken; the syphilitic Wolf seems to outdo the poem in his sense of sin and punishment, and this may be among the settings most affected by personal feeling. On any interpretation the effect of the final vocal phrase is so central to the song that an emphatic pause on 'Schuld' seems justifiable.

2. The sorrow or remorse of motif 22 resound throughout; the postlude is interestingly comparable to that of *Wie viele Zeit verlor ich* (223).

3. Cf. Reichardt; Zelter (two settings); Schubert, D 478 (three settings); Schumann, Op. 98a no. 4; Liszt (two settings).

89 (G 4) Spottlied aus 'Wilhelm Meister' (*Pasquinade from 'Wilhelm Meister'*)

2 November 1888   F major   c'–f''

I, my lord baron, am just a poor devil who envies you your rank, your place so near the throne, and many a fine piece of ploughland, your father's solid castle, his game-preserves and shoots.

But it seems, my lord baron, that you envy me, since nature has always been motherly to me from boyhood on. My light mood and mind have made me a poor man, it's true – but not a poor specimen.

So, my dear lord baron, I thought we might leave things just as they are, you would remain your esteemed father's son, and I my mother's child. We live free of envy and rancour, neither coveting the other's titles; no place on Parnassus for you, none in the Peerage for me.

The Baron in Goethe's novel has artistic pretensions. He patronizes, in every sense, the troupe of itinerant actors with whom Wilhelm is associated; this satirical poem is circulated anonymously at the castle. The piano introduction, which also serves for two interludes and a postlude, is a delightful piece of high-spirited and mocking effrontery, beginning innocuously enough with hints and allusions and finally poking outright fun. But the rest of the song has to depend for its appeal on vocal melody, which is not one of Wolf's most felicitous or inventive; indeed the persistent four-square crotchet movement in voice and piano, with its thirtyfold iteration in each of three verses, will risk tedium in any but inspired performance, despite its undeniable effectiveness as an image of the ceaseless flow of sarcastic comment. It is not until the serene impudence of the last two lines that the voice part fully attains that melodic charm, the piano that lightness of touch, which could successfully serve as saving graces; but by then it may well be too late.

NOTES 1. If the song is to be performed for maximum interpretative effect, the indicated tempo ('mässig') seems too slow.

2. The rising phrase that ends the prelude wherever it occurs is a Wolfian coinage for high spirits, motif 7. The lifting and dipping and sixths of the piano part suggest the idea of singing, motif 10. The stoutly-built ancestral castle attracts the manly motif 6, though this is less apt in its later contexts. Motif 8 is released in the horn passages at the word 'Titel'; the final squib is set off at that moment. At 'und keinen ich in dem Kapitel' the harmony and key are shared with the equally impudent climax of *Ich hab in Penna* (232): cf. motif 36.

3. The sometimes indifferent verbal accentuation ('um', bar 11, 'und', bar 16) suggests that the piano part is the basic and dominant inspiration.

90 (G 5) Mignon I (Heiss mich nicht reden)

19 December 1888   F major   c'–f''

Bid me not speak, bid me be silent, for secrecy is my duty. I should willingly show you all my inmost heart, but fate has willed it otherwise. In due time the sun's course dispels the dark night, and it must grow bright; the hard rock opens its bosom, and does not grudge the earth the deep-hidden springs.

Everyone seeks peace in the arms of a friend, there the breast can pour out its laments; but my lips are closed by a vow, and only a god can release them.

Unlike most of the other *Wilhelm Meister* lyrics, this is not set in any particular scene; it is simply appended to Book V, chapter 16 as a poem that Mignon had 'recited once or twice, with great expression'. The intense inward secrecy of these lines render them perhaps only dubiously suitable for musical setting. At least it seems to have been mainly the metaphors of imparting the secret that inspired Wolf. In the passage beginning 'Zur rechten Zeit' (in due time) the majestically rising octaves in which the sun appears and the springs come to light are a fine imagining, and the shifting stresses in the voice part are subtle and sensitive. Similarly the piano phrase that forms both prelude and postlude offers not only a graphic picture of a look or gesture of refusal, but an effective frame for it. The rest of the musical material however somewhat lacks these qualities of evocation or distinction, and the music of keeping secret remains predictably uncommunicative.

NOTES 1. No doubt the text is imagined by Mignon, like that of *Kennst du das Land?* (94), as addressed to Wilhelm himself, protector and beloved. Her duty of keeping secret is a painful one, if the chord at 'Pflicht' affords any clue; it echoes 'Pein' in the first Harper song (motif 34).

2. Perhaps this song's opening bars for voice and piano were in Wolf's mind

when he began the masterly *Dass doch gemalt* (195) in the same key and with similar progressions, though there is no clear conceptual link.

   3. Cf. Reichardt; Zelter; Zumsteeg; Schubert, D 726 and D 877; Schumann, Op. 98a no. 5.

91 (G 6) Mignon II (Nur wer die Sehnsucht kennt)

18 December 1888   G minor   d'–g''

Only those who know yearning can fathom grief like mine. Alone and sundered from all joy I scan the skies to the south.
  Ah! he who loves and knows me is far away.
  My senses reel, my inmost being burns.
  Only those who know yearning can fathom grief like mine.

This world-renowned poem is described by Goethe as being sung by Mignon and the Harper, with the most heartfelt expression, as an irregular duet (Book IV, chapter 11); and one of Schubert's five settings treats it thus, most memorably. But most of the composers who have been moved by it into music have chosen to set it as a solo song for a woman's voice. We are also told that the music corresponded to the dreaming and yearning mood of Wilhelm Meister at the time he heard it. But the usual conception is that the emotion expressed is one of profound grief. Wolf's setting is typically complex and ambitious; the accompaniment suggests the Harper's presence, if not his participation, and the music seeks both to dream and to grieve. His Mignon experiences the words as she sings them, in excited reverie. Even in the piano prelude, with its lightly-drooping treble octaves that sing and pulsate over slender throbbing chords throughout the song, the tempo fluctuates from bar to bar, as if already under the changing stress of strong emotion. The music anticipates the ground of that emotion: it will later be heard as the piano part at the crucial phrase 'Ach! der mich liebt und kennt ist in der Weite' (Ah! he who loves and knows me is far away). The voice at first shares the ensuing piano melody, which consists of the prelude's tune forced steadily downwards, semitone by semitone, in a brief but vivid image of depression. Then both recover together at the recollection of joy, and the voice lifts yearningly to that word ('aller Freude'). Similarly throughout the song; the vocal line rises or falls, the tempo slackens or quickens incessantly. At the same time there is little or no change in the finespun seamless texture of the music, which is designed to be modelled and displayed for maximum effect by singer and pianist. Such a degree of reliance on dramatic interpretation is rare in a Wolf song; but it is invariably justified in skilled and sensitive performance.

NOTES 1. Mignon and the Harper are imagined as singing about their Italian homeland; 'nach jener Seite' implies the south.

2. The insistent rhyming on 'ennt' and assonance on '–eide/–eude/–eite', with concomitant intensity of expression, all demand special equivalence. Within an unusually wide vocal compass, all the 'ennt' rhymes save one are confined within the same third, G to B. The exception is the powerful 'brennt', on a high note. Then all the disyllable rhymes are set by either a falling semitone ('leide', 'Seite') or a falling sixth ('Freude', 'Weite', '–weide'). These two intervals together make the piano interlude motif at bars 40–5; the ubiquitous falling semitone is also evidently thematic as the sorrow-motif 22. The southern-sky-scanning interlude at bars 21–5 has the intense interrogation of motif 32 – an apt and perhaps deliberate allusion to the 'kennst du es wohl' music of the previous day (see 94, note 4), where also the singer faces south. The eight-bar prelude is extrapolated from bars 26–33, where the initial motif 21 of reflection or narration is apt. Note how the voice suddenly enters with 'es schwindelt mir' before the eight-bar sentence has ended. This central theme has much of the air and mood of the Harper's recurrent prelude in *Harfenspieler III* (88), as if to imply his presence. The frequent augmented fifth chords of heightened emotion are motif 23; the dominant ending is motif 31.

3. Cf. Reichardt; Zelter (three settings); Beethoven (four settings); Schubert, D 310, 359, 656 (TTBBB), 877/1, (duet), 877/4; Loewe, Op. 9/III/5; Tchaikovsky, Op. 6 no. 6; Medtner, Op. 18 no. 4.

92 (G 7) Mignon III (So lasst mich scheinen)

22 December 1888   A minor $c^{\#}$–g''

Let me seem to be an angel until I become one; do not take my white dress from me. I am hastening away from this fair earth to that long home. There I shall rest awhile; then my eyes will open, renewed; then I shall leave behind this pure raiment, the girdle and the garland. And those heavenly forms, they make no question of man or woman; and no clothes, no folds, trammel the transfigured body. True, I have lived without trouble and care; but I felt deep pain enough. I grew old with grief before my time; now let me be made for ever young.

The girl Mignon was dressed as an angel, white-robed and golden-winged, for her part in a children's charade. The younger children were a little frightened at first, believing her to be a real angel; and even when they recognized her they were still unsure, 'and did not venture to approach nearer to the wondrous apparition. Here are your presents, she said, and reached out her basket. They gathered round her, they looked, they touched, they questioned her. Are you an angel? asked one child. Would I were, Mignon replied. Why are you holding a lily? So pure and so open should my heart be; then I would be happy. What are the wings like? let us see them! They represent lovelier ones not yet unfolded. So she replied significantly to every innocent light question. When the curiosity of the small company was satisfied, and the impression of the apparition had begun to fade, it was time to change her costume. This she resisted, took her zither, sat here on this tall writing-desk and sang a song with unbelievable charm'. In the lyric, the scene and the whole context there is deep tragic feeling; Mignon is to die young. Wolf was no doubt familiar with this passage from *Wilhelm Meister* (Book VIII, chapter 2). The piano left hand suggests a zither accompaniment. The slow high chords of melody in the right hand tinkle in tinsel finery and at the same time dance an angelic pavane, in a clear image of the heavenly figures envisioned by the singer. The slender voice part is, so to speak, the form under the piano's dress. Grace and grief and childlike gravity sing together in this matchless music. Particularly memorable is the last vocal line, where long octaves fall, die away, and then rise again bright in A major on the final word 'jung'.

NOTES 1. The construction repays analysis: bars 1–6 = 18–23; 7–9 become 24–5; 10–13 become 24–29; 14–17 = 30–3. A 'himmlische Gestalten' motif occurs at those words, bars 18–19. The sorrow of motif 22 is most evident at the moment of greatest grief – in the piano part at 'hinab in jenes feste Haus', bars 7–9. The falling semitones are then taken downwards into the left hand, bars 10–11; and they are also transformed into a hidden figure within the right-hand octaves at bars 10–17(24–34). The ubiquitous rhythm of motif 1, with the weak beats of motif 2 thrown into relief throughout in the higher octave, is apt for the withdrawn child Mignon. The key of A minor is often associated with a girl's grief or distress; the major mode at 'jung' is overtly expressive of innocent hope and faith.
    2. Cf. Reichardt; Zelter; Schubert D 469, 727, 877/3; Schumann, Op. 98a no. 9.

93 (G 8) Philine

30 October 1888   A major   e'–g''

Do not sing in mournful tones of the loneliness of night; no, fair ladies, it is made for companionship.

As woman was given to man for his better half, so is night half of life, and the better half by far. Can you rejoice in the daytime, which only interrupts our pleasures? It may be useful as a distraction, but for nothing else.

Yet when at night-time the lamp's sweet half-light flows, and laughter and love pour out from lip to nearby lip; when the wanton fleet-foot boy, who at other times flashes past like wildfire, will often, in return for some small gift, tarry awhile and join in the games; when the nightingale lovingly sings its song for lovers, which to captives and mourners conveys only pain and lament;

then, with how light a heartbeat do you not hear the bell that with twelve solemn strokes announces rest and security?

Therefore during the long daytime remember this, dear heart; every day brings its troubles, and the night has its pleasures.

Philine is the soubrette of the company of itinerant actors that Wilhelm Meister meets and joins while on his travels. She is light-hearted, charming, easygoing and undemanding; so is her music here. In the novel, Book V, chapter 10 begins with an earnest colloquy about *Hamlet*, which Philine interrupts, first impatiently, then teasingly. She claims that everyone has missed the most beautiful thought to be found in the play, and one in which the Prince himself took pleasure. Goethe proceeds:

> The others wondered what she meant, and there was a lull in the conversation. The company had risen, it was already late; they seemed to be on the point of dispersing. As they stood there undecided, Philine began to sing a ditty with a very graceful and pleasing melody.

This is precisely what Wolf provides; and his music in its playful delicacy adds more than a hint of the playful indelicacy that is Philine herself. The recurrent saucy prelude and the main melody with its flirtatiously fluttering and chirruping accompaniment are entirely delightful. But the eight verses demand varied countermelodies, and here Wolf is arguably less successful. The alternating strains are less overtly attractive, and rely perhaps overmuch on keyboard commentary and illustration which is not equally apt in all contexts. Thus the little figurations marked 'zart' (delicate) at 'wenn in nächt'ger Stunde' (when at night-time), like the twinkling points of staccato at 'süsser Lampe Dämmerung fliesst' (the lamp's sweet half-light), serve brilliantly for the sheen and sparkle of soft lights and sweet talk; but they sound artificial when imported into the second verse at 'Wie das Weib dem Mann gegeben' (As woman was given to man) etc. Similarly the lightly skipping semiquavers that announce the arrival of Cupid, 'der rasche lose Knabe', are not only unsubtle but perhaps even elide the real point of the verses, namely that the normally light-foot love-god is now lingering and loitering. Again, the nightingale's trilling triplets are rather over-elaborate, while the continued light-hearted skipping pays no heed at all to the 'Gefangnen und Betrübten', the captives and mourners, who seem fully as entitled to musical representation. But all such cavils are instantly forgotten as soon as the main theme reappears. On its final recurrence it is followed by a thoughtful mock-philosophical moment at 'Darum an dem langen Tage'

(Therefore in the long daytime) which emerges from a favourite progression in sudden brightness at the word 'Nacht', with an impudent flouting of convention which is echoed and applauded in the postlude. Here the piano prelude figure is heard appearing and disappearing for the last time, as if taking a culminating curtain-call. The graphic effect becomes especially vivid when considered in conjunction with Goethe's own prose postlude to Philine's song:

> She gave a little bow when she had finished, and Serlo [manager of the theatre company] gave her a loud 'Bravo!'. She skipped through the door and ran off laughing. They could hear her still singing and clattering with her heels as she went down the stairs.

NOTES 1. The grace-notes in the piano (bar 9 etc) and later in the voice ('einer kleinen Gabe' etc) are indications of the suppressed laughter and mischief underlying words and music (motif 4). Wolf's special pleasure in the character, and characteristics, of Philine, is already manifest in his review (1 March 1885) of a performance of the opera Mignon by Ambroise Thomas:

> In taking her farewell of the Vienna public, Mme L'Allemand could hardly have made a happier choice than the role of Philine. How charming she looked, how coquettish!

2. The sparkling staccato of the 'süsse Lampe' is motif 25; the skipping semiquavers of Cupid and the 'Scherz und Liebe' motif are equally depictive. The confusion at the half-bar ('von', 'zur' etc) caused by the addition of a bar of 2/8 shows that the musical thought is dominated by the piano part, passim.

3. Of special constructional interest is the relation of the prelude (which also serves as two interludes and postlude) to the last four bars for voice and piano. In Goethe's last clinching lines 'Jeder Tag hat seine Plage/Und die Nacht hat ihre Lust' the essence of the poem is stated epigrammatically; part of the point is that, in German, day is masculine and night is feminine. The prelude's four bars begin with Wolf's setting of 'jeder Tag' and end with his setting of 'ihre Lust'; and the two are sequentially linked in an ingenious yet natural-sounding chain of musical thought.

4. Cf. Reichardt; and Schumann, Op. 98a no. 7, which for all its rather puzzling omission of Goethe's effective second verse ('Wie dem Weib' etc) is also a masterpiece of the 'graceful and pleasing melody' stipulated in Wilhelm Meister.

94 (G 9) Mignon (Kennst du das Land)

17 December 1888 (orchestrated 31 October 1893, to replace a lost version of 1890)   G♭ major   b♭ –a♭ ''

Do you know the land where the lemons blossom, where oranges glow golden among dark leaves? A soft wind breathes from the blue sky, the silent myrtle stands there and the tall laurel.

Do you know it? [Do you know it?] There, there, I long to go with you,
my love.

Do you know the house? Its roof rests on pillars, the hall shines, the
room gleams, and marble statues stand and look at me – 'What have they
done to you, you poor child?'

Do you know it? [Do you know it?] There, there, I long to go with you,
my protector.

Do you know the mountain and its cloudy paths, where the mule seeks
its way in the mist; in caves the old brood of the dragons dwells, the rock
falls sheer and the torrent over it.

Do you know it?
[Do you know it?]
There, there lies our way; oh, father, let us go.
[Let us go.]

The evocative 'Kennst du das Land wo die Zitronen blühn' is among the
best-known lines of German poetry. But the rest of the poem is less well-
known, and indeed can hardly be understood without some knowledge of
its context in *Wilhelm Meister*. The child Mignon had been born in Italy
but abducted by vagabonds and brought into Germany, a beaten and half-
starved waif who was forced to dance and sing in a troupe of travelling
entertainers. In this lyric she remembers as if in a dream the beauty of a
southern homeland, the splendour of her home, and the mountain paths
over which she was brought by her captors. One morning her protector
Wilhelm hears music at his door.

He thought at first that it was the Harper come again to visit him; but
soon he made out the tones of a zither, and the voice that began to sing
was Mignon's voice. Wilhelm opened the door, the child entered and
sang the song set out above. Melody and expression pleased our friend
especially, although he could not understand all the words. He asked
for the verses to be repeated and explained, wrote them down and
translated them into German. But the originality of the turns of phrase
was such that he could only imitate them from afar; and the childish
innocence of expression vanished when the broken language was
repaired and the disjointed thoughts reunited. The charm of the
melody, moreover, was quite incomparable. She began each verse with
stateliness and solemnity, as if she wished to draw attention to
something remarkable, as if she had something important to convey. At
each third line the singing became duller and gloomier; the 'do you
know it?' was uttered mysteriously and deliberately; in the 'There!
There!' lay an irresistible longing, and her 'let us go!' was contrived to

change subtly with each repetition, now pleading and urgent, now compelling and full of promise.

Wolf faithfully follows these indications with a setting which despite its apparent complexity is basically in simple strophic form. A piano prelude of haunting melodic beauty introduces each verse. Each begins with expressive solemnity, with a darkening harmonic change at the third line. The voice sings out hushed amid passionate piano interludes for the repeated 'Kennst du es wohl?'; then voice and piano combine with thrilling effect at each 'dahin!'. The vocal line at the end of each verse is subtly modified to reflect the changing appeal to Wilhelm, innocently idealized as lover, protector and father. Upon this pattern Wolf superimposes his own interpretation of the poem. The excitement and tension are made to increase from verse to verse, as the music becomes steadily more ecstatic and exalted. The first verse is quiet and beautiful to match the words. The second is heightened by adding rhythmic interest in the piano part. The third is treated dramatically to conform with what Wolf knew of the fate of Mignon. Her memory is playing her tricks, the music suggests, her imagination is running wild; she will never go there, there is no such place, it is a dream, she will die. Indeed, some such thoughts might well have harrowed the mind of the listening Wilhelm, then or later; and it is clear from the context that the song and its implications are designed to disturb him and make him fearful for the child. For 'when she had sung the song a second time, she paused for a moment, looked sharply at Wilhelm, and asked – Do you know the land? It must mean Italy, said Wilhelm; where did you learn that song? Italy! said Mignon significantly – if you are going to Italy, take me with you, I'm freezing here. Have you already been there, dear little one? asked Wilhelm. The child was silent and no more could be got out of her'. On any interpretation the music of the third verse is superbly overwrought, perhaps depicting an irrational confidence in the reality of a dream and heightening the contrast between that dream and the sad truth. The intense power of the music, even in the piano version, remains a splendid conception, quite beyond anything attempted or imagined by any other of the composers who had set this poem. It may not quite succeed; but it far outstrips all ordinary successes. It stands high among the world's most memorable songs.

NOTES 1. The piano counterpoint in small notes in bars 7–12 comes from the flute part of the 1893 orchestration (an earlier version was lost by Wolf, and not discovered until after his death). It was not included until the second edition of the Goethe songs, at a time (June 1897) when Wolf's judgement may have been clouded by incipient brain disease. It is perhaps best omitted.

2. In some Peters editions a sharp needs to be added to the D at 'ihn' in 'über ihn die Flut', a flat to the F on the syllable 'hin' in the twelfth bar from the end, and a dot to the piano's final minims.

3. The second 'Kennst du es wohl?' in each verse and 'lass uns ziehn' at the end, are Wolf's repetitions, not Goethe's. But there is some textual justification; Goethe expected his composers to repeat words in the contemporary style, and he expressly says '"Lass uns ziehn" wusste sie *bei jeder Wiederholung* dergestalt zu modifizieren...', although those words occur only once in his text.

4. The prelude has the adoring motif 11. After each second 'kennst du es wohl?' (e.g. bars 28–30) occurs the longing dominant seventh of motif 32 in the same form as *Mignon II*, dated the following day (bars 25, 47–8); see 91, note 2.

5. For a similar harmonic scheme in the same keys with G♭ minor again notated enharmonically as F♯ minor see *Der Mond hat eine schwere Klage erhoben* (193). That resemblance seems merely fortuitous. But the parallels with *Geh', Geliebter* (see 180, note 3) may argue a further element in Wolf's interpretation of Mignon.

6. At 'in Höhlen wohnt der Drachen alte Brut' the music assumes the shape of the dragon in the cave in *Siegfried*, at 'Fafner, der wilde Wurm'.

7. Cf. Reichardt; Zelter (six settings); Beethoven, Op. 75 no. 1; Schubert, D 321; Schumann, Op. 98a no. 1; Liszt (two settings).

95 (G 10) Der Sänger (*The minstrel*)

14 December 1888   E major   A–f'

'*What do I hear outside resounding before the gate, and upon the bridge? Let the song re-echo in our ears here in the great hall!*' So spoke the king, the page ran, the boy returned, the king cried '*Let the old man be brought in to me!*'

'*Accept my greetings, noble lords, and you fine ladies! How rich a heaven, star on star! Who could know your names?*

In this hall full of grandeur and magnificence close you, my eyes; here is not the time for amazed delight'.

The minstrel shut his eyes and sang in full tones. The knights looked at him boldly, the ladies demurely down into their laps. The king, pleased with the song, commanded a chain of gold to be brought to honour the minstrel for his performance.

'*Give this golden chain not to me but to your knights before whose fierce countenances the enemy lances splinter; or give it to that chancellor of yours, and let him add its golden burden to his other burdens.*

I sing as the bird sings that lives in the boughs; the song that wells freely from the throat is its own rich reward. But if I may ask a boon, I will ask for one thing; let me be brought a beaker of the best wine, in pure gold'.

*He raised it to his lips and drained it down. '*O drink full of sweet refreshment! A blessed house indeed where this is but a small gift. If* *fortune favours you, think of me, and thank God as warmly as I thank you for this drink.'*

This is the Harper's first, and least characteristic, song in *Wilhelm Meister* (Book II, chapter 11). It had already been set, not especially memorably, by both Schubert and Schumann. Wolf fares no better. But a poem thought worthy of musical treatment by the three greatest of song-writers cannot be without interest or significance. No doubt all three sincerely responded to some central truth in Goethe's allegory of the artist in society, particularly perhaps the idea that song is its own reward. Each treats the given text deferentially, with earnest and copious musical illustration. In Wolf the piano prelude is so to speak set singing outside, overheard by the king after one bar's solo, and invited in. Meanwhile it has continued with its song, up to 'widerhallen!' (re-echo). Then it ceases, just in time for the kingly commands to be powerfully accompanied by falling fifths in bass octaves, at 'Der König sprach's' and again at 'Der König rief'; the page's excursion and reappearance are illustrated by scampering treble figures in much smaller note-values. Harp-chords resound as the minstrel greets the court in his best recitative; they rise and brighten at the contemplation of the star-studded assembly, 'welch reicher Himmel! Stern bei Stern!', and almost applaud the splendour of the décor at 'Herrlichkeit' (magnificence). Then after the appropriate preliminary flourishes we hear the original song, now presented as an on-stage solo. Once again the lordly left-hand gestures of royal command dominate the music, as the golden chain is brought in with a commensurately generous vocal gesture at the last word of 'eine goldne Kette reichen'. At its rather cool rejection the left-hand melodies take a more expressive turn, in single notes, but these soon don octaves and come thundering up like the imagined knights; and the minstrel's theme song resumes, to orthodox spread or broken chords from the harp, at 'Ich singe wie der Vogel' (I sing as the bird). After the request for wine, Wolf tells us, since Goethe omits to do so, that the king issues the necessary command with further imperious gestures; and the minstrel's song resumes softly, after a thunderous re-introduction, to point the moral that bird and bard are alike content with very little reward, being already so rich in song. This one is finely effective for a resonant and flexible bass-baritone; but its construction is undeniably diffuse, and its repeated central ideas and their musical equivalents risk tedium when extended through well over a hundred bars of moderate time.

NOTES 1. The text shows that the Goethe source was one of the later revised editions, not (as in Schumann's setting) the inferior early version. If (as textual evidence suggests, see 112, note 1) Wolf was using the 1861 *Gedichte*, then he changed the last word of 'Eine goldne Kette bringen' (bar 59) to the more impressive 'reichen', which the poem reserves for the later bestowal of wine. The musical treatment renders the change irreversible.

2. The kingly gesture of falling fifths, motif 29 (bars 9, 12, 54–7, 90–2) recurs in an analogous context of the creating gesture of divinity in bars 7–11 of *Gesegnet sei* (190); for a further possible parallel see 98, note 4. The mediant harmonic changes for the notional brightness of sky and stars, bars 24–6, are motif 24, while the flourishes at 'Herrlichkeit', bar 32, finishing on a top G# recall the treatment of 'Sieg' e.g. in *Der Genesene an die Hoffnung* (13). The piano part at bar 60ff. has something of the loneliness of motif 15; renunciation and detachment are the sentiments expressed ('Die gold'ne Kette gib mir nicht'). The single notes then change to octaves for the doughty knights, and come pounding up in mortal combat to the strains of the manly motif 6 after 'Lanzen splittern', bars 67–8. The postlude in praise of wine, motif 38, is recalled in the frankly bibulous songs of the *Westöstlicher Divan*, e.g. *Ob der Koran* (119).

3. Cf. Reichardt; Zelter; Schubert, D 149; Loewe, Op. 59 no. 2; Schumann, Op. 98a no. 2.

96 (G 11) Der Rattenfänger (*The ratcatcher*)

6 November 1888 (orchestrated 5 February 1890)   A minor   c'–f''

I am the well-known-minstrel, the much-travelled ratcatcher, of whose services this famous old city evidently has special need. And however many rats there might be, and even if weasels were running with them, I'd still rid this place of them all, they'd have to be off forthwith, the whole pack of them.

Then the good-humoured minstrel is also a child-catcher, who tames even the wildest when he sings his golden fairytales. And however obstinate the boys might be, and however startled the girls, I just strike my strings and they all have to follow after me.

Then the highly versatile minstrel can on occasion become a girl-catcher. He never yet arrived in any town without winning many a heart. And however foolish the girls, and however prudish the women, they all become so tremulous with love at my magic strings and song.

[I am the well-known minstrel, the much-travelled ratcatcher, of whose services this famous old city evidently has special need. And however many rats there might be, and even if weasels were running with them, I'd still rid this place of them all, they'd have to be off forthwith, the whole pack of them.]

The thirteenth-century legend of the Pied Piper of Hamelin is familiar to English readers from the Browning version. In any language he is a fairy-tale figure with magic powers that make rats and children follow his music. Goethe, with his penchant and gift for making legendary figures human, presents us with his own reflections on the character. His ratcatcher is a boastful and worldly (rather than other-worldly) spellbinder with natural (rather than supernatural) powers over women. As befits a Don Juan, he is a serenader as well as an enchanter, a lutanist instead of a piper. But above all he is the poet and musician, whose spells and charms are those of art. This presents an almost personal challenge to the composer. To match the lyric, a musical equivalent had to be found to suggest in its rhythm an irresistible force, in its melody a compelling lightheartedness and magic, turning at times to tenderness; a strain to bring everyone trooping after it. The result in Wolf's song is a dazzling *tour de force*.

The piano part, which rivets attention from the very first notes, has the rhythmical strength and urgency of Schubert's *An Schwager Kronos* or *Erlkönig* enhanced with a brilliance that is pure Wolf. The prelude falls in volume and pitch to a soft strumming accompaniment; the voice enters, and all is lilt and fire. During each verse the piano leaves its neutral figurations from time to time and vies with the voice, whether in Mephistophelean swagger and abandon or in delicacy and tenderness. After each verse the brilliant prelude flares out again. The song abounds in especially illuminating moments. After the army of rats has been notionally reinforced by a troop of weasels ('und wären Wiesel mit im Spiele') the whole lot suddenly swarm into a brief bar of piano interlude. But then the boast is audibly made good; powerful octaves halt the downward movement and force it back to the original level, despite its evident reluctance (also amusingly expressed in contrary motion between voice and piano); they *have* to go, the voice insists on a sustained note, which as it were underlines and italicizes the word 'müssen'. At 'wenn er die goldenen Märchen singt' (when he sings his golden fairy-tales) the vocal melody is hushed and lingered out lovingly. 'In meine Saiten greif ich ein'; here the strings are struck with full octave power, again in contrary motion with the voice, this time with directions reversed; again the word 'müssen' is stressed by prolongation. The third verse is climactic in both poem and song. After the sighing and swooning of voice and piano at 'liebebang' (tremulous with love), the magic strings and singing suddenly emerge with a new brightness in A major. To round off the musical form, the first verse is repeated. In the postlude the Rattenfänger motifs are heard again in their original minor mode, expanded and extended in ecstatic figurations, like virtuoso string-playing (an exacting task for all but virtuoso pianists). Having thus pointed the worldly moral, Wolf, if not Goethe, is content to let the fabulous figure return to fairyland. The themes rise and vanish into thin air, like the elfin music of *Nixe Binsefuss* (57)

NOTE 1. Goethe's poem has only three verses; but at the end of the 1861 edition appear the words 'Vom Anfang', i.e. *da capo ad libitum*, which provides Wolf's repetition with any necessary justification.

2. Some Peters editions omit the staccato dot over the penultimate right-hand chord (cf. the last two left-hand chords).

3. The rising lilt at the end of the piano prelude, and *passim*, is motif 7. For the postlude's string effects, see 166, note 4. In the orchestral version (which as so often in Wolf's scores markedly increases the already formidable difficulties of maintaining the needful fiery tempo) the colour and brilliance are further enhanced, by added chromatic runs for flutes.

4. Cf. Schubert's completely contrasting monochrome setting, D 255.

97 (G 12) Ritter Kurts Brautfahrt (*Sir Kurt's wedding-ride*)

9 December 1888   F major   c'–g''

With a bridegroom's élan Sir Kurt mounts his steed, which is to carry him to his wedding at the castle of his noble beloved. When in a rocky desert place a menacing foeman appears, without hesitation, without a word, they soon proceed to swift action.

The tide of combat is slow to turn, but at last Kurt rejoices in victory. He quits the spot, a sorely bruised victor. But what's this he now perceives among the flickering leaves of the thicket? A young mother with a baby at her breast glides through the grove.

And she beckons him to her: 'Not so fast, dear sir! Have you no thought for your sweetheart, no gift for your child?' Sweet flames glow through him, so that he has no desire to ride on, finding the mother just as lovable as he found the maiden.

But he hears the servants sounding their trumpets, and recalls his high-born bride; and now the annual fair and market are clamorous on his path, and in the booths he chooses many a pledge of love and devotion. But alas, here come Jews with expired IOUs.

So courts of justice detain the nimble knight. Oh what a tangled tale is the hero's career! And how am I to remain patient today, with similar serious embarrassments? Adversaries, women, debts, alas, no gentleman ever gets free of them. [alas, no gentleman ever gets free of them.]

This is a brilliantly effective and original song which might have established many a lesser man's reputation. It contains dozens of themes and accompaniment figures, as if the poem, perhaps by striking a personal chord, had inspired fresh musical invention on a lavish scale. But on analysis much of the music is heard to contain, if not indeed to consist of, echoes of previous work. This song and the next (to which much of the present commentary also applies) were written at a time when the Goethe inspiration was showing some signs of abatement. Technically the music is deft and effective enough, but the consistent musical annotation of the extended poetic text can seem contrived and even tedious. The long unfolded narrative canvas fails to cohere and convince as it should; and this is doubly disappointing as some of the individual scenes and sketches are drawn in the liveliest lines and colours. Thus the prelude's mounting and trotting, the blithe singing concealed in the accompaniment, the sudden rhythmic compression of 'Schreiten sie zu rascher Tat' (they soon proceed to swift action) to illustrate those words, the battle interlude, the gently lambent music of the old flame and its rekindling, and so on down to the last detail of the postlude's spirited determination to gallop at full speed far out of reach of the hero's hazards; all these are highly engaging in isolation, though they arguably outstay their collective welcome.

NOTES 1. In the Peters edition and the *Gesamtausgabe* a B natural seems to be needed in the right-hand chord on 'freut' in bar 44, as in 43 and 45. The final repetition of the text is Wolf's, not Goethe's.

2. The main sources of the material are *Der Feuerreiter* (56) and *Seemanns Abschied* (82). The defiant phrases heard in the piano at 'als am öden Felsenorte' anticipate *Prometheus* (134) and the main march themes *Epiphanias* (104) – if those two masterpieces, dated somewhat later, were not in fact earlier in conception.

3. The high-spirited motif 7 at the end of the prelude (bar 12) explains that what follows is to be mock-heroic. The piano right-hand theme at 'aber ach!' etc recurs in the crowd scenes of *Was in der Schenke* (123).

4. Wolf's first biographer, Ernst Decsey, records the sources of the musical description of Jewish moneylenders. The left-hand melody at 'aber ach!' etc. is in debt to Carl Goldmark's *Queen of Sheba*, the right-hand counter-melody at 'da kommen Juden' is on loan from Adalbert von Goldschmidt.

5. Wolf's own occasional indebtness to Loewe in the depictive piano writing is far less specific and deliberate, though rather more readily identifiable. But the Wagner echoes of trumpeting servants (heralds) and mortal combat are no doubt meant to be recognized, with amusement, as a polite parody of *Lohengrin*.

6. Cf. Reichardt; Zelter.

98 (G 13) Gutmann und Gutweib (*Goodman and goodwife*)

28 November 1888   D major   c'–g''

It is the eve of St Martin; and goodwife, who loves her husband, has been kneading puddings for him and baking them in the pan.

Now they're both lying in bed, and a wild west wind is howling; and goodman says to goodwife, 'You, bolt the door shut'. 'I've only just stretched out, and I'm not warmed up yet, how will that help me to rest? Let it clatter a hundred years, I'm not bolting the door.'

So then they made a bet, in quiet whispers; whoever spoke the first word was to slide the bolt.

Two travellers arrive at midnight and don't know where they are; the lamp was out, the fire was out, nothing to be heard or seen. 'What kind of hell-hole is this? Our patience has snapped!' But there was not a syllable in reply – that was because of the door.

They ate the white pudding, and then the black one, quite unperturbed. And goodwife said plenty to herself, but nothing out loud.

Then one of them said to the other, 'How dry my throat is! The cupboard's gaping and smells of spirits; that's bound to be where they keep it! And here I grasp a flask of Schnapps; that's a lucky find! I'll give you a sip, you give me one, we'll soon revive'. But goodman bounded furiously out of bed and came at them menacingly – 'Whoever takes my Schnapps will have to pay for it in hard cash!' And goodwife too jumped out, delighted, with three jumps as if she'd come into a fortune: 'You, goodman, spoke the first word – now just you go and bolt the door.'

As in the preceding song, Wolf lavishes a mint of music on a text that is perhaps over-long for song-writing treatment. The composer again imagines the scene with vivid depiction, but without that deep evocation of mood and character that is the life of the Lied. Though the music is full of verve and brilliance, and interprets the changing scene with sustained inventiveness of a high order, the result remains stage scenery and stage effects. Among the subtler felicities are: the canonic treatment of the opening melody, to symbolize the potential disunity of the marital state; the alarmed recurrence of that St Martin's theme when those celebratory puddings are eaten ('Den weissen Pudding speisten sie' etc); goodman's angry and violent leaps out of bed ('Doch Gutmann sprang so heftig auf') compared with goodwife's merry hopping and skipping ('Und Gutweib sprang auch froh heran'); and the way in which the postlude summarizes the whole story in motivic key-phrases – St Martin's eve, then the arrival of travellers simultaneously with an argument about the door, as two themes graphically combine, and finally general hilarity as the door slams securely shut.

NOTES 1. Goethe's source is *Get up and bar the door*, which he no doubt found in *Ancient and Modern Scots Songs* (Vol. I), ed. David Herd, Edinburgh 1769, and which he adapts rather than translates. The same text appears as No. 110 of the *Oxford Book of Scottish Verse* (1966).
2. On the last page of some Peters editions the first right-hand chord at the beginning of the bar containing 'nun riegle die' has its flat misplaced from B to D.
3. In addition to the suggested motifs of St Martin (bars 1–2 etc), marriage (bars 5–8), the door-barring (at 'riegle die Türe fest', bars 20–21), goodwife (bars 22–9 and later), the travellers (bar 51ff. at 'Zwei Wanderer') and perhaps the

wager (the falling fifths of bars 47–9, transformed to falling ninths after 'keine Silbe laut', the notes of which reappear as sevenths in the postlude), there are many other significant themes. For example: the high-spirited motif 7 at the end of the prelude (bar 12, just as in the preceding song) again shows that what follows is not to be taken too seriously; the travellers' theme combines the unrest of motif 5 with the companionable thirds (e.g. at 'kommen um Mitternacht') of motif 16 and the exaggerated pathos of motif 23. Finally the exultant postlude has the laughter of motif 4.

4. Wager theme or not, bars 47–9 have the typical ebullience of F♯ major tonality, motif 40; the falling fifth anticipates the falling ring in *Dies zu deuten* (127) and the gestures of motif 29; see 95, note 2. For the piano part at 'Im Bette liegen beide nun', and its recurrence after 'ich riegelte sie nicht zu', see motif 17, the music of wakefulness at night. For a further possibly motivic analogy, see 117, note 2. The fact that goodwife frisks about to the strains of *Der Rattenfänger* (right hand at 'Gutmann, sprachst') may be coincidence: but minds closely attuned to Wolf may find it meaningful.

5. Cf. Loewe, Op. 9/VIII/5.

99 (G 14) Cophtisches Lied I (*Coptic song I*)

28 December 1888   A♭ major   c'–f♭''

Leave quarrelsome argument to scholars; leave austere deliberation to teachers. All the wisest men of all times smile and nod and agree with one accord: Foolish, to wait for fools to learn better! Children of wisdom, deal with fools according to their folly, as is right and proper.

Merlin the Old, in his shining tomb, where I consulted him in my youth, instructed me with a similar rejoinder: Foolish, to wait for fools to learn better! Children of wisdom, deal with fools according to their folly, as is right and proper.

And on the windy peaks of India, or in the dark tombs of Egypt, I have heard only this same sacred word: Foolish, to wait for fools to learn better! Children of wisdom, deal with fools according to their folly, as is right and proper.

This and the following poem, as Wolf may have known, appear in an early play of Goethe's, *Der Grosskophta*. Coptic, as the language of the Christian descendants of the ancient Egyptians, is clearly a suitable tongue for oracular utterance. Goethe's dactyls are translated into the measured tread of processional feet, ♩ ♫♩ ♫ , in full piano chords. This gives the song a basic solemnity to which the vocal melodies add grace and the harmonies wit. For example the last words of the refrain 'wie sichs gehört' (as is right and proper) are accompanied each time by a deliberately orthodox and academically correct cadential progression. The interlude at the end of each verse serves as synopsis and final postlude. It is derived from the piano part at 'Töricht, auf Bessrung der Toren zu harren!' (Foolish, to wait for fools to learn better!), a point hammered home with left-hand accents and right-hand grace-notes suggesting clinching arguments, interspersed with the wagging of an admonitory forefinger and cackles of ironic amusement. Each verse offers refined variations. Thus the grave of the wizard Merlin shines in outlandish tonalities; his voice from the oracle is heralded by three sepulchral drum-strokes, like the tolling cauldrons on Dodona. In the third verse the same moment of awaited response is again heightened by a tonally ambiguous interlude. There is also a variation of texture. The Indian heights and the Egyptian depths had already been generally indicated at the words 'der indischen Lüfte' and 'ägyptischer Grüfte'. But when the oracle again speaks, it is from both sources simultaneously, as the immensely wide spacing of the piano chords tells us. There could be no more comprehensive or convincing consensus, especially with the further impressive effect of oracular awesomeness, as if the final answer had issued from some huge cavernous echoing vault.

NOTES 1. This song usefully exemplifies Wolf's way of blending prototypes into a new and original mixture. Practically every bar has been heard before somewhere in his work. The singing of the opening melody (motif 10) looks back to *Der Schreckenberger* (74, note 2). There is the mystery of motif 19 at bars 8–12 and, in an extended form, at 'Merlin der Alte' etc. There is the narrative of motif 21 at bars 1–2, with the ironic acciaccaturas of motif 4 in bar 18 etc (cf. note to *Rat einer Alten*, 53). The clinching arguments are driven home by motif 27, e.g. in the postlude. Even the piano's echoing heights and depths described above are borrowed from the last page of *Der Feuerreiter*, at the eerie sights and sounds in the mill cellar (after 'husch! da fällt's in Asche ab'). Yet the total effect is novel not derivative. For a further possible motivic kinship, see 117, note 2.

2. In the absence of a prelude the first two lines of poem and song seem essentially introductory, which suggests a deliberate pause on the C-major chord on 'sein!' in bar 4.

3. Cf. Max Bruch.

100 (G 15) Cophtisches Lied II (*Coptic song II*)

28 December 1888   D minor/D major   c'–e''

Go! obey my indication, use your young days, learn to be wiser in good time: On the great scales of fortune the pointer is seldom at rest.

You must climb or sink, you must dominate and win or serve and lose, suffer or triumph, be anvil or hammer.

The poem has the savour of a text from a secularized Book of Proverbs. The two halves of the song – the first solemn and pensive, the second strong and decisive – are in marked contrast of key, texture and rhythm. They are linked by a passage that vividly suggests the swinging movement of a balance before a definite tilt is established, in response to the pivotal image 'auf des Glückes grosse Wage' (on the great scales of fortune) etc. A piano interlude thoughtfully extends this idea, borrowing for the purpose the vocal melody just heard, as if carefully weighing the whole question. In this way Wolf is perhaps suggesting his own view – there isn't much in it either way, and the merest touch might decide. But he has no doubt at all about which one had better be, given the choice – anvil or hammer? The second half, from 'Du musst steigen' (You must climb), is wholly conclusive on that point. The piano's sharp crotchets begin to sink and become abject in cringing octaves at 'dienen und verlieren' (serve and lose). Then the music struggles manfully for its independence, with both hands; and the last nine bars of piano solo are unequivocally hammered out in thirty ringing blows of prodigious power.

NOTES 1. For the poetic text, see 99.

2. The mystery motif 19 occurs at 'auf des Glückes grosser Wage' etc. The two-fisted pounding at 'leiden oder triumphieren' is motif 27.

3. Both halves of the song begin in the minor and end on the *dominant* of the relative major; which is also a way of hammering Goethe's point home, as well as creating harmonic unity (beginning in D minor, ending in D major). Perhaps the notation was deliberately designed to achieve this effect; the D-major climax is surely really heard, and meant to be heard, as a full close (not motif 31), although the key-signature is G major.

4. The exultant climax of the voice part at 'Hammer', with its strong swing as of Donner's hammer in *Das Rheingold*, rings in the more exalted conclusion of *Wohl denk ich oft* (240) at 'alle Leute': again, motif 27. The anvil is also heard clanging at the end of *Prometheus* (134).

101 (G 16) Frech und froh I (*Free and easy I*)

14 November 1888   F major   e'–g''

Getting on well with girls, knocking about with men, and more credit than cash; that's how you get through life. With a lot, you can live like a lord; with a little, you can still manage. To make a lot from a little, just add pleasure. If it won't come, take it. If someone stands in your way, chase him off. Let others begrudge what they can't get; just be truly carefree, that's the alpha and omega. Continue to write verses, conform with the world, and always remember, in good times and bad, this golden ABC [this golden ABC].

102 (G 17) Frech und froh II (Free and easy II)

2 February 1889   F minor/F major   e'–a''

With all my heart I despise the pangs of love, the gentle groans, the sweet distress. All I want to hear about is the practical side; burning glances, rough kisses. Only a sad dog could be refreshed by pleasure mixed with pain. Girl, give my young heart nothing of pain, and all pleasure.

The two songs, related in meaning and music, are of no great account; but each is lively and effective and would make a welcome addition to the standard repertory. Continuous quick bouncing scale-passages and repeated chords in the piano part set the tone of the first song; sharp dynamic contrasts indicate its temper. It is the precise counterpart of the ironic detachment advocated by Goethe, the pushful thrust of his philosophy, the urgent vehemence of his voice. The accompaniment, like the character described, proceeds on its way with reckless independence; the vocal line interjects its pithy phrases at key moments. There are the usual telling touches; thus the idea of pleasure twice kindles the harmony into a bright A major, at 'schafft nur die Lust herbei' (just add pleasure), and again at 'froh' (carefree) etc, while the irresistible impetus of the piano postlude is well designed to sweep aside all opposition and win the argument hands down. A highly Schumannian jest is the emphatic setting of the letters ABC to those same notes (B = B♭ in German) in unison with piano octaves in both hands. That allusion, like the song as a whole, exemplifies a sense of wit and fun perhaps more readily apparent in study than in performance, an inward quality recognizable elsewhere in the Goethe volume (e.g. 89 and 118).

The second song begins with heartfelt sighs and groans. Then the expression changes markedly to show that the first six bars, down to 'süssen Schmerz' (sweet distress) were intended as deliberate burlesque. 'Frech und froh', says the music, taking its cue from the free and easy motifs of the first song, presented with added jauntiness and vigour. Again double octaves are brought in for extra emphasis as the sufferings of the sad dog are contemptuously kicked aside, at 'sei ein armer Hund' etc; and the last words 'alle Lust' make an effective climax pleasurably prolonged by the postlude.

NOTES 1. The first poem occurs as a robber's song in the Singspiel *Claudine von Villa Bella*. The ascription of the 'Frech und froh' title to both poems is only editorial; it really belongs solely to the second.

2. The first song bristles with stereotypes. The accompaniment figure, motif 27 *passim*, regularly culminates in the high spirits of motif 7. The horn passages at bar 4 etc, and the progression at 'das wenig vieles sei' etc are familiar formulae

(motifs 8 and 19) though without any clear motivic significance here. The outspoken ABC octaves are motif 30.

3. The second song (the words of which form a telling rejoinder to those of *Nimmersatte Liebe*, 21) opens with more than a hint of self-parody. The first six bars resound to the sorrow of motif 22, so conspicuous in the *Wilhelm Meister* songs. The two-handed (or footed) gestures of rejection and dismissal at 'sei ein armer Hund' etc are cognate with the physical efforts of 'leiden oder triumphieren' in the second *Cophtisches Lied* (100), motif 27. At the last words 'alle Lust' the piano has the enhanced awareness of motif 36.

4. The 'frech und froh' motif has the brusque horn passages of the peevish Beckmesser (Entrüstungsmotif) in Act III scene 2 of *Die Meistersinger von Nürnberg*; the repeated notes combined with rising scale passages in parallel tenths faintly echo the cudgelling riot at the end of Act II (cf. strings at 'Mein', seht nur dort' etc). Perhaps Wolf construed the poem as exasperatedly aggressive and hitting out at convention.

5. Cf. (for 101) Beethoven (with orchestra); and, as part of the Singspiel setting of *Claudine von Villa Bella*, Reichardt and Schubert (*Räuberlied*, D 239/7).

103 (G 18) Beherzigung (*Counsel*)

30 December 1888   A minor/A major   d'–a''

Ah, what should a man desire? Is it better to live quietly, firmly clasping and holding on, or should he be up and doing?

Should he build a house? should he live in tents? Should he trust the rocks? Even the solid rocks can shake.

There is no universal answer. Let each man decide for himself how to act, where to dwell; and let him who stands take heed lest he fall.

Goethe's very secular sermon is preached on texts in I Corinthians X, about our sinful fathers and their punishments.

Many transgressed and were overthrown, some in the wilderness. [verse 5] Wherefore let him that thinketh he standeth take heed lest he fall. [verse 12]

The music is full of latent strength, being built on a specially constructed motivic foundation. The idea that Wolf seeks to convey is implied in his odd injunction 'Quite moderate tempo, yet with powerful inward excitement'. This suggests that the singer's mind, like the poet's, is made up before his exhortation begins. The piano's introductory motif says as much in a phrase that suggests discontent rather than indecision. The vocal questions are set to falling inflexions, as if interpreted rhetorically rather than literally. So when in the graphic interlude after 'Felsen beben' (rocks shake) the unifying motif above is finally transformed, after many repetitions, to usher in the final section in A major

the effect doubtless intended, namely that of a clarion call to action, sounds more like the slogan of a political manifesto, or the peroration of a sermon. The conclusion thus suffers from being sententious rather than inspiring; indeed the whole song gives some impression of contrivance in the way in which it is all rather ostentatiously developed in successive sequences from one single phrase. But this procedure may well be Wolf's way of saying, here as in *Cophtisches Lied II* (100), that the poem is really all on the same theme, that *pace* Goethe there *is* one answer, namely to stand on one's own two feet, as further emphasized in the final triumphal march music of the last page and the postlude. The resulting unity and power of the music can make a thrilling impression in performance.

NOTES 1. Note the harmonic tensions of motif 23 in the opening bars and motifs 32 or 33 for the later questioning inflexions. For the word 'treiben' and in the two following bars the piano has an analogue of the 'unrest' motif 5 which is used in a much simplified and strengthened form in the great *Prometheus* (134) dated only three days later (e.g. at bars 18–19).

2. Conversely, the postlude here owes much to that of *Cophtisches Lied II* dated only two days earlier. Compare also the sudden surge of self-confidence at 'wo er bleibe, und wer steht' with the analogous mood of pride in possession and self-possession at 'und ein Bettler sein' in *Hätt ich irgend wohl Bedenken* (128), only a month later. Perhaps there is again some subjective element in the music.

3. Cf. Zelter.

104 (G 19) Epiphanias (*Epiphany*)

27 December 1888   G major   d'–b♭''

The holy three kings with their star, they eat, they drink, and are loath to pay; they like to eat, they like to drink, they eat, drink and are loath to pay. The holy three kings are come here, there are three of them, not four of them, and if to the three a fourth were added there'd be one holy three-king more. 'I the first, am the white and also the handsome one; by day is the right time to see me. Yet, oh dear, despite all my spices, I shall never pleasure any girl again.' 'But I'm the brown and I'm the tall one, well known to women and for song. I bring gold, not spices, so I shall be welcome everywhere.' 'I, lastly, am the black and I'm the little one, and I'd like to enjoy myself too for once. I like to eat, I like to drink, I like to eat, drink and say thank you.'

The holy three kings are well-disposed; they seek the mother and the child. Pious Joseph sits there too; the ox and the ass are lying in the straw. 'We bring myrrh, we bring gold, and frankincense, beloved of the ladies. And if we have wine of good vintage, we three will drink as deep as any six. As we see here only fine gentlemen and ladies, but no oxen or asses, we cannot be in the right place, and so must proceed on our way.'

Wolf spent the Christmas of 1888 with his married mistress Melanie Köchert and her family. As a footnote in his first edition indicates, this song was written in celebration of her birthday (which happened to be on Epiphany, 6 January) and was then sung and acted by her three young daughters in costume as the three kings. One hopes that the family was as pleased with it as posterity has been. Wolf may have known that in offering such a presentation, in his music as well as his stage-management, he was following Goethe's own precedent; for the poem was similarly enacted before the Weimar court in 1781. It went well then; and its pawky humour is still not unamusing. At one level it evidently relates to the old traditional house-to-house visits of waits in costume, with a cardboard star on a pole. But, as often in Goethe, there is a deeper earnestness underlying the broad effect. Similarly, Wolf's setting, though high-spirited burlesque, also gives the impression, in its strong rhythms and sturdy construction, of a certain basic seriousness.

Its broad swinging melodies have a popular appeal; in addition Wolf takes full advantage of the opportunities for graphic illustration. Each of his three kings is distinctively costumed in colourful and contrasting music. Their collective Three-King theme is sedately sober and processional, with voice and piano almost in unison, all three marching along as one. But then as the theme continues in the piano, the voice

206

separates, with a hint of hidden hilarity in the piano staccato after 'kommen allhier', anticipating the forthright jollity of the following line about the added fourth king ('und wenn zu dreien der vierte wär"). Here the voice remains independent, not to say supernumerary, until it covertly rejoins an inner line within the accompaniment at 'so wär' ein heil'ger Drei-König mehr'; whether deliberate or not, this is a brilliant illustration of the poem's playfully absurd paradox. The following three episodes are sharply characterized, as if they were played as separate roles under their traditional names, Gaspard, Melchior and Balthasar. The first is tuneful and charmingly diffident; the voice part waits for its cue from the independent piano march theme, which briefly allows a proper pride to shine through at 'bei Tage solltet ihr erst mich sehn!' (by day is the right time to see me). One contributory cause of Gaspard's celibacy, the staid rhythm and harmony suggests, may be his unadventurous temperament. Melchior, on the contrary, is ebullient and graphically tall, with alert and erect piano figures and a vocal phrase climbing to a high B♭ at the word 'lang'. The third role is mock-lugubrious, full of suppressed laughter and with staccato semiquavers that sparkle and twinkle their way back to the original joint march theme. After a complete reprise, down to 'ihrer sechs' (any six), an ironic bewilderment comes into the music, and the repeated piano notes mark time. The three kings have lost their orientation. They are helped by noticing that the company consists solely of fine ladies and gentlemen, with not a single ox or ass: 'aber keine Ochsen* und Esel schaun'. The story goes that on one occasion when the composer was accompanying this song at a public performance he was seen to look quizzically at the audience at this point, in a quiet echo of Goethe's jest at the expense of the court of Weimar. In the long postlude we are to imagine each king making a separate bow and exit, each to his characteristic rhythm. Then they reassemble and proceed on their way, as their joint theme is heard gradually fading and finally disappearing in the distance.

NOTES 1. The Peters edition has 'kein Mädchen mir erfrein' (never woo and wed) in bars 24–5; the *Kritische Gesamtausgabe* (like Wolf's putative source, the 1861 *Gedichte*) offers the racier 'mehr erfreun', translated above. Both versions appear in various editions of Goethe; the former may be a bowdlerization.

2. 'Heiligen' at bar 1 and the reprise, instead of 'heil 'gen' as in other Goethe editions, is found in the 1861 *Gedichte* which however also has 'heiligen' at bar 9.

3. The Three-King theme (in plain octaves, motif 30) divides neatly into three parts: (a) a rising fourth, (b) a group of quavers, and (c) three strong crotchet chords incorporating an Amen cadence. Each king is allotted, in addition to his new distinctive rhythm, a portion of this material; thus the first king has (a), left hand *passim*, the second has (c) in bars 26 and 28, and the third (b) in bars 38–41.

4. The effect of irresolution at 'Da wir nun hier' etc is achieved by unresolved

---

*'Ochs' also means 'blockhead'

chords, first dominant sevenths (bars 62–3) and then diminished sevenths (63–4); motifs 32 and 33. The very decided resolution comes at 'so sind wir nicht am rechten Ort', which is after all in its context a vital conclusion. Another harmonic allusion may be the F♯ (G♭) tonality for the idea of gold, motif 40. The piano part of the third king's episode ('Ich endlich' etc) qualifies for the smallness of motif 3 (at 'sein') and the merriment of motif 4, *passim*; he is described as 'klein' and at least potentially 'lustig'.

5. There is a fragmentary orchestral version (introduction and twenty-one bars) dated 25 April 1894.

6. Cf. Zelter (SATB).

105 (G 20) St Nepomuks Vorabend (*The eve of St Nepomuk*)

15 November 1888   G major   d'–a♭ ''

Points of light are floating on the river, children are singing on the bridge, bells great and small from the cathedral join in the reverence, the delight. Lights fade, stars fade; so the soul of our saint passed away. He could not divulge a confessed misdeed. Float again, lights, play, children; children's choir, oh sing, sing! no less proclaiming what shall bring a star among the stars.

St Nepomuk was martyred by drowning for refusing to divulge the sins confessed to him by Queen Johanna of Bohemia. In the fifteenth-century legend, stars shone round his body as it floated down the river Moldau. The effect was simulated with floating candlelights as part of the annual celebration of the saint's feast-day (15 May), in pious memory of the miracle. Wolf's music is an image of floating lights, distant bells, joyous singing. The gently rocking accompaniment, with thirds and sixths high in the keyboard, suggests the quietude and reverence of a starry night and at the same time a pious carillon of praise. From these background scenes the voice part emerges like the quiet thoughts of a bystander moved and impressed by the spectacle, while the changing piano harmonies gleam and fade. 'Slowly and with the utmost delicacy throughout' is the composer's express direction. Even the ecstatic leaping phrase 'sing, sing!', with its long high A♭ is subdued and absorbed within the impressionist picture of lights floating and shining, sounds ringing and singing, the reverence and delight of the poem made manifest in music.

NOTES 1. Wolf can have had no qualms about the time-signature; the last two bars are carefully written out in a deliberate 6/4. But the vocal line is more like 3/2. One explanation is that the nocturnal motif 18, the essence of the piano part here, demands cross-rhythms or syncopations for its lulling effect. The rocking chords are placed high in the keyboard, as in the star motif 25, and are textured in thirds and sixths like the carillon in *Zum neuen Jahr* (39). The harmonic light effects

208

(e.g. A♭ C, E, in successive bars 4–6) are motif 24. At 'singe, singe' is the lifting and dipping song motif 10 writ large.

2. It is worth noting how any possible asperities of harmony have been deliberately smoothed; thus the first two quavers of bar 17, right hand, have been altered from bar 2 to avoid a clash with the voice.

3. Cf. the duet setting of Zelter, whose eye-witness description of the ceremony inspired Goethe's poem.

106 (G 21) Genialisch Treiben (*Creative activity*)

10 February 1889   A minor   c'–f♯''

Unremittingly, like Saint Diogenes, I trundle my tub.

   Now it is earnest, now jest; now it is love, now hate; now it is this, now that; it is a nothing, and also a something.

   Thus unremittingly, like Saint Diogenes, I trundle my tub.

The saintly Cynic philosopher Diogenes was reputed to live in a tub. Goethe's half-humorous, half-wry use of this garbled tradition as a description of the artist's way of life compresses the relevant ideas into a few laconic lines; austerity, energy, curiosity, changeability and occasional achievement. And the poem's recurrence (only one rhyme) and circularity (last two lines repeating the first two) powerfully reinforce the central tub-trundling image and its peripheral meanings. The extended Chopinesque piano scherzo that Wolf provides as musical equivalent is similarly crammed with zest and significance, and is audibly symbolic in its restless rolling and rumbling. It is the austere and self-denying aspects of the poem that the composer wishes to emphasize; his own creative life was more arduous than joyous, and only intermittently rewarding. So there is nothing winning about the piano part except its drive and force, which are exceptional even for Wolf. The voice part is as it were caught up, contained in and carried away by this surge of energy, but is always buoyed and supported by it, never submerged. At 'Fass' (tub) the vocal line is sustained over four dotted minims in a graphic image of ceaseless motion, and even when it stops the propulsive impetus thus generated pushes the piano part on for four further bars until it is abruptly brought to a halt – by a collision rather than retardation, the sharp final chord suggests. There is a brief well-earned pause, and the piano is off again; this time more effortfully, as it were gradually uphill, achieving its lighter moments of love or jest ('Spass') against the force of gravity. A moment of relieving brightness occurs at 'Was' (something), the notion of occasional positive achievement; the accompaniment's chromatic rolling becomes diatonic rollicking. But no real respite or remission is allowed; the relentless quaver movement is only momentarily halted; octaves in both hands soon roll helplessly downhill again into the main theme to end the song as it began.

NOTES 1. The basic left hand theme that begins and dominates the accompaniment is a Wolfian coinage for the idea of restless or unremitting activity; motif 5. If the minor key and falling phrases (piano octaves, bars 1–4 etc) are any guide, the mood is a sad one, motif 22. The piano's variant melodies are engagingly used to provide further commentary; thus after 'bald ist es Ernst' the right hand sings 'wälz' ohne Unterlass'.

2. The music alludes to the Phrygian mode; the only example in Wolf. It is tempting (if fanciful) to interpret this as a tribute to the reputed birthplace in Asia Minor of Diogenes himself. Such a device would be, since Schumann's inexhaustible ingenuity of extra-musical allusion, wholly within the Lied tradition. Fauré, perhaps under that latter influence, had already set a precedent in referring, in his song Lydia, to the Lydian mode.

3. Cf. Zelter, who also in his different way preserves the poet's image of perpetual motion, by setting the poem for three-voice six-part canon.

107 (G 22) Der Schäfer (*The shepherd*)

4 November 1888   C minor   b–d''

There was a lazy shepherd, a real sleepy-head, who cared nothing for his sheep. When a girl took his fancy the poor fellow became forlorn; goodbye to appetite and sleep! He took to aimless roaming, counting the stars at night, moaning and complaining mightily. Now that she's accepted him, it's all come back again; thirst, appetite and sleep.

This pleasant song, tailored to the verses in attractive musical material, is by no means as homespun as the words might suggest at first reading. Goethe's deceptively simple lyric comes from his Singspiel *Jery und Bätely*. Wolf's brief prelude adumbrates a character-sketch, beginning with a stretch and a yawn.

Then we hear octaves in unison with the voice, a Wolfian device for rendering direct statements or questions. The listless phrases droop and saunter in set patterns of boredom; at 'ihn kümmerte kein Schaf' (cared nothing for his sheep) the piano yawns again, as in the prelude. But the music perks up and develops a livelier interest as soon as the girl is mentioned: 'Ein Mädchen konnt ihn fassen.' The octaves reappear, appropriately broken, to describe the shepherd's distraught wanderings, at 'Es trieb ihn in die Ferne' etc. Finally, to a gradually more animated accompaniment, comes the comparatively happy ending: 'Durst, Appetit und Schlaf.' Wolf is still full of ironic finesse; his final 'Schlaf' is set to a loud interrupted cadence. Then the piano gives one last yawn and settles down to sleep again.

NOTES 1. Some Peters editions have B♭ instead of G at the last quaver of the first bar.

2. The octaves and unisons are motif 30. The yawn's seventh is a respectful parody of the dragon Fafner's yawn in *Siegfried*; 'lass mich schlafen' is the common denominator.

3. This song again foreshadows refinements of Wolf's style in the brief wryly humorous genre piece. The main kinship here is with *Ich liess mir sagen* (212), in the same key and on much the same theme.

4. Cf. Reichardt (with orchestra).

108 (G 23) Der neue Amadis (*The latter-day Amadis*)

5 February 1889   G minor   c'–f''

When I was still a boy I was cooped up, and so I sat for many a year on my own as if in the womb. But you were my pastime, golden day-dreams; and I became a warm hero, like Prince Pipi, and roamed through the world. I built many a crystal castle, and shattered them too; hurled my shining spear through the belly of dragons; yes; I was a man. As a knight-errant, I rescued the Fish Princess; she was vastly civil and invited me to dine, and I was gallantry itself.

And her kiss was ambrosia, glowing like wine. Oh, I wellnigh died of love. She was spangled all over with sunshine. Oh, who has stolen her from me? Are there no magic bonds to hold her back from swift flight? Say, where is her country? Where is the road that leads there?

The title refers to Amadis de Gaul, pseudo-historical chivalric hero of fourteenth-century Spanish romance. Goethe's verses are warmly and imaginatively nostalgic and are suddenly filled with real pathos in the last two lines. In re-creating the poem, Wolf adds typical touches of picturesque and picaresque detail, most brilliantly at 'und ich war galant', where voice and piano combine hilariously in a brief but splendid moment of comic invention. The voice exults on a rising arpeggio and dreams on a sustained note; the piano performs an imaginary gavotte in the *style galant*. But the music throughout is as bright and vivid as the world seen through the eyes of childhood. The small prelude enters to a crisp hobby-

211

horse rhythm, the knightly charger of boyish fantasy. This is interspersed with motifs of constraint and release; but at each day-dreaming escapade, the little knight-errant rhythm recurs – defending the 'goldne Phantasie', bearing off the 'Prinzessin Fisch' and finally trying in vain to trot off again in search of her, as the last page is filled with a fervent yet unsentimental Goethean feeling for the lost innocence of young love.

NOTES 1. In some Peters editions a flat needs to be added before the lowest bass note on the third quaver of bar 66.

2. The lyric was chosen by Goethe to be the first in his collected poems. His boyhood recollections here are no doubt the fruit of his mother's famed 'Lust zu fabulieren', from French fairy-tale sources in which princes are changed into birds (hence 'Pipi'), and princesses into fish, by wicked wizards whose wiles and black arts our hero duly circumvents.

3. Much of the song, and in particular the last vocal note sustained over a characteristic rhythm, is akin to *Der Tambour* (17), also about wishful and wistful thinking, with reality breaking in via a sharp final chord. Each has the élan of motif 7, e.g. here at 'und durchzog die Welt' in voice and piano. In this song however the mood remains more fluid, less resolved; hence the dominant ending, motif 31. For other echoes, see 120, note 2 and 202, note 3.

4. As often elsewhere in Wolf (e.g. 107 etc) there is a tone of affectionate Wagnerian parody. The idea of boyhood restrictions on a heroic young dragon-slayer may well have conjured up in Wolf's mind (e.g. at bars 4 and 8) the frustrated motif of Siegfried's irritation with Mime, in Act I.

5. Cf. Reichardt.

109 (G 24) Blumengruss (*Flower greeting*)

31 December 1888   F major   e♭'–f''

The garland that I have gathered, may it greet you a thousand times. I have stooped down, oh, surely a thousand times, and pressed it to my heart, how many hundred thousand times! [How many hundred thousand times].

This is a perfect page. The persistent quiet accompaniment figure

epitomizes the character of the poem, all humble and devoted stooping and drooping. The continual caressing tenderness of this phrase with its subtle inflexions of pitch and harmony blends with the wistful cadences of the melody to re-create most movingly the love and sorrow behind these simple words; briefly hopeful at the first 'tausendmal', bending submissively at 'gebücket' (stooped down) and still resigned but even more steadfast in the last words and the brief postlude.

NOTES 1. The repetition is Wolf's, not Goethe's.

2. Here is a paradigm of one aspect of Wolf's harmonic procedures. The tonality is a clear F major. But the stress of emotion leads it away, via the hint of a brighter A major (bar 4), back again through the flat side (with an augmented fifth, motif 23, in bar 6) via an interrupted cadence in bar 12, to the final tonic simplicity of the closing words. This song (like the next) looks forward to the refinements of the Italian Songbook in its compression of deep feeling within a miniature frame.

3. The opening vocal melody seems to have had special significance for Wolf; it recurs in the same key and similar harmonies, in analogous verbal contexts of self-surrender in *Nicht Gelegenheit* (124) and *Ach des Knaben Augen* (142). For a further echo, see 124, note 2.

4. Cf. Zelter (duet with chorus); Reichardt.

110 (G 25) Gleich und Gleich (*Like with like*)

6 November 1888   E major   f#'–ab''

A little flower-bell had burgeoned early up from the ground in lovely blossom. There came a bee and sipped daintily. They must surely be made for each other.

Another miniature masterpiece. The tiny prelude has two components, each diminutive, each made for the other; as if the composer's mind were first saying to itself, and then singing, 'Ein Blümlein und ein Bienelein'. Five staccato quavers swing like a bell; a small accented motif thrusts like a bee in a flower. The spacing and placing of these musical metaphors, the shapely grace and sensitivity of the vocal line, combine to make a radiantly perfect little summer idyll, full of spirit and significance. And to capture the likeness with total truthfulness to life, there are one or two surprising final touches with the tip of the brush. At the moment when complete assurance is expected, 'wohl beide für einander sein' (surely made for each other) the harmony momentarily falters into wistful chromatic uncertainty before recovering to end brightly in the brief postlude.

NOTES 1. Since it is clear that the poem's symbolism of human love had not escaped the composer, it is amusing to note that the bee-and-flower relationship is presented in musical terms akin to those used in *Mausfallen-Sprüchlein* (6) for a cat-and-mouse (or even a mouse-and-mousetrap) relationship.

2. Like other Goethe songs (e.g. 107, 109) this is an interesting blend of earlier and later styles. In recapturing the charm of *Mausfallen-Sprüchlein* it anticipates the technical perfection and deep emotion of such songs as *Heut Nacht erhob ich*

mich (227). The piano part's construction here is noteworthy, e.g. in the general balance of each phrase by a complementary equivalent, like with like; and in such details as the simplification, at 'naschte fein', of the expected rhythm ♪♪♪ , because that is needed in the voice part and its duplication would mar the delicate texture.

    3. Cf. Zelter; Franz, Op. 22 no. 1; Medtner, Op. 15 no. 11; Webern, Op. 12 no. 4.

111 (G 26) Die Spröde (*The coy shepherdess*)

21 October 1889   C# minor/E major   d#'–g#''

On the clearest of spring mornings the shepherdess went walking and singing, young and fair and carefree, so that it resounded through the fields – so la la! le ral [la] la! [So la la, ralla la!]. Thyrsis offered her, just for one kiss, two lambkins, three, on the spot. She looked at him roguishly for a while, but then went on singing and laughing: so la la! le ral [la] la! [So la la!]. And another offered her ribbons, and the third his heart; but she jested with heart and ribbons as with the lambs: just la la! le ral [la] la! [Just la la, ralla la!].

Goethe's carefree poem and its sadder sequel (112), written in the mock-pastoral convention, are full of life and warmth. Such verse was perfectly suited to Wolf's own genius for infusing melodic and harmonic grace and fire into formal thematic constructions. The flouncing piano figure heard in the short prelude goes coquetting through the song, as the shepherdess moves through the meadows; and it mirrors her moods and thoughts. It is briefly forgotten as she loses herself in song and mirth; at each refrain the accompaniment shifts into an impersonal strumming, rounded off with an exuberant pizzicato. In the middle verse, Thyrsis makes a brief appearance to a new serenading strain. After his proffered bartering exchange of 'zwei, drei Schäfchen' for a kiss, the 'drei' syncopated and accented to show his quick-witted improvement of the original offer as he notices what a bargain he will be getting, the harmonies become faintly troubled. Then after 'ein Weilchen' (for a while) there is a moment of detectable hesitation before the advance is rejected and the song resumes even more triumphantly than before. But the refrain now ends on a pensive sustained top G#, dwindling away into silence. Evidently the shepherdess is not wholly displeased or unmoved by the proposal. Indeed, all the music has, among its blend of beauty and brilliance, a certain wistful unease that prepares the listener, if not the heroine, for a sadder sequel.

NOTES 1. The *Kritische Gesamtausgabe*, no doubt correctly, restores the autograph's natural (omitted in all previous editions) before the voice's D on the 'sie' of 'doch sie sang und lachte fort'.

2. The two poems were made for music in every sense; in their earliest version as one single work they were published as an underlay to the melody of 'Mama mia' from Cimarosa's opera *L'impresario in angustie* (1786). In this version (see *Die bekehrte Schäferin*, No. 207 of Erk's *Deutscher Liederschatz*) the 'so la la' refrain is repeated ad lib. The translation above shows Wolf's additions to the Goethe source (*Gedichte*, 1861) which he seems to have used. See also 112, note 1.

3. The smallness motif 3 in the minor seconds of the piano prelude etc suggest that Wolf had imagined a Dresden shepherdess figure. The cheerful grace-notes in voice and piano stand for mocking laughter, motif 4. The vocal melody at 'so wie mit den Lämmern Scherz' is found in contexts suggesting contentment, often, as here, associated with the open air (motif 9); it also has Wolf's rollicking F#-major tonality (motif 40) already heard at the exultant 'lachte fort'.

4. The thematic relationships with 112 are of interest. Of course Wolf intended to set both texts in February 1889; and the sketch of a (quite different) prelude to *Die Spröde* dates from that time. But it was abandoned as unsatisfactory, and was then perhaps replaced by sketches for the present version, which in turn proved intractable. In any event this song was not completed until eight months after all the other Goethe lieder, but only a week before the first Spanish songs; and it has certain characteristics, such as the uncertainty of accentuation at the half-bar indicating the piano part as the basic concept, in common with the latter style. There is a further foreshadowing in the serenading accompaniment devised for Thyrsis here, which reappears in a more extended form in *Ein Ständchen euch zu bringen* (208).

5. Cf. Zelter (also in a pastoral *siciliano*); Medtner, Op. 18 no. 1.

112 (G 27) Die Bekehrte (*The repentant shepherdess*)

12 February 1889   A minor   d#'–a''

In the red glow of sunset I walked silently through the wood. Damon sat and blew his flute so that the rocks resounded; so la la! [ral la la! ralla la la la ral la la la!]. And he drew me down to him and kissed me so gently, so sweetly, and I said 'blow again' and the good-hearted lad blew. So la la! [ral la la! la la la!].

My peace of mind is now lost, my joy has flown away, and I hear in my ears only the old tones of so la la! ralla [ralla la la la ral la la la! la la!]

We are to imagine the song as sung by *Die Spröde* of 111; the German title here means that she has now been 'converted', almost in a religious sense. Wolf's music maintains perceptible if tenuous thematic links, and also mirrors the poetic change from the third person to the first; in this beautifully intimate and personal song all is direct simplicity and tenderness. As before, the prelude imparts a basic shape and rhythm. A

215

fervent rise and fall in the piano's melodic figures, now stripped of their flounces, convey both the emotional state of the singer and the symbol of its cause – the sound of the flute. After 'den Wald entlang' (through the wood) there is a long pause as if the strains of the flute, heard from a distance, had halted the walking stride in its tracks. The music of the second verse, 'und er zog mich' (and he drew me) unobtrusively introduces a new and firmer figure which begins at a lower level, like the seated Damon. Despite the hint of passion and regret in the restrained crescendo at 'süss' (sweet) the main motif retains its poise and its pitch. Yet after the refrain the tiny interlude slows down and muses, breaks off wistfully and pauses, before resuming in a reprise of the first verse, with final insistent flute-notes. An especially subtle and sensitive touch is the way in which the 'so la la' refrain has been melodically varied and also made gradually more restricted and inhibited at each appearance; first with two top A's, then with only one, and lastly with none.

NOTES 1. The *Kritische Gesamtausgabe* assumes, implausibly, that Wolf altered Goethe's 'und er zog mich, ach, an sich nieder' into his own 'und er zog mich zu sich nieder'. It seems much more likely that he found the latter reading in the volume he was using; it actually occurs in a Cotta edition (Stuttgart, 1861), which therefore has strong claims to be regarded as Wolf's textual source. The poem as there printed has 'Glanze', 'Ruhe', 'höre'; and it seems reasonable to suppose that the omission of the final 'e' from each word, for the sake of melodic smoothness, was indeed Wolf's own deliberate choice. So are the repetitions of the refrain; but both the Cimarosa adaptation (see 111, note 1) and Goethe's own text, ending with 'So la la, le ralla, *etc*', can be construed as conceding the composer a certain discretion, if not *carte blanche*.

2. The shepherdess figure is here draped in much plainer material or shown in bare outline. The rising minor seconds now suggest less smallness (motif 3) than the unease of motif 5 (as in bars 5 and 10, right hand). They lift and dip in an analogue of the singing motif 10. The long dominant seventh deliberately left unresolved after bar 36 is motif 32.

3. Wolf was fond of using A minor for women's songs in distressful or wistful mood. If his interlude after the second verse here should remind the listener of the faltering and cessation of the spinning-wheel accompaniment in Schubert's *Gretchen am Spinnrade*, that may be because the following words 'Meine Ruh ist nun verloren' reminded Wolf of Goethe's 'Meine Ruh ist hin', and hence of Schubert's setting.

4. Cf. Zelter; Medtner, Op. 18 no. 2; Busoni.

113 (G 28) Frühling über's Jahr (*Spring all the year round*)

21 December 1888   A major   d#'–a''

Already new growth is breaking up the flower-bed; snow-white snowdrop bells are swaying there, crocuses unfold their intense glow, some budding is emerald, some blood-red. Pert primroses are on parade; roguish violets are assiduously hidden; so much else is stirring and moving, in short, Spring is here, active and alive.

But the richest flowering in all the garden is the sweet disposition of my darling; her ever-glowing glances, stirring song, enlivening talk, an ever open, a blossom-heart, kindly in earnest, and pure in jest.

Even though summer brings rose and lily it vies with my love in vain.

Goethe's radiant poem is a spring song and a love song together. Wolf's music captures both aspects most beautifully. The delicate swaying and pealing of the brief prelude dominate the music, as if the composer had been captivated by the imagined white chiming of the second line 'Da wanken Glöckchen so weiss wie Schnee'. The imagery of continuous budding and flowering is sustained by separate melodies high in the piano right hand and in the voice, the former high and regular in pattern like a lightly-built trellis round which the latter is loosely twined and festooned. Of Goethe's first sixteen short lines (down to 'lebt', alive) only one begins on a down-beat; several words and syllables are tenderly trailed over the bar-lines. This outline picture is carefully coloured by changing harmonies; the bright home key of A major for snowdrops ('weiss wie Schnee'), the higher mediant for the stronger glow ('Glut') of crocuses, an added seventh for the blood-red budding ('Blut'). Then the vocal melody adds its own further felicities of line drawing, becoming bold for the pert and parading primroses ('Primeln stolzieren so naseweis') and then slyly unobtrusive for the hidden violets ('schalkhafte Veilchen' etc). All this culminates in a top A fortissimo at the first climax of the song to hail the new life of Spring ('der Frühling, der wirkt und *lebt*!'). Thus far the poem has described the fair field; now fresh enhancement is called for as the loved one appears, herself a fairer flower. Wolf's response is to relax and gentle his music. 'Innig' (rapt) is his direction for the singer, 'weich' (tender) for the pianist. The song becomes more reflective and restrained in vocal melody, smoother and deeper in keyboard touch and texture. The poet's telling word 'Blütenherz' (blossom-heart) is allowed to unfold slowly on a high hushed phrase. After 'Scherz' (jest) the poem returns to its previous theme of garden flowers. At this moment, the music returns to its first floral metaphors of the chiming prelude and the interweaving melodies in voice and accompaniment. But now those metaphors are

217

further enriched by the comparison which is the essence of the poem. The voice has a new melody; at 'vergebens' (in vain) a little jet of irrepressible delight bubbles up from the piano. Now for the first time in the song, just for one bar, the continuous semiquaver rhythm on the first crotchet beat is momentarily halted, so that the key word 'Liebchen' can sound out with an especially sweet clarity before a few more bars of chiming and swaying end the song.

NOTES 1. The *Kritische Gesamtausgabe* prefers the autograph D on 'wenn' at 'wenn Rose und Lilie der Sommer bringt' to the C♯ of all previous editions.
2. The flexibility of the vocal phrasing supersedes the bar-lines; thus the scansion of the first four bars for the voice is 3 + 3 + 2 crotchets, and similarly at bars 13–16.
3. The right-hand figures are akin to the restless energy of motif 5. It is noteworthy that their upward semitonal movement is reversed and relaxed into more soothing strains just for the eight bars of direct comparison at 'Doch was im Garten am reichsten blüht' etc; and the tension resumes as the effect of that fairer flowering is described at 'Da glühen Blicke' etc. The bold melodic line at 'Primeln stolzieren' recalls the opening phrase of that bold spring song *Er ist's* (18). This one is a prime example of the brightness of A major for Wolf; among so many colourful harmonic touches, it may not be by chance that the ebullient primroses are painted in F♯ major (motif 40). The mediant change from A to C♯ (from 'Schnee' to 'Glut') is motif 24.
4. The chimes appropriate to a 'Schneeglöckchen' are treated not dissimilarly in Schubert's *Viola*, D786, which begins 'Schneeglöckein'.
5. Cf. Loewe, Op. 79 no. 5.

114 (G 29) Anakreons Grab (*The grave of Anacreon*)

4 November 1888 (orchestrated 13 November 1893, to replace a lost version of 1890)   D major   d'–d''

Here, where the rose blooms, where vine and laurel entwine, where the turtle-dove calls its mate, where the cicada sings for joy, whose grave is this, so beautifully planted and adorned with life by all the gods? It is Anacreon's resting-place.

Spring, summer and autumn were enjoyed by the happy poet; and at last this mound has sheltered him from the winter.

The Greek poet Anacreon is traditionally the laureate of nature, love, and wine as well as song; hence the symbolic decoration of his resting-place. Goethe's beautiful lines, replete with reverence, are rounded by their elegiac metre into a classical object of shapely perfection. Wolf's music re-creates their form and content, and further adds a new reverence and beauty of its own. His setting seems to express not only the poem but the actual experience he imagines as having inspired it, namely the unexpected chance discovery of a real tomb in a living landscape. The two bars of prelude are tranquil and meditative. At the entry of the voice the piano has evocatively falling minor thirds, at 'blüht' (blooms) and 'schlingen' (entwine). A brief semitonal clash moans at the word 'Turtelchen' (turtle-dove); at 'lockt' (calls its mate) the piano phrases gently rise. A slight shadow darkens the tonality into the minor for a moment at the word 'Grab'; and now the music both illustrates and meditates upon the contrast of rich exuberant life that makes this grave so beautiful. The harmony becomes richer and more complex; tendrils of melody stray across the bar-lines; the word 'Leben' (life) is lingered out and relished in the voice part. Then we hear the rising semitones of the first two chords of the prelude repeated with a quiet insistence. From the outset they were already posing the question which the voice, turning their tenderly probing tensions into simple satisfied harmonies, now most memorably answers, 'Es ist Anakreons Ruh'. Everything that has so far been heard combines to charge this magical phrase with emotive effect. The voice seems to read the inscription. 'It is' – then a slight pause – then, slowly and almost amazedly savouring the admired and beloved name – '*Anacreon's* resting-place'. On this last word 'Ruh' the piano's relaxing harmonies come finally to rest. The music resumes with a variant of the prelude; the voice adds its last loving epitaph, in music warm and peaceful as before, which the singer's art can now render new-radiant with the spirit of Anacreon. The postlude meditates on themes of release and sleep.

NOTES 1. Similar slow rising semitones have been heard elsewhere in moments of mystic comfort and joy; see e.g. 32, note 4.

2. The postlude's horn passage after 'geschützt' suggests the open-air feeling of 'release', motif 8; cf. also the call at 'lockt'. The rocking quavers of the postlude are akin to the music of night and sleep (motif 18) in e.g. *Um Mitternacht* (31). For a later resemblance see 172, note 2.

3. If the descending minor thirds making a diminished seventh chord – bars 3 and 4 – were felt by Wolf as depictive or symbolic of trailing foliage, that would account for an echo of the Brahms *Alto Rhapsody*, op. 53, where exactly that figuration, on two flutes (also Wolf's scoring in his orchestral version of this song), seems to be used in much the same sense – to introduce the words 'schlagen die Sträuche zusammen' as the bushes close up again behind the lost traveller. The *Rhapsody* was one of the few works by Brahms that Wolf could tolerate and even enjoy; he heard and reviewed a performance of it in April 1886.

115 (G 30) Dank des Paria (*Gratitude of the outcast*)

9 November 1888   A♭ major   c'–g♭''

Great Brahma! now I recognize that you are the creator of all worlds! I name you as my lord; for all men have value in your eyes. And even to the lowliest you close none of your thousand ears. Us, the deeply degraded [us, the deeply degraded], and all men, you have born anew.

Let all here address their prayers to this woman whom pain has transformed into a goddess. Now I steadfastly await the vision of him who alone can cause and act.

The poem is one of a group central to Goethe's mature thought, and highly productive of literary footnotes. But these quatrains in isolation can hardly be understood; and the daunting task of objectively matching and clarifying their intensity of thought and feeling by means of musical equivalence, in a genre depending for its effect on immediacy and intimacy of appeal, has arguably proved too much even for Wolf. He has audibly prayed in aid from Wagner; and with the piano part orchestrated the work might prove effective and even impressive as a fragment of unwritten opera. As a song, it may regretfully be reckoned among Wolf's few failures.

NOTES 1. The poem is the third of a trilogy *Paria* (I. *Des Paria Gebet;* II. *Legende*). The woman mentioned is no doubt the heroine of II; unjustly beheaded by her jealous husband on suspicion of infidelity, she is miraculously restored, but with her head transposed on to the body of an executed woman criminal; henceforth she will dwell among the gods 'weisen Wollens, wilden Handels', wise in will, wild in deed, an epitome of the human predicament, in Goethean terms. Wolf's textual repetition here however suggests that his chief interest and sympathies lie with the figure of the despised outcast or pariah, perhaps for personal reasons.

2. The piano part, with its Wagnerian overtones, was no doubt the primary inspiration; the resulting imperfection of accentuation ('*von* den tausend Ohren') needs care in performance.

3. There are interesting affinities with *Wie glänzt der helle Mond* (186, see note 2). The situations depicted are somewhat analogous in their humble visions of godhead. In this song bars 13–16 and 22–5 correspond closely to the two main themes of the later and greater work. In the former passage here, the star motif 25 lends poignancy to the contrasting mood of self-abasement; in the latter (as also in 186) a woman is passing through affliction into the next world. Note also the exultant transition to F♯ major here at the word 'Welten', motif 40, and the semitonal clash of the pain motif 34, at the word 'Schmerz'.

4. Cf. Loewe, in Op. 58.

116 (G 31) Königlich Gebet (*A king's prayer*)

7 January 1889   C major   c–e'

Ha, I am the master of the world! The nobles who serve me, love me. Ha, I am the master of the world! I love the nobles whom I command. O grant me, God in heaven! that I am not made overbearing by this eminence and this love.

There is perhaps more lording than loving in the music, and more pride than prayer. But the song is effective and by no means negligible. There is nobility in the vocal line and great strength in the piano part, the first two bars of which already cry out a lusty Amen. The separating chords in both hands graphically indicate the weight and width of the world, and the commensurate scope of its mastery, at each occurrence of the opening phrase 'Ha! Ich bin der Herr der Welt!' The striding bass octaves are modestly inclined at 'mich lieben die Edlen' (the nobles love me); but they rise in renewed pride at the converse pronouncement, 'ich liebe die Edlen'. After the final invocation the postlude is convincingly majestic, yet humble enough to add a further heartfelt Amen.

NOTES 1. The 'master of the world' theme, bars 1–4 and 9–12, has the rhythm, key and mood of the overture to *Die Meistersinger von Nürnberg*. Again the composer's feeling may have been personal, this time an intimation of the artist's dominance or supremacy; the contrasting counterpart of *Dank des Paria* (115).

2. A comparison of the postlude with the same music at bars 16–19 suggests some arbitrariness about the barring, often an indication that the piano part was primary and the voice superimposed; the rather wilful scansion of the latter ('Edlen' in two different rhythms, bars 6 and 14) reinforces that view.

3. The strong themes of the piano part find a truer use, shorn of any suspicion of bombast, in the middle section of the mighty *Grenzen der Menschheit* (136) dated only two days later.

4. One may compare the early Mörike song *Der König bei der Krönung* (8) on a similar theme.

117 (G 32) Phänomen *(Phenomenon)*

aus dem 'Buch des Sängers' (from the 'Book of the Minstrel')
19 January 1889   A major   d'–e♭''

When Phoebus couples with a wall of rain, up springs a curved rim shaded in colour. I see the same arc described in mist, and though the bow be white, yet it is a bow of heaven. So, blithe old man, do not lose heart; though your hair too is now white, yet you will love.

Goethe had a lasting interest in physics as well as metaphysics; particularly in the science of optics, a field to which he made some original

221

if heterodox contributions in his day. He felt that natural phenomena had their own inward life and love; hence their service in his work as powerful symbols of the human condition. He saw colours for example, in a typically vivid phrase, as 'the actions and sufferings of light'. The phenomenon here is the lunar rainbow, the rim of which remains white though potentially containing all colours; an encouraging image of old age. Given the strength and consistency of Wolf's instinctive musical response to verbal concepts, and especially his harmonic depiction of light and colour, it will not be by mere coincidence that this is among the most intensely chromatic of all his songs; for in German, even more than in English, the concept of chromaticism instantly connotes the idea of colour. The key-signature is A major; but that chord is heard only in the first half of the first bar. The music, before ending on (if anything) the dominant E major, uses a whole palette of tone-painting. Its sixteen bars contain major or minor chords on each of the twelve semitones. But each brief phrase is harmonically self-contained, with an effect of colours changing and dissolving in a rainbow of progression. And with all this the music has great charm. The vocal melodic flow is separately sensitive to words and ideas; thus in the opening phrase 'Wenn zu der Regenwand Phöbus sich gattet' the sun twice stoops to meet the rain. The next two bars are notated in flats within the key of three sharps; thus the colour is shaded ('farbig beschattet'), and the piano echo adds a further faint reflection. At the end the brief postlude's new brightness in tonality and pitch, its new frailty of texture, blend to make an old man's voice ('doch wirst du lieben') tremulous with promise.

NOTES 1. The tonality is worth examining in some detail. In addition to its fluctuation, which entails some 160 accidentals in sixteen bars, there is the frequent use of ambiguous chords (augmented fifths, diminished sevenths, cf. motifs 23, 33) as well as ambiguous notation. In a song consisting of the juxtaposition of unrelated chords, the expected mystery motif 19 has some protective colouring; but it is detectable enough at the direction 'geheimnisvoll', bars 6–7. There the low left-hand octave pedal point is also expressive, motif 39. The first two bars have the narrative or reflective harmony of motif 21 (see also the related passages mentioned in 74, note 2); the dominant ending, here with a question expecting or at least much hoping for the answer 'yes', is motif 31.

2. The four-part writing in the piano part at bar 11, with harmonic change at each chord, is rather rare in Wolf. The only clear parallel occurs at bars 3–4 of *Gutmann und Gutweib* (98); in each case the words relate, perhaps just by coincidence, to happiness and love in old age. The piano interlude after 'nur gehört' in *Cophtisches Lied* (99) is not dissimilar in feeling-tone. All three songs are near-contemporary.

3. Cf. Brahms, Op. 61 no. 3 (SA).

4. For the moon-rainbow in English verse, see Browning, *Christmas Eve and Easter Day (VI)*.

222

118 (G 33) Erschaffen und Beleben (*Creation and animation*)

aus dem 'Buch des Sängers' (from the 'Book of the Minstrel')
21 January 1889   E minor–E major   c#'–e''

Jack Adam was a clod of earth that God made into a man; but he brought
with him much that was earthy from his mother's womb. Then Jehovah
breathed the best of spirits into his nostrils; whereupon he showed signs of
real life – he began to sneeze.

But even with bones, limbs and a head he was still half a clod, until at
last Noah found just the right thing for the creature – a bottle of wine.

The clay felt the effect straightaway, the moment it was moistened, just
as dough is fermented by yeast. So, Hafiz, let your sweet song, your sacred
example, lead us, to the accompaniment of clinking glasses, into our
Creator's temple.

The poem is racy and clever in its account of human creation and
evolution; and as usual with Goethe there is a tinge of reverence, even of
philosophical reflection. So Wolf's genius for matching music leads to a
rather odd blend of flavours. The brief prelude of thumping crotchet
octaves promises a plain diatonic treatment of Goethe's broad humour.
Instead, the music is thoughtful in its melodic refinement and tonal
complexity. The piano interludes restore the expected balance, with a fit
of sneezing after 'er fing an zu niesen' and a hilarious outburst at the
mention of wine ('den Humpen'). In the last verse, with its appeal to the
great Persian poet Hafiz as intercessor, all constraint is thrown aside. The
crotchet rhythm of the voice relaxes into comfortable minims, the piano
arpeggios provide the stipulated accompaniment of clinking glasses, and
both march off together in a bibulous procession to the promised land,
from man's genesis to his exodus in five spirited verses.

NOTES 1. Older Peters editions omit the bass C sharps at the word 'netzet'.
2. Processional exit is a favourite device of Wolf's for dramatizing his settings;
cf. *Der Schreckenberger* (74) and *Epiphanias* (104) among many others.
3. There is motif 19 at bars 12–15 for the mystery of creation at 'die Elohim'
etc. At the mention of wine ('den Humpen') the music arrives with sudden éclat in
Wolf's rollicking key of F# major, motif 40. The final major key and the Amen
chord are also typically expressive.
4. Cf. Zelter; Richard Strauss, Op. 87, no. 2.

119 (G 34) 'Ob der Koran von Ewigkeit sei?'

aus dem Schenkenbuche (from the 'Book of the Cup-bearer')
17 January 1889   A minor   b♭ –g''

*Has the Koran existed from eternity? I don't ask about that. Was it
created? That I can't tell. That it is the Book of Books, I believe as a good
Moslem in duty bound. But that wine has existed from eternity, I have no
doubt. Or that it was created before the angels were, that too may be no
mere legend. The drinker, be all that as it may, sees the countenance of
God more clearly.*

The task of setting a poem which in the guise of a theological disputation
is devoted to the praise of wine presents its own special difficulties. Wolf's
achievement is such that one is not conscious of them; the song is a perfect
treatment of the words. With a fine sweep of rising octaves for piano and
voice in unison, the music announces a solemn inquiry. The piano echoes
the last part of the phrase, 'Ewigkeit sei' (from eternity) softly, as if in
meditation. 'Darnach frag' ich nicht' is in vernacular contrast, a
throwaway line in the poem as in the quasi-spoken voice part; the tone is
lowered, with the implication that the question is not only difficult but
boring. 'Ob der Koran geschaffen sei?' – or was it created? Again the
echoing pause for reflection. Again the contrast of tone and tenor; 'das
weiss ich nicht', I don't know. And, as the piano part now hints by
borrowing the vocal phrase for 'darnach frag' ich nicht', I don't much
care. But of course, the voice part adds hastily, though without much
conviction, I believe it to be the Book of Books, 'aus Mosleminenpflicht'.
The song now audibly turns to a far more congenial topic, and announces,
this time with enthusiastic certitude, its considered view on the genesis of
wine, with a spirited 'hear, hear!' from the piano. A rhythmic excitement
in repeated chords begins to ferment within the music, which becomes
steadily more lively and assured. It bursts out suddenly into a bright A
major (the first time this chord has been heard so far) on 'Gott', at the
thought of seeing through a glass clearly, already face to face. This
continues in a blithe postlude which is first syncopated, then rollicking,
then ecstatic, thus conveying in its eight bars a potted idealized history of
the effects of wine-bibbing.

NOTES 1. The unison with voice and piano in bars 1–2, 6–7, is motif 30; the
implied dominant question-marks in those bars are motif 31; the A-major
tonality connotes freshness ('blickt Gott *frischer* ins Angesicht') here as in the
spring songs; the postlude's Amen cadence is ironically apt.

2. The note of mellow elation in the postlude is heard in some of the love-song
settings of the *Westöstlicher Divan*, e.g. the postludes to 128 and 129. The

syncopations here, motif 38, may derive from the postlude to *Der Sänger* (95) which also follows a paean in praise of wine.

3. The throwaway inflexion of 'das weiss ich nicht' somewhat recalls Hans Sachs's 'Das sag' ich nicht' in Act II scene 4 of *Die Meistersinger von Nürnberg*.

120 (G 35) 'Trunken müssen wir alle sein!'

aus dem Schenkenbuche (from the 'Book of the Cup-bearer')
18 January 1889   F♯ minor   e♯'–f♯''

We must all get drunk! Youth is drunkenness without wine; and if old age can drink itself back to youth again, that's a marvellous virtue. Dear life takes care to bring us cares, and what should take them away again but the vine?

So no more disputation; wine is seriously forbidden, and if we can't help drinking, let it be the best vintage. You'd be a heretic twice over, if damned for bad wine.

[So we must all get drunk! drunk! drunk!]

In this bravura display piece the purely musical interest is subordinated to dramatic effect; and the riotous result can be one of intoxicating intensity. In the first section the piano is boisterously robust. Its bunched chords in both hands and rolling 6/8 rhythm makes a fitting vehicle for the vocal line, a chariot for the god of wine himself ('Bacchantisch' is Wolf's direction). A slightly more solemn (though hardly more sober) note is struck at the mention of old age; 'trinkt sich das Alter' etc. But the revelry breaks out again with ever more fervid elation at 'Reben' (vine). Then the time-signature changes to 2/4 and the tempo quickens, as if to distract attention from the dubious theology of the text and increase its persuasive powers. At the word 'Krätzer' (bad wine) the piano part's powerful protest comes thundering up in octaves in both hands to the final outburst of drunken revelry from voice and piano that ends the song.

NOTES 1. The inebriation extends to the treatment of the verses; Wolf quite uncharacteristically conflates two different poems (the second begins at 'Da wird nicht mehr nachgefragt!') and brings back the opening line of the first, with further repetitions, to make an effective coda. This, intentionally or not, greatly enhances the contrast of the middle section; so the first section should not be taken too fast.

2. The contented vocal line at 'Trinke nur vom besten Wein' is a variant of motif 9. The piano interlude at 'Reben' offers the tipsy elation of F♯ major (in a blend of motifs 40 and 7). The F♯-major music is finally whipped into a frenzy of repetition, much as in *Erstes Liebeslied eines Mädchens* (54), at the last sustained 'trunken!' etc. The piano part of the middle section seems to have served as a source for some

of the characteristic phrases of *Der neue Amadis*, e.g. at bars 4 and 8; see 108, note 3.

4. A more deliberate allusion perhaps is to the Schubert drinking song *Zum Punsche*, D492, where the piano interludes in bars 6–7, 12–13 sound like the source of the main thematic material here.

121 (G 36) 'So lang man nüchtern ist...'

aus dem Schenkenbuche (from the 'Book of the Cup-bearer')
16 January 1889   A minor   d'–f#''

So long as one is sober, badness pleases; when one has drunk, one knows what is right. But then excess is imminent; Hafiz, oh teach me your interpretation.

For my own opinion, in no way exaggerated, is that if one cannot drink one should not love. Yet you drinkers should not think yourselves better off; if one cannot love, then one should not drink.

The knotty words may seem unpromising timber for a lyric; but Wolf's plain treatment uncovers good grain and sweetness. The piano part is mock solemn, with an independent melodic dignity that remains serenely unruffled despite the hiccuping demisemiquaver rests. At 'das Rechte' (what is right) the voice soars in pontifical declamation, while the piano is rectitude itself, in clipped military rhythm. The music becomes stridently philosophical at 'Übermass' (excess) and then quietly tender, in a higher register, at the mention of Hafiz, great poet and admired mentor, the Persian Hans Sachs. The interlude has a quiet pensive satisfaction; a problem has been posed, a conclusion will follow. This the resuming voice announces, at 'Denn meine Meinung' (For my own opinion) etc. It seems that a new train of thought is about to intervene. Instead, piano and voice together glide back to the music of the first page; which is then repeated with only slight variations. The piano concludes the song with its interlude themes, a question asked and answered, this time with the complete conviction of a final sforzando chord. It may be conceded that the modified strophic form is not wholly satisfactory as an equivalent for the text, the material used to cover both verses being arguably not equally fitting to each context. But the poem is so appealing, yet difficult to set, and the music so delightful, that the composer seems justified in subordinating verbal significance to musical impulse wherever a choice has to be made.

NOTES 1. The structure is interesting; in the twice 21 bars, 22–5 are varied from 1–4, but the seams stitch together again from 26 onwards. The four-bar interlude-postlude is clearly expressive of doubts resolved. It sounds apt, in a context

226

bounded by 'Übermass' and 'übertrieben', to hear the exaggeration of motif 23's augmented fifths (= übermässige Quinten) briskly dismissed by diatonic resolution. The tonal progression of each half of the song from A minor or E minor to D major is unprecedented in Wolf.

2. As so often in Schubert, the strophic form leaves some loose ends; thus the converging love motif 13 occurs pat at 'nicht lieben kann' (meaning '*I* can love as well as drink'), second half of bar 31, as well as for the beloved Hafiz, bar 15; but it seems non-thematic at bars 16 and 27. Similarly the mystery of motif 19 occurs at 'Nur ist das Übermass', about an unresolved and perhaps insoluble problem; but the same music in the second verse is unthematic. The contentment of motif 9, conversely, is delightfully apt for 'wenn man nicht lieben kann' but less clearly so in the first verse.

3. Cf. Zelter (SATB); Mendelssohn, Op. 75 no. 3 (TTBB).

122 (G 37) 'Sie haben wegen der Trunkenheit...'

aus dem Schenkenbuche (from the 'Book of the Cup-bearer')
18 January 1889   G minor $c^{\#'}-f''$

They have repeatedly accused us of drunkenness, for years; they can never find enough to say about our drunkenness. Lying in a stupor until dawn is the usual effect of drunkenness, yet I am harried around all night by my drunkenness. For what torments me so wretchedly is love's drunkenness; from night to day, from day to night, it wavers in my heart – in my heart, where the drunkenness of song so swells and towers that no sober drunkenness dares to raise its head. It is love-, song- and wine-drunkenness, whether by night or day, the most divine form of drunkenness, that overjoys and torments me.

The first line, used as title, leads us to expect another of Wolf's Bacchantic outbursts. But he has rightly delved deeper. Although the sound and sense of 'Trunkenheit' resound through the music as through the poem, Wolf scrupulously follows Goethe in following and supporting this idea with a changing interpretation. The first page is devoted to the mundane variety of inebriation. 12/8, a rarity in Wolf, is called upon for this purpose. The crotchet-quaver movement slides and sways grotesquely with uncertain harmonies and slurred vocal line. The usual effect of drunkenness ('Gewöhnlich der Betrunkenheit'), i.e. lying in a stupor all night, until dawn, is graphically illustrated by long and low-lying left-hand chords, towards which the right-hand octaves slither helplessly down the keyboard. But all this turns out to have been part of a metaphor for the total abandon and oblivion that characterize lovers and poets. When the main trouble is diagnosed as 'Liebestrunkenheit' the music rallies and becomes much more coherent and compelling. On the last page the original slipping and slumping themes are rehabilitated and set to work as the emphatic bass of the piano part, as if to illustrate the point that all possible kinds of drunkenness are similar in their effects, if not indeed in their cause. The postlude thickly attempts some further portentous utterance, but loses the thread and dozes off instead. All this is brilliantly done; but perhaps Wolf has followed Goethe too closely in insisting on his one theme. In verse, the point is ingeniously made by the alternation of one single word with one solitary rhyme; and even the latter inspiration is feigned to be exhausted long before the end of the poem, so that 'tagt' and 'plagt' have to be repeated at the end. With musical equivalents for fuddled paucity of discourse and obsessive limitation of topic so densely superimposed, the balance seems to be overweighted towards the words.

NOTES 1. The right hand piano part at 'Es ist die Liebestrunkenheit' recalls *Lied eines Verliebten* (55), and is in turn the forerunner of similar passionate themes, e.g. in 132 and 133 below as well as in many of the Spanish love-songs (e.g. 154, 164, 176, q.v.).
2. The low-lying and supine left-hand chords of bars 7–8 are one aspect of motif 39; the inebriated syncopations from bar 13 onwards are motif 38.

123 (G 38) 'Was in der Schenke waren heute...'

aus dem Schenkenbuche (from the 'Book of the Cup-bearer')
16 January 1889   D minor $e^{b\,'}$–g''

What an uproar there was at the inn when day broke this morning! The landlord and girls! Torches, people! Such haggling there was, such insulting! Blowing of flutes, beating of drums, it was life in the raw. Yet there was I in the thick of it, loving it and revelling in it.

That I have learnt nothing of propriety, is what everyone reproaches me for; yet at least I have stayed prudently aloof from the quarrels of critics and professors.

The sunrise scene at the Levantine inn must have presented itself very vividly to Wolf's imagination. 'Extremely fast and whirling' is his direction; his setting begins like the musical equivalent of a whirling dervish. The prelude has an insistent figure in 6/8 quaver octaves; the voice enters, and is instantly swept away in a tumult of quaver chords. Impetus is sustained by further repetition of this piano passage, first at the same pitch, then a tone higher, and then an octave higher in the right hand; and now the widely separated chords in the two hands, melody in the right, pounding in the left, make a lively image of instrumental accompaniment at the mention of flute and drums ('Die Flöte klang, der

Trommel scholl'). Among further images of turbulence, the first two lines of verse are set to four bars of music (down to 'Tumulte') while the second two lines, because of the vocal interjections and pauses, take eight bars (down to 'Insulte'). By that time the musical and verbal phrase-lengths have become hopelessly out of phase, like the confusion described. The impetus continues unslackened throughout the poet's avowed enjoyment of the scene and bursts out in a rough and wild piano interlude that repeats the music already heard at the words 'ein wüstes Wesen' (life in the raw). This changes into portentous octaves that set the scene for the weighty pronouncements of the last verse, to new musical material. But there is still no slackening of the tempo; and the running quavers in the bass are slightly syncopated from time to time, as if to hint that wine is among the sources of inspiration of the new philosophy. It appears that the change of mood in the last verse has rather disconcerted the composer, who discovers that what has pleased and excited him most about the poem is not after all its main message; and Goethe's moral that the quarrels of real life are preferable to academic disputation is not an easy one to infer unaided from the song as such. It is with evident relief that the piano, after the final sung phrase 'vom Streit der Schulen und Katheder', returns in full strength to the opening theme with a splendid bravura passage that relives and relishes the tumultuous scene at the inn.

NOTES 1. Goethe has 'es' (not 'das') 'war ein wüstes Wesen'.

2. The rhythmic construction is interesting. The four-bar phrases, regular for the first twenty bars, modulate (as it were) into 3 + 3 + 2 + 2 at 'das war ein wüstes Wesen' before forming fours again at bar 31. Similarly the relation between verse-line and bar-line is loose in the first two verses, strict in the last; which might have been one way, and a highly ingenious one, of interpreting the poem. The musical sentence-structure has been collapsed and rebuilt to make images of order arising out of chaos. Of Goethe's twelve lines, the first takes eleven consecutive quaver beats, the second thirteen, the third an intermittent twenty-five, the fourth eighteen. Much as in the poem, no clear and consistent pattern emerges until the final quatrain. This irregularity in turn entails that the four-bar musical phrases are soon out of step with the tetrametric lines of verse; order is restored with the final quatrain.

3. Those last four lines are introduced by portentous octaves with augmented intervals (motif 23) which anticipate the theme of the Corregidor in Wolf's opera of that name, written six years later; again, it seems that Goethe is being idiosyncratically interpreted by the composer. The following repeated accented octaves in both hands, as it were laying down the law, are motif 27.

4. It is perhaps relevant that the bass line at 'Dass ich der Sitte' has not only the syncopations of motif 38 but also the characteristic shape of motif 15 as in some of the Spanish songs, e.g. *Wer tat deinem Füsslein weh?* (176); the text implies estrangement ('entfernt'). There is also some kinship between this song and the music of the alienated *Das Köhlerweib* (185), also in D minor.

5. The genesis of the 'tumult' motif here occurs in *Ritter Kurts Brautfahrt* (97),

dated only two months earlier, where the music depicts a crowd scene. Each passage has affinities with the crowd-music (e.g. at bar 15) of *Der Feuerreiter*. The final accented chords of the postlude here, with their diminished sevenths (motif 33) suggests the hard knocks sustained by jostling, as perhaps also in the postlude to 97.

124 (G 39) 'Nicht Gelegenheit macht Diebe...' (Hatem)

aus dem 'Buch Suleika' (from the 'Book of Suleika')
21 January 1889   F major $c\sharp'-g''$

No, opportunity does not make thieves; it is itself the greatest thief, for it stole all the love that I still had left in my heart, and gave it to you, all my life's savings, so that I am now a pauper and dependent solely upon you. But already I feel compassion in the tender sapphire of your gaze, and in your arms I rejoice in a new destiny.

125 (G 40) 'Hoch beglückt in deiner Liebe...' (Suleika)

aus dem 'Buch Suleika' (from the 'Book of Suleika')
23 January 1889   B♭ major $e'-a''$

Greatly rejoicing in your love, I do not chide opportunity; even though it may have stolen from you, how that theft has delighted me! But why speak of stealing? Give yourself to me from free choice. I should love to believe that it was I who robbed you. What you have given so willingly brings you a splendid reward. My peace of mind, the richness of my life, all this I give with joy; take it from me. Do not, even in jest, speak of poverty; does not love make us rich? When I hold you in my arms, my joy is as great as any ever known.

These two songs are considered together because they are deliberately linked by both poet and musician. They share the same vocabulary, the same melodies. Yet the effect of each is quite different. The first song, the loving protestation of Goethe-Hatem, begins with some rather banal strumming by way of prelude. The rest sounds like a scrap-book of previous Wolf songs, compiled with scissors and paste. The construction lacks the customary tautness and tensions; and the accentuation is awry. Yet there are passages of intense beauty; the vocal melody redeems the song, irradiating the music in the middle verse and heightening the closing words with a tenderness that transcends criticism. In the piano part of the reply from Suleika, variations are worked out with great inventiveness. The zest and vitality of the music are impressive. But the song suffers from its self-imposed task of reworking given themes, in conformity with the poem. Though more carefully constructed than its companion piece, it is felt to be less moving. This, it may be argued, is precisely the relationship of the two poems; the first rather laboured yet deeply-felt, the second highly ingenious yet unconvincing. Perhaps it is Wolf's instinctive grasp of the strength and quality of his poetic material that has produced these rather disparate results in what should have been a matching pair. If the strong emotion of the former and the fresh invention of the latter could have been recombined the world would be richer by two very considerable masterpieces.

NOTES 1. Some of the *Westöstlicher Divan* lyrics, including one or two that inspired Schubert (D717 and 720) and Schumann (e.g. his Op. 25 no. 9) have been accepted (on no very clear or demonstrable grounds, it would seem) as the work of Goethe's beloved Marianne von Willemer. No doubt there was much loving collaboration; and there is some independent evidence of her poetic talent. But Wolf's music does not seem to derive from the second of these poems the sustenance that his art craved. Its comparative failure among the Goethe songs might be the more readily explicable in proportion as the text is less authentically Goethean. Whatever its provenance however, and whatever Wolf's source, the universally accepted reading 'ward sie auch' in bar 16 appears to make better sense than Wolf's 'ward sie gleich', which might well be amended accordingly.

2. The first poem makes great play with a trite proverbial expression: 'Gelegenheit macht Diebe', opportunity makes thieves. It is conceivable that Wolf strove to match that sententiousness in his prelude. But the following almost continuous reminiscence of his own work could hardly have been intentional. For what it is worth, some selected echoes are as follows. Bars 7–10, piano, see the first page of *Frage und Antwort* (47) and of *Nimmersatte Liebe* (21). Bars 13–16, voice, see the opening vocal line of *Blumengruss* (109). Bars 13–16, piano, cf. *Ganymed* (135) at 'ach, an deinem Busen'. Bars 19–20, voice, cf. bars 7–8 of *Blumengruss*. Bars 17–21, piano, cf. *Mignon III* (92) at 'dort ruh ich' etc. Similar reverberations can be heard, though more faintly, in the second song, which is deliberately derived from the same material (most manifestly in the opening vocal melody of each). Here the musical allusions become more obscure, rather as if Suleika is capping Hatem's proverb with an adaptation of her own: 'Gelegenheit macht Liebe'. We hear the music of word-play throughout; hence perhaps the clear anticipation of some of the techniques of the Spanish Songbook, in particular *Bitt' ihn, o Mutter* (162).

3. The postlude of 124 and the prelude of 125 are (just as in the Peregrina songs, 45 and 46) linked by the converging melodic lines of the love-motif 13.

126 (G 41) 'Als ich auf dem Euphrat schiffte...' (Suleika)

aus dem 'Buch Suleika' (from the 'Book of Suleika')
24 January 1889   A major   e♭'–e''

As I was sailing on the Euphrates, there fell from my finger, down into the watery gulfs, the gold ring that I recently received from you. So I dreamed. Then the red dawn shone into my eyes through the trees. Say, O poet, say, O prophet, what is the meaning of this dream?

127 (G 42) 'Dies zu deuten, bin erbötig...' (Hatem)

aus dem 'Buch Suleika' (from the 'Book of Suleika')
24 January 1889   A major   c♯'–f♯''

Willingly I interpret this. Have I not often told you how the Doge of Venice is wedded to the sea?

So from your fingers the ring fell into the Euphrates; oh, sweet dream, you inspire me to a thousand heavenly songs!

Me, who from Hindustan travelled to Damascus to journey with new caravans as far as the Red Sea, me you wed to your river, the terrace, this grove, and here, until the last kiss, my soul shall be dedicated to you.

Again two songs are related musically as well as verbally. The first, recounting a woman's dream of drifting on the river, is ideally matched by a delicate 12/8 barcarolle movement. It is as if the voice is in the present, telling the story, and the piano part is in the past, musingly reliving the dream and re-creating its wavy outline. At 'fingerab' (from my finger) the tonality flattens, and the falling left-hand melody goes down further still. It re-emerges at 'Also träumt' ich', as if to show that it was only a dream; that realisation dawns slowly through a long drawn harmonic change that finally awakes in a bright A major again. In that key the original music returns, before modulating again into an unresolved question; what can it mean? Hatem's reply takes the same themes, now transferred to a sturdy terra firma of repeated quaver chords in 4/4 time, and gives them a forthright interpretation. They begin in the same key as before, and undergo the same transformation; again the tonality flattens at the mention of the falling ring, symbol of the Doge's mystic union with the sea. At 'so von deinen Fingergliedern' (so from your fingers) the bass melody begins to sing the left-hand tune of the previous song; in a brief one-bar interlude the ring theme falls into the depths of the keyboard. The opening music is repeated for the following itinerary, which Goethe introduces to show how seasoned a traveller and how experienced a human being his hero is. Then a further development is needed to express the correlative idea that Suleika is offering a correspondingly wide and warm welcome; her dream weds her lover to the river and the whole surrounding terrain, herself included. Now comes a fine flowing peroration; the wedding ring theme, worn on the left hand, makes a circling and embracing gesture of lordly allegiance that slowly traverses two downward octaves with a joyous cry from the voice at 'bis zum letzten Kusse' before coming to rest in a tenderly musing postlude.

NOTES 1. In the first song, the tonal structure is of special interest. The change from A to A♭ major is further nuanced by a brief G♯ (= A♭) minor chord (almost the only time any minor triad is heard) just at the sad little moment between 'Ring' and 'fingerab' (not, as some Peters editions wrongly have it, 'Ringfinger ab'). Then the word 'träumt' seems to be characterized by an F♭, heard elsewhere in the key of A♭ as an expression of sleep (motif 37). The highly Schumannian ending asks a question in the dominant (motif 31), but that of the relative minor; as if Suleika has a covert fear that her dream may bode ill. (Cf. Schumann's *Im wunderschönen Monat Mai*, Op. 48 no. 1, where an A-major song ends on a dominant seventh of the relative minor.)

2. When this tonal structure is adapted in Hatem's reply it inevitably loses a little of its verbal appositeness; thus the A♭ change though apt enough for the new idea of the Doge has no clear motivic force when it recurs at 'um mit neuen Karawanen'. But this second song has subtleties of its own; thus the repeated bass keynote goes on falling a semitone (A in bars 1–4, A♭ in 5–8, G in 9–11) before finishing on F in bar 17, which in bar 18, two octaves lower, symbolizes the falling ring as it reaches the river-bed – of course on the lowest note in the song.

3. During these bars the shared theme is clearly brought out in the piano left hand, because Hatem is directly describing Suleika's dream; and it recurs for the same reason at 'mich vermählst du'.

128 (G 43) 'Hätt' ich irgend wohl Bedenken...' (Hatem)

aus dem 'Buch Suleika' (from the 'Book of Suleika')
26 January 1889   A major   e'–e''

Would I think twice, my sweet love, if I had the chance of making you a present of cities like Balch, or Bokhara, or Samarkand, with all their excitement and splendour? But just ask the emperor if he would give you those cities? He is grander and wiser; but he doesn't know what loving is. No, my sovereign, you'll never reconcile yourself to bestowing such gifts. For that, one needs to have a girl like mine and be a beggar like me.

There are thematic affinities with the previous song. Hatem-Goethe is again in joyous mood. Again voice and left hand vie in delighted melodies; but this time the right hand has quaver triplet chords in a lively tempo; the music is alive with amused excitement in response to the poet's hyperbole.

At the same time, the lovingly tender question and answer of the earlier dialogue is not forgotten; the symbolic pledge of the falling ring is thoughtfully recalled, e.g. at 'Samarkand' and again after 'Rausch und Tand' (excitement and splendour). The bass line becomes ponderous and the right hand slightly dissonant when the oddly ungenerous views of the Shah are mentioned, at 'Aber frag einmal den Kaiser'. He is much grander, the poem then explains; 'er ist herrlicher'; here the left hand theme appears robed in a display of octaves, which are instantly removed when his human limitations are instanced; 'doch er weiss nicht wie man liebt'. Now the dissonances return, more markedly than before, as the ruler is actively criticized. And now Wolf's music adds a gloss to the meaning of the poem. For true kingly generosity, says Hatem, one has to be a beggar. But this must be meant ironically; to enjoy a love such as Suleika's is to be no beggar but a king. Here Hatem's theme smilingly carries out a small *coup d'état*, and emerges wearing the royal octaves, which billow out magnificently in the long trailing phrases that bring this engaging song to a close. Thus the postlude offers an anticipatory tone-translation of the last line of the next poem; we hear Hatem crowned Shah.

NOTES 1. The left-hand theme is clearly akin to the corresponding melodies of 126 and 127; in particular its instant diminution in the voice part derives from the former. Again the transition to A♭ major is maintained, though here it is notated as G♯ major, at bar 10 (cf. bar 17 of 127).

2. It sounds as if the Shah on his throne is awarded the loneliness idea of motif 15, bars 11–14 and 20–2; serve him right, one feels, for his niggardliness. The question-mark at bar 9 is motif 31; at bar 14, motif 32.

129 (G 44) 'Komm, Liebchen, komm...' (Hatem)

aus dem 'Buch Suleika' (from the 'Book of Suleika')
25 January 1889   A♭ major   e♭'–a♭''

Come, my love, come and put on my turban. Only your hand can wind it so beautifully. Not even the Shah himself, on the highest throne of Persia, could have his head enfolded so gracefully. A turban was the head-dress that fell in folds from the head of Alexander, and well pleased all the rulers that succeeded him, as a royal embellishment. A turban is what arrays our emperor; they call it a crown, but what's in a name? Jewels and pearls may delight the eyes, but the most beautiful adornment remains muslin. And so wind this turban here, pure white and striped with silver, about my brow, my love. What then is majesty? It's well-known to me; for if you but look at me, I become as great as He.

Once again we hear the Hatem love-song style and themes, Schubertian in their melodic felicity. Again the left hand vies with the vocal line; again they share the same tone of voice, the same inflexions. Here the piano is heard singing 'Komm, Liebchen, komm' before the voice does. The music becomes more characteristically Wolfian at 'Ein Dulbend war das Band' (a turban was the head-dress). Lighter and cooler in texture, it goes spiralling sedately round in winding melodic figures and key-changes, culminating on the softly sustained last syllable of 'Musselin', fittingly the longest note in the song, as being not merely a testament of beauty but a confession of faith. The first strain reappears and is taken to a resoundingly accented climax on the last line 'ich bin so gross als Er', a bold, even revolutionary, claim to parity with the Shah himself. At this passionate avowal the turban is set aside, as if forgotten. The long piano postlude meditates on the measure and melody of the opening words 'Komm, Liebchen, komm'. This theme is deployed first appealingly, then imploringly, in eloquently syncopated left hand octaves under the persistent six-quaver rhythm of right hand chords. At the close we are meant to hear it hushing to a whisper and saying (quietly, tenderly) 'come, my love'.

NOTES 1. In some Peters editions, the highest left hand piano note at the first quaver of the interlude bar after 'umher' is misprinted as $D^\flat$ instead of a tied $E^\flat$.

2. The right hand quaver chords reappear in 128; the simple cadence at bars 8–9 recalls bar 5 etc in that song and bar 17 of 127. Again Hatem's single notes at the outset are contrasted with the Shah's octaves, bar 11ff.; and these, further embellished as chords, are finally appropriated by Hatem to bolster up his culminating claim ('Ich bin so gross als Er').

3. For the postlude's syncopations, see 119, note 2; for a later application of the cooling muslin texture, see 163, note 2.

130 (G 45) 'Wie sollt' ich heiter bleiben...' (Hatem)

aus dem 'Buch Suleika' (from the 'Book of Suleika')
23 January 1889   F minor $e^\flat{}'-f''$

How should I remain carefree, sundered from day and light? Now I wish to write, and have no taste for wine. When she drew me to her there was no need for talking, and as my tongue faltered then so does my pen now. Come then, beloved cup-bearer, and fill my cup in silence. All I need say is 'Remembrance'; he already knows my wish [he already knows my wish].

131 (G 46) 'Wenn ich dein gedenke...' (Hatem)

aus dem 'Buch Suleika' (from the 'Book of Suleika')
25 January 1889   F minor   c'–f♭''

*When I remember you, my cup-bearer always says: 'Sir, why so silent?
For Saki would gladly listen for ever to your teaching.' When I lie lost in
thoughts under the cypress-tree, he learns nothing from me; and yet in
that silent sphere I am so profound, as wise as Solomon.*

Another pair of songs, linked in music (key and 6/8 time) as in words (the
rhyme of 'Schenke – Gedenke', cup-bearer and memories, occurs in each).
Each mode contains the same mood, an inward thought of the loved-one
pervading the mind, in all its musings. As in 124 and 125 the very clarity
of the poetic image as reflected in Wolf's music may account for the
difference of quality in the two songs. The first is directly concerned with
the thoughts of love; its tenderness is explicit. The second is, so to speak,
about the thoughts of the thoughts of love; it is an implied love-song,
deliberately distanced from actuality, and it sounds that much more
remote. The dreamy wistful lilt of the first begins with a questioning
prelude, which turns into the rhetorical inquiry of the first two lines,
down to 'Tag und Licht?' (day and light?). New major chords sound
mellow and tender, with a sustained left hand note, for the wish to write
love-lyrics; 'Nun aber will ich schreiben'. After the tense and insistent
recurrences of memory at 'Wenn sie mich an sich lockte' (when she drew
me to her) the major chords return to reinforce the meaning; as the singer
returns to his thwarted desire to write ('und wie die Zunge stockte, so
stockt die Feder auch', as my tongue faltered then, so does my pen now)
the accompaniment quotes the music for 'Nun aber will ich schreiben'. A
new major triad, heard for the first time in the song, appears at 'Gedenke',
contradicting the minor key; the memories bring happiness to the
harmony in a wholly Schubertian style. In the second song, again in
conformity with the poem, the harmonies shift obscurely throughout, as if
the feeling were experienced through a haze or veil. Further, the semitonal
rocking movement of the first song

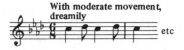

is now made less obtrusive and is given a new pivot

while sustained inner voices are sensed rather than heard throughout the music, like the hidden and unspoken thoughts that Goethe describes. The harmonies are deployed in sinuous sequences that fluctuate uncertainly between major and minor tonalities. Both songs are marked 'traumhaft', dreamily. But in the first song the mood though elusive is clearly caught and held; in the second, except in superlative performance, the emotions never really quite succeed in shining through the surrounding subtlety.

NOTES 1. In 131, some Peters editions omit the flat before the left-hand G in bar 10.
2. The rocking rhythm and semitonal alternation of the first song throughout suggests the dreaminess of motif 18, even without the syncopations. The C-major chord at 'Licht?' is the dominant questioning of motif 31. The change from that tonality to the warmer A♭ major at 'Nun aber will ich schreiben' strikingly anticipates the Spanish Songbook, see 142, note 4.
3. The thematic material of the second song, with its melodies in contrary motion based on the span of a minor third, is again akin to some of the Spanish songs; see also 122, note 1. Here the shifts between minor and major, e.g. at bars 21, 23, 24, recall earlier Hatem songs.

132 (G 47) 'Locken, haltet mich gefangen...' (Hatem)

aus dem 'Buch Suleika' (from the 'Book of Suleika')
29 January 1889   A major   d♯'–a''

Let her tresses bind me fast within the circle of her face! You beloved tawny serpents, I have nothing to match you.

Only this heart is durable, and swells in the most youthful of blossomings; under the snow and mists an Etna bursts molten out towards you.

Like the red dawn you bring a blush to the grave face of those mountain-tops; and once again Hatem feels the breath of spring and the heat of summer.

Cup-bearer! one more flagon; I pledge this bowl to her! If she finds a heap of ashes, she can say 'He burnt himself up for me'.

133 (G 48) 'Nimmer will ich dich verlieren!...' (Suleika)

aus dem 'Buch Suleika' (from the 'Book of Suleika')
30 January 1889   A major   d♯'–a''

Let me never lose you! Love gives strength to love. May you adorn my youth with your powerful passion.

Oh, how flattered my own impulses feel, when my poet is praised; for love is life, and mind is the life of life itself.

The light and ironical passion of the first song in this concluding duologue is deliberately exaggerated, in the music as in the poem. The piano part tears away, the voice strikes in exultantly; at 'zu erwidern hab ich nichts' I have nothing to match you, the piano is all rippling coils and ringlets, silencing the poet's voice, compelling his admiration (not to say envy). But when it resumes, at 'Nur dies Herz' (only this heart), there is after all a response to Suleika's beauty, and a passionate one. If the poet's white and no doubt scant hair is like a snowy mountain peak, then his heart is a hidden volcano; as promised in the first of the *Westöstlicher Divan* songs, *Phänomen* (117), he can still love. This realisation brings new life into the music. The sinuous triplet quavers are relegated to the left hand, and subordinated to dominant rising virile right-hand figures. The thrust and fire of the voice part also vividly suggest hidden sources of power about to burst out. The first theme reappears higher in the keyboard, lighter in texture, as befits the invigorating air of the mountain peaks; then the rippling piano music returns in renewed brightness for the sustained words 'Frühling' (spring) and 'Sommer'. The concluding declamatory phrases die away in mock pathos at the mention of ashes and then revive in *crescendo* for the amused last words 'Der verbrannte mir' (he burnt himself up for me). The postlude emerges unscathed from the ashes to relive the first moments of the song; 'Locken, haltet mich gefangen', it says, in a passionate outcry including a final glimpse of the rippling tresses themselves. The second song is Suleika's reply. The words (whatever their intention or authorship) find no very clear musical equivalent in Wolf's setting, which brushes aside their rather obscure intellectual implications and overtones. The composer's concern is to complement the previous declaration of love with an acceptance fully as fiery and as fervent as its own. There is a smouldering quietude at 'Ach! wie schmeichelt's' (how it flatters) as the rising figure common to both songs is restrained and damped down, only to leap up at the culminating phrase 'Denn das Leben ist die Liebe' etc in a great climactic flare of pitch, dynamics and texture (sustained top A, *ff*, followed by piano tremolandi) that makes a fitting finale to the Oriental love songs of the *Westöstlicher Divan*.

NOTES 1. Both texts set intractable problems which the composer seems sensibly to ignore. In the first, the deft substitution of the name 'Hatem', at the point where the reader and perhaps the listener will expect a rhyme to '-röte', tells us confidentially that Hatem is an alias for Goethe. The second is presumably written in a style suitable for Marianne, whether by Goethe or by the lady herself (if the latter, then the reference to being flattered when she hears her poet praised takes on a further meaning). But that style seems rather refractory to musical equivalence, at least on the present evidence.

2. The opening piano music of 132 has off-beat quavers; the poem asks to be bound and helpless (motif 2). When the volcano's lava erupts, we hear the dotted rhythms ♪♪♩ which in Wolf as in Wagner (Parsifal's meeting with the knights) and Schubert *passim* betoken virile activity.

3. The rhythmic impetuosity rivals that of *Der Feuerreiter* (56). It seems that at the reference to ashes here ('Findet sie ein Häufchen Asche') the piano passages on the last page of the earlier song ('Husch! da fällt's in Asche ab') are deliberately quoted. For the piano part of 132 at bars 8–10 etc, see 122, note 1. Its equivalents for the idea of ringlets may be compared and contrasted with Schubert's re-creation of the same image to a poem on the same theme from the same Goethe source, in *Versunken*, D715.

4. The music of 133 shares some general thematic relation with 132 (e.g. the runs and chords in the opening bars of each) as well as key and compass; but there is little clear motivic equivalence.

134 (G 49) Prometheus

2 January 1889 (orchestrated 12 March–April 1890) D minor   Bᵇ–f'

Cover your heaven, Zeus, with cloudy vapour,
    and, like a boy lopping thistles, practise your skills on oak-trees and mountain-tops.

Yet you must leave me my earth still standing, and my smithy which you did not build, and my hearth whose fire you envy me.

I know nothing under the sun so mean as you gods! You nourish your majesty miserably on levied sacrifice and the breaths of prayer, and you would starve, were not children and beggars optimistic fools. When I was a child, not knowing which way to turn, I too used to lift my misguided gaze to the sun, as if there above were an ear to hear my lament, a heart like my own to pity me in my affliction.

Who helped me against the overbearing Titans?

Who saved me from death, from slavery?

Did you not accomplish all this yourself, my holy glowing heart? And did you not, youthful well-meaning dupe, glow your thanks to the slumberer in the skies?

I, honour you, Zeus? Why? Have you ever eased the pains of one heavy-laden? Have you ever dried the tears of one dismayed? Have I not been forged into a man by all-powerful time and everlasting fate, my masters and yours? Perhaps you thought I would hate life and flee into the wilderness because not all my blossoming dreams bore fruit? Here I sit, making men in my own image, a race like unto me, to suffer, to weep, to enjoy and rejoice, and to ignore you — as I do!

The demi-god Prometheus was represented as man's ally against the tyranny of the gods. In some myths he is even the creator of mankind who to animate his creation stole fire from heaven. His punishment was to be chained to a mountain in the Caucasus, with an eagle feeding on his liver; from this plight he was rescued by Hercules. He is a powerful symbol of all humanist ideals, from artistic inspiration to rebellion against harsh authority. Goethe's great dramatic monologue inspired both Wolf and Schubert to magnificent music. Here, as in the next song, Schubert's setting is outstanding for human strength and nobility, while Wolf chooses to attempt to write above a mortal pitch. Everything about his Prometheus is larger than life. He orchestrated nearly thirty of his songs, but only of this one can it confidently be claimed that it is better so arranged. The piano part, magnificent though it is, sometimes seems inadequate as sheer sound to exploit the full range and resource of this prodigious music, which shares with Milton's Satan

> ... th'unconquerable will,
> And study of revenge, immortal hate
> And courage never to submit or yield ...
> And what is else not to be overcome.

The long heaven-storming prelude has a Titanic defiance, like a huge clenched fist rising and shaking and striking out at the gods. The music hushes and relaxes to gather strength and is then repeated in full, this time with the voice part adding its snarling contempt – 'Bedecke deinen Himmel, Zeus', etc. After 'Bergeshöhn' (mountain-tops) both hands return together from their punitive expedition and come down to earth with unshakeable confidence, at 'musst mir meine Erde doch lassen stehn' (Yet you must leave me my earth still standing). Great massed octaves, again in both hands, surge up invincibly and turn into a further outburst of pride and rage at 'beneidest' (envy). Now the piano part begins to crawl with loathing and contempt at 'Ich kenne nichts Ärmeres' (I know nothing so mean). For some fifty bars a sinuous mock-whimpering motif with frequent semitonal clashes sounds in the right hand. Under it the left hand marches in strong octaves as Prometheus sings, in slowly rising phrases or broader melodic sweeps, of the manifest inadequacies of the gods. Another insurgent climax is reached after 'sich des Bedrängten zu erbarmen' (to pity me in my affliction). The right hand motif has meanwhile risen menacingly higher; now its gestures grow ever more insistent until the left hand joins it and both suddenly strike out together again in a frenzy. There is again a pause to recover breath and strength and control. Then at 'Wer half mir' (who helped me) the music of the prelude returns once more, as past wrongs are remembered and Zeus himself is again attacked in angry declamation. Here the whole giant frame of Prometheus begins to shake in tremolando chords at 'heilig glühend Herz!' (holy glowing heart). After 'Schlafenden da droben?' (slumberer in the skies?) there are stunning roars of rage in the piano interlude and then of defiance as the resuming voice fairly shouts 'Ich dich ehren? Wofür?' (I, honour you? Why?). The initial quietude of the following indictment much enhances its final effectiveness. The piano has repeated triplet quaver octaves in the right hand, as the voice sings its pitying melodies; 'Hast du die Schmerzen gelindert' (have you ever eased the pains) etc. The ponderous minim octaves in the left hand that carry the full weight of the grave charges preferred are interspersed with involuntary outbursts of revulsion and indignation, reverting to the angry rhythms of the prelude. The right-hand octaves thicken into chords, the left-hand octaves surge challengingly up the keyboard as Prometheus dares to assert his parity with the gods, in a common subordination to Time and Fate, 'meine Herrn und deine' (my masters and yours). At this last word a *fff* is reached for the fourth and last time. Gradually the rage dies out of the music, the mood changes from defiance to affirmation. With 'Hier sitz' ich' (here I sit) Prometheus is absorbed in his creative task. In the piano the strokes of hammer on anvil ring out. Now Zeus is irrevocably denied, his power usurped. So the anger and pride of the prelude reappear; and the final words 'wie ich' are echoed and reinforced by strong hammering chords, as the forger of mankind with one and the same gesture turns his back on heaven and resumes his human creation.

NOTES 1. The *Kritische Gesamtausgabe*, no doubt rightly (in view of bar 143), corrects the last left-hand octave of bar 139 to F natural, not F#.

2. The magnificent poem (misrepresented in the Peters edition, which twice gives 'jedes' instead of 'je des', in bars 139 and 143) is strong enough to bear many different interpretations. But clearly neither words nor music are about 'Prometheus bound' as is sometimes suggested – a position hardly compatible with the words 'hier sitz' ich' etc.

3. Nonetheless Wolf is as ever concerned to create human character on his own account, and arguably goes beyond his poet in doing so. His interpretation can be to some extent deduced from the music, in particular the prelude. This contains in essence almost all the song's thematic material, the later expressive significance of which may be inferred from its later verbal contexts. It could perhaps be expounded thus. A solitary giant figure towers up (bars 1–4) and conscious of its strength becomes proud, angry, self-assertive (bars 4–8) and then moves through defiance (bars 9–16) to open rebellion and menace (bars 17–19). With that frame of mind established, there is a more conventional two-bar prelude, bars 20–1 (perhaps the point at which the song in its first conception originally began). Now the music begins again, with bar 23 as bar 1 etc, except that the right hand tremolandi have been lightened to make room for the voice. For bars 39–49 there is a sudden change of mood and texture. Two new themes appear; minim chords

241

in a characteristic harmonic progression, followed by rising octaves. But as in the poem there is continuity as well as change. The gaze shifts from heaven to earth, but the observer's basic viewpoint and stance remain unvaried. So the minim chords in bars 39–40 are evolved from bars 9 and 11 (= 30 and 32); and the rising octaves in bar 40 are evolved from bars 17–19 (= 37–8). At this latter point, bar 38, the expected continuation 18–19 etc is omitted; so the impression is of sudden shift of perspective, just as in the poem. The switch to the lower register at bar 39 further confirms a change of ground. Finally the asperities of the original statement are modified and mitigated in each case, transforming the expressive effect from defiant threat to unshakeable self-confidence. In this highly Wolfian way the whole song is constructed from the building-blocks of the prelude, which are continually cut, dressed and shaped anew in conformity with the sense of the words, their character-study, scene-painting and dramatic conflict.

4. The structure may be further exemplified by the study of two separate strands. First there are the variations of rhythm and texture in bars 4–8 etc, 129–32, 140 and 144 etc (left hand) and the way in which these motifs of self-assertion culminate first in the massive anvil-strokes of 160–2 and then in the final outburst of the closing bars. Then there are the various melodic and harmonic guises in which the chords of bars 39–40 and 45–6 etc reappear in bars 115–16 etc, 123–4 etc, and 139–40 before the basic progression common to all of them is lingered out in the almost forgiving passages in bars 159–60, recurring in similar mood in bars 167–9. These two strands, which perhaps correspond notionally to the ideas of the Titan's anger and of something approaching filial respect or even esteem, unite and part again, especially at the pivotal point of both words and music, namely the change of mood in bars 159–61 with the words 'Hier sitz' ich' etc.

5. The hammer-blows of motif 27 resound throughout. Other associative writing includes the falling bass of the first four bars, which later suggests the idea of isolation, motif 15. The defiant ring of bars 9ff. has a milder parallel in bars 23–6 of *Ritter Kurts Brautfahrt* (97), where Kurt meets a foeman; the menace of bars 18–19 is related to the restless energy of motif 5 in a version already used in *Beherzigung* (103); the rising octaves of bar 40 are the last and truest use of the manly motif 6 often heard in the Eichendorff songs. The questioning and tensions of motifs 31–3, and the violence of motif 27, are also much in evidence.

6. Wolf orchestrated this song in 1890, at the height of his powers. The grandeur of subject and scale combine to give his sonorous imagination a Wagnerian quality in thematic material as well as scoring; thus the music at 'wähntest du etwa' in particular recalls a passage in the Act III prelude to *Siegfried*. No doubt Wolf also knew Liszt's symphonic poem *Prometheus*; this too audibly grows in strength and stature in its opening bars.

7. Cf. also Reichardt; Schubert, D674.

135 (G 50) Ganymed (*Ganymede*)

11 January 1889 (orchestrated 1890; lost)   D major   f#'–g''

In the radiance of dawn how you glow upon me from all sides, beloved
Springtime! With a thousandfold bliss of love the holy sense of your
eternal warmth presses against my heart, unending beauty! If only I could
clasp you in these arms [in these arms].

Oh, I lie on your breast, I languish, and your flowers, your grass, press
against my heart. You cool the burning thirst of my bosom, sweet wind of
morning! The nightingale calls me lovingly from the misty valley. I come,
I come! But where, oh, where?

Above; I am impelled above. The clouds float down, the clouds descend
to my yearning love. To me! To me! In their embrace aloft, enfolding and
enfolded! Aloft to your breast, all-loving Father!

Goethe takes the legend of the Trojan prince Ganymed, gathered up to
Olympus by Zeus to be the cup-bearer of the gods, and puts it to profound
uses as a symbol of union with God and Nature, mysticism and
pantheism. The poem thus arguably presents an even more difficult task
to a composer than its opposite counterpart *Prometheus* (134). The
defiance in that poem is one single impulse. But the self-surrender here is
an infinitely more far-reaching concept. Wolf's and Schubert's settings
are utterly different from each other and still leave whole areas of the
poem unexplored. Even Schubert's demi-god Prometheus is an
endearingly human figure. His prince Ganymed naturally remains
entirely earth-bound throughout his setting, responding to the springtime
beauty of the real world; the apotheosis takes place, if at all, at the end of
the song, as it were off-stage. So relaxed and amiable an approach was
alien to Wolf's passionate and intellectual cast of mind. He justified his
own attempt to set both poems again on the ground that Schubert had
simply failed to understand them. But Schubert's simplicity is the secret of
his   success;   and   the   same   applies   to   Wolf's   complexity.   He
characteristically seeks to express the whole transcendent significance of
Goethe's poem, including its highly-charged erotic symbolism. As a
result, his music sounds much more metaphysical in conception than
Schubert's. Already at the outset it is in a hovering trance of ecstatic
communion with nature, irradiated by the spring dawn-shine. The
piano's soft high single quavers fall and rise, float and drift, in languorous
curves and suspensions, over softly shining staccato chords. These are
further brightened by a progression from D major through F♯ major to B♭
major, while the voice sings its warm melodies based on the tonic triad of
each successive key. D major is again reached for the cry of 'Dass ich dich

243

fassen möcht' (If only I could clasp you) set for the voice alone, but interspersed with slow expressive piano phrases ending in sustained rich chords with added dissonance, like tears of joy. Piano echoes voice at 'in diesen Arm!'; and for the succeeding vision of beauty in nature an almost voluptuous swaying movement begins. A new semiquaver sighing is heard in the left hand as the winds of dawning blow, at 'du kühlst die brennende Durst' (you cool the burning thirst). The music is all yearning at the repeated question 'wohin' (where), ending on the sustained tension of a long interrogative dominant seventh chord and an inquiring pause. Then the first strains are repeated, so that the ensuing music, exactly like the words, falls on the ear as the answer to a question: 'wohin? ... hinauf!'. The left hand is now arrayed in rising tremolandi instead of steady chords; the music is made cloudy and sent billowing slowly upwards. From that turning-point until the end of the song the appeal to Zeus is sonorously unified with the previous appeal to nature; a passionate pantheism is made audible. At the final climax voice and piano divide and continue that dual effect in separate strains. As the singer cries out in love of God 'all-liebender Vater!' the postlude sings of love for springtime, to the melody of 'in diesen Arm', with which passionate invocation the song ends.

NOTES 1. The repetition of 'in diesen Arm' is Wolf's, not Goethe's.

2. The nature of the text offers special insights into Wolf's musical equivalence. Love of God and of Nature, with mystic transfiguration, are expressed with unparalleled intensity of phrase-structure and vocabulary in both words and music. In Goethe's poem, each of three key notions attracts a cluster of synonyms or echoes. The radiance of beauty ('-glanze', 'anglühst', 'Frühling', 'Schöne' etc), the warmth of love ('Geliebter', 'Liebeswonne', 'Herz', 'Wärme', 'Gefühl') are linked and latched together by the idea of motion towards, from all directions ('an', 'drängen', 'fassen', 'hinauf', 'abwärts', 'neigen', etc). So the music too is heard in its most verbally intensified and saturated forms. In the beginning, light comes in through the mediant key-change of motif 24 as well as through the staccato chords of motif 26, which may also have the added significance of tears, as in Mühvoll komm ich (143, note 3). At the end, from the first 'hinauf' onwards, the love music of motif 13 is writ large, and on the grandest scale. The descending melodic line is met and converged upon not just by another melody but by throbbing handfuls of chords. The actions and aspirations of the central character are as it were charted on the stave; the lowest note occurs at the end of the word 'abwärts'. Similarly the piano part is a map of movement and feeling, on a commensurately broader scale. The whole song is articulated by changing rhythms merging and almost modulating one into the other. The 3 + 3 + 2 quavers are made to billow as in Grenzen der Menschheit (136, note 3), motif 38. The other syncopations include a generous and apt measure of the childlike helplessness of motif 2. The questioning dominant seventh before the reprise is motif 32.

3. Like *Prometheus* (134) the music might gain from orchestration. Wolf made an orchestral version in 1890, but it was later lost. Even the piano score, not surprisingly, has something of the atmosphere of *Siegfried*, also at dawn, on the hill of magic fire (in Act III).

4. Cf. Reichardt; Schubert, D544; Loewe, Op. 81 no. 5 (and a choral setting without opus number).

136 (G 51) Grenzen der Menschheit (*The limits of mankind*)

9 January 1889   A minor   F–e♭ '

When the holy eternal father with serene hand sows the benison of his lightnings from rolling thunderclouds over the earth, I kiss the lowest hem of his garment, with childlike awe in my faithful heart. For no man shall measure himself against gods. If he arise and touch the stars with the crown of his head, then his unsteady soles find no foothold, he becomes the plaything of clouds and winds.

If he stands with firm marrowy bones on the steadfast and enduring earth, then his stature cannot compare even with the oak tree or the vine.

What distinguishes gods from mankind? Before the gods, many waves roll on, an eternal stream; us the waves first lift, then engulf and drown.

A little ring encompasses our life; and many generations link in lasting succession on the endless chain of their existence.

This final song of the Goethe volume explores the ways of the universe, the nature of gods and men. Within this mighty music the conflicting moods of the two previous songs – emulation of godhead in *Prometheus*, surrender to divinity in *Ganymed* – are absorbed and reconciled. The piano begins with slow majestic chords resolving into bass tremolando octaves; an epitome of the image of eternal majesty enthroned serene above the thunder. The voice part responds with its worshipping words set to a tranquil and long-flighted melodic line. The harmonies, at first strange and remote, gradually resolve into a warm major cadence, thus expressing the dual human response of awe and love for an eternal father, as defined by the voice at 'kindliche Schauer treu in der Brust' (childlike awe in my faithful heart). At 'Denn mit Göttern' (For no man shall measure himself against gods) etc the music aspires, climbs and then falls in both pitch and volume; the philosophical assessment is made graphically vivid. At 'Hebt er sich aufwärts' (if he arise) voice and piano together stir and gesture and strain upwards to a new and spaciously sustained climax at 'Sterne' (stars). Widely separated octaves and augmented chords now speak with eloquence and grandeur about uncertain walking on sheer dizzying space. There is unsurpassable strength and solidity in the starkly contrasting section at 'Steht er' (If he stand). Here the heavy and deliberate crotchet tread of the wide-ranging bass octaves resounds under the repeated notes of the voice; and the following piano interlude merges into an everyday matter-of-fact theme. It is worth considering what demands the poem makes on the composer in this passage. If the latter is to fashion a worthy musical equivalent for these splendid verses he must find music that speaks first of exalted uncertainty, then of unexalted certainty, thus compressing into a few bars the paradox of the human condition as Goethe conceives it. The music must first of all have starry grandeur but also a certain instability; then it must have complete steadiness and strength but also a certain down-to-earth or homely quality. The result is not likely to be part of a conscious thought-process; but it is a searching test of the song-writer's intuitive feeling for his art. Schubert and Wolf both succeed triumphantly. At 'Was unterscheidet Götter von Menschen?' (What distinguishes gods from men?) there is a minatory reminiscence of the previous equivalent for 'no man shall measure himself against the gods'. After a solemn pause, the gods themselves are evoked, or rather the endlessly flowing sea of time that rolls before them. The awe-inspiring chords of Father Zeus are sent billowing up in a succession of great waves. The vocal phrases are first reverent at 'ein ewiger Strom' (an eternal stream), then heart-rending at 'verschlingt die Welle' (the waves engulf), then endlessly resigned at 'und wir versinken' (and we drown). After 'Ein kleiner Ring', set in a little ring of semibreves, the tolling minims of the first page reappear in a chain of high widespread chords, each closely linked to the other, as the huge intervals of the voice part plunge and rear into the final words 'an ihres Daseins unendliche Kette' (on the endless chain of their existence). In the postlude the music dissolves into an eerie and sombre vision of an eternity beyond our imagining.

NOTES 1. The word at the beginning of bar 36 in older Peters editions should be corrected to 'hebt' from 'heb'.

2. The constructional use of rhythm in the piano part is far more extended and elaborate than usual even in Wolf. It seems that an even minim rhythm is associated with gods or eternity, and an even crotchet rhythm with mortal man, with complex compromise when the two ideas are interfused. This correspondence might be charted thus, to show one aspect of background form and structure.

Bars	Idea	Rhythm in 2/2 time
(a)	1–27	emotions aroused by the gods
(b)	28–35	men unlike gods
(c)	36–43	men emulating gods
(d)	44–73	the human condition
(e)	74–77	men unlike gods
(f)	78–95	men and gods in time
(g)	96–99	the limits of mankind; a ring (!)
(h)	100–126	the eternity of the gods

It will be noted how the rhythms expand and develop like the verbal themes, with eternity the same at the end as in the beginning; alpha and omega. Similarly (b) and (e) have the formal identity that the words imply, while (c) and (f) aptly stand in the relation of augmentation or diminution.

3. Those last two 3 + 3 + 2 arrangements are found in *Ganymed* (135, dated two days later) and practically nowhere else in Wolf's work. In both contexts their function is to render ideas of time and space in a more fluid or amorphous form, and thus to provide an equivalent for the imagined billowing of waves or clouds as symbols of eternity: motif 38. The harmonic correspondence between bars 46–9 and 96–9 is also meaningful, in the pathetic sense of motif 23 applied to mortal uncertainty ('unsichern Sohlen' etc) and mortal limitation ('Ein kleiner Ring'). In the whole passage at 44–50 the augmented fifths of motif 23 wear the mysterious aspect of motif 19, which also suffuses the strange unrelated chords of the opening page.

4. Those chords predictably owe something to Wagner's motif for Wotan the Wanderer in the first act of *Siegfried*, e.g. at the words 'Heil dir weiser Schmied!' There is also a less explicable but manifest affinity with Schubert's *Wehmut*, D772, e.g. its minim chords compared with the first page here, and the last bars of each postlude where Wolf gravitates towards the Schubertian D minor, leaving his own A-minor tonality illustratively hovering in mid-air. The Schubert song in its far more modest and limited way is also a powerful evocation of the nature of the universe and humanity, and the transience of the latter.

5. Cf. Schubert, D716.

V. The Spanish Songbook

The Romantic movement in Germany was insatiably avid for poetry of all kinds, from all lands. In the eager quest for national and folk themes, the Romance languages and traditions were especially sought after. As German painters had craved the clear air and warm light of Italy, so German writers and musicians found their own native art-forms revivified and irradiated by Southern grace and lightness of rhyme and metre, melody and cadence. Further, the ideas of Spanish local colour and costume, pride and passion, guitar and castanets made a particular appeal to the lighter lyric poets such as Emanuel Geibel (1815–84) and through them to great song-writers such as Schumann, whose Geibel setting *Der Hidalgo* of 1840 was among the very first to put Spain on the map of the Lied. There had been earlier importations into literature, and translations from the Spanish were a flourishing trade by the early nineteenth century; thus the successful printing and publishing firm founded in Zwickau, near Leipzig, by Schumann's father had brought out a popular sixteen-volume edition of Cervantes between 1825 and 1829. But even earlier (1821–5) there had appeared in Hamburg a comprehensive three-volume anthology of poetry* in Spanish, with notes and commentary for German readers, which was to serve as the main source for the selection of Spanish verses translated by Geibel and Heyse as the *Spanisches Liederbuch* (1852). Predictably, Geibel had been among the first to translate Spanish lyrics in his *Volkslieder und Romanzen der Spanier* (1843), from sources including George Borrow's handbook on Spanish gypsy life and art *The Zincali* (1841). Schumann in 1849 was equally a pioneer of their musical composition, notably in his *Spanisches Liederspiel,* Op. 74, and *Spanische Liebeslieder,* Op. 138, in which Geibel's translations were treated in quasi-dramatic form, with modest touches of local colour, for one, two or four voices with piano solo or (in Op. 138) duet accompaniment. No doubt it was Wolf's familiarity with those works and their novel and successful adaptations of a notional Spanish idiom that

---

* *Floresta de Rimas Antiguas Castellanas*, ed. J. N. Böhl de Faber, 1821–5

predisposed him to explore and exploit such sources on his own account, though he may well also have known other settings (e.g. by Brahms or Jensen) from the *Spanisches Liederbuch* of Geibel and Heyse.

They were both prominent among the North German poets who went to Munich in the early 1850s at the invitation of Maximilian II of Bavaria, who had a modest literary talent and a penchant for the society of gifted writers. Paul Heyse (1830–1914) shared Geibel's love of Romance languages and literature, and was also a compelling translator, whose later versions of popular Italian lyrics were also to inspire Wolf (in the *Italienisches Liederbuch*, see pp. 311ff). Geibel revised some of his 1843 translations and added new ones. He also, with typical generosity, gave his younger and as yet unrecognized protégé the run of his own comprehensive library with its anthologies of Spanish and other Romance-language poetry; and he was happy to see Heyse's translations standing beside, and indeed sometimes supplanting, his own in their joint compilation, the *Spanisches Liederbuch* of 1852.

In that book, questions of the sources, authorship and correct text of the original Spanish poems were, perhaps designedly, left rather obscure. They have recently received their first full scholarly elucidation in a detailed monograph.* The attributions given in the notes below are mainly restricted to the incipits and poets cited by Heyse and Geibel themselves, with some brief additional notes on dates or floruit. For those interested in further research, a page reference is provided to the Böhl de Faber anthology† where most of the original Spanish texts are to be found. It has however long been known that some of the German lyrics are not translations but original work offered under the transparent pseudonyms of 'Don Manuel del Rio' for Emanuel Geibel ('of the river', perhaps in honour of his native Lübeck on the river Trave) and 'Don Luis el Chico' for Paul Ludwig Heyse (Luis = Ludwig; perhaps 'the lad' because of his youth and quasi-adoptive status). In addition there are grounds for supposing that some of the other lyrics for which no original Spanish sources can be traced are also the work of Geibel or Heyse, as Sleeman and Davies have suggested. This would be quite typical of anthologies designed to make foreign or domestic literature and tradition available to a contemporary German readership; in just the same way, some of the poems included in the supposed folk-anthology *Des Knaben*

---

* 'Variations on Spanish Themes: The Spanisches Liederbuch of Emanuel Geibel and Paul Heyse and its reflection in the songs of Hugo Wolf' by Margaret G. Sleeman and Gareth A. Davies, in *Proceedings of the Leeds Philosophical and Literary Society*, Literary and Historical Section, 18 (1981)

† op. cit.

Wunderhorn were written by the compilers Arnim or Brentano.*

For Hugo Wolf, the thought of Spain and the Spanish tradition was no doubt musically inspiring; and he would in due course turn to a German translation of Pedro de Alarcon as the textual basis of his two operas, *Der Corregidor* (1895) and the unfinished *Manuel Venegas* (1897). In his *Spanisches Liederbuch* too the imported themes of religious and secular passion, together with the metrical equivalents of dancing feet, snapping fingers, guitars and castanets, and the structural effect of complex rhyme patterns and repeated refrains, must have done much to mould the music into new lively and colourful shapes, as suggested in the separate commentaries below. Conversely the occasionally stilted style, with its classical conventions of Cupid and other mythic or allegorical devices, sometimes audibly inhibits the musical invention. Whatever the outcome, however, the essential source of the art-work, whether considered as the composer's raw material or the poets' finished product, is the German text with its own technical deftness as translation and its own merits and limitations as lyric verse by Geibel or Heyse. One would expect to find a few of their poems in a representative anthology of nineteenth-century German verse; but even as original lyricists their talent was for perfection of form rather than depth of content. And no doubt this was part of their attraction for Wolf, who at this stage of his development, after a comparative subservience to Mörike and Goethe, needed a lesser genre of poetry that his music could assimilate and even dominate. At the same time he would be paying due homage to such famed masters as Lope de Vega and Cervantes, together with many lesser names and much anonymity. The Spanish Songbook thus provides Wolf with a logical transition from great national literature to European folk-art, from the Mörike and Goethe settings of 1888–9 to the Italian songs of 1891–6.

Wolf follows his source-book, as Geibel and Heyse in turn followed theirs, in separating *Geistliche Lieder* (sacred songs, abbreviated as S.g. below, Nos. 137–46) from *Weltliche Lieder* (secular, S.w., Nos. 147–80). He set all but three of the sacred lyrics selected by the translators, and about a third of their ninety-nine secular pieces, almost all love-songs. Seven of the love-songs that he passed over had already been set by Schumann; but so had six of those Wolf chose. So his selection of secular lyrics was unfettered as well as fully representative. His special concentration on the sacred songs however, with their heavy emphasis on guilt and redemption, may well have had some personal significance.

---

* see E. Sams: 'Notes on a Magic Horn', *The Musical Times,* July 1974

137 (S.g. 1) 'Nun bin ich dein...'

15 January 1890   F major   c'–f'

*Now I am yours, you flower of all flowers. My sole and continual song is
in your praise. I strive to be assiduous in dedicating myself to you and to
your suffering. Chosen among women, all my hopes aspire to you, my
inmost being is ever open to you; come to rescue me from the curse of evil
that has so sorely beset me! You star of the sea, haven of bliss, through
whom the afflicted in their sorrow have found salvation, before I die, look
down from heaven, you queen of the suns. The fullness of your mercy can
never fail, you help to victory him who is bowed down with shame. To
cling to you, to lie at your feet, heals all grief and pain. I suffer heavy and
most deserved punishment. I am so afraid of having soon to sleep the sleep
of death. Turn you to me and pilot me through the sea into harbour.*

Heyse's translation of this prayer to the Virgin Mary consists of five verses
in a rhyming and metric scheme which in German (where double rhymes
are rarer than in Spanish) sounds somewhat selfconsciously adroit. Under
the weight and strength of Wolf's musical response, all the frills of the
versification are ironed out into a single simple penitential garment, each
line of which expresses a sinner's prayer and praise. Now nothing
distracts attention from the central theme of supplication that rings
through this beautiful song like a litany. The opening words dictate the
basic 4/2 rhythm ♩ ♩ ♩ 𝅝 round which the harmonies and vocal line
are sensitively inflected, so that despite the slow tempo and the insistent
beat there is no monotony. The opening bars manifest a mood which is
thereafter created afresh in every bar, even in the postlude. This
incorporates not only the rhythm but the vocal melody with which the
song began, with the effect of resolving all that has gone before into an
unshakeable certitude – 'now I am yours'.

NOTES 1. 'Quiero seguir' (Böhl I, p. 1) by the fourteenth-century poet Juan Ruiz,
Archpriest of Hita, is translated by Paul Heyse.
    2. Within the strong structure each variant is meaningful. Note in particular the
basic identity of bars 5–6, 14–15, 23–4, 39–40 plus the two following bars in
each case, compared with the softer and lighter texture of 31–2 etc, 'an dich zu
schmiegen' where the music imagines itself enskied. All those four-bar phrases
come at the ends of verses. The same music also occurs twice at the beginning of a
verse, in the second, 'Frau auserlesen' (with its affinity to motif 19), and the third
'Du Stern der See' where the queen of heaven is directly addressed and described.
But in the first and last verses, where the sinner is reflecting on his own
unworthiness, the music has the yearning inflexion (motif 12) of the first two bars
(compare 1–2 with 35–6, 'Ich leide schwer'). In that last verse, only, there are
heavy bass octaves for 'schwer und wohlverdiente Strafen'. The remaining fourth

verse ('Nie wird versiegen') is differentiated harmonically by divergence from the basic key of F major, showing that this is the emotional climax of the song; especially, within the new tonality, the F#(G♭) major treatment, motif 40, of 'heilt alle Harm und Schaden'.

138 (S.g. 2) 'Die du Gott gebarst...'

5 November 1889   A minor   e'–g''

You who gave birth to God, you pure one, who alone have released us from our chains, make me glad, me who weep, for only your grace and mercy can save us. Lady, turn me wholly to you, so that this torment and this dread may have an end, so that death may find me unafraid, and the light of the heavenly pastures not blind me.

Because you were born immaculate, chosen to dwell among eternal praise, although suffering enfold me I am not lost, if you consent to save me.

Again the highly-wrought Spanish rhyme-scheme preserved in Heyse's translation seems contrived in German; again the unifying piano rhythm, this time ♭𝄴 ♪ ♩ ♩ ♩ ♩ ♩ (which is one way of scanning the first four words, as before, though here the vocal line itself is far more protracted), is so inflected as to avoid all feeling of monotony while creating the impression of a single overmastering emotion. These first two songs are complementary, just as the two poems are; the second has fewer felicities of melody or phrase, but closer structural unity and control.

NOTES 1. 'O Virgen que á Dios pariste' (Böhl I, p. 7) by the fifteenth-century poet Nicolás Nuñez is translated by Paul Heyse.

2. The parallelism with 137 extends to the harmonic and dynamic structure. Again the heaviest bass line (bar 17ff) relates to the heaviest burden of torment and dread, 'Qual und Grauen'; again the song is in the same key almost throughout, with accidentals that are only incidental. The tonality truly diverges only at the emotionally climactic moment where death is mentioned; 'dass der Tod mich furchtlos fände' etc.

3. Here however there are only three verses, and the first and last are linked by the word 'retten' and its rhymes. So the music is in quite strict ABA form (1–16 = 37–49, including a repeated two-bar phrase at 9–10, 42–3). That strictness plus the added bar at 33 permits the inference that the voice has been held back from its expected reprise at bar 34; a Wolfian image of rapt contemplation.

4. Instead of the certitude of 137, 'nun bin ich dein', there is here a prayer as yet unanswered; hence the dominant questioning of motif 31 in the final chords.

139 (S.g. 3) 'Nun wandre, Maria...'

4 November 1889   E minor   g'–f#''

You must journey on, Mary, journey ever onward; already the cocks are crowing and the place is near. Journey on, beloved, you my jewel, and soon we shall be in Bethlehem. Then you can have a good rest, and a sleep. Already the cocks are crowing and the place is near. Well I see, lady, that your strength is failing; alas, I can do little to ease your pains. But take comfort; we shall surely find a lodging there. Already the cocks are crowing and the place is near. If only your time were come, Mary, I'd give a good reward for the good tidings. I'd even give our donkey in exchange. Already the cocks are crowing; come; the place is near.

The poem is in a long Christian tradition of devout imaginative embroidery on the Gospels. The source is Luke II, 1–5:

> ... there went out a decree from Caesar Augustus that all the world should be taxed... And all went to be taxed, every one into his own city. And Joseph also went up from Galilee, out of the city of Nazareth, into Judaea, unto the city of David, which is called Bethlehem... To be taxed with Mary his espoused wife, being great with child.

In these touching verses, Joseph speaks; all he knows at the time is that they have had to undertake a long journey, and that his dear wife is in need of loving comfort. It is this human situation that Wolf's song re-creates, with ineffable tenderness, as if the music were a soothing response to a cry of distress. This reassuring tone keeps the voice mainly within the small span of a fourth, B to E, within which the same notes are heard repeatedly. Yet the typically Wolfian effect is one of shapely singable melody. Similarly the dynamics are calmingly restrained. The music never rises above *mf*, and that for only two half-bars; all the rest is marked *p* and *pp* The journeying figures of the prelude continue throughout the song. Companionable thirds low in the right hand sound out their steady equal quavers over a trudging bass, with a processional effect as the level rises from the lower to the middle register, suggesting an uphill journey. As they level out, and journey on, the quiet comfort of the voice part begins. By 'du Kleinod' (you jewel) a falling left-hand gesture has been unobtrusively added to the walking movement. As soon as the word 'Bethlehem' is reached, that movement is halted, hushed and reflective, as if brought to a standstill by a sudden vision of anticipation. Then, with another upward movement and a few added semiquavers to give a hint of extra effort, the steady plodding resumes at 'Dann ruhest du fein' (then you can have a good rest). Troubled harmonies tell of Joseph's helpless anxiety and solicitude at 'Wohl seh ich, Herrin, die Kraft dir schwinden' (Well I see, lady, that your strength is failing); the left hand, while still maintaining its dotted crotchets and quaver rhythm, again adds its falling gestures. Thus there is extra effort and pain in the piano part; each step is a pang. But the disturbed music relaxes into a brief bright A major at 'Getrost!' (take comfort). The steady journeying resumes, the music is all solace. At 'das Eselein' etc (the donkey) the left hand again gestures, though now in a more consonant context of contentment, even amusement. Finally the piano part moves downhill and away, to a destination already in sight. The voice is heard as if from a far distance singing: 'Komm! nah ist der Ort'. As the little procession moves out of earshot, the piano postlude in its lower register finds and holds, for the first time in the song, the tonic-major key, with a moving warmth and assurance of rest and sleep soon.

NOTES 1. 'Caminad esposa' (Böhl I, p. 16) by Ocaña (floruit c. 1600) is translated by Paul Heyse.

2. The parallel thirds of companionship are motif 16; the music at 'wohl seh' ich, Herrin' etc has the aura of the mystery motif 19; at 'Schmerzen' we hear the painful clash of motif 34. The final soothing *tierce de Picardie* is interestingly anticipated in Schumann's *Mein Herz ist schwer*, Op. 25 no. 15.

140 (S.g. 4) 'Die ihr schwebet um diese Palmen...'

5 November 1889   E major   g'–g'

You who hover around these palm-trees in night and wind, you holy angels, hush the tree-tops, my child is asleep.

You palm-trees of Bethlehem in the raging wind – why must you thresh so angrily tonight? Oh roar not so, be still, lean calmly and gently over us; hush the tree-tops, my child is asleep.

The child of heaven suffers distress; oh, how weary he has grown with all the sorrows of the world. Oh now in sleep his pains are gently eased and dissolved; hush the tree-tops, my child is asleep.

A fierce coldness comes roaring down; with what shall I cover my baby's limbs! Oh all you angels soaring on wings in the wind, hush the tree-tops, my child is asleep.

The verses approach nearer to fine poetry in their own right than is usual in this song-book; and for Wolf it is not enough to represent poetry; the mood and the scene must be re-created afresh. So the music for this song must speak eloquently of winds and wings and tenderness, prayer and lullaby. The piano prelude sets the scene with a semiquaver winnowing of broken chords followed by a soughing melody in the left hand, in which the voice joins. The whole essence of this song is in these few bars, the figurations and melodies of which persist throughout in a ceaseless flow. Dynamic contrasts help to depict the changing bright and dark patterns of sound and sight in the windswept treescape. At 'Ihr Palmen von Bethlehem' bass octaves come blustering up and the voice cries imploringly. The long high melodic line is heard as if shining out through the dark storm and controlling it for a while; a long easeful lull takes possession of the music, until the winds blow down again grim and chill at 'Grimmige Kälte sauset hernieder'. But they are still as it were held in check by the high sweetness of the voice part, and are conjured into peace at the moment of final invocation. Here the composer's imagination is seized by the picture of winged angels riding the wind. Without any halt in the flow or change in the texture of the music the middle syllable of the word 'geflügelt' (winged) streams out over five beats. Then the small miracle is made audible. The piano semiquavers are hushed as the voice sings its final heartfelt appeal – 'stillet die Wipfel! es schlummert mein Kind'. In the postlude the winds abate and are still.

NOTES 1. In the Peters edition, 'die' should be substituted for Wolf's slip 'ihr' in bar 43; 'stillet die Wipfel' is an appeal to the angels, not the tree-tops, each time it occurs.

2. The Virgin's Carol, *Cantorcillo de la Virgen* ('Pues andais en las palmas', Böhl III, p. 13) of Lope da Vega (1562–1613) is translated by Emanuel Geibel. Here as quite often in the so-called Spanish and Italian songs the patterns of rhyme and special felicities of vocabulary that inspired Wolf are contributed by the translator; the original is assonantal but rhymeless.

3. The mediant modulations are so persistent and formative that they seem to have for Wolf here as elsewhere the significance of changing effects of light, motif 24. Within that frame (e.g. E major bars 1–3, G♯ (= A♭) major 6–8, C major 10–12, etc) the flattened sixth of each successive key-centre, C natural, E natural (F♭), A♭, may suggest the idea of continuing and unbroken slumber, motif 37.

4. Cf. Brahms, Op. 91 no. 2 for contralto and piano with viola obligato.

141 (S.g. 5) 'Führ' mich, Kind...'

15 December 1889   A major   e'–f♯''

Lead me, child, to Bethlehem! You are my God, I long to behold you. Who, who could ever succeed in coming to you without your aid? Shake me awake, call me and I will stride out, give your hand to guide me, that I may be on my way; that I may see Bethlehem, there to behold my God. Who, who could ever succeed in coming to you without your aid? I am deep and sore smitten with the heavy sickness of sin. If you will not come to my help I must stumble, I must stagger. Lead me to Bethlehem, you are my God, I long to behold you. Who, who could ever succeed in coming to you without your aid?

The idea of a painful journey to Bethlehem, spiritual or physical, again evokes the undulating quaver thirds and occasional semitonal clashes of *Nun wandre Maria* (139). This later song, though inevitably overshadowed by that masterpiece, has a quiet radiance of its own. The poetic structure with its repeated refrain dictates the ABABA form, and Wolf re-creates that pattern to perfection. The design also adds significance to the verses. 'Führ' mich, Kind, nach Bethlehem', the main vocal melody entreats. The piano part is pining for the desired journey, already setting out. But there is a hint of anxiety among the slight but unresolved harmonic tensions of 'Wem geläng' es, wem' (Who, who could ever succeed). In each of the contrasting B sections this musical material is converted into a penitential garment. At 'Rüttle mich' (Shake me) the strong bass octaves are coloured with the same shade of anxiety. Later, at 'der Sünde schwerem Kranken' (the heavy sickness of sin) there are distressed augmented intervals, suggesting the unquiet thought 'perhaps no help will come'. But after each such passage an intimate reassurance returns. The momentous piano octaves are steadied, even at the words 'sträucheln' and 'schwanken' (stumble, stagger); the tone is hushed, the journeying thirds reappear with their processional melodies, and the music advances and believes again. In the postlude, as in the more comforting moments throughout the song, the journeying hands at last cease to overlap and go on their way together, in full accord.

NOTES 1. The anonymous 'Llevadme, niño, á Belen' (Böhl II p. 37) is translated by Paul Heyse.
   2. The strong and consistent structure permits the inference that any variations will be deliberate and meaningful; thus the words 'dich, mein Gott, dich' are in dotted rhythm at bars 3–4 but in equal crotchets at 37–8 because the singer has gained in confidence.
   3. The processional character of the music, and the quasi-vocal nature of its four-part harmony in the accompaniment, later put into Wolf's mind (admittedly a mind then not far from terminal breakdown) the notion of including this song as an *a cappella* introit for tenor solo and mixed chorus in his unfinished opera *Manuel Venegas*, also based on a Spanish source (letter to Melanie Köchert, 7 July 1897).
   4. The independent melodies in the piano part are certainly noteworthy, especially as a developmental stage in Wolf's own songwriting. The linear thirds of *Nun wandre Maria* (139) are doubled here with an added effect of rhythmic canon; there are two imagined journeys, and the fear is lest they remain unsynchronized. Finally all the ideas of 137 and 141 are blended and distilled into the independent melodies of 142, q.v.
   5. The unresolved chords at 'Rüttle mich' etc recall bars 7–8 of 137. The bass

octaves at e.g. 10–11 have the unease of motif 5; perhaps this theme is remembered from *Blindes Schauen*, 155 (q.v., note 3), written less than three weeks earlier.

142 (S.g. 6) 'Ach, des Knaben Augen...'

21 December 1889   F major   e♭'–f''

Oh, the child's eyes look so clear and beautiful, and they have a nameless radiance that wins all my heart. If only with those sweet eyes he would look at mine! If then he should see his own image there, he would surely smile at me lovingly. So I surrender myself to the sole service of his eyes, for they have a nameless radiance that wins all my heart.

The song itself has a heart-winning radiance. The plain thirds in both hands of the piano part achieve an extraordinary limpidity and grace of melodic rise and fall, quite independently of the vocal line, whose equally steady flow is mainly in repeated notes or else moves by step. It is thus the voice that speaks, and the piano that sings; and yet the recitative is so beguiling as to outshine the broader tunes of the accompaniment. The whole song, with its perpetual fount of fresh melody in five, sometimes six, parts, symbolizes a great and continuous outpouring of simple adoration. In the first verse the swaying and soothing piano chords are heard as a lullaby; they and the voice rise tenderly together to 'Ein Etwas strahlt aus ihnen' (they have a nameless radiance). But then the two lines diverge; the vocal melody falls quietly, as if averting its gaze, while the piano's lullaby goes chiming softly upward. They resume at the earlier lower pitch with 'Blickt' er doch' (if only he would look); the thought returns for a time to the human level, and is there further mellowed by the magical change from F to A♭ major at 'säh' er dann' (if then he should see). The music has a maternal tenderness, as if for all children. And this dual idea, the infusion of warmth into worship, enriches the reprise of the first strain, at 'und so geb ich ganz mich hin' (and so I surrender myself). The postlude is a brief prayer and lullaby together.

NOTES 1. 'Los ojos del niño son' (Böhl II, p. 40) by the fourteenth-century priest Lopez de Ubeda, is translated by Paul Heyse.
2. There is a slight uncertainty of accentuation at the half-bar; no doubt the song, in typical Spanish style, was conceived as a piano piece. The two different scansions of 'ganzes Herz gewinnt' (bars 7–8, 24–5) are surely not intended as deliberate contrast; so the song needs to be sung as if in 3/4 with only slight stress on the first beat.
3. The consecutive thirds of 139 and 141 recur; but here (as in *Zum neuen Jahr*, 39) the thirds and sixths are perhaps more decorative than motivic. Nevertheless

Wolf uses thirds for lullaby music elsewhere, e.g. in the early piano piece *Wiegenlied*.

4. The contour of the first long vocal phrase 'Ach ... erschienen' has been heard elsewhere, e.g. in *Blumengruss* (109), where the same notes in the same key occur in an analogous mood of surrender and abnegation. Its use here may be an involuntary reminiscence of that context. The change to A♭ from the dominant of F (minor) was also heard in the Goethe songs, e.g. *Wie sollt ich heiter bleiben* (130), with a similar effect of infused warmth but without any clear verbal parallel.

5. For the theme of beauty in eyes, see 44, note 2.

143 (S.g. 7) 'Mühvoll komm ich und beladen...'

10 January 1890   G minor   d'–g''

Toilful I come and heavy-laden; receive me, you haven of mercy! See, I come in scalding tears, with humble gestures, grimed with the dust of the earth. You alone can make me as white as the fleece of lambs. You will redeem the wrongs of him who embraces you in repentance. Take then, Lord, this burden from me; toilful I come, and heavy-laden.

Let me kneel before you beseeching that I may anoint your feet with scented spikenard and tears, like the woman you forgave, until my guilt disperses like smoke. You who once told a malefactor 'Today shalt thou be in Paradise!', oh receive me, [receive me] you haven of mercy.

Wolf's genius lay in music which is not only masterly in itself, but gains further lustre and meaning from an intimate connection with the essence of the words. But here music and verse seem to be drawn from rather different sources, and the second part of the contract is arguably unfulfilled. Neither the self-abasement of the poem nor its orthodox pietism was ever anything but alien to Wolf's normal character and temperament. In his music, the helplessly clinging remorse is accorded a new stance and strength, which are then used for self-flagellation. The song takes place as it were within one personality, as one single obsession in one mind; there is hardly a hint of any outside source of mercy or redemption. The poetic address to an implored saviour takes on the tones of soliloquy. Piano chords foreshadow the characteristic obsessive rhythm ¾ ♩ ♪♪♪♪ | ♪.♪ ♩. But in the two-bar prelude those accented quavers are held in reserve; they appear in an inner voice after the vocal entry, so that the piano too can be heard crying out 'Mühvoll komm ich', as well as sounding toilful and heavy-laden. Soon those accented notes on the second and third beats of the bar change to full but staccato chords, at the words 'Sieh, ich komm in Tränen heiss' (see, I come in scalding tears). Thus the accompaniment labours and weeps its way among intensely rich chromatic dissonance, followed by the voice in broken and abject falling phrases. A first emotional climax is reached at 'Nimm denn, Herr!' (Take then, Lord); here the tensions are resolved in a strong affirmation of the main theme in more diatonic terms. But this is soon reabsorbed into the chromatic texture at the repetition of the opening words, further intensified by the piano with a return to its main theme. The music of the first page reappears, with the staccato chords again falling pat for more tears, leading on to the diatonic climax at 'O nimm mich an!' (oh receive me). Here the voice is briefly high and ecstatic before bowing in submission down to the closing words. The postlude restates the obsessive rhythm that has resounded throughout the song.

NOTES 1. Wolf repeats 'nimm mich an' in the last line.

2. The text is not in Böhl, and differs markedly from most of the other cited sources in being basically biblical. Nearly every line calls for a concordance, and the language of the Old Testament is as much in evidence as the familiar Gospel references, e.g. Luke XXIII, 43 for the words from the cross. The anointing conflates three sources; the tears of forgiveness are Luke VII, 37–8 and 48, and the spikenard John XII, 3. The *Spanisches Liederbuch* of Heyse and Geibel cites a notional Spanish first line, 'Vengo triste y lastimado'. But the supposed author, Don Manuel del Rio, seems otherwise unknown to literary history, and the text sounds much more German-Protestant than Spanish-Catholic. No doubt Don Manuel was really Emanuel Geibel, as his biographer suggested. See also 177, note 1, and p. 249.

3. The keynote of agonized obsession in the verses is struck (motifs 27 and 33) with superb technical assurance. In 69 bars of slow 3/4 the two-bar piano rhythm ♩ ♫♫♩ | ♪·♪ ♩ is heard some thirty times. Within the firm frame of prelude and postlude, the second thirty bars of accompaniment are essentially the first thirty repeated in varying transpositions. Of the first thirty, the second four echo the first four; the next two bars are twice repeated. Each idea is the same idea, and that consists either of repeated emphatic single notes, conveying the burden of 'mühvoll komm ich' or else of repeated dissonant staccato chords, giving the sense of 'ich komm in Tränen' (motif 26 as in *Ganymed*, 135). The augmented fifths at e.g. bar 26 are motif 23; the final dominant is motif 31.

4. In the repetition of the second thirty bars there are certain variants explicable as following the inflexions of the vocal line. But there seems no clear reason why the piano part should not be exactly parallel in bar 17 as in bar 47, in which case one would expect D sharps in the last left-hand chord of the former.

5. The cyclic patterns of the piano's melodic lines (e.g. bars 19–24, 49–54) recur at moments of intense inwardness or constraint, e.g. in 189, 218, 222, and 240.

144 (S.g. 8) 'Ach, wie lang die Seele schlummert...'

19 December 1889   E♭ major   c'−a♭''

Alas, how long the soul slumbers! The time has come for it to awaken. Deserving the name of death is its sleep, so heavy and fearful, since it was overcome by that intoxication it gulped from the poison of sin. But now the light it has longed for breaks blindingly into its eyes; the time has come for it to awaken. Though it may now seem deaf to the sweet angel choirs, yet if it timidly listens upwards, it will hear the weeping of God as a little child. After a long night of slumber such a day of mercy now laughs upon it; the time has come for it to awaken.

Voice and piano join forces to provide the prelude. Its seven-bar setting of the opening phrases (down to 'sich ermuntre', awaken) summarizes the entire thematic material – a basic rhythm to a falling motif plus a rising semitone for the sleeping of the soul, and a rather jaded harmonic progression for its awakening. The two are related by the dotted rhythm, which contains the sound and sense of 'sich ermuntre' as it were potentially in the sleep motif and actually in the awakening. The piano's falling intervals lengthen and recur as the voice bewails the soul's protracted slothfulness. But at 'doch nun ihrer Sehnsucht Licht' (but now the light it has longed for) the coming change is gently intimated. The rhythm is strengthened by bass semibreves on the beat; the sleep motif is inverted; the voice sings out softly in free, almost rousing, melodies. In the second verse, at 'Mochte sie gleich taub erscheinen' (though it may now seem deaf), the soul's harmonies are a little more hectic; its sevenths now turn upwards, or attain new heights in the keyboard, in response to the new visions and sounds in the verses. This time the diatonic contrast, when it recurs at 'Da nach langer Schlummernacht' (After a long night of slumber), is even more reassuring. The bass semibreves almost seem to doze off again inadvertently. True, the text says only that the hour of the soul's awakening is at hand; but one feels it should offer a more alert response to the blinding light of heaven. The apparent discrepancy between the restrained gentleness, even gentility, of the music, and the sublime transcendence of its subject sounds atypical.

NOTES 1. The anonymous 'Mucho ha que el alma duerme' (Böhl I, p. 25) is translated by Emanuel Geibel.

2. As in 143, voice and piano share the prelude, no doubt because both poems begin with an extrapolated refrain.

3. For other uses of rising semitones in somewhat analogous verbal contexts, see 32, note 4. The falling sleep theme incongruously recalls the yawning of *Der Schäfer* (107); the waking is motif 36; the bass semibreves are motif 39.

4. There are evident rhythmic affinities between this song and the next, 145, dated some three weeks earlier. This suggests that Wolf, consciously or not, is recomposing an earlier inspiration. This phenomenon occurs elsewhere, e.g. 222 is (perhaps intentionally) based on 224, while part of 225 is (no doubt inadvertently) based on 214.

5. The melody of the refrain recalls the joyous bridal motif that shines through Act II of *Götterdämmerung*.

145 (S.g. 9) 'Herr, was trägt der Boden hier ...'

24 November 1889   E minor   b–e''

Lord, what grows in this ground that you water so bitterly? 'Thorns, dear heart, for me; and for you the beauty of flowers.' Oh, where such streams flow, shall there a garden thrive? 'Yes, and know this, garlands of many different kinds are woven there.' Oh my Lord, for whose adornment are those garlands woven, say! 'Those of thorns are for me; those of flowers I hand to you.'

This song and its following counterpart (146) are imaginary colloquies between sinner and redeemer. Wolf reaches great heights in his re-creation of the bittersweet dramatic paradox of the poems. It is the redeemed sinner who questions in anguish, while the Saviour answers from Gethsemane or Golgotha in tones of beatific calm and comfort. The solemn phrases of the piano prelude continue as the voice enters; they seem to suggest with each stab of pain an involuntary gesture of sympathy and love. Each time the voice poses its insistent questions, four sharp dissonances are gently resolved. At each reply, the piano chords are deeper in pitch, fuller in sound, firmer in rhythm, sweeter in harmony; similarly the vocal melody warms and brightens, suffused with comfort. So the song proceeds until the last reply summons all that has gone before into one compelling final phrase, first sombre with dark octaves in the piano at 'Die von Dornen sind für mich', then ineffably tender, with a simple chordal accompaniment, at 'die von Blumen reich' ich dir'.

NOTES 1. The anonymous 'Qué producirá mi Dios' (Böhl I, p. 31) is translated by Paul Heyse.

2. The two contrasting rhythms (e.g. bars 6 and 7) recur in 144 (e.g. last two bars); see note 4 to the latter song.

3. The resolving dissonances of the piano prelude (cf. the pain motif 34) recall those of Schubert's *Dass sie hier gewesen* (D775) where the conjunction of sorrow and love, though solely on the human level, is also the theme; there is a further verbal link in the flowing ('rinnen' in both texts) of tears. Wolf's last bar also shares a Schubertian echo (cf. the last bar of *Wanderers Nachtlied*, D768). The final *tierce de Picardie* is motivic, as in *Nun wandre, Maria* (139)

4. A timeless atmosphere is conveyed by the piano's constant omission of the first beat in each bar; conversely its appearance in the last three bars lends a new presence to the last phrases. Dramatic though Wolf's intentions manifestly are, however, they are not best served either in this song or 146 by performance as a duet for soprano and baritone.

146 (S.g. 10) 'Wunden trägst du, mein Geliebter...'

16 December 1889   B minor   f#'–f#''

You bear wounds, my loved Lord, and they cause you pain; would that I bore them in your stead.

Lord, who dares so to stain your brow with blood and sweat? 'Soul, these marks are the price of your salvation. Of these wounds I must die, for my great love of you.' Lord, would I might bear them for you, for they will be your death. 'If this suffering moves you, child, say rather that they will be your life; there was not one of them struck from which life does not flow for you.' Oh how my heart and mind ache with your anguish! 'Gladly would I endure far worse to save you, for he alone knows how to love who has been consumed by love's fire!'

You bear wounds, my loved Lord, and they cause you pain; would that I bore them in your stead.

This fitting finale to the sacred songs has much in common with its previous counterpart. But it stands nearer to the Passion. The agonized questions are now accompanied by the middle register of the piano, the comforting replies by the higher register, becoming at times remote. Into this fine song Wolf pours a libation of his Spanish devotional music, resuming and reuniting the earlier responses to love and compassion that resound throughout the cycle. The thematic connections with the former colloquy are manifest enough, for example in the distressful dissonances and the frequent absence of a first beat in the piano part; both harmony and time are again in suspension. Wolf's music also implies, by a concordance of thematic cross-reference, that the Saviour's interlocutor in each song was also the pilgrim of *Führ' mich, Kind, nach Bethlehem* (141) who there beheld the eyes of the holy child, as in *Ach, des Knaben Augen* (142). It further suggests, whether intentionally or not, that the sinner in question was Wolf himself, whose own guilt-feelings and craving for love and forgiveness were exceedingly deep and durable.

NOTES 1. 'Feridas teneis mi vida' (Böhl I, p. 37) by José de Valdivielso (1560–1638) is translated by Emanuel Geibel.

2. The typical structure is derived from the poem; the same three lines at beginning and end provide a symmetrical frame (bars 1–10 and 47–60, with the

dominant ending of motif 31) for an interior threefold strophic repetition, bars 11–22, 23–34, 35–46. This repetition demands a G♯ on the second and third right-hand chords of bar 37, just as in 13 and 25 – a correction made in the *Kritische Gesamtausgabe*, but still needed in older Peters editions.

3. Within that pattern, bars 15–16 have the opening melody of *Ach, des Knaben Augen* (142), while bars 11–14 suggest the Bethlehem pilgrimage of *Führ'mich, Kind* (141) at bars 10–11, 27–8; further, bar 10 here recalls bar 8 of 141.

4. 'Wunden' and 'schmerzen' evoke the painful dissonances of motif 34: The dominant ending is motif 31.

147 (S.w. 1) 'Klinge klinge, mein Pandero...'

20 November 1889   G minor   d♭'–f''

Jingle, jingle, my tambourine, but my heart is thinking of other things.

If you, joyful instrument, could understand my torment and experience it, every tone you emit would lament for my grief. For the twirling and bowing of the set dances I wildly beat time, trying to silence the thoughts that remind me of my grief.

And oh, sirs, while I'm brandishing my tambourine, my heart often feels like breaking, and my singing becomes a cry of pain; for my heart is thinking of other things.

The simultaneous musical portrayal of a tambourine ringing out gaily and a heart suffering in silence has perhaps proved rather too taxing a task even for Wolf. The piano thrums and jingles exhilaratingly in its solo passages; even so, some of the singer's sorrow has infiltrated the instrument. Yet the measured pulse of the accompaniment with its incessant staccato semiquavers jingling and tinkling over a strongly-stamped Spanish dance rhythm provides the usual strong framework within which the subtle and flexible vocal line is free to choose and develop its expressive points. Thus the opening words are set to the predictable 3/4 rhythm ♪♩♪♪♪♪ | ♩ ♩; but the answering phrase at 'doch an andres denkt mein Herz' (but my heart is thinking of other things) is wistfully extended over four whole bars, to show that the balance of happiness is already disturbed. The verses thrice introduce three consecutive rhyming lines the sense of which sometimes overruns the end of the line. So in arranging for each rhyme to fall on the first beat of a two-bar phrase, Wolf makes space within the metric scheme for the sound and significance of particular words to be specially savoured, e.g. the high and sustained 'Qual' (torment) in the first quatrain, 'wild' (wildly) in the second, 'oftmals' (often) in the last. Similarly the leaps and curves of the vocal line are themselves verbally expressive, as if the melody were a mode of choreography; thus after each of those three highlights the voice suddenly droops and darkens, exhausted by effort and grief. The whole song manifests a creative intelligence fashioning and reshaping musical material which, though not itself of the finest quality or most original design, is memorably remodelled for maximum pictorial, dramatic and emotive effect.

NOTES 1. 'Tango vos, el mi pandero' (Böhl I, p. 289) by the sixteenth-century poet Alvaro Fernandez de Ameida is translated by Emanuel Geibel.

2. The piano's persistent semitones are motif 4, here indicative of forced gaiety. The notionally Spanish snap and flounce of sforzando chords, grace notes and trills recall Schumann's settings of Geibel's translations, such as *Der Contrabandiste* Op. 74 (e.g. its bar 24).

3. Of course Wolf knew his *Carmen* (cf. Act III prelude). There is another less explicable echo; the piano interludes here (bar 10ff) seem indebted to Beethoven's Sonata Op. 53 ('Waldstein'), bars 62–3 of the first movement.

4. Cf. Anton Rubinstein, Op. 76 no. 6; Jensen, Op. 21 no. 1. Schumann's Op. 69 no. 1 (SSAA) sets the same poem in Eichendorff's translation – 'Schwirrend Tamburin, dich schwing' ich'.

148 (S.w. 2) 'In dem Schatten meiner Locken...'

17 November 1889 (orchestrated 1895)   B♭ major   d'–f''

In the shadow of my tresses my lover has fallen asleep. Shall I wake him up now? Ah, no. I carefully combed out my curling tresses early each morning. But in vain is my labour, for the winds dishevel them.

Shadowing tresses, sighing winds, sent my love to sleep. Shall I wake him up now? Ah, no. I'll have to hear how grieved he is by his long yearning, how my sunbrown cheek gives him life and takes it away again.

And he calls me his serpent; and yet he fell asleep at my side. Shall I wake him up now? Ah no.

This justly famous song exemplifies the category of slight yet perfect work which is so typical of one aspect of Wolf's genius. The poem is not especially felicitous; indeed some of the syntax seems too evidently contrived for the sake of the rhyme-scheme. But the imagined situation and character-sketch are appealing; and Wolf was moved by them to make a song full of melodic enchantment and harmonic subtlety. The soft bolero rhythm of the prelude's first bar persists almost throughout the song, a motif of amused and loving thoughts; the singer is immobilized, but her mind is dancing. This theme is delicately varied in tempo and harmony to reflect her changing mood. The question-and-answer refrain

'Weck ich ihn nun auf? Ach nein!' is delightfully interpreted as finding her in two minds. Mischief and affection impel her to wake him, the music suggests. But tenderness, as of a mother watching a sleeping child, supervenes. So the mischievous rhythm soon slows down. 'Schlief mir mein Geliebter' is sung to a marked rallentando, lingeringly and lovingly. Then the movement halts altogether, on a sustained arpeggio chord at 'ein'; the lover has fallen asleep in music as well as words. Mischief returns in a new bright key: 'Weck ich ihn nun auf?' with a rising and questioning inflexion at 'auf'; shall I wake him up? The piano echoes its own question; Shall I? . . . Shall I?'. 'Ach nein', sings the voice in a sweetly resigned fall. But the piano is not yet quite convinced. The chord within which the word 'nein' is being sustained turns out to be the wrong chord, and is gently changed so that the piano can ask its question yet again, reaching, with the same small sigh, the same conclusion. It is characteristic of Wolf at his most inventive that elusive subtleties of this kind are not obtruded into the music. What we hear is a fresh flow of melody in brightening harmonic sequence. Intuitive forces are at work moulding the music into the shape of an idea, infusing it with the relevant emotion, making that emotion audible. The dancing piano figurations now reappear until a more even rhythm in spread chords is heard at 'schläferten den Liebsten ein' (sent my love to sleep). The tender musing recurs and flares into the brightness of F♯-major tonality for the words 'braune Wange' (brown cheek) before resuming in the original key. After a final reprise of the question and answer the song ends with a summary from the piano postlude; two bars of the dancing rhythm for the singer's temperament, one bar for her question and the last two notes for her answer 'Ach nein', this time subdued and without key-change; the final reprieve.

NOTES 1. The anonymous 'Á la sombra de mis cabellos' (Böhl I, p. 283) is translated by Paul Heyse, whose 'zerzausen' is preferable to Wolf's first edition's 'zersausen'.

2. Mediant modulations occur elsewhere in passages suggesting the changing effects of light (motif 24). Their use here may be even more metaphorical, to suggest brightening and fading smiles of intending and relenting, or in more general terms sleeping and waking. But the harmonic parallels with *Die ihr schwebet* (140) might also suggest a changing pattern of light and shade among wind-blown or otherwise parted leaves or curls as a basic image.

3. The analogous arpeggios in *Und willst du deinen Liebsten* (203), together with the word 'strählen' (comb) in both, strongly suggest that the arpeggios here are an image of the rhythmic gestures of hair-combing and their lulling effect, e.g. at 'schläferten den Liebsten ein': motif 28.

4. The elated F♯−major tonality at 'braune Wange' is motif 40. For the dividing melodic lines of the main piano theme, see motif 14: the mood is one of almost maternal tenderness.

5. The song was orchestrated by Wolf and incorporated into his opera *Der Corregidor* (1895) where it is sung by Frasquita in Act I.
6. Cf. Brahms, Op. 6 no. 1; Jensen, Op. 1 no. 4.

149 (S.w. 3) 'Seltsam ist Juanas Weise...'

14 November 1889   G minor   d♭'–f♯''

Strange are the ways of Juana. When I stand in grief, when I sigh and say: today, she softly says 'tomorrow'. She is glum when I am glad, she sings merrily when I weep. If I say I find her attractive, she says she'll always shrink from me. Proofs of such cruelty break my heart with grief; when I sigh and say: today, she softly says 'tomorrow'. If I lift my eyelids, she always contrives to lower her gaze, only to raise it again the moment I lower mine. When I praise her as a saint, she contentiously calls me a demon; when I sigh and say: today, she softly says 'tomorrow'. I am instantly called hopeless if I should modestly mention some small achievement; if I dare hope for the joys of heaven, she prophesies hell for me. Yes, her heart is so icy that if she saw me dying of grief and heard my last sigh: today, she'd still say softly 'tomorrow'.

The cautious triggering phrase 'Wenn ich seufz'und sage heut' cunningly changes the pressure of its importuning from brusque demand to sustained request, then to hesitant entreaty. Each time the vocal melody is differently harmonized and inflected, with an insinuating appeal. Each time the pistol of rejection is fired with the same fatal result, no less deadly for being fitted with a silencer; the soft but unyielding answer always falls on the same notes. Yet these too are very slightly varied in value, in both voice and piano. We are to understand that for the singer, at any rate, the situation is not entirely desperate; he will go on making his proposals, always on a major chord, hoping one day to receive a response in the same encouraging tonality. The soft answer turns away wrath; there is always tomorrow. Thus the poem is interpreted by the music as wryly rueful and not without humour. The piano part has a wistful guitar-theme of detached spread chords introduced by a sustained bass note, the very model of the persistent serenader. The chords break off abruptly and lapse into sad silence on the first beat of every other bar. It is precisely at this moment that the plaintive two-bar phrase of the voice begins. Thus vocal line and accompaniment alternate and overlap ceaselessly; but, like Juana and her unfortunate lover, they never really come to terms. In much of the song the voice is heard alone save for the aftermath of a quaver chord spun out by the sustaining pedal – as tenuous a relationship as that described. The effect is that of the quaint mechanical figures sometimes seen on old cathedral clock-towers; as one emerges, the other retires. Voice and piano pursue their separate ways with a flawless delicate dovetailing which is irresistible when sung with the perfect intonation that the musical logic of the chromatic movement demands.

NOTES 1. The anonymous 'Estraño humor tiene Juana' (not in Böhl) is translated by Emanuel Geibel.

2. The drooping chromatic sorrow of motif 22, so characteristic of Goethe's Harper, is here put to mock-tragic uses for the Spanish guitarist. 'Lebe wohl' resounds much as in the Mörike song of that name (48); though the mood here as evinced e.g. in the final sharp piano chord is one of affectionate exasperation rather than passionate despair.

150 (S.w. 4) 'Treibe nur mit Lieben Spott...'

15 November 1889   G minor   d'–f''

Just go on mocking at love, my dearest; the god of love will mock at you too, one day. You may thrive on mockery now, as you please; women bring joy and sorrow to us all. Just go on mocking at love, my dearest; the god of love will mock at you too, one day. If you are now too haughty for wooing, believe, oh believe that love will seize you as its prey; if you mock at my need, my dearest, the god of love will mock at you too, one day. Whoever lives in flesh, let them always ponder this – Cupid sleeps but then suddenly stirs and inflicts wounds. Just you go on mocking at love, my dearest; the god of love will mock at you too, one day.

This is perhaps intended by Wolf, though without any clear textual justification, as a pendant to the previous song, a reproof to the heartless Juana; the key and time-signatures are the same, the moderate tempo hardly different ('mässig' replaces the previous 'sehr mässig'), the harmonies similar and the spread guitar chords (though here restricted to a brief prelude) entirely analogous. The mood, now more incisive, is still not without a certain tenderness. Yet a deliberate foot-stamping and finger-snapping dance-measure dominates the song; the local colour is applied pictorially as an illustration of petulance and disdain. The first vocal phrase of the recurring refrain has the characteristic rhythmic shape ¾ ♪♪♪♪♪ ♪ ♪ ♪ imposed by the opening words, with an added dotted-note snap at 'Geliebte mein' (my dearest). Voice and piano freely interchange musical ideas throughout, transforming the monologue into an imagined colloquy. In the quicker contrasting section at 'Magst an Spotten nach Gefallen du dich weiden' (You may thrive on mockery now, as you please) the piano jars and clashes peevishly. But these asperities are softened at the corresponding passage beginning 'Bist auch jetzt zu stolz zum Minnen' (If you are now too haughty for wooing); and the refrain is, as always, douce in its remonstrance. The final slight slowing and hushing reveal the singer's real feelings.

NOTES 1. The anonymous 'Burla bien con desamor' (not in Böhl) is translated by Paul Heyse.

2. As so often, the variations from the basic four-bar structure imposed by the poem are used as expressive device; hence the lengthening to five bars in order to emphasize 'Leiden' and 'Wunden' by prolongation. Both those passages are interestingly akin to the mystery motif 19.

3. In a song where mockery is mentioned one would expect motif 4; in this one, which is about nothing else, the thematic acciaccaturas are at times exaggerated into semitonal clashes, in a parody of motif 34. See also 162, note 2. The quasi-horn-passages at bar 5 etc may be motivic in the sense of casting off or escape (motif 8).

151 (S.w. 5) 'Auf dem grünen Balkon . . .'

12 December 1889   A major   e'–f''

On the green balcony my girl is looking at me through the trellis. With her eyes she blinks fondly, with her finger she tells me: No! Fortune, though it never constantly favours young love in this world, has yet granted me one joy, and there too I must falter. I hear now flattery, now petulance, when I come to her window-shutter. Always, after the custom of girls, a drop of pain falls into my joy. With her eyes she blinks fondly, with her finger she tells me: No! How can she reconcile her coldness and my fire? Because she is my heaven, I see darkness alternating with light; in vain are my laments that the sweet little creature has never yet twined her arms around mine. Yet she keeps me so delicately in suspense, with her eyes she blinks fondly, with her finger she tells me: No!

Many elements combine to make this perhaps the most instantly compelling song that even Wolf ever wrote. First, the poem is attractive in its own right; the charm and chime of phrase and rhyme clamour for musical expression. Then this pleasure is enhanced by the perfect matching of the vocal melodies and piano part with the sound and sense of the words, evoking an irresistible tenderness and exaltation. Add to this again, on the purely musical plane, the rhythmic understanding between voice and piano, each contributing to a continuous swing and sway. Yet again, add the ceaseless flow of lilting melody in three separate strands; not only the vocal line, not only the beguiling arabesques of the right hand but the spread guitar-chords of the left have a melodic part to play. All these elements act and interact, play and interplay, in a continuous counterpoint; and yet are marvellously brought together by the sheer quality of the musical ideas and their treatment into one single organic whole, in which there still remains room for such special felicities as the amorously melting surrender of the surrounding harmonies at the sustained notes of 'ihr Fensterlädchen' (her window-shutter) and later at 'schlang um meine' (twined around mine). Those are the two moments when the notional serenader mentally approaches closest to his coy mistress. And Wolf, temperamentally much in sympathy with that predicament, has ventured on a little prophecy by way of consolation. The song-form is ABABA, where A contains the sad 'she tells me: No!' The first 'Nein!' has piano support. At the second, the piano note is slightly shifted away from the first beat of the bar. At its last appearance the piano remains silent on the subject. The point is also made separately, and almost as subtly, by the voice. The first time we hear the phrase 'Sagt sie mir: Nein!' it is clearly 'She says: No!' The second is much less positive in its negation. The third is clearly 'She *says*: No! ...'. It is a very winning song.

NOTES 1. The anonymous text 'Mirandome está mi niña' (not in Böhl) is translated by Paul Heyse.

2. Again, as in 150 (see note 2), the departures from basic structure are expressively significant; thus the expected seven-bar sentence is extended to eight at bar 29 to permit the long and longing extension of arms at 'meine'.

3. There is a hint of the rising and falling sixths of the song-motif 11, e.g. in the opening vocal melody.

152 (S.w. 6) 'Wenn du zu den Blumen gehst...'

1 November 1889 (orchestrated 5–6 December 1897)   A major   d#'–g''

When you go to gather flowers, pluck the loveliest to grace yourself with; oh, when you stand in the garden, it is yourself you must gather. All the flowers well know that your beauty is past compare; any flower that beheld you would have to turn pale and droop. When you go to gather flowers, pluck the loveliest to grace yourself with; oh, when you stand in the garden, it is yourself you must gather. Sweeter than roses are the kisses that your lips bestow, for the charm of flowers ends where your love-charm but begins. When you go to gather flowers, pluck the loveliest to grace yourself with; oh, when you stand in the garden, it is yourself you must gather.

Wolf's rich and beautiful music is a response to the poem's intense insistence on formal conceit and pattern, the colour and design of its verbal flower-garden. In combining the expressive fluency of Schumann's songwriting with the contrapuntal sureness of Bach himself the music at first follows well-known paths, but soon strikes out in new directions of its own. None of the Spanish songs is authentically Spanish, or is intended to be, or indeed could be, given the characteristic cadence of their translations; but this one is quintessentially German. Voice and piano begin together with a simple walking tune that simultaneously sets the words and the image of the opening phrase 'Wenn du zu den Blumen gehst'. At first the accompaniment is like a simple two-part invention, to match the naive thought of the two kinds of beauty. But at the words 'Ach, wenn du in dem Gärtlein stehst' (oh, when you stand in the garden) the music is set flowering. In the piano left hand the two original strains are crossed to form a new idea; that is to say, the bass and alto parts of the initial walking music are recombined, in a brief reminiscence of the loved one's entry into the garden. Over this an added treble part peals out in high repeated accented notes and then comes chiming downwards. Now it is the voice's turn to grow and develop. At 'müsstest du dich selber pflücken' (it is yourself you must gather) the sedate walking is abandoned. These words are wedded to a curving melody that goes straying amazed among the bar-lines, as if the thought expressed were among the most novel and striking ever uttered. Now the piano accompaniment further burgeons into a fourth voice; and so the song proceeds, with strands of melody weaving and interweaving a garland of their own. Again the voice decorates and prolongs the verbal conceit at 'lieblicher als Rosen' (sweeter than roses) etc. But at the final repetition of 'müsstest du dich selber pflücken', the music indicates that the singer has now grown more accustomed to this idea. It seems to him now not quite so breathtaking but more familiar and even more beautiful; so the vocal melody finds an easier and more flowing curve down to the end of its line. Two bars of piano postlude say dulcetly 'wenn zu Blumen gehst' as the song ends with a quiet meditation on those key words.

NOTES 1. The anonymous 'Niña si a la huerta vas' (not in Böhl) is translated by Paul Heyse. The 'die' before 'Küsse' in bar 29 seems to be Wolf's own interpolation, designed to keep the melody flowing.

2. The regular nine-bar ABABA construction is noteworthy, especially the extension of bars 15–18 into 33–6. Among so much that is identical and symmetrical the left-hand crotchet D of bar 27 (so in the *Kritische Gesamtausgabe*) ought surely to be a quaver, as in bar 9.

3. The recombining idea described above is an unprecedented image, even for Wolf. From bars 1–2 he takes right-hand notes 1–6, left-hand notes 5–8, and thus makes a new ground, left hand bar 5, in which a new melody can grow. The bell-notes plus thirds and sixths recall *Zum neuen Jahr* (39), also in Wolf's bright or

springtime key of A major. *Frühling übers Jahr* (113) has the same poetic mood and the same basic idea as this song (152).

4. There are internal Spanish affinities; e.g. in key, structure and texture, with *Auf dem grünen Balkon* (151), the 'dramatic' equivalent to this lyric setting. See also 153, note 4.

5. The song was orchestrated with a view to inclusion in Wolf's unfinished opera *Manuel Venegas* (1897).

153 (S.w. 7) 'Wer sein holdes Lieb verloren...'

28 October 1889 (orchestrated 1–4 December 1897)   F# minor   f#'–f#''

Whoever has lost his sweet love through not understanding love – better if he had never been born. I lost her there in the garden, as she plucked roses and blossoms. Brightly on her cheeks glowed shame and joy in gentle grace, and she spoke to me of love. But I, greatest of all fools, could find no answer for her – would I had never been born. I lost her there in the garden as she spoke of the pangs of love, for I dared not tell her how I am hers alone. She sank down amid the flowers. But I, greatest of all fools, gained no advantage even from that – would that I had never been born! [Whoever has lost his sweet love through not understanding love – better if he had never been born.]

As in 149 the singer's misfortunes are described plaintively, even querulously, but not without affection or humour. The doleful phrases of the prelude lie mainly within a compass of just two semitones, a melody fully as inhibited as the hapless hero. These wistful vocal lines combine with similar sad little phrases from the piano, enlivened with soulful leaps. Like the singer, the music is made to lag behind long after the event. At 'Hell auf ihren Wangen glühten' (Brightly on her cheeks glowed) etc the piano is still saying to itself the words of four bars earlier, borrowing the previous vocal line for that purpose; 'Ich verlor sie dort im Garten' etc. But the love thus parodied, though belated, is enduring; the piano interlude after 'von Liebe sprach sie mir' (she spoke to me of love) is replete with grave tenderness. Voice and piano now vie in self-reproach; but again the besetting sins of delay and inertia are amusingly mirrored in the music. As the voice says 'ich wagte nicht zu sagen' (I dared not tell), the piano is still singing 'ich verlor sie dort im Garten', four bars too late as usual. The tender piano interlude recurs after 'In den Blumen sank sie hin' (she sank down among the flowers), followed by the same outburst of self-reproach; finally the song reverts to its original strains of helpless and childlike inhibition.

271

NOTES 1. The final repetition comes from Wolf, not his source, which is the anonymous 'Quien gentil señora pierde' (Böhl I, p. 280) translated by Emanuel Geibel.

2. A structural comparison shows that the three bars 19–21 correspond to the two bars 40–1; the former passage has been extended to linger out the mixed feelings of shame and pleasure.

3. The idea of childish helplessness is well conveyed by motif 2, most manifestly in the piano part at the key phrase 'ich verlor sie dort im Garten'.

4. Thematic affinities, and the placing of the song in the volume, suggest that Wolf envisaged this as a sad sequel to 152. It too was intended for inclusion in the unfinished opera *Manuel Venegas* (1897). But the former song embodies too contented and articulate a lover for the juxtaposition to be wholly convincing.

5. The time-signature of 2/4 is perhaps not quite accurate; the tonic stress is felt in practice on the first beat of every other bar, as if the song were really in common time with extra barlines inserted. Once again this effect implies that the piano part was the primary inspiration.

154 (S. w. 8) 'Ich fuhr über Meer ...'

31 October 1889   B minor   d'–g#''

I sailed over sea, I fared over land; happiness – that I found never. The others around me, how they rejoiced. I rejoiced never! Happiness I hunted, from sorrows I suffered, as a right I demanded what love refused me. I hoped and dared, but no happiness flourished for me, and so I never beheld any. I bore without complaining the sore suffering, and thought the bad times would pass by. But it was the happy days that fled away, and I never caught up with them.

The verses sound barren; despite their protestations, they are hardly more than a rather tedious series of complaints, unrelieved by any illuminating thought or insight. Perhaps this hard luck story struck a responsive chord in Wolf, whose own biography contains long chapters of isolation and depression. Taking his cue from the first words 'Ich fuhr über Meer', he attempts to infuse a passionate intensity into his music by means of a relentlessly rolling and tossing theme worked out with some ingenuity and force in the piano part. But then he has to retard this driving rhythm by extensive and repeated rallentandos in order to match the limp pathos of the text. This saps the vitality of the song, which thus becomes reckonable among Wolf's comparative failures. But the detailed musico-verbal imagery is as noteworthy as ever. The wide-ranging left-hand melody of the first three bars, roaming over land and sea, the peremptory knocking accents at 'Verlangt' ich' (I demanded) clamouring for admittance at love's closed door, the image of fleeting days at 'Tage, wie eilen sie' — all these would have proved fierily effective for a less dampening poem.

NOTES 1. The anonymous 'Las tierras corrí', (not in Böhl) is translated by Paul Heyse, whose 'und' before 'ich jubelte nie!' is omitted by Wolf, presumably in order to secure uniformity among the three clinching final phrases (each beginning on the second beat of the bar).

2. The thematic material based on the interval of a minor third is characteristic of this song book; see also 122, note 1.

3. Given the theme, some form of the unrest of motif 5 was to be expected; indeed, the piano left hand relies on this formula perhaps overmuch. Its knocking at 'verlangt' ich' is cognate with motifs 27 and 33.

155 (S.w. 9) 'Blindes Schauen...'

26 November 1889   B minor   f#'-g''

Blind seeing, dark light, sad glory, dead life, calamity that seemed prosperity, happy weeping, pleasure full of fear, sweet gall, parched moisture, war in peace on all sides; love, your promise of blessing was false, for your curse has robbed me of my sleep.

For the piano part of this song, Wolf has devised a motif of great strength and unifying force. Perhaps it deserved a better fate than that of uneasy yoke-fellow to these verses. There is no attempt at a musical equivalent for their literary figure of oxymoron, in which contrasting terms are juxtaposed to give special rhetorical pungency to the expression. Instead, the cue is taken from the last sentence. The light, the glory, the pleasure and the sweetness of love are left to one side; it is all malediction, no blessing. From the very first bar of prelude the music begins to rage and tear; the postlude is a shouted outburst of thwarted anger. The song has superlative dramatic effect, but not the same order of musico-verbal equivalence.

NOTES 1. 'Vista ciega, luz oscura' (Böhl I, p. 301) by Rodrigo de Cota (floruit 1510) is translated by Paul Heyse.

2. Perhaps the piano part was preconceived. The introduction of its left-hand rhythm $\frac{4}{4}$ ♪ ♩. ♪♩ into the vocal line at bars 15 and 17 is not motivated by the scansion of the words. The inversion of the right-hand theme at bars 11–13 is not motivated by the sense of the words. Each sounds more like absolute than expressive music.

3. Yet Wolf may after all have found some equivalent for the paradox of the poem; the apparently strong left-hand rhythm concentrates on the weak beats of the bar (cf. motif 2). The main motif recurs in *Führ mich, Kind* (141) in contexts expressive of anxiety or fear; its hammered diminished sevenths in the postlude are motif 27.

4. The poem taxed its translators as well as its composers. Heyse's version replaced Geibel's earlier (1843) attempt, 'Dunkler Sichtglanz...', which was set by Schumann as Op. 138 no. 10 (SATB).

156 (S.w. 10) 'Eide, so die Liebe schwur...'

31 March 1890   B minor $c^{\#\,\prime}-f^{\#\,\prime\prime}$

The oaths sworn by love are but weak sureties. When love sits in judgement, then, Señor, do not forget that such proceedings always go by favour, never by rights and duties. The oaths sworn by love are but weak sureties. There you'll find unhappy wretches binding themselves with promises that are blown away in the wind, like the flowers of the field. The oaths sworn by love are but weak sureties. And as clerks of the court you'll see idle thoughts; because their tiny hands are trembling, none of them can record you aright. The oaths sworn by love are but weak sureties. And when the sureties are assembled and all await the verdict, they pronounce sentence but never carry it out. The oaths sworn by love are but weak sureties.

The verses are in a rhythmic pattern similar to that of 157, dated some five months earlier; but Wolf has few changes and no improvements to suggest. The nature of the poem inhibits the composer from deploying his most characteristic gifts. There is no musical equivalent for allegory as such; and no single particular emotion can be identified here, let alone re-created in musical terms. The result is just a song, unilluminated by the usual Wolfian brightness of perception, and relying overmuch on a portentous and rather uneasy playfulness that runs parallel to the sense of the words without really intercommunicating with them. But the general equivalents are engaging enough; the dry ironic tone of voice is neatly represented in the cutting and jabbing left-hand octave figures at 'Sitzt die Liebe zu Gericht' (When love sits in judgement) which then broaden out and sway up and down in a symbolic see-saw after 'vergesset nicht' (do not forget) in a colourful picture of ostensibly decisive indecision. And where Wolf finds a verbal phrase that especially pleases him, as at 'die Blumen auf der Flur' (the flowers of the field), the musical response is most appealing.

NOTES 1. The anonymous 'Juramentos por amores' (not in Böhl) is translated by Paul Heyse, whose 'von Vollziehen' seems preferable to Wolf's first edition reading 'vom Vollziehen', at bar 48.
2. It is fair to record that Wolf himself was delighted with this song, and referred to it in a letter of the same day to his mistress Melanie Köchert as 'The crown of all the Spanish [songs]. In the highest degree hidalgo'. This at least

affords some clue to its performance and the expected degree of bravura and panache.

3. At bars 9–11 appears the sort of rollicking music that Wolf often contrived to write in F#-major tonality, motif 40. In this B-minor song he need make no special effort to reach it; the rollicking is itself rather lackadaisical, and not clearly relevant to the sense of the words when the same music recurs at bars 33–5.

4. Perhaps the rising octave hint of *Heiss mich nicht reden* (90) in the single bar of prelude here is not accidental; the music of having taken an oath and being disposed to break it.

5. It may be the same notion of oath-taking that brings a suggestion of Wotan's world-dominating spear motif (cf. *Götterdämmerung* Act I) in the left hand *passim*, in an effective parody of the majesty of the law.

157 (S.w. 11) 'Herz, verzage nicht geschwind...'

19 November 1889 (orchestrated 1895)   E minor   b–f#''

Do not despair too soon, my heart, just because women are women. Teach them to know mistrust, they, who call themselves shining stars but burn like sparks of fire. So do not despair too soon, just because women are women. Do not let them confuse your mind when they coo sweet melodies; they would like to hoodwink you with their wiles, blind you with their tricks, because women are women.

They are always in league with one another, and are doughty fighters with their tongues, they want what the moment forbids, they build castles in the air, because women are women.

And so contrary are their minds that if you praise anything praiseworthy they will instantly rant against it, although in their hearts they agree with you, because women are women.

The words certainly suggest a degree of misogyny, with more snarls than smiles. But the music is teasing and playful; the mood, much as in 149 above, is never more than wry, and never that for long. Behind this apparent condemnation of women in general lies an exasperated but tender affection for at least one woman in particular. The opening mock solemn recitative is punctuated by despairing gestures from the piano which lapse into repeated chords of moody acquiescence. The refrain 'weil die Weiber Weiber sind' (because women are women) is subtly varied at each repetition; first sad, then tender, then declamatory, and finally drawn out and almost sentimental. Meanwhile the ostensible disapproval of the voice fires off its complaints in bursts of triple rhymes, while the piano smiles and twinkles. A left-hand motif crosses hands into the treble like an obsessive thought perpetually popping up into consciousness; its repeated rhythm ¾ ♪ ♪ | ♪ ♪ ♪ ♪ keeps on saying 'die Weiber'. The postlude chuckles indulgently and is clearly about to drop its guard when it is suddenly recalled to its right defensive frame of mind by a final interrupting chord.

NOTES 1. The anonymous 'Corazon no desesperes' (not in Böhl) is translated by Paul Heyse.

2. The sense of the concealed melodic line within the persistent dotted rhythm is closely akin – most clearly in the postlude – to the love motif 13; the recurring rising triplet figure speaks of gaiety, motif 7, but it is heard as an ironic suppressed ebullience, low in the left hand; the snapped falling semitones at bars 8–9 are the laughter of motif 4.

3. Conformably with the hypothesis offered in the commentary above, the song was orchestrated in 1895 and allotted to the philandering Corregidor, in Act II of Wolf's opera of that name, to express exasperated and frustrated infatuation with the beguiling Frasquita.

158 (S.w. 12) 'Sagt, seid ihr es, feiner Herr ...'

19 November 1889   G major   f'–g''

Tell me, sir, aren't you the fine gentleman who was dancing so nimbly, dancing and singing with us here the other day? Weren't you the one who talked so much that no one else could get a word in? and talked so loudly and boastfully? and sang so well and faultlessly? Yes, upon my soul, you're the one, who was dancing about with us, dancing and singing. Weren't you the one who said he was not at home with castanets and singing, who had never known love, who had escaped the chains of women? Yes, you're the one; and I bet you have held many a girl tight, dancing and singing. Weren't you the one who praised dance and song to the skies, weren't you the one that sat in the corner, too tired to move his limbs? Yes, you're the one, I'd know you anywhere, who tired us out too with all that dancing and singing.

For this soubrette song Wolf invents a whole musical vocabulary of coquetry. The left-hand piano part sets up a ceaseless thrumming of even quavers, usually with open fifths on each beat of the bar to emphasize the rhythm, as in 147. To this tambourine accompaniment, the staccato right hand and the voice go dancing and singing. These two separate lines intertwine, part, meet again, bow and curtsey, in a continuous outpouring of bright duetting melody. Technical device is lavished on the identification of the culprit: 'ja, ihr seid's' (yes, you're the one). This central idea is furnished with a harmonic equivalent (the home key of G major each time it occurs), a melodic equivalent (the insinuating off-beat motif of the piano introduction as if singing the words 'ja, ihr seid's' though not quite with total conviction – 'I'm pretty sure it was you') a rhythmic equivalent (the accusingly accented crotchets like the repeated jabs of an accusing forefinger – as if enunciating *'ja, ihr seid es'*) and a pitch equivalent (at the final repetition the piano is an octave higher as well as a degree louder). An amusing further point is the fact that this motif was already announced by the prelude; suspicions are aroused, and the piano pastes up a Wanted poster in sound, before the verbal interrogation begins. But the young gentleman thus identified must surely have been more delighted than embarrassed at having his prodigious feats (in the gypsy encampment?) recalled in this ebullient and charming music.

NOTES 1. 'Dezi si soys vos galan' (not in Böhl) is translated by Paul Heyse, whose 'nicht' should be restored at bar 28 in preference to Wolf's first edition's 'nie'; otherwise that latter word loses the effect of greater emphasis intended in bar 30.
2. The accented crotchets (bar 8 etc) are motif 27 decorated with the mockery of motif 4, also found in contexts of accusation in *Rat einer Alten* (53) and *Cophtisches Lied I* (99).
3. Mediant modulations are a manifest feature. In other contexts they have motivic significance, motif 24 – but perhaps not here, unless the dancing and singing are imagined as having gone on all night? There may be an analogous effect in *Die ihr schwebet* (140).

159 (S.w. 13) 'Mögen alle bösen Zungen...'

3 April 1890   D major   e'–f#''

All those wicked tongues can just go on saying what they please; I return the love of him who loves me, and I love and am beloved. Wicked, wicked words your tongues whisper, unsparingly; but I know that they're just thirsting for innocent blood. So it will never trouble me, chatter as much as you please; I return the love of him who loves me, and I love and am beloved. Only those people lend themselves to slander who lack love and favour, because their own lives are wretched and nobody woos or wants them. Therefore I think that the love they revile does me honour; I return the love of him who loves me, and I love and am beloved. If I were made of stone and iron, then you might insist that I should reject the greetings and entreaties of love. But as it is, my heart is unfortunately soft, of the kind that God gives to us girls; so I return the love of him who loves me, and I love and am beloved.

An occasional ponderousness in the German rhythm and vocabulary of these verses might have veiled their intended irony; but not from Wolf. We know from a dozen deft touches that he hears the words as bewitchingly light of heart, and indeed light of head, not to say love. Even the small prelude sounds coquettish, as its little rhythmic figure ♪♪♪ is heard flirting with different beats of the 3/8 bar. As the voice enters with 'Mögen alle bösen Zungen' the piano's staccato right hand suggests chattering tongues, while the left-hand figure already heard continues to pirouette in different positions with cheerful unconcern. The voice part in words and melody recombines both those ideas; the ill-natured gossip described leaves the lilting melody unperturbed. At each refrain 'Wer mich liebt, den lieb ich wieder' (I return the love of him who loves me) the single notes give place to staccato chords, as if applauding the sentiments expressed, and even conveying a broad hint of 'Whoever loves me, I'll love him'. Then the staccato chattering of the gossips is allotted to the left hand, in a further lively image of their banishment to the back of the mind, while the right hand has slight repeated chords from which the voice picks out its melodic line. The closely woven pattern of the poem enables the composer, as so often in the Spanish Songbook, to achieve a formal perfection of design more common in instrumental music than in song; and this structured effect greatly enhances the irony of the freedom, not to say licence, expressed and advocated in words and music. But there is still room for special felicities, such as the tenderly modulating spread chords and rising phrases illustrating the irresistibility of 'Liebesgruss und Liebesflehn' (the greetings and entreaties of love).

NOTES 1. The anonymous 'Dirá cuanto digere' (Böhl I, p. 298) is translated by Emanuel Geibel.

2. The structure is worth close analysis. Note in particular the identity of bars 5–8 with 21–4, 39–42, and 56–9, to different words, while the recurrent verbal refrain is subtly varied, and even reharmonized for clinching effect in the last four bars; note too how the four-bar periods have an extra bar added at 37 and 55 to enhance the expressive effect of 'minnt und mag' and 'Liebesflehn'. That last happy sigh from the piano reaches F♯ major, motif 40, like the similar amorous sigh on the last page of *Nachtzauber* (73). Wolf may well have heard this latter effect in Schumann, e.g. at the close of the latter's *Verratene Liebe*, Op. 40 no. 5, or *Mädchen-Schwermut*, Op. 142 no. 3.

3. Conformably with the interpretation offered, the prelude recalls that of *Tretet ein, hoher Krieger* (181, also in D major), a song with more than a hint of flirtatiousness, while the piano phrase heard in the two bars (28–9) preceding 'Zur Verleumdung' here has off-beat octaves (motif 2) as in *Ich hab in Penna* (232), an unabashed avowal of coquetry. The all-purpose staccato is motif 26.

4. Another parallel with the Italian songs is in the descending bass line accompanied by a steady left hand, e.g. bars 13–18, which is here perhaps illustrative rather than motivic as in *Mir ward gesagt* (188).

5. Cf. Schumann, Op. 74 no. 9 (SATB).

278

160 (S.w. 14) 'Köpfchen, Köpfchen, nicht gewimmert...'

31 October 1889 $\qquad$ B♭ major f'–g''

Little head, little head, do not whimper; hold up bravely, hold up cheerfully, put two sturdy props under you, wholesomely carpentered from patience. Hope shines, however bad things may become and vex you. But you mustn't take anything too grievously to heart, least of all any fairy-story that might make your hair stand on end. God, and the giant Christopher, forfend that. [God, and the giant Christopher, forfend that.]

A pleasant trifle on which the composer has lavished lashings of deftness and wit. The accompaniment's clashing semitones in single quavers suggest a series of tiny but persistent pangs, easing into relieved consonance at the invocation of 'Geduld' (patience). The semitones are now translated into melody along right-hand octaves, with added staccato chords in the left hand as the rays of hope sparkle and shine. This effect vanishes at the mention of taking things too seriously, 'musst mit Grämen', and with the warning against hair-raising stories, 'ja kein Märchen', the small discords resume. Their interval of a minor second is graphically transformed into the wide rising interval of the minor ninth to hint at hair standing on end at 'zu Berg dir stehn die Härchen'. But at the moment of final intercession the music becomes firmly diatonic. In the postlude the tiny top notes are tapped out delightedly free from any suspicion or hint of semitonal clash; the prayer is answered, the headache is cleared.

NOTES 1. 'Cabecita, cabecita' (not in Böhl) comes from the short story *La Gitanilla* by Miguel de Cervantes (1546–1616). Wolf repeats the last couplet of Heyse's translation (which at bars 20–1 reads 'dir *nur* nichts' etc). In Cervantes the words are spoken by the heroine Preciosa: but the German title *Preciosas Sprüchlein gegen Kopfweh*, her prescription against headache, given in the source book and reproduced in Wolf's score, seems to be Heyse's own invention. In fact the Cervantes story makes no mention of any headache; Preciosa repeats these lines laughingly to her lover who has fallen into a swoon on learning that she has other admirers.

2. Wolf seems to suppose, naturally enough, that Preciosa is soliloquizing, almost in the style of a nursery rhyme. This conforms with her naïve reference to St Christopher, traditionally of gigantic stature and with powers to ward off harm and distress. The music is on a minuscule scale suitable for a young girl. Thus the high staccato minor seconds of motif 3 further emphasized by the off-beat rhythm of motif 2 fit the idea of a childish predicament and prayer; the clashes also evoke tiny stabs of pain, motif 34. It is not surprising that this song is liberally sprinkled with semitone chords or intervals, which recur fiftyfold in forty bars of 4/8 time.

3. The horn passages in the postlude are motivic in the sense of release or relief; motif 8. The staccato left hand at bars 12, 14, etc, as a response to the idea of sparkling or shining, is motif 25.

4. Cf. Cornelius, op. posth.

161 (S.w. 15) 'Sagt ihm, dass er zu mir komme...'

4 April 1890   B minor   d'–f#''

*Tell him to come to me, for the **more** they chide me about it, oh, the more my passion grows! Oh, nothing **on earth** can make love falter; by their scolding, it is but doubled. Not all the **raging** of the envious can imperil it, for the more they chide me about it, oh, the more my passion grows! They have locked me in my room many a long day, they have tirelessly punished me with painful torments. But I bear all my afflictions with the courage born of love, and the more they chide me about it, oh, the more my passion grows! My tormentors often say I must quit you, but that just makes us the more united at heart. Even if I must die for it, it is seemly to die for love, and the more they chide me about it, oh, the more my passion grows!*

The verses, with their recurrent refrain 'je mehr sie mich drum schelten, ach, je mehr wächst meine Glut!' consist of alternately shorter and longer lines, dimeter and quadrimeter, arranged in a basically trochaic pattern, rhyming a b a b b c, where c is a rhyme to the refrain's 'Glut'. Wolf's typically close-patterned piano part condenses and clamps all this versifying technique within a regular framework of two or three bars of even quavers in 3/4 time. To avoid monotony, semiquavers are sometimes added to the second beat thus ♪♩ ♫♫♪♩ . This rhythm throbs through the song as obsessively as the love it expresses, while the voice is left free to declaim its passions and devotions more flexibly. The music is perhaps a little laboured, but lovingly so, with intense concentration on its craftsmanship. Intricate variations of harmony in Chopinesque chromatics are sustained by the undeniably vital rhythmic force of the main motif, just as in the poem the vicissitudes of misfortune are sustained by an enduring passion; and the dual force of verbal and musical metaphor makes an uncommonly compelling song.

NOTES 1. The anonymous 'Decidle que me venga á ver' (Böhl I, p. 283) is translated by Paul Heyse. In bar 16 the first word 'ihrer' is a mistranscription of the original 'aller', and should be corrected. Less significant but still in principle rectifiable is Wolf's substitution of 'denn' for the original 'und' in bar 29.

2. The passionate love-motif 13 is strongly in evidence, e.g. in the piano interlude of bars 20–1 and the postlude. There it appears in the ecstatic key of F# major (motif 40), which also evokes the bliss of dying for love at 'Tod um Liebe lieblich tut'; the ending on that key, the dominant, is motif 31; the semitonal pangs are motif 34.

3. The heavy and strange chords that begin bars 22 and 24 are clearly expressive in the verbal context of isolation and punishment: so it will not be mere coincidence that they are heard in analogous usage in *Mühvoll komm'ich* (143), bars 21 and 51.

162 (S.w. 16) 'Bitt' ihn, o Mutter...'

26 November 1889   G minor   d'–a♭''

Ask him, oh mother, ask the boy not to aim at me any more, because it is killing me.

Mother, oh mother, capricious love scorns yet appeases me, shuns yet attracts me. I saw two eyes last Sunday, wonder of heaven, terror of the earth.

When I saw them, oh mother, my heart experienced what people say about basilisks.

Ask him, oh mother, ask the boy not to aim at me any more, because it is killing me.

In both words and music there is over-insistence on somewhat jaded themes; the persistent twang of Cupid's arrows and the concomitant pang as they find their mark arguably concentrate too closely for comfort on one single point and its effect. But the music goes with a fiery impetus, there is strong erotic feeling in plenty, and the song can be superbly effective given the requisite virtuoso performance.

NOTES 1. The anonymous 'Rogaselo madre' (not in Böhl) is translated by Paul Heyse. 'What people say about basilisks' is of course that the very sight of them is fatal.

2. It sounds as though Wolf had been reminded, perhaps by the idea of Cupid in both poems, of *Treibe nur mit Lieben Spott* (150), dated eleven days earlier. The key, the opening melodies, and especially the chains of first inversions with added semitonal clashes (at 'was man sagt, o Mutter' here and at 'Magst an Spotten nach Gefallen' in 150, are the very same chords) make it clear that the same thematic material is being unrolled again. This may have been intentional, to suggest that the singer of this song was the girl addressed in 150, and that the prophecy that she will one day in her turn be mocked by Cupid has been duly fulfilled. On the other hand it was Wolf's normal practice in the songbooks to juxtapose those unrelated texts into which he has introduced a deliberate thematic relationship (e.g. 14/15, 74/75); and it seems that this may well be an example of involuntarily recomposing an earlier inspiration.

3. *Unfall* (80), another painful encounter with Cupid, also affords an interesting comparison.

4. The piano figurations recall those of *Die Spinnerin* (3, note 2) in the passage about 'fliegen wie Vögelein', whether by coincidence or because in Wolf's mind Cupid is not only winged but diminutive (motif 3). Apart from any possible depictive function the snapping semitonal fall of these piano semiquavers has the mockery of motif 4. The rising triplet semitones *passim* are a form of the unrest motif 5 ('sehr unruhig' is the composer's direction) The semitonal clashes are motif 34; the mortal nature of the wounds inflicted is driven home by the pang of that motif at bars 10 and 41. At 'ich sah zwei Augen' and again at 'da ich sie sah' is the mystery of motif 19; one interesting consequence is that both those verbal phrases are set to the same notes, A B♭ E, though in quite different rhythms – an

281

unusual but not ineffective way of linking cause and effect. The dominant ending is motif 31; will the appeal be heeded? is the verbal implication of the musical question.

163 (S.w. 17) 'Liebe mir in Busen zündet...'

2 April 1890   A minor   e'–f#''

Love in my bosom kindles a blaze; water, dear mother, before my heart burns away.

Do not punish the blind child for my sins; at first he cooled my soul so gently.

Then it suddenly caught fire, alas for my folly; water, dear mother, before my heart burns away. Oh, where is the flood that could quench this fire? For so great a blaze not all the seas would suffice. Because it gives me such pleasure I weep incessantly; water, dear mother, before my heart burns away.

Again the verses are formular and not over-inspired; Wolf fails fully to take fire from them. But again the *tour de force* effect in virtuoso performance is irresistible. After the short kindling fuse of the piano prelude and the exploding piano chords and bright melody of the declamatory opening phrases, a tearaway rhythm runs like wildfire through the music, cooling down or flaring up as the words dictate.

NOTES 1. The anonymous 'En mi helado pecho' (not in Böhl) is translated by Paul Heyse. 'Das blinde Kind' is Cupid again.

2. As in 162, this song suggests that Wolf is recomposing previous inspirations, this time going back to the Goethe songbook. The unrest of motif 5 occurs at bars 11–12 etc in a context reminiscent of *Genialisch Treiben* (106). At bar 23, where the music expresses the idea of cooling, its texture is curiously akin to the piano part of the passage praising muslin as a head-dress in *Komm, Liebchen, komm* (129). Again, the key (A minor for a girl's distress), time-signature and opening melodic line of this song alike recall the far superior *Trau nicht der Liebe* (165). The opening vocal line here may be compared with bars 65–6 of that song, dated only four days earlier. It also recalls the beginning of two other songs referring to Cupid, especially 150 (see 162, note 2).

164 (S.w. 18) 'Schmerzliche Wonnen...'

29 March 1890   A major   e'–a''

Sorrowful bliss and blissful sorrow, water in the eyes, fire in the heart, pride on the lips and sighs in the mind, love is a mixture of honey and gall. Often, when a soul quits the body, St Michael seeks to carry it up into heaven. But the Devil is also trying to devour it. Neither will give in, and they tussle for it. Tormented soul, you feel yourself tugged this way and that in a fearful seesaw, up and down; in just such a turmoil, love hurls us between heaven and hell. Oh mother, at seventeen I have felt this suspense and terror, and renounced it with tears of remorse; yet already I am in love, already in love again!

Wolf's difficulties in finding a musical equivalent for allegory have already been noted. Here he is at least given a clear central theme of conflict to deal with. St Michael traditionally receives the souls of the dead; his struggle with Satan recalls Revelations XII, 7–9. But the episodic nature of the verses, and the literary device of oxymoron (as in *Blindes Schauen*, 155) resist tonal expression. The result is a rather idiosyncratic mélange of song and ballad, expression and depiction, depending for its effect (as in other songs in the Spanish volume) on the sustained rhythmic and declamatory excitement that can be achieved in virtuoso performance. However, the effects achieved by tonal analogue are often novel and by no means negligible. The emotional tug-of-war oscillates among a selection of musical equivalents ranging from the unobtrusive canon between right and left hands that subtly italicizes the opening words 'Schmerzliche Wonnen und wonnige Schmerzen' to a variety of contrary motions. These are again split between the two hands at 'in ängstlichen Wogen' (in a fearful seesaw) and in emphatic octaves, at 'aufwärts und abwärts', where the voice part also has its rather predictable ups and downs. Finally the postlude has a witty and amusing synopsis to offer, compressed into fourteen presto bars. First we hear the veering octaves of oscillation, with bright and dark harmonies as well as up and down movement, affording brief glimpses of heaven and hell. Then the rhythm steadies with a new sense of firmness and resolution; octaves in both hands take a solemn vow of continence. There follows a brief pause, a loud discord, and the resolve is heard collapsing hopelessly but happily; here I go again! says the music, 'schon lieb ich aufs neue!'.

NOTES 1. The anonymous 'Triste piacer' (not in Böhl) is ostensibly translated by Emanuel Geibel; but his letter of 23 February 1852 to Paul Heyse (*Briefwechsel*, ed. E. Petzet, 1922, p. 77) hints that it is wholly or partly his own work. His text has 'vom Leib sich geschieden' at bars 23–5; Wolf's first edition reading 'vom Leibe geschieden' is either an inadvertence or an attempt to render the text more readily articulate at the required tempo. Perhaps the same applies to the substitution of 'in Frieden' for Geibel's 'zum Frieden' in bar 29. The original text should surely be restored in both passages.

2. Some of the motivic writing sounds engagingly apt, for example the isolation and separation of motif 15 as soul sunders from body at bars 22–8 followed by the bliss of F# major (motif 40) at the idea of heavenly peace in bars 29–30. The

left-hand gestures at bars 31–6, like the quasi-canonic effects in the piano (left hand bar 3, right hand bar 4ff.) are vivid metaphors of tussle, as described above; and even the repeated major seconds that serve as piano prelude are essentially small-scale images of the clash that is the poem's theme. At bars 12–15 etc there is an interesting anticipation of *Dass doch gemalt* (195), dated six years later.

3. But there are also affinities between this and earlier songs which are less impressive and indeed sometimes sound like jaded echoes of previous inspirations. Bars 3–9, piano left hand, recall *Lied eines Verliebten* (55); cf. also 122, note 1. Bars 18–19 plus the echo at bars 20–1 strongly recall the Hatem songs (127–9) and their typical cadence mentioned in 129, note 2. At 'aufwärts und abwärts' etc the piano has reminiscences of *Der Rattenfänger* (96), while the movement of the vocal line nods in the direction of the mystery motif 19. That turmoil ('Getriebe') briefly reverberates (bars 59–60) in the tones of the 'Tumulte' from *Was in der Schenke* (123, prelude etc). The end of the voice part recalls the same moment in *Hätt ich irgend wohl Bedenken* (128).

165 (S.w. 19) 'Trau nicht der Liebe...'

28 March 1890   A minor   c#'–a''

Put no trust in love, my darling; take care! It will make you weep, where you laughed today. And do you not see the moon's shape dwindle; the shape of happiness is no less changeable. Then it takes swift revenge, and as for love, take care! it will make you weep, where you laughed today.

So be well on your guard against foolish pride! the crickets may chirp in the Maytime woods, but then they fall asleep, and as for love, take care! it will make you weep, where you laughed today.

Where are you roaming? take my advice – the child with the arrows has pranks in mind. The days speed by, and as for love, take care! it will make you weep, where you laughed today.

It is not always bright, not always dark, but the sparkling of joy fades so fast. A false fellow is Cupid, take care! he will make you weep, where you laughed today.

Here is that perfect blend of technique and felicity that characterizes the best of the Spanish songs. As in the previous song, the verses offer variations on the theme of change and contrast. But here the poem is more lyrical, less dramatic; and the dichotomies described are correspondingly less stark and more subtle. Similarly the musical colours are less primary and more pastel. The preluding bass fifths suggest a strumming guitar, in a solitary mood of wistful melancholy. Voice and piano vie in melodies, which are related yet pursue their separate ways in a meaningful duality of counterpoint. At 'gelacht' (laughed) the lilting piano echoes exult gleefully until they are gently but firmly cut off by a sforzando chord, pointing the moral that the laughter is to be short-lived. Then a persistent swaying rhythm further suggests fluctuating fortunes; and when the refrain reappears there are fresh admonitions in the music. This time at 'gelacht' a little phrase in staccato quavers goes twinkling down the middle register of the keyboard and vanishes like a fading smile; and again the laughing piano phrases in the tonic major are suddenly silenced by a peremptory chord. So the song proceeds in an extended metaphor of its theme; duetting melodies, swaying rhythms, each alternating with the other, always telling the same sweetly melancholy tale and always with the same sad ending. The piano postlude, suddenly louder, faster and more emphatic in two concentrated and clinching minor chords, explains that the ironically graceful music has all along been making light of its true feelings and suppressing its real despair.

NOTES 1. The anonymous 'En los tus amores' (not in Böhl) is translated by Paul Heyse.

2. The typical wistfulness of A minor suggests that Wolf thought of this as a woman's song; the minor-major nuances are engagingly Schubertian (cf. *Blanka* D631), as are the dark and bright nuances of staccato. At bars 59–60 staccato is further used for the playful touch of 'Possen'. The descending chromatics of 'gelacht' in bar 27 have the laughter of motif 4; a similar sforzando cut-off chord ends *Erstes Liebeslied eines Mädchens* (54).

3. Again there are the Goethe echoes found in other songs dated March or April 1890 (cf. 164 above, note 3). Here the swaying motion of left-hand fifths at bars 13 etc recalls *Wie soll ich heiter bleiben* (130) bars 14 etc, where also two different periods of time are being contrasted. The scampering of Cupid at 'ein falscher Geselle', which may well have been the primary inspiration repeated for the form's sake at bars 22 and 24, recalls the scampering in *Der Rattenfänger* (96).

166 (S.w. 20) 'Ach, im Maien war's...'

30 March 1890   A major   e'–g#''

Oh it was in Maytime, in Maytime, when the warm breezes blow and people in love are wont to seek their sweethearts. I alone, I poor sufferer, am lying languishing in a dungeon cell; and I cannot see when day dawns and I do not know when night falls.

But I could tell by a bird that sang outside in the Maytime until a marksman killed it – may God send him the worst of rewards!

This enchanting song is unique in the Spanish volume, and indeed in Wolf's work as a whole, in that its music stands in no clear or definable relation to its words. The composer audibly disbelieves in what the poet says; so far from being confined in a subterranean and windowless dungeon, the singer seems to be imagined as bathed in bright sunshine, inspired to fluent melody and accompanying himself on the guitar. It is true that the death of the bird ('das hat mir ein Schütz getötet') remains the emotional climax of the song, as evidenced by the troubled harmonies generated at that moment which are released and resolved only gradually in the piano postlude. But otherwise the music seems manifestly more inspired by the idea of warmth and love and Maytime than by the actual subject of the verses. Perhaps (as arguably in *Der Freund*, 66) Wolf was directly inspired by the first line before completing his reading of the poem; perhaps he envisaged a song within a song, a ballad describing how an itinerant musician entertains the company with an old tale of forgotten sorrow from long ago, with its pangs of grief soothed into an occasional touch of mild melancholy.

NOTES 1. The anonymous 'Que por mayo era por mayo' (Böhl I, p. 247), was translated by Paul Heyse under the title *Romance del Prisonero* (which may itself have suggested that the words need not be treated too realistically). Heyse also added rhymes to the Spanish text, again preferring lyricism to realism.

2. Wolf changed 'nachzugehen' into 'nachzugehn', atypically marring the rhyme (with 'wehen') for the sake of the melody. His further presumably inadvertent substitution of 'im Maien sang' for the original 'im Baume sang' should surely be corrected.

3. The generally indifferent accentuation also suggests that a preconceived melody is being imposed on the text. It may even have been an instrumental conception; Wolf had his *Italian Serenade* in mind at this time, see 171, note 3. The melodic line at 'war's, im Maien', heard again in *Nein, junger Herr* (198), recalls the last movement of Schubert's Violin Sonata D384.

4. The guitar accompaniment is perhaps also influenced by the idea of a serenade; at any rate it is clearly akin to that of *Ein Ständchen euch zu bringen* (208). The piano postludes of those two songs, and also of *Der Rattenfänger* (96) have much in common. The effect is so striking and so unusual in keyboard music that one wonders whether Wolf was reproducing a particular style of guitar-playing familiar from his own experience.

5. This is the third consecutive song noted as having affinities with *Der Rattenfänger* – which Wolf had been orchestrating only a month or so earlier.

167 (S.w. 21) 'Alle gingen, Herz, zur Ruh...'

2 November 1889   F major   d'–f''

All things have gone to rest, my heart; all sleep, save you alone. For hopeless sorrow has scared slumber away from your bed, and your thoughts drift in speechless grief to their love [to their love].

This fine song combines the mood and style of some of the Mörike settings, both devotional and amorous, with the poignant harmonies and strict structure so characteristic of the Spanish volume. A continuous rhythm ♩ ♩♩♩ ♪♩ etc suggesting the uneasy throb of the sorrowing heart is announced in the single left-hand notes of the prelude. Like a heartbeat, it is unobtrusive, almost unnoticed, until a moment of passionate stress. Even then it never distracts from the richly expressive cantilena that is the singing voice in this exquisite duet for mind and heart. It begins with single bass notes in the prelude, and is then heard through slow quiet chords as an accompaniment figure while the voice sings its equally heartfelt opening melody. It is transferred to the right hand in octaves at 'Denn der hoffnunglslose Kummer' (For hopeless sorrow). Gradually it rises in pitch and is transformed into fuller chords with a quickening extra beat in the rhythm at 'und dein Sinnen' (and your thoughts). It reaches a climax as the voice sings its final repeated phrase, first passionately then tenderly. The piano postlude incorporates allusions to the opening vocal melody, saying again 'Alle gingen, Herz, zur Ruh' before itself hushing into silence.

NOTES 1. The anonymous 'Todos duermen corazon' (Böhl I, p. 303) is translated by Emanuel Geibel. The final repetition of 'seiner Liebe zu' is Wolf's.

2. At 'Denn der hoffnungslose' etc, bars 7–13, appears the clearly-minted Wolfian coinage for wakefulness at night, motif 17. The heartbeat motifs are also heard at the end of *Geh, Geliebter* (180).

3. The harmonies of the second 'seiner Liebe zu' may perhaps have been lingering in Wolf's mind when two years later he came to set the closing words of *Dass doch gemalt* (195), also in F major.

4. Cf. Schumann's duet setting (ST) Op. 74 no. 4.

168 (S.w. 22) 'Dereinst, dereinst, Gedanke mein...'

11 April 1890   F minor   d♭'–d♭''

Some day, some day, my mind, you will be at peace. Though now you know no relief from the fires of love, yet in the cool earth you will sleep well. There without love or pain you will be at peace. What in life you have never found will be granted when life has ended. Then without wounds and without pain you will be at peace.

The German verses verge on the maudlin. Wolf's noble music enriches and redeems them. The abject sorrow, the yearning for release, are implied rather than stated; the mood created by the composer is one of immense weariness of spirit. The continuing slow accompaniment rhythm 𝄴 ♩ ♩ with its total absence of impulse, assists this impression; but what makes it unforgettable is the falling of the vocal and piano themes. Falling tones, falling semitones, resound throughout, as if the melodic lines themselves were being flattened and crushed by an intangible but intolerable burden. When the voice sings of the coming lightening of this load, the melodic line counteracts the downward pressure sufficiently to enable it to rise somewhat, though slowly and with palpable effort, step by step up the scale for three notes. This happens at the first 'ruhig sein' (be at peace), echoed by the piano, at 'schläfst du gut' (you will sleep well) and again at 'wird's dir gegeben' (will be granted). Otherwise the vocal line either falls or else has its attempts to rise thwarted by this great weight of weariness. Even the further repetitions of the key-phrase are compounded of two falling semitones –

This was no doubt the composer's central concept, the germ-theme from which this whole beautiful song grows and develops.

NOTES 1. 'Alguna vez' (Böhl I, p. 295) by Cristobal de Castillejo (1492?–1550) is translated by Emanuel Geibel.

2. The song has a striking thematic kinship with Wolf's music for Goethe's Harper (86–8). Indeed the poem here on its lower level expresses exactly the underlying mood of the Harper lyric and so evokes an analogous musical equivalent (e.g. the grief of motif 22 *passim*).

3. There are also occasional affinities with the Mörike setting *Heimweh* (49) with its shared theme of thoughts wandering back to the loved one; its opening vocal melody provides the postlude here, and the impression of melodic lines flattened by the weight of grief is vividly conveyed by both songs.

4. The persistent omission of the first beat of the bar conveys the helplessness of motif 2, particularly evident at 'ruhig sein' and at 'in kühler Erden, da schläfst du gut'.

5. Cf. Schumann's duet setting (SA) Op. 74 no. 3; Jensen Op. 4 no. 7.

169 (S.w. 23) 'Tief im Herzen trag' ich Pein...'

12 April 1890   C minor   c'–e♭''

Deep in my heart I bear grief, outwardly I must be serene. I conceal my dear grief deep within, well out of sight of the world, and it is felt by the soul alone, for the body does not deserve it. As the spark, free and bright, hides itself within flint, so I bear grief deep within.

We are told little about the nature of the poet's grief and nothing about what causes it. But Wolf succeeds marvellously well in the daunting task of finding a musical equivalent for so unknown and unknowable an inward sorrow. His song is strangely and hauntingly sad, with an independent piano part like a Chopin mazurka (indeed, it might well pass for one of the finest). The vocal phrases wear this mysterious music like a veil over their grief-stricken expression. Its downward melodic movement is semitonally secretive, as befits the passive mood, until the moment when the words mention the new idea of active concealment. Then, at 'verhehle' (conceal) the semitonal intervals are graphically transformed into downward sevenths, the picture of introversion. For the vivid simile of spark in flint ('wie der Funke frei und licht sich verbirgt im Kieselstein') the mazurka movement halts and turns aside to accompany the voice in warmer harmonies. A brief gleam of the E major triad is heard before darkening again into C minor as the voice sings, most movingly, the last words 'trag' ich innen tief die Pein', with an octave drop on to 'tief'. In the postlude the solemn mazurka measure resumes and ends the song; in the last bars the final minor melody is heard hidden in the left hand, quietly reaffirming the poetic theme of ingrained grief.

NOTES 1. 'De dentro tengo mi mal' (Böhl I, p. 291), one of the occasional lyrics written in Spanish by the Portuguese poet Luis de Camoens (1525–1580), is translated by Emanuel Geibel.

2. Wolf much admired Chopin; earlier evidence of that influence is found in *Karwoche* (38). Another fine mazurka-like invention appears in *Mein Liebster singt* (206), where the independent piano part emerges with even greater clarity as an expressive device derived from the poem.

3. The falling semitones, as in 168 above, are the grief motif 22 of the Harper songs 86–8. After 'stille sein' the piano part lies still at exactly the same level, and wearing much the same expression, as at 'Anakreons Ruh' in *Anakreons Grab* (114). The successive brightening of the main chords, with roots in A^b, C and E, at the spark-in-flint image, bars 16–19, is motif 24.

4. Cf. Schumann, Op. 138 no. 2.

170 (S.w. 24) 'Komm, o Tod, von Nacht umgeben...'

14 April 1890 D^b major $e^{b\,\prime}-g^{b\,\prime\prime}$

Come, O Death, shrouded in night, steal towards me quietly so that my joy in embracing you does not recall me to life. Come as lightning moves us when unheralded by thunder, until it suddenly flares and deals a double blow. So may you be vouchsafed to me, stilling my longing so suddenly that my joy in embracing you does not recall me to life.

'Half in love with easeful death' is the mood of this marvellous song, from which all suspicion of maudlin sentiment has been excised by the music, leaving an unaffected warmth and longing. The piano prelude gives a deep sigh at being disturbed, but emerges serenely enough from its depths of meditation to join in a long sweet duet with the vocal melody; and this typically Wolfian image for the poetic idea of serene union is further embellished with persistently rhythmic lulling phrases to say that death is a sleep. A first dynamic and harmonic climax is reached at 'Lust, dich zu umfangen' (joy in embracing you). Here the music warms into sudden life, in brighter tonalities, and thus as it were becomes aware of the danger of which it sings; it instantly hushes and fades back into the half-lights of the home key, at 'nicht zurück mich ruf' (does not recall me). The resounding sharp-key radiance recurs for the image of sudden lightning dealing a double blow, at 'und den Schlag gedoppelt führet'. Then the quiet invocation of the first verse resumes, with the repetition of the poet's words; and now the musical depiction of warmth and brightness and their gentle renunciation are even more moving and effective than before. The piano postlude sings again 'Komm, o Tod'; then the music grants its own request and ceases to be.

NOTES 1. 'Ven muerte tan escondida' (Böhl I, p. 268) by Comendador Escriva (c. 1450–c.1520) is translated by Emanuel Geibel.
   2. The harmonic procedures are a clear paradigm of Wolf's style; the flat key-centre radiates into remote regions notated in sharps to emphasize the contrast, thus identifying the emotionally climactic moments and translating their meaning into musical terms.
   3. The persistent lulling accompaniment figure is a brother of Wolf's sleep music, motif 18. The prelude's gradual upward movement into life is somewhat akin to the opening of *Der Genesene an die Hoffnung* (13); cf. also the prelude to *Alles endet* (241).
   4. It would be surprising if the conjunction of joy and death had not put Wolf in mind of the 'Liebestod' in Wagner's *Tristan und Isolde*, of which this song is an independent lyric counterpart.

171 (S.w. 25) 'Ob auch finstre Blicke...'

16 April 1890   B minor   b–f#''

Although sombre glances came gliding from your eyes, my love,* at least it cannot be disputed that you have looked my way.

   No matter how those glances strove to wound my heart, is there any sorrow that would not be richly requited by the joy of seeing you? And however fatally my feelings have been stricken by your anger, at least it cannot be disputed that you have looked my way.

This sad little song of hopeless devotion may make no very great first impression; but it can make a lasting one. The voice echoes the prelude's

---

* 'Augenstern' means both 'pupil' (of the eye) and 'darling'

wistful melody and adds a further dying fall of its own, in a sad sequence made sadder still by the addition of glum little accompaniment chords. The minor mood cheers up briefly into a major chord at the very end of the refrain 'du hast geblickt nach mir' (you have looked my way). But we are to understand that this is comparatively cold comfort; the major tonality instantly fades back into the wistful theme of the prelude. The deeper meaning of this theme is now made manifest; its melody is loaned to the voice to express the words 'ist's ein Leiden' etc (is there any sorrow). These are the strains of humble and hopeless devotion, a musical wringing of hands. Then the opening music returns, delicately varied and with added fervour in the intonation; this time for example the word 'abgestritten' (disputed) is allotted an almost defiant rising inflexion. The brief dominant chord shines out again as before, at 'mir'; then the prelude appears once more to end the song, again on a wistfully enquiring note, hoping against hope.

NOTES 1. The anonymous 'Aunque con semblante airado' (Böhl I, p. 274) is translated by Paul Heyse.

2. The formal refrain construction is typical, like the ambiguous accentuation (e.g. when the voice sings the prelude theme at bar 17 etc it is shifted half a bar, and an extra bar of 3/8 has to be inserted to get back into step). The refrain pattern suggests that something is amiss with either bar 9 or bar 29 as given in the Peters edition and the *Kritische Gesamtausgabe*. The two bars should surely be identical; perhaps the former like the latter should have a D as the lowest note of the second chord, as in the autograph.

3. The identity of prelude, interlude and postlude is a favourite unifying device of Wolf's in songs devoted to one single idea. The linking theme here recalls one of the melodies of his *Serenade* for string quartet, a work manifestly expressive of some emotional or literary context, to which the words of this song are no doubt relevant. There is a further connection; it was on 16 April 1890, the day this song was written, that Wolf (in a letter to Oskar Grohe) first called his string quartet an *Italian Serenade*.

4. The questioning dominant ending is motif 31; for the drooping semitones see 180, note 2.

172 (S.w. 26) 'Bedeckt mich mit Blumen...'

10 November 1889   A♭ major   d'–f''

Cover me in flowers; I am dying of love. So that the breeze with its soft breath does not waft the sweet fragrance from me: cover me. Indeed it is all the same, the breath of love or the fragrance in flowers. Here you must make ready my grave of jasmine and white lilies; I am dying. And if you ask – of what? I reply: among sweet torments, of love [of love].

From this verbal potpourri of sickly yearning Wolf makes a most beautiful song, lush yet not sentimental. The piano has a languorous melody sustained in Chopinesque style over chords which though full are marked *staccato* in both hands; the composer's imagination responds to the idea of the thick soft touch of a flower-petal shroud. The voice, like a second violin, adds a counterpoint; and the two intertwine continually in a further floral tribute, this time to Wagner. The vocal line is constantly renewed and varied to match the inflexions of the words. Thus at successive mentions of 'Liebe' (love) the melodic curve reaches a top F (the highest note in the song, held in reserve for these moments). Then for the last 'Liebe' the voice descends to a lower register to expire in ineffable yearning, dying away under a reprise of the opening piano melody which in turn dies away.

NOTES 1. 'Cubridme de flores' is translated by Emanuel Geibel, into whose text Wolf inserts 'mir' in bar 7. The Spanish poem is said to be anonymous in the German source; but Böhl (I, p. 35: Annex, pp. 3, 14) ascribed it to one Maria Doceo. Its form is unique. The first couplet is split into four phrases which are separately added in that order as a rhyme at the end of each further couplet. Something of the effect can be gleaned by reading the first sentence of the translation above, and then looking at the last two or three words of the next four sentences. The setting disturbs the pattern by repeating 'vor Liebe' at the end; and no doubt it could hardly be reproduced exactly in music without sounding too conspicuous and contrived. Yet Wolf has, deliberately or not, offered one exact equivalent; 'mit Blumen' in bars 2–3 has the same notes as 'von Blumen' in bars 20–1.

2. Again the heady blend of death and flowers (as in *Karwoche*, 38) is redolent of Chopin and Wagner. For the former, cf. the G-minor *Ballade*, Op. 23 (e.g. bars 101–2); for the latter, the 'Liebestod' in *Tristan und Isolde*, also about love and death among flowers. The piano melody at bars 24–5 here recalls bars 7–8 of *Anakreons Grab*; the words of both passages are about a flowery grave. The Italian song *Sterb ich so hüllt in Blumen* (219) is a more austere treatment of the same poetic idea.

3. The yearning of the piano part *passim* is motif 12; for the allusive use of staccato see motif 26.

4. Cf. Schumann's duet setting (SA) Op. 138 no. 4.

173 (Sw. 27) 'Und schläfst du, mein Mädchen...'

17 November 1889   E♭ major   e♭'–g♭''

If you are asleep, my girl, arise and open the door to me, for the hour has come, we are leaving this place. And if you have no shoes on, stay unshod; through raging waters our way lies, through the deep, deep water of the Guadalquivir, for the hour has come, we are leaving this place [we are leaving this place].

The fierce urgency of the words is somewhat abated by Wolf's music, which presents a more static though still attractively colourful picture. Despite the quick tempo the persistent 6/8 rhythm announced in the prelude gives the impression of a barcarolle, as though the musical imagination is already water-borne, from the first bars. The delightful vocal melodies have typical touches: 'denn die Stund' ist gekommen' (for the hour has come) all on one note, like an ominous chime; 'reissende Wasser' (raging waters) on a rising arpeggio, like Schubert's water-music; 'tief-tiefen Wasser' to a deeply falling interval. The piano part too has characteristic harmonies, such as the mysterious and conspiratorial darkening of the tonality at 'und bist ohne Sohlen' (if you have no shoes on) and its corresponding brightening at 'geht unsere Bahn' (our way lies). The home key is effectively reserved solely for references to leaving this place, thus subtly saying that home is anywhere but here. The postlude is heard leaving home and disappearing into the distance, with the implication that the story may eventually find a similarly happy ending elsewhere.

NOTES 1. 'Si dormis doncella' (Böhl I, p. 302) by the Portuguese Gil Vicente (1465?–1537), who like Camoens wrote occasional lyrics in Spanish, is translated by Emanuel Geibel. The final repetition is Wolf's.

   2. There is the mystery motif 19 in the piano part at 'und bist ohne Sohlen'. The key, the words 'wandern von hier', and especially the identical final chords, recall the Mörike setting *Auf einer Wanderung* (27), also a song of travel, which has the happiest of endings.

   3. Cf. Schumann's duet setting (TB) Op. 74 no. 2.

174 (S.w. 28) 'Sie blasen zum Abmarsch...'

13 December 1889   B♭ major   e♭'–f''

The bugles are sounding for the march off, dear mother, my lover must depart and leaves me alone!

   In the sky the stars have scarcely faded, and already infantry fire can be heard in the distance. Hardly has he heard the call but he straps his pack and marches off, with my heart following behind. My lover must depart and leaves me alone.

   I am like a day bereft of sun, my sorrow will be long in healing; I have nothing to ask, no pleasure to seek, I just commune with my grief.

   My lover must depart, and leaves me alone!

Like *Klinge, klinge mein Pandero* (147) this delectable song is a duet for two aspects of a situation. The bright bugle-calls and clear drum-taps of the piano part make an admirable foil for the veiled pathos of the words and their mourning melodies. The quietly summoning staccato thirds of the prelude dissolve into soft bugle-calls as the voice enters; 'Sie blasen zum Abmarsch'. The simple drooping melodies of the sad village girl linger wistfully among the bustling preparations for departure. At the first 'lässt mich allein!' the voice is illustratively left alone for a moment or two. Then drum-taps are heard and the piano prelude music swells out, in military band fashion, before marching away again at the hushed re-entry of the voice. Now the march-themes appear, as faded and pale as the dawn: 'die Sterne sind kaum noch geflohn' (the stars have scarcely faded). The refrain is repeated, to sad sighs and a grieving echo from the piano. Here a doleful reverie intervenes. The vocal melodies are muted; the accompaniment's march, already some distance away, is interspersed with muffled drum taps. The music slows down, dreams and broods darkly in troubled harmonies, drooping vocal lines, low bass octaves. The refrain recurs, with sighs and echoes as before; and now the last words 'lässt mich allein' are lingered out in a final fond farewell. The postlude returns to the military march theme, *a tempo*, quite cheerfully at first, with some high ringing bugle notes, then softer with little poignant harmonic clashes, then receding into the distance, then fading into inaudibility. The singer is left alone.

NOTES 1. The anonymous 'En campaña, madre' (Böhl I, p. 300) is translated by Paul Heyse.

2. Bars 14–15 have the drumming of *Der Tambour* (17); in the left hand after 'meiner Pein' is the unrest of motif 5; the postlude has the processional exit effect very dear to Wolf e.g. in *Epiphanias* (104).

3. The pathos of this song may be compared with the tender gaiety of *Ihr jungen Leute* (202) with exactly the same background scene, with similar colouring and effects, including the companionable thirds of motif 16, but creating a very different impression.

175 (S.w. 29) 'Weint nicht, ihr Äuglein...'

29 March 1890   B minor   f#'–g''

Weep not, you dear eyes! How can one so woefully weep for jealousy who kills with love? One who deals death himself, how can he wish for death? Whoever can resist his tears would be won over by his smiles. So weep not, you dear eyes! How can one so woefully weep for jealousy who kills with love?

The mood of the German verses is unclear. So in the music; Wolf alternates between earnest and jest, cajoling and reproach, with beguiling melodies to begin and end, and troubled chromatics in the middle section. As in *Ich fuhr über Meer* (154) numerous changes of tempo are directed; in each context the song relies to a much greater extent than usual on interpretation and correspondingly less on purely musical expression. The intention seems to be to convert this monologue into an imagined duologue. The piano prelude theme as it were portrays the person addressed; it begins with a two-bar outburst of petulance, answered in a vocal line 'Weint nicht ihr Äuglein' which is deliberately held back like an ingratiating gesture of soothing restraint. The passionate prelude theme recurs, *a tempo*, unmollified. But now the salve is again applied; 'wie kann so trübe weinen vor Eifersucht...' (How can one so woefully weep), and this time exactly the right emollient flattery is rubbed into the bruised ego: 'wer tötet durch Liebe' (who kills with love?). The unhappy piano theme is blandished into lilting major melody. The voice seizes this opportunity to pursue reassuring arguments at the same brisk tempo, 'Wer selbst Tod bringt' (One who deals death himself), before slowing down again to press the point home with rhetorical emphasis; the lover is irresistible, and can have no conceivable cause for jealousy. Now the entire first section is repeated, as the words dictate, beginning with the piano prelude, which still sounds unconvinced. Then the previous dialogue is resumed with enhanced effect. 'Weint nicht' (weep not); oh yes I will, says the piano. But you are capable of killing with love; 'tötet durch Liebe'. Oh, am I, says the piano; come, that's more like it; and it sings the major melody to itself again with quiet delight.

NOTES 1. 'No lloreis ojuelos' (Böhl III, p. 209) by Lope de Vega (1562–1613) is translated by Paul Heyse.

2. As in 171 above, the lilting themes and transparent texture are somewhat reminiscent of the *Italian Serenade* for string quartet. This song is also linked more specifically with the next, 176 (compare the first dozen bars of each). For the falling semitones, see 180, note 2.

3. The piano bars expressing (it is suggested) delight are in Wolf's blissful F# major (motif 40); that tonality, dominant in the context of B minor, is also motif 31, standing for the final question mark.

176 (S.w. 30) 'Wer tat deinem Füsslein weh...'

5 December 1889   A major   c#'–g''

'Who has hurt your poor foot, la Marioneta, hurt your snow-white heel, la Marion?' I'll tell you what ails me, not one word will I withhold from you. I went to the rosebush at night and plucked a rose from its branches. On the way I trod on a thorn, la Marioneta, and now it has pierced my

heart, la Marion. I'll tell you all my grief, friend, and won't mislead you, I went into a wood to pick myself a lily. There a sharp thorn pricked me, la Marioneta, it was a sweet word of love, la Marion. I'll tell you, in all sincerity, of my sickness and my wound. Today I went into the garden, where the fairest carnation grew. There a splinter hurt me, la Marioneta, the wound bled and is still bleeding, la Marion. 'Fair lady, by your leave, I am a skilled surgeon, I can soothe your wound so gently that you will scarcely be aware of it. You will soon be healed, la Marioneta, soon free of all pain, la Marion'.

Wolf is clearly attracted by the poetic use of the refrain 'La Marioneta . . . la Marion' which comes tripping in with a vivacity so irresistible as to disarm criticism. There is much wit and resource in the elated rhythmic pulse, the thrumming and tinkling guitar and castanet effects of the accompaniment, the captivating melodies in voice and piano. The girl does not so much sing as dance her reply, which is full of suppressed mischief as well as glee. In each of her three verses the words constantly protest their sincerity; the truth ('mit Aufrichtigkeit', in all sincerity), the whole truth ('will kein Wörtlein Euch verschweigen', not one word will I withhold from you) and nothing but the truth ('will euch nicht berücken', I won't mislead you). But really, says the piano part chuckling and skipping and snapping its fingers, it's nothing *like* the truth. The erotic symbolism of bloom and thorn is made joyously manifest in the music. In the last page the first speaker assumes a new character. The pace is significantly slower, the left hand draws itself up proudly in a repeated octave theme, as the professional services are offered. But after the portentously protracted phrase 'kaum gewähren sollt' (scarcely be aware of it) the singer is unable to keep up the burlesque pretence a moment longer; the first themes return at the initial lively tempo and race off to a spirited conclusion with the repeated 'la Marion'.

NOTES 1. The text is Emanuel Geibel's translation of the anonymous 'Qui tal fet lo mal del peu' (not in Böhl). In the German source-book and in Wolf's first edition it bears the superscription 'Limusinisch', i.e. stemming from Limousin, the old *département* of Corrèze and Haute-Vienne. The original language is evidently not strictly Hispanic but a form of Provençal; the varied refrain 'la Marioneta, la Marion' sounds more French than Spanish.

2. The consecutive thirds, right hand bar 13 etc, and the mordents, bar 15 etc, may convey motivic expression (16 and 4 respectively) as well as local colour. The delightedly skipping octaves, recalling the fun and games of Cupid in *Philine* (93) are always F$^{\sharp}$ major (motif 40) each time they occur (first in bar 27).

3. For the melodic curve of the left-hand piano theme (bars 2–9 etc) in other love-songs, see 122 note 1.

4. The thorn-in-flesh symbolism of the tribulations of love recurs in the Italian song *Ich esse nun mein Brot* (210).

177 (S.w. 31) 'Deine Mutter, süsses Kind...'

2 April 1890   F♯ minor   c♯'–f♯''

*Your mother, sweet child, as she lay in labour, heard the roaring wind.
And so she bore you with your fickle veering wind-like ways. If today you
have chosen a heart, tomorrow you faithlessly discard it. But I reckon him
a fool who reproaches you for infidelity. Your fate was against you; for
your mother, sweet child, as she lay in labour, heard the roaring wind.*

A waywardly syncopated dance-rhythm

symbolizes the variety of different postures that one small figure can
adopt. As it strums through the guitar-like accompaniment, the
harmonies too are heard veering between dark and bright. After 'brausen
hörte sie den Wind' (heard the roaring wind) we hear it too, in a moment
of brief and unobtrusive bluster. Similarly after 'treulos hin' (faithlessly
discard it) caution is thrown to the winds with a flamboyant gesture in the
upper register. Throughout this highly-wrought and subtle song the last
two left-hand quavers of each bar are set softly dancing. At the words
'dein Geschick war dir entgegen' (your fate was against you) the wind-
motif recurs with a regretful sigh to underline what that fate was and to
show that the singer too in his own way is also victim of it. But the vocal
tone remains gentle; the inflexions of the voice part suggest affectionate
reproof rather than scolding, much as in *Herz, verzage nicht geschwind*
(157).

NOTES 1. The text is said to be 'La tu madre o mis amore', by one Don Luis el
Chico, a name otherwise unknown to literary history. No doubt it was a
pseudonym for the young Paul Heyse himself. See also 143, note 2 and p. 249.
  2. The structure equates bars 1–4 with 23–6; so it is far from clear, even in a
song about veering affection, why the vocal line at 'süsses' at bar 24 is reversed
from bar 2.
  3. The wind-motif (used as it were literally in bars 7–8 and 29–30 but
figuratively in 21–2) has an interesting affinity with Wolf's love-motif 13. But here,
aptly enough, it is mostly unilateral; the lower voice yearns upward, but the
higher remains rather unmoved. The accompaniment hugs the off-beat *passim*,
motif 2, perhaps influenced by 'Kind' in the first line, which may also have
inspired the playful downward octave skips, *staccato*. The wry mordents of the
right hand are the ironic motif 4.
  4. Much of the writing here is derivative; the texture and some of the thematic
material recall *Auf dem grünen Balkon* (151) of some five months earlier, while
the shifting rhythm of wilful waywardness (remembered in *Mögen alle bösen
Zungen*, 159, dated the following day) was also Wolf's way of characterizing the
gusting passions of his epic heroine Penthesilea in his tone-poem of that name

(1883–5): e.g.

etc

In this song too the shifting notation of sharps in flats is expressive.

178 (S.w. 32) 'Da nur Leid und Leidenschaft...'

20 April 1890   B minor   e'–f#''

As only sorrow and passion have assailed me while in your custody, I am now offering my heart for sale. Tell me, are there any offers?

If I am to give my own valuation, three-farthings would not be too much. It was never the wind's plaything, it obstinately stayed in your toils.

But driven by necessity I am now offering my heart for sale, to be knocked down to the highest bidder. Tell me, are there any offers?

Every day it silently grieves me, and never delights me any more. Now who'll bid? who'll give more? Away with it and its whims, which are obviously bad, yet I am offering my heart for sale. If it were happy, I'd gladly keep it. Tell me, are there any offers?

If you buy I can live without grieving, so anyone who likes can have it. Who's buying, who'll take it? Let everyone say what they'll give. Once more before the hammer comes down, I am now offering my heart for sale, so that you can make up your minds. Tell me, does anyone want it?

Well, then, going, going, gone! Well done; may it bring you happiness. Take it, my darling, brand the slave-mark into it with a hot iron; for even though you have no wish to purchase, I shall give you my heart.

As already noted, Wolf (like music itself) finds difficulty in expressing verses that embody extended figures of speech. Here the whole poem is a rather trivial and tedious allegory, so that the composer has little opportunity for changes of mood and no great success in establishing what the prevailing mood actually is. The piano part, no doubt the primary conception, has some racy and effective moments, such as the crankily self-willed interlude after 'eigensinnig blieb's' (it obstinately stayed) and the 'going, going, gone' effects at 'Nun zum ersten und zum zweiten' etc. But in general the vocal line has to carry all the highly repetitive burden of meaning and expression; and in the absence of broad melodic appeal the task proves intractable. The music sounds as if the creative springs of the Spanish songs are now at last running dry, leaving only a rather arid arroyo of symmetrical structure without any real flow, freshness or sparkle of content.

NOTES 1. The anonymous 'Pues que no me sabeis dar' (Böhl I, p. 358) is translated by Paul Heyse, who has 'jetzt', not 'nun', in bars 11 and 41.

2. Again the song is somewhat derivative, e.g. from the postlude to *Komm, Liebchen, komm* (129). The verbal accentuation has been adapted to the pattern of the piano part, not always convincingly (e.g. the stresses on 'und' and 'mit'). The jollification of the rising motif 7, bars 19–20 etc, and the ensuing raciness of F♯ major, motif 40, with the questioning of motif 31 for 'Lust darauf?' are all rather jaded. Before the final 'zum Kauf' the piano acciaccatura, motif 4, and the vocal grace notes, show that the mood is not too desperately serious.

179 (S.w. 33) 'Wehe der, die mir verstrickte...'

27 April 1890   A minor   f'–a''

Woe to her who lured my loved one from me, woe to her who lured him!
  Oh, the first man I loved was caught in Seville, my much loved man,
  woe to her who lured him!
He was caught in Seville with the chains of my tresses, my much loved man,
  woe to her [woe to her] who lured him [woe to her]!

This was the last of the Spanish songs to be composed; and the previous torrent of inspiration already perceptibly dwindling a week earlier, in 178 above, has now thinned to a brackish trickle. Wolf seems to be recomposing the already rather unsatisfactory *Liebe mir im Busen* (163), in an attempt to rekindle the passion invoked in that song. Perhaps the link is intentional. But the words here have no energy of their own to impart to the music, no sustenance to offer; the effort to impel them along is too palpable. There is the usual cleverness; thus when the mood briefly turns to reverie and the voice sings of the lost lover, at 'Ach, der erste' (Oh, the first man), the piano theme is derived from the opening vocal melody, as if to imply that while the voice is ostensibly dreaming of love for him, the hurt mind is still really brooding on hate for her. But the musical material is not fine enough to compel total attention, let alone express emotive subtleties; and its main hope for survival lies in the dramatic scope it affords to a powerful soprano with a ringing high A and a sufficiently menacing aspect. Otherwise it is hard to believe in either the verse or the music.

NOTES 1. 'Mal haya quien los envuelve' (Böhl I, p. 302) by Gil Vicente (1465?–

1537) is translated by Paul Heyse. The verbal repetitions on the last page are not his but Wolf's.

2. The drooping opening phrase, in the typical A minor for a woman in distress, is echoed from *Trau nicht der Liebe* (165) and more closely still from *Liebe mir im Busen* (163), the opening piano bars of which are served up here again.

3. The opening vocal line, transferred to the piano at bar 13 etc, is the sorrow-motif 22.

180 (S.w. 34) 'Geh', Geliebter, geh jetzt...'

1 April 1890   F♯ major   c♯'–g♭''

Go, beloved, go now; see, the morning dawns.

Already people are going through the streets, and the market is bustling so busily that pale morning must already be lifting its white wings. And I am afraid of our neighbours, that you will give offence, for they do not know how deeply I love you, and you love me. So, beloved, go now; see, the morning dawns.

When the sun shining in the sky banishes the clear pearls from the field, so must I, weeping, lose the pearl that was my treasure. What to others looks like daylight remains night-time to my eyes, for the darkness of parting looms before me each time the sunrise awakes. Go, beloved, go now; see, the morning dawns.

Flee, then, from my arms, for if you let the time slip by we may pay with long sorrow for our moment of loving warmth. Yet we can surely endure a day in purgatory while hope allows us to see the radiance of heaven shining afar. So, beloved, go now; see, the morning dawns.

The operatic breadth and sweep of this long marvellous song make a fittingly climactic conclusion to Wolf's most highly-wrought songbook. A scene of ill-starred or illicit love, whether a village Romeo and Juliet or a more prosaic liaison, is vividly enacted in a setting of flawless construction and great depth of feeling. Wolf himself, a man with a married mistress and living just such a life of passionate but clandestine devotion, must infallibly have reacted with intense empathy to the predicament described. That response is embodied in music of a power and quality that not only transcend the stilted traditional language of the poem, with its white-winged morning and shining pearls of dew, but even justify its dramatic convention. 'Go now', the song commands, and goes on commanding for some hundred bars of moderate 9/8 time. But no listener would wish the order obeyed earlier. The piano prelude contains in a mere three bars the whole essence of the song. The first bar establishes an urgent cajoling rhythm. The second holds it back with tenderly drooping semitones. In the third bar, without any change in the feeling or the texture of the music, the two ideas are combined – insistently pressing rhythms in the left hand, gently falling quavers in the right – a command and a caress together. The scene is thus set for the entry of the voice to a melody as apt as it is beautiful. It too combines the elements of warmth and urgency from which the entire song is compounded. It begins on an unexpected note, on a chord out of the home key, as if reluctantly breaking away from warm closeness into cold separation; 'Geh, Geliebter'. It shifts again briefly out of the key and off the beat at 'Sieh', as if just noticing the grey light of morning, only to plunge and reappear deep and vibrant at 'dämmert' (dawns). Then in a brief piano interlude the gestures of affection already heard in the prelude melt again into tenderness on a high bright arpeggio. All this takes place in eight words and eleven bars, but they comprehend a world of feeling and tension. What follows is evolved by a process of continuous creation. So far all the music has been bound together and fixed in place by a long tonic pedal note sounded or sustained in the left hand. The tonality is suspended, like the scene and the time. But now the voice begins to describe the external activity, with the increasing bustle and business in the market-place, 'der Markt wird so belebt'. So the musical movement too quickens its pace and quits the home tonic, reverting to the prelude themes as the voice proclaims its urgent and tender concern for the avoidance of scandal and the continuance of reunion, at 'Und vor unsern Nachbarn bin ich bange' (And I am afraid of our neighbours) – thus reinforcing the expressive significance that Wolf attaches to those three bars. Sequences of new and sumptuous melody reflect the appearance of sunlight at 'Wenn die Sonn am Himmel scheinend' (When the sun shining in the sky); there is urgent grief at 'Fliehe denn aus meinen Armen' (Flee then from my arms). Each of the long episodes is introduced, separated and rounded off by the recurring refrain 'Drum, Geliebter, geh jetzt' (So, beloved, go now). In the postlude tenderness and anxiety are heard hushing to a murmur of heartbeats and an empty embrace. All this may sound exaggerated; but admirers of this great song may well find that such a description savours of culpable understatement.

NOTES 1. The anonymous 'Vete amor, y vete' (not in Böhl) is translated by Emanuel Geibel. For once Wolf has pruned his given poem, and with good reason. The omitted third strophe (before 'fliehe denn') reads as follows:

> *Willst du feste Wurzel fassen,*
>   *Liebster, hier an meiner Brust,*
> *Ohne dass der Neider Hassen*
>   *Stürmisch uns verstört die Lust;*
> *Willst du, dass zu tausend Malen*

Ich wie heut dich sehen mag,
Und dir stets auf Sicht bezahlen
Unsrer Liebe Schuldbetrag:
Geh, Geliebter, etc

This is not only indifferent verse, but might well have been regarded by the composer, given his own personal temperament and circumstances, as in dubious taste. In any event the song is already just long enough.

2. The drooping semitones of the piano prelude seem to have had special significance for Wolf in the Spanish songs. They appear in nearly the same notes and similar tonality in 171 and 175 (e.g. piano prelude and bar 22 in each), both dated about the same time. These passages are clearly related to the loving and grieving music of motifs 13 and 22 respectively. The staccato at 'Perlen klar' is a shining example of motif 25; the heartbeats in the piano postlude are as in *Alle gingen, Herz, zur Ruh* (167) *passim*; the final chords are also those of two other songs of travel or departure, *Auf einer Wanderung* (27) and *Und schläfst du* (173).

3. There are surprising musical affinities between this song and Mignon's *Kennst du das Land* (94). Even discounting such evident parallels as the keys and key-changes of the two songs, their common 3/4–9/8 rhythmic structure, the falling quaver semitones (here *passim*, after 'wohl' in 94) there is an unmistakable feeling of identity of impulse behind the music. For example the prelude to 94 with its adoring motif 11 recalls the recurring melody of the refrain here. More specifically still, the passages at 'Kennst du es wohl' in 94 are distilled here into the music of 'fliehe denn aus meinen Armen'. Such resemblances at the high creative level common to both songs will not be merely superficial; so there is room for speculation about the causes of the kinship. There is no evidence that Wolf had imagined Mignon as being passionately in love with Wilhelm Meister and thinking of this love as guilty or illicit, though it is fair to say that much in Goethe's novel could be adduced in support of such a view. Perhaps the link is simply that 'Geh, Geliebter' forcibly reminds Wolf's creative mind of the words 'möcht ich mit dir, o mein Geliebter ziehn' in Goethe's poem and hence of his own music for it. Such an association could readily have been reinforced if Wolf's 1890 orchestration of the Mignon song had overlapped the composition of this one.

4. This in turn was orchestrated in 1892, but only fragmentarily.

302

VI. The Keller songs

We have already met the Swiss writer Gottfried Keller (1819–90) for his pleasant valediction to Mörike (p. 59). He is perhaps best known for his novels and short stories; but he was also a considerable poet. Like both Goethe and Mörike, he devoted much of his time and talent to community service; and he always adopted a staunchly didactic and moralist stance. Again like his great predecessors, Keller had an impressive gift for visual art and the correspondingly vivid verbal image. But in the lesser artist and minor poet the individual *aperçu* remains more personal than universal; and Keller's cantonal quirks and constraints of thought and expression tend to limit the brightness and breadth of his poetic vision.

Wolf, who much admired Keller's prose works (especially the quasi-autobiographical novel *Der grüne Heinrich*) had planned these songs as a tribute for the writer's seventieth birthday. But he was late in starting, the music did not flow as freely as usual, and Keller died before the songs were completed. The six poems Wolf chose are taken from the collection known as *Alte Weisen* or, as one might say, old songs resung. Each is by or about a woman; each offers a portrait of an actual acquaintance or an imagined persona. This common characteristic was made manifest in earlier separate editions of Keller's poems (*Gedichte*, 1846) where each of the *Alte Weisen* was allotted a woman's name. Those titles were omitted by the poet from later revisions. But the linking theme of feminine character and personality would have remained apparent, and attractive, to Wolf whatever his textual source (very possibly, here as in his Eichendorff selection, the first or *Gedichte* volume of the collected works; Keller's had appeared in 1883).

In any guise the verses are typically elusive and evocative; the old songs recall the stirrings of memory or desire in the poet or his creations. The musical settings attain vivid and enduring life whenever the character-drawing or scene depiction are at their clearest and most graphic. Wolf wrote to his mistress Melanie Köchert on 24 June 1890 to say that the spell had finally been broken and the last three songs were completed; the apple-blossom was set, St Peter cobbling away, and the charcoal-burner's drunken wife howling hideously. Elsewhere the music audibly labours in its efforts to follow Keller's meaning and direction. As one of the poet's most perceptive and admiring commentators, Jethro Bithell, has written 'What this or that poem of Keller's may leave in the memory is not verbal music, but a picture clearly limned, though set at a distance by the strangeness of the thought'.* Wolf's settings sound as though they had had to contend with that latter difficulty in particular.

181 'Tretet ein, hoher Krieger...'

25 May 1890   D major   c#'–g''

Enter, noble warrior who has surrendered his heart to me. Lay aside your crimson cloak and your golden spurs. Yoke your steed to our plough, as a salutation to my father; give me the crested saddle-cloth as a carpet for my feet. Your sword-hilt must yield its gold and gems to me, and the gleaming blade will be a poker. And the snow-white plume on the blood-red cap will be handy as a cooling fan in the summertime. And the marshal must learn how we bake white bread and how we mince sausages and stuffing at Yule-tide. Now commend your soul to the Lord Jesus, for your body is sold where it cannot be redeemed.

An odd poem, and therefore an odd setting. The fate of the captive knight in bondage serves as an ironic allegory of love or matrimony. But Keller's fun seems to be taken just a little too far; the last lines, intentionally or not, strike a decidedly serious note. Wolf matches the dry humour with some irony of his own; the music is lilting and playful in style, and coquettishly transparent in texture. But the singer and pianist are directed to perform it 'sehr gemessen und mit Anstand', with precision and decorum, throughout, and yet at times 'zart', with tenderness. This continual contrast between ostensible and actual meaning, in both words and music, offers perplexing problems of style and interpretation. But if the elements of formality and informality can be aptly alloyed in performance, the result is an integrally delectable song, full of the colouring and sparkle of real and attractive human features vividly imagined and presented. The prelude as it were seeks to encourage a hesitant visitor across the threshold; once over, the music displays amusingly meaningful patterns of free melodies weaving themselves ingratiatingly around a rather restricted and scarcely perceptible inner voice, like Circe enchanting Odysseus. The texture becomes lighter still at the mention of the richly embroidered saddle-cloth, 'die Schabrack'; at

---

* *An Anthology of German Poetry, 1830–1880*, Methuen, 1947, p. xcix

'Euer Schwertgriff' the left hand makes an audibly covetous grab for the sword hilt. The whole song effectively parodies the male swagger of a military march; see the conquered hero comes.

NOTES 1. The Peters edition notation would be clearer if the tied B flats were repeated in the piano as in the voice, bars 14 and 38.

2. Wolf may be using the poem as a lay-figure round which to drape pre-conceived musical material. This procedure is unobjectionable and indeed often impossible to detect if the fit is good; but here it is bursting apart at the seams. When 'in', 'und', 'auf' and even the second syllable of 'Vater' are allotted to the first beat of a strongly metrical bar, something must be awry. It is clear that the stress in the voice-part is felt at the half-bar, *passim*, while the piano part is best barred as written. Wolf has conceived the latter in rhythmic terms before finding a correspondingly complete concept of the vocal line. The result is a kind of rhythmic canon at the half-bar, which can itself have an expressive quality, e.g. in stressing the independence or separation of two ideas, almost as a musical equivalent for irony.

2. The piano prelude echoes the introduction to *Mögen alle bösen Zungen* (159), also interpretable in terms of coquetry.

3. Cf. Pfitzner, Op. 33 no. 7.

182. 'Singt mein Schatz wie ein Fink...'

2 June 1890   A major $c^{\#}{}'{-}a''$

If my sweetheart sings like a finch, I'll sing a nightingale's song; if he is a lynx, then I'll be a snake! O ye maidens in the country, from the mountains and over the sea, render my fairest love to me, or you will do me harm. He must surrender, to our glory and our praise, and he must not stir, whether loudly or softly. O you dear playmates, render to me that proud man; he shall see how love can be a fiery sword!

Wolf seems unusually baffled and ill at ease. At first his music seeks to impose significance on the text, rather than drawing sustenance from it. In the first few bars, the piano part is devoted to a rather trivial rendering of finches and nightingales, chirping and trilling. It is not until the word 'Schlang' (snake) that the song deploys any consistent image; and then the continuous sinuous depiction of toils and coils from voice and right-hand octaves in writhing chromatics seriously outstay their welcome, despite lavish accelerandos and crescendos and a climax at 'ein feurig Schwert' (a fiery sword) which is finely effective in its way. The postlude whirls and strikes, like a rapier and viper, sword and snake in one.

NOTES 1. The words should read '(zum Ruhm) uns und Preis', not 'uns zum Preis' as in the Peters edition.

2. As in 181 above there is some (though much slighter) confusion at the half-

bar, e.g. at 'ist mein Liebster ein Luchs'. This might have suggested a preconceived accompaniment, but for the comparative dullness of the one provided.

3. The nightingale is also allotted semiquaver triplets in the same key in *Philine* (93). The postlude has the passionate love-music of motif 13; cf. also the postlude to *Erstes Liebeslied eines Mädchens* (54).

4. In a letter of 20 August 1890 to Melanie Köchert, Wolf was very scathing about Brahms's setting of these verses, Op. 69 no. 8 under Keller's first-edition title of *Salome* (apparently just a woman's name, with no reference to the biblical character). But there seems little to choose between them. Cf. also Pfitzner, Op. 33 no. 5.

183 'Du milchjunger Knabe...'

16 June 1890   A minor   d'–f''

You milk-young boy, why do you look at me so? What a question it is that your eyes have asked! All the town councillors, and all the world's wise men, remain dumbfounded by the question that your eyes have put! But there's an empty snail-shell, look, lying there in the grass; just put that to your ear, and you'll hear something whispering!

We too have a question – what is it about this poem that suggests such curiously convoluted music, such subtle emotional overtones? A wistful questioning starts up in the piano part,

and there it persists until transmuted at 'Schneckhäusel' (snail-shell) into the gentle meaningless demisemiquaver whisper which is all that is offered by way of reply. With its wistful delicacy, its tentative groping for the key, the music seems to be an exquisite portrayal of calf-love itself, not of the character who has inspired it. On this view it is the young man, in effect, who is singing. The song is all question, murmur and mystery, representing a response to the words by their naive hearer. The vocal line seems almost a reverie in reported speech; 'this is what she said to me'. There is little trace of the woman's mature and affectionate good nature; only (since she is singing) her instinctive empathy and understanding for a boy's perplexities, which she shares and even teasingly imitates, like Susanna and the Countess with Cherubino. The dramatic point is neatly made at 'alle Ratsherrn in der Stadt' etc (all the town councillors); even during this comprehensive assurance that the question is wholly unanswerable, the piano helplessly goes on posing it.

NOTES 1. The suggested evocation of calf-love in the music is somewhat supported by its mild resemblances to *Nimmersatte Liebe* (21) and *Wie lange schon* (197) where the same impulses are perceptible. The questioning dominant sevenths are motif 32.

2. Wolf was also uncomplimentary (see 182, note 4) about Brahms's splendid setting Op. 86 no. 1 under the title *Therese*; in particular he correctly deduced that it drew on an earlier edition of Keller's poems. It is worth noting that in Brahms the last verse reads 'Eine Meermuschel liegt/Auf der Schrank meiner Bas'/Da halte dein Ohr dran/ Dann hörst du etwas', which was no doubt altered because of the too obviously intrusive invention of a female cousin, or aunt, (Base) just for the sake of a rhyme. Brahms's booming deep-sea tones, and hence his idea of the low-voiced maternal D major Therese, like Wolf's fluting snail-shell whisper in his typical A minor, derive equally from the vicissitudes of textual emendation. The Wolfian inflexions of teasing or mockery (e.g. in the grace notes of motif 4, or in the sudden vehemence of the last two chords, threatening disillusionment as in the last bar of *Trau nicht der Liebe*, 165) might well have been anathema to Brahms.

3. Cf. also Pfitzner, Op. 33 no. 3.

184 'Wandl' ich in dem Morgentau...'

8–23 June 1890   A major $e'-g^{\#''}$

When I walk in the morning dew through the scent-filled meadow, I must feel so shamed by the flowers all around!

Dove on the church roof, fish in the millstream, and the snake silent in the weeds; they all feel and call themselves brides.

The apple blossom in bright sunshine proudly thinks of itself as a young mother; even though it is so early in the year, the butterfly pair dies joyously.

God, what have I done then that I without a mate in springtime, without a sweet kiss, must die unloved?

Again Keller poses a problem, this time by introducing the contrasting notion of death at the end of his poem. Wolf again sensibly bypasses this perplexity; it would have been a pity to disturb with overt tragedy the lilting longing of this song in his favourite springtime key of A major. The prelude's slightly syncopated 6/8 rhythm ♩ ♪♩♩♩ – perhaps suggested by the first four words of the German text – dominates the music within a pattern of changing harmonies; the image is one of constant progression through a brightness intermittently dimmed by dark shadows, as at 'Täublein auf dem Kirchendach' etc (Dove on the church roof). In the last verse, 'Gott, was hab ich denn getan?', yearning is portrayed with characteristic delicacy in a new treatment of the opening vocal melody. Voice and right hand are first heard in unison, then in wistful separation, singing similar strains that are kept tantalizingly apart though languishingly close. The postlude is notably more hopeful than the poem about the singer's future prospects.

NOTES 1. In conformity with the verses, both aspects of Wolf's love-music are contained in this song; *storge* or mother-love *passim*, motif 14, and *eros* or sexual love, motif 13, at 'Gott, was hab ich' etc.

2. Here the Italian songs are directly foreshadowed, perhaps because of the specially intense yet homely quality of personal feeling evinced in the verses. For example the piano part at 'Braut' has the same essence as the similar phrases in *Wir haben beide* (205) at the words 'Die Engel Gottes'.

3. The uncertainly fluctuating rhythm is one aspect of motif 38.

185 'Das Köhlerweib ist trunken...'

7–23 June 1890   D minor   c'–g''

The charcoal burner's wife is drunk and singing in the wood. Hear how her voice echoes shrilly around the countryside! She was the fairest flower far-famed in the land; rich and poor sued for her hand. She preened so proudly about in her chatelaines; choosing a bridegroom was too much trouble for her. Then red wine outwitted her; how transient all things must be! The charcoal burner's wife is drunk and singing in the wood; how her song resounds shrilly through the twilight!

The poem is full of pity; the music brims with bitterness and mockery. 'What a shame', says Keller, as his verses move gently from daylight to dusk, like the fate of his heroine. 'Serve her right', says Wolf, focussing his music in an even harsher glare at the victim's inexorable end. The song begins with a brilliant evocation of wild singing interspersed with whoops of hysterical laughter. Even in the sudden flash-back reminiscence of 'Sie war die schönste Blume' (she was the fairest flower) we are not allowed any moment of real regret or tenderness. Indeed the word 'Blume' is allotted the slightly tipsy rhythm already heard at 'trunken' (drunk). A new theme clearly associated with the idea of queening it and strutting about

is disapprovingly introduced long before the poem mentions it; and the same theme itself conveys more than a hint of an imminent loss of decorum. Indeed after 'fiel ihr zu schwer' (was too much trouble for her) it sags blowsily and collapses; and the original sharply observed and sharply critical theme takes over and ends the song. Even the pitying words 'wie müssen alle Dinge vergänglich sein!' (how transient all things must be!) are swept away in the blazing bitter crescendo that summons the music back to its opening strains for the repetition of 'Das Köhlerweib ist trunken'. This leads on to a climax first in the voice, which makes the song resound anew by stressing and prolonging those words ('Lied' and 'erschallt') and then in the piano postlude, which with implacable mastery unforgettably conveys the vivid impression of shrill screaming laughter, mirthless and terrible in the twilit wood.

NOTES 1. The Peters edition would be improved by a tie in the vocal line between bars 31 and 32, at 'Arme'. Given the splendidly strong formal construction, an image of inexorable fate, it is far from clear why the left-hand chords at bar 43 should not exactly parallel the repetitive pattern elsewhere (cf. bar 26).

2. The 'queening' theme illustrated above has few analogues elsewhere in Wolf, but its motivic status and function are manifest. The acciaccaturas *passim* are the dry laughter of motif 4; the alternating minor seconds in the right hand at bars 5–7 and at regular four-bar intervals thereafter have the same mocking inflexion. It will not be merely coincidence that this figuration dominates the music at 'da hat sie überlistet der rote Wein' etc; wine is also a mocker, by long tradition. The postlude's diminished sevenths are motif 33.

3. The slightly tipsy 'trunken' syncopations recall motif 38 in the bibulous songs of the *Westöstlicher Divan*; for a closer kinship see *Was in der Schenke*, 123, note 4.

186 'Wie glänzt der helle Mond...'

5–23 June 1890   G minor   b–e''

How cold and distant the bright moon shines, but farther still glimmers my beauty's star! Far from me the sea beats on the shore; but farther still lies the land of my youth. There is a little cart without wheels or shafts, and in it I shall soon be journeying to Paradise. There sits the mother of God on her throne, with her blessed son asleep on her knees. There sits God the father, feeding the Holy Ghost* from his hand with the grains of heaven. In a silver veil I'll be sitting then and looking at my white fingers. But Saint Peter will grant himself no rest; he'll be squatting in front of the door cobbling old shoes.

Wolf had little sympathy for the drunken charcoal-woman in the previous song. But his heart went out to the old peasant woman in this one. The result is the masterpiece of the Keller songs and one that takes an assured place among the best of Wolf's work. By his own standards it is open to criticism; for example, the ABA song form has no very clear relevance to

---

* For the dove as emblem of the Holy Ghost see Matthew III, 16

the poem. This is partly attributable to Keller's style and idiom, with which Wolf was never entirely at ease. The old woman is of a rather literary turn of mind and phrase in her first two carefully-balanced couplets, and this is hardly consistent with the ostensible naïvety of her descriptions of the coffin's journey and destination, touchingly expressed though these are. But the underlying thought is coherent enough; and the sheer quality of the musical material defies criticism. Soft open repeated chords in the piano's upper register suggest the heights and spaces of the night sky. The vocal melodies end with a rising inflexion for the first part of each of the two comparisons and then droop again for the second, making the melancholy points most movingly – 'the moon – my beauty; the sea – my youth'. A whole lifetime of pious tranquillity and resignation is made audible. The idea of heaven is then depicted in sweet strong chords over an affirmingly upturned bass line, the music of an old woman's naive and touching faith. At 'in einem Silberschleier' (in a silver veil) the original themes and figurations return, and Wolf proceeds without incongruity to round off the music with a graphic illustration. The final section at 'hockt vor der Tür' (squats in front of the door), continued in a short piano postlude, contrives by the simplest of means and in a short compass to suggest the tableau of St Peter, traditionally a cobbler, working among the otherwise motionless radiance of a picture-book Heaven.

NOTES 1. The high piano chords presenting moon- and star-shine, bars 1–8 etc, are motif 25, as at the end of *An die Geliebte* (44). The music is suffused with the brightness of F$^\sharp$ major (motif 40); the childhood memories are imagined as happy though distant. The rasp of awl through leather is rather reminiscent of the analogous Wagnerian effect in *Die Meistersinger von Nürnberg*. The repeated octave introduction to 'ohn' Rad und Deichsel' recalls the outset of another anticipated journey heavenward, before 'o führt mich ganz' in *Zur Ruh, zur Ruh* (12); see also 188, note 2.

2. The curious affinities between this song and *Dank des Paria* have already been commented on (115, note 3); even more interesting and perhaps revealing are the less marked but still detectable affinities between this song and that extremely unflattering vision of the religious life *Geselle, woll'n wir uns in Kutten hüllen* (200, note 3). The composer's scepticism enhances both the irony of the last-named song and the pathos of the other two.

3. Cf. Pfitzner, Op. 33 no. 8.

VII. The Italian Songbook

Paul Heyse (1830–1914) has already been mentioned (p. 249) as a gifted translator from Romance languages. His share of the *Spanisches Liederbuch* so impressed his patron Maximilian II of Bavaria that he was granted a perpetual pension for a literary career that lasted into the twentieth century and earned much esteem, affluence and a Nobel prize. It had begun with a slender but genuine lyric talent that prompted Schumann to some late (1850) Lieder; and these in turn may have inspired Brahms to those few solo and choral settings which have secured a modest but enduring place in the history of song for Heyse's own original poetic achievement. But Heyse's skills were always deployed to better advantage in the work of translation; and his versions of Italian poets, notably Leopardi, are still highly regarded. His linguistic interests and gifts had developed early. He studied classical and Romance literature in Berlin and Bonn, and then travelled in Italy researching and editing poetic manuscripts from the times of the troubadours. As with Spanish literature, German translation from the Italian had become a commercially viable enterprise with the advent of the Romantic movement. Early versions of Petrarch and Dante lyrics for example had appeared in Leipzig in the 1810s, while Wilhelm Müller, who was not only the poet of the great Schubert song-cycles but also an accomplished linguist and translator, had travelled in Italy and published *Egeria* (1817), a collection of Italian folk-songs recovered from oral tradition and broadsheet ephemera.

By the middle of the nineteenth century Italy's own national and romantic resurgence had stimulated widespread indigenous interest in folk and traditional poetry which had been extensively collected and published in the volumes on which Heyse drew for his translation in the *Italienisches Liederbuch* of 1860, notably Tommaseo's two-volume *Canti popolari* (1841) and Tigri's *Canti popolari Toscani* (1856) with occasional contributions from Marcoaldi's *Canti poplari inediti* (1855) and Dalmedico's *Canti del popolo Veneziano* (1848). The notes to each of Wolf's settings (nos. 187–232 below) offer, for those interested in further

311

research, a page and first-line reference to Heyse's stipulated source.

The genre of Italian popular or traditional song has not been extensively studied. Textbooks tend to by-pass the topic, and it has evoked few echoes of interest or imitation in other literatures. One of its verse-forms, the two- or three-line *stornello*, was re-created in English by Browning, who had no doubt encountered many examples during his years in Italy. In *Fra Lippo Lippi* we read e.g.

> Flower o' the broom,
> Take away love, and our earth is a tomb

or

> Flower o' the quince,
> I let Lisa go, and what's good in life since?

and these are admirable specimens of the style. A standardized catch-phrase is capped with a longer rhyming line, as in an improvised party-game; but the outcome is a gracefully cadenced reflection on life and love. This blend of the racy with the courtly, as if naïve village folk-poets were writing under the influence of Petrarch and Dante, typifies all the verses selected and translated by Heyse from the Italian anthologies cited above. No doubt this duality stood high among the reasons for their appeal to all the collectors and translators, as well as to their composers from Brahms to Joseph Marx and Wolf-Ferrari. These verses seem to incorporate a living tradition, as if in Italy more than anywhere else in Europe the earliest classics of literature had been absorbed into the national consciousness. In particular it is the eight- or ten-line Tuscan *rispetto* (and its Venetian equivalent the *vilota*) that will appeal most powerfully to all Romantics. Much of the anthologies, most of Heyse's selection, and almost all Wolf's settings, are in this form. 'Rispetto' means an elegant conceit or compliment paid by lover to lover; in its worldlier forms it may be wrily humorous, even woundingly sarcastic. Among many possible variations a basic prototype is readily discernible: eight lines of ten or eleven syllables (iambic pentameter, usually with feminine rhymes or disyllabic assonances) are arranged in the rhyme scheme a b a b c c d d, in which the last two couplets are interlinked by phrase-reversal. For example the original Italian text of No. 27 (213 below) reads as follows:

> *E m'ero spolto per andare a letto:*
> *Bella, tu mi venisti in fantasia.*
> *Presto mi rizzo, mi calzo e mi vesto;*
> *Piglio il mi ribechino e vado via.*
> *E per tutta la via e canto e suono:*
> *Fo innamorar le citte, e le abbandono.*

E per tutta la via e suono e canto:
Fo innamorar le citte, e poi le lasso.

This might be rendered in English, retaining one of the assonances and the phrase-reversal in lines six and eight, thus:

I had lain down in bed and closed my eyes:
    Then in a dream I saw your face, my pretty.
I leap from bed, I don my clothes and shoes:
    I take my lute and wander through the city.
Along the city streets I play and sing:
Enchant the girls, then leave them languishing.
Along the city streets I sing and play:
Enchant the girls, and then go on my way.

Thus a germinal idea is developed through an opening quatrain into two couplets of repeated and clinching conclusion, reinforced by added and varied rhyme. The structure is typically far more complex than the thought, as if (to suggest an English equivalent for the Italian genre) a lost Shakespeare sonnet had been collected in simplified form as a Somerset folk-song; and there seems little doubt that the sung tradition of the *rispetto* ultimately derives from the Italian poets of the renaissance. But no doubt it was the popular melodies that kept the lyrics alive in rural Tuscany. More than one *rispetto*-collector confirms that his informants were often unable to recall the words in a spoken as distinct from a sung context. The typical example cited in the original Italian above has the fluid rhythms and nonchalant assonances of a sung lyric in a popular oral tradition. Heyse's equally typical aim, on the contrary, is a translation into written German verse suitable for reading or declaiming by sophisticated poetry-lovers. And only thus could the words have offered any appeal or challenge to the great masters of the Lied, who were inspired by poetry as an independent art-form and not by the verbal component of popular songs. The latter aspect of the *rispetto* of course retains its own special charm and style, which can be heard in full measure in Wolf-Ferrari's settings of the original Italian *stornelli, rispetti* and other traditional verses. But Hugo Wolf's Muse was wedded to literary German, as in Heyse's beautifully accomplished translation of the given example:

Schon streckt' ich aus im Bett die müden Glieder,
    Da tritt dein Bildniss vor mich hin, du Traute.
Gleich spring' ich auf, fahr' in die Schuhe wieder
    Und wandre durch die Stadt mit meiner Laute.

313

Ich sing' und spiele, dass die Strasse schallt;
So manche lauscht – vorüber bin ich bald.
So manches Mädchen hat mein Lied gerührt,
Indes der Wind schon Sang und Klang entführt.

Here the rucked rhythms of the original Italian are carefully ironed out into a smooth iambic regularity; the assonances are corrected, in an almost schoolmasterly fashion, into exact rhyme ('letto/vesto' becomes 'Glieder/wieder' and 'canto/lasso' becomes 'gerührt/entführt'). Heyse thus insists that his verses are to be considered as competent poetry, not amateurish bungling. The result is a thoughtful lyric well worthy of later inclusion in his collected works; but it is less a translation than a transportation from its oral rural Italian folk-tradition into a printed metropolitan German bourgeois art-form. Even the characteristic phrase-reversal of the *rispetto* ('canto e suono' … 'suono e canto') is subordinated to the easy and elegant flow of Heyse's verse.

In other poems however that effect is retained; and Wolf would certainly be as familiar with the form as with the content of the *rispetto* from the German text alone. There is no evidence, and no reason to suppose, that he was even aware of, let alone familiar with, the original Italian. So the musical quality of his Italian (as of his Spanish) Songbook derives directly from the German text. As he wrote to his friend Emil Kauffmann, 'A warm heart, I can assure you, beats in the small bodies of my youngest children of the south, who cannot, despite appearances, deny their German origins. Yes, their hearts beat in German, though the sun shines on them in Italian...'*

The same may be said of other Lied settings from Heyse's *Italienisches Liederbuch*. Soon after its publication in 1860, that volume came into the hands of another lifelong admirer of Heyse's fluent and civilized artistry, namely Brahms, whose exquisite *Am Sonntag Morgen*, Op. 49 no. 1, thus anticipated Wolf's first Italian songs by some 25 years. The special success of Brahms's setting and its evident indebtedness to poetic theme and structure might well have impelled Wolf to further exploration of its source-book, just as Wolf's work in turn influenced later song-writers, notably Joseph Marx, to make their own Heyse selections. On any hypothesis the *Italienisches Liederbuch* was the ideal choice for Wolf in 1890–91, when he composed the twenty-two songs that comprise the first volume, and perhaps selected or even sketched the twenty-four others that followed five years later. These brief anonymous lyrics are often repetitive and sometimes trivial; but the collection as a whole succeeds in creating a vivid picture of a true and real world where Wolf's creative imagination

---

* 11 December 1892

314

could dwell and function without constraint. Its local colouring had already proved inspirational for him, as in the *Italian Serenade* of 1887; its lively vignettes were well designed to bring out his genius for small-scale drama and characterization. Admittedly the occasional artifice in Heyse's renderings can sometimes suggest an idealized summer landscape 'wo die Zitronen blüh'n'. But in the main Heyse's treatment of the original Italian lyrics preserves their sense of close communal life, the living reality of the street, the church, the market-place, and above all the men and women, happy or sad, in love or despair, accepted or ostracized. Even the first lines by which the songs are generally known serve to illustrate this personal and intimate background. 'They tell me...', 'I'm told...', 'I asked them and they said...' Practically the entire songbook is about what 'I' or 'you' feel, what 'they' say or do. From this context, and within the strongly unified miniature structure of the verses, Wolf creates an apotheosis of classical poetry and popular song, each raised to the highest imaginable pitch of musical art. As Frank Walker says in his definitive biography of Hugo Wolf, 'The Italian songs are as fresh today as on the day when they came into existence and no amount of repetition can impair their charm. It is impossible to imagine that they can ever fade or lose their significance while civilized humanity endures'.*

187 (I 1) 'Auch kleine Dinge...'

9 December 1891   A major e'–f#''

Even small things can delight us, even small things can be precious. Consider how we love to adorn ourselves with pearls; they are costly, and are only small. Consider how small the olive is, yet it is sought after for its goodness. Just think of the rose, how small it is, yet it smells so sweet, as you know.

This justly famous song, simple in style yet deeply moving in effect, was chosen by Wolf to stand at the forefront of a collection containing many of his rarest masterpieces; and the world has applauded his choice ever since. Yet the song's meaning is far from self-evident. The feeling goes too deep for a love of miniature things as such – though Wolf would certainly have been convinced that, as this work goes far to demonstrate, the miniature art-forms of the Lied can offer as precious a gift as music has to bestow. In one anthology of Italian popular poetry the original verses are classified under 'Amore Ineguale', as if social disparity were the theme, here as in e.g. *Wohl kenn ich Euren Stand* (215); in another, the heading is

---

* op. cit. 2nd Edn. 1968, p. 304

'Bontà e Bellezza di Donne', as if the meaning were a courtly compliment. Wolf's quiet and intense music suggests rather that he has read and interpreted the German text as a love-song, a humble avowal of lonely and perhaps hopeless adoration.

The piano prelude is a marvellously subtle foreshadowing of the thematic material to be used as accompaniment throughout; broken chords in semiquavers in the right hand, a falling melodic line in the left. Smallness and self-effacement are tenderly and unobtrusively written into this music. The soft sound is barely audible, the slow rhythm barely perceptible. The treble notes converge into minor and diminished intervals; the bass moves constrictedly stepwise; the voice is introduced by tiny chromatic beads of staccato, in a beautiful image of a small separate series like a row of pearls. This mood of absorbed concentration is further reinforced by quietly-emphasized soundings of the keynote that command attention, first when the voice begins and then at each successive admonition. 'Bedenkt', 'bedenkt', 'denkt'; consider, reflect, think, the music implores, sustained by a vocal line which is among the very finest of Wolf's many similar inspirations. It is all delicacy and restraint, closely moulded to the words, yet making an instantaneous and unforgettable appeal as sheer melody.

NOTES 1. For the original Tuscan *rispetto* 'Le cose piccoline son pur belle!', see Tommaseo, I, p. 244; also Tigri, p. 39.

2. The smallness themes are related to motif 4, but modified to obviate any trace of humorous or ironic connotation. The pearling staccato at bar 4 links motifs 25 and 26.

3. Some additional pointers to the interpretation suggested above are as follows. A melodic line in the left hand, falling away from a steady level of figuration in the right, often appears in Wolfian contexts evocative of separation or loneliness, motif 15; the next song, *Mir ward gesagt*, is a striking example. Here the first chord has the pang of motif 34, while the left-hand melodic line runs very closely parallel to that of a later song of humble and lowly love, *Wohl kenn ich Euren Stand* (215). Further, the piano part centres throughout on the weak beat of the bar in a way often associated in Wolf's music with the idea of child-like dependence, motif 2. The moving gentleness and simplicity in the quiet climax of the last lines and the piano postlude is typical of the Italian love-songs; see in particular, 204, note 5.

4. The subtle harmonic techniques repay study. As in e.g. *St Nepomuks Vorabend* (105) the chords are altered to avoid any unwanted clash with the vocal line (compare e.g. bar 1 here with bar 21). This careful avoidance of all non-thematic discord or modulation gives a special flavour to the deliberate mellowing of the tonality into the flat supertonic at 'Güte'. The Schumannian chain of dominants at 'teuer' suggests that master's love-motif, as e.g. in *Frauenliebe und-leben*.

188 (I 2) 'Mir ward gesagt...'

25 September 1890   E minor/G major   d'–f#''

I was told you were journeying far away. Oh where are you going, my love, my life? I would like to know the day of your departure. I will give you an escort of tears. I will bedew your path with tears. Think of me, and hope will shine upon me! With tears I shall be beside you everywhere; think of me, do not forget, dear heart!

The sadness in much of the music adds poignancy by suggesting that this is fated to be a final farewell. The right hand with its slow quaver chords in common time is central to the song. The voice part emerges from and is sustained by these chords, while in the left hand a melody in single notes, with a distressed discord on the first beat of the bar, goes grieving downward on its separate way. The steady rhythm, the troubled harmonies, and the dividing melody respectively suggest a journey, a sorrow, and a separation; and all three are blended by great art into exactly the emotion described in the verses. And Wolf further finds an added emotional climax. For the winning final words 'vergiss es nicht, mein Herz!', in a sweetly loving and resigned recitative, the steady movement of the accompaniment is momentarily halted as if the imagined journey has disappeared into inaccessible distance, where words can no longer follow it, leaving only imploring gestures of supplication from the piano postlude as it is finally left alone.

NOTES 1. For the original Umbrian *rispetto* 'M'è stato detto che voli partire', see Marcoaldi, p. 44.

2. The piano part of the whole song is composed of the isolation of motif 15. The thrice repeated right-hand octaves introducing an impending journey (in the 2/4 bar before 'Mit Tränen') recur, perhaps by coincidence, in *Wie glänzt der helle Mond* (see 186, note 1). The final phrase is lifted by its diatonic harmonies out of the prevailing chromatic mood; the tonality shifts from the relative minor to the dominant of the home key, with the final questioning or pleading effect of motif 31. This favourite procedure of Wolf's is a clear indication, if one were needed, that the last line is the emotional climax of the song.

3. The discord on the first beat of the bar looks forward to the opening of *Wie viele Zeit verlor ich* (223) and suggests a somewhat similar mood.

189 (I 3) 'Ihr seid die Allerschönste...'

2 October 1890   A♭ major   e♭'–g♭''

You are the loveliest of all, far and wide, much fairer than the show of flowers in Maytime; not Orvieto cathedral, not the greatest of Viterbo's fountains rises in such majesty. So high a grace and magic are your own, that Siena cathedral must bow before you; oh, you are so rich in grace and charm, that not even Siena cathedral itself can compare with you.

This is hardly among the outstanding successes of the Italian songs. The tonality and rhythm are square, and the special responses to the text are atypically conventional, e.g. the rather infelicitous fussing in the piano part as it rises and falls at the mention of fountains, after the sustained 'Brunnen'. The courtly compliments of the verses are conventional, and offer little real sustenance to the musical imagination. It is not until the comparison at the final couplet that an image from the poem clearly sensitizes the music. The chord just before 'der Dom von Siena selbst' is suddenly quiet, and sustained, in a brightly remote tonality. Thus we hear that Wolf's characteristic empathy enables him to share the lover's experience of being suddenly as moved by a woman's human beauty as by the timeless radiance of a great cathedral. But it takes more than one such moment to make the typical Italian masterpiece; and elsewhere the music, though full of the charm of which the *rispetto* speaks, arguably misses the magic.

NOTES 1. For the original *rispetto* 'E sete la più bella mentovata', see Tigri, p. 20.

2. The marked speed of crotchet = 100 seems rather too fast for the seriousness with which Wolf interprets the poem's conceits. On the second page he adds indications of restraint; but the moderate tempos demanded at the 'poco rit.' passages may still seem too incisive a contrast with the following 'bewegt'. Here too the impression is one of somewhat disparate elements not wholly fused together.

3. Again, the repeated bars 7 and 8 and the postlude's restatement of the previous four bars suggest that the inspiration is not yet flowing freely.

4. For the piano part at bars 12–15, see 143, note 5.

190 (I 4) 'Gesegnet sei, durch den die Welt entstund...'

3 October 1890   E♭ major   d'–g''

Blessings on him through whom the world came into being; how finely he created it on all sides! He created the sea with its unfathomable depths, he created the ships that glide over it, he created Paradise with its eternal light, he created beauty and your countenance.

The basic material of this masterpiece is simplicity itself. The piano part offers ordinary dotted rhythms, falling octaves or fifths, quietly moving chords, repeated seconds rising by step. The voice part too proceeds by repeated notes or the simplest of sequences. It is an elementary treatise on the rudiments of musical theory, set out in seventeen bars of common time. Yet by these slender means some undistinguished verses have been transmuted into great music. The poetic form helps by providing a progressive framework of thought round which the song can construct its cumulative effect. Further, its transcendent theme of creation is treated in human terms; God is presented as an artisan as well as an artist. So the divine is naïvely brought down to earth, in words and music. There is great power in the falling octaves of the first bar, with its image of the creating gesture in the right hand; there is great strength in the chromatically rising bass line. The voice echoes the falling gesture in its opening words, and again at 'entstund' (came into being). At 'wie trefflich schuf er sie' (how finely he created it) there is an exultant fanfare for voice and piano in a new bright key. The voice rings out here, in the supposed climax. But we soon learn that there is a still greater glory. The meditation resumes and continues: 'Er schuf das Meer ...' (He created the sea). Here the right-hand piano part turns to a neutral orthodox accompaniment of repeated quavers, as if epitomizing the continuous movement of sea and ships, and this lightening of texture gives greater prominence and clarity to the repeated creating gestures of falling fifths, now in the left hand. Finally the true climax is reached. 'Er schuf die' (he created) – and now the composer makes us believe that at this instant the thought of the loved one's face takes possession of the singer's mind and takes his breath away, so that the voice first swells out triumphantly and then suddenly hushes in adoration – 'Schönheit und dein Angesicht'; the ideas blur together in a hushed murmur, as if that face had all the beauty in the world. At this moment we hear the tonic chord for the first time in the song since its opening bar; and the final vocal syllables echo the same dotted rhythm and the same key note as the first sounds of the prelude. Thus the original motif of creation finds its true *raison d'être*. In the postlude the piano goes on meditating upon that moment of adoring insight.

NOTES 1. For the original *rispetto* 'Sia benedetto chi fece le mondo', see Tigri, p. 28.

2. The sudden decrescendo at 'Schönheit' should not be exaggerated; the previous 'Licht' need be no more than a *mf*.

3. The lordly gesture of the falling fifths (bars 7–11) has already been heard in *Der Sänger* (95). It is a less intense version of the falling octaves in the prelude etc; these return in the left hand at the final climax. The harmonic procedures are typically motivic; the remote bright outgoing D major occurs at the survey of the

external world, while the more inward and tranquil home key of E♭ major is heard, in effect for the first time, at 'die Schönheit' etc. The postlude's Amen effects and the high octaves as in motif 25 (with the same tonic E flats and the same rhythm as the first notes of the piano, and the last notes of the voice) recall the postlude to *An die Geliebte* (44), where a similarly starry ecstasy is expressed; see note 4 to that song. Perhaps the conceptual link is that the 'Paradies mit ewigem Licht' contemplated here puts Wolf in mind of 'zum Himmel auf, da lächeln alle Sterne' in Mörike's poem.

4. Words about the beauty of a woman's face always struck a powerfully responsive chord in Wolf's songs; see also 44, note 2.

191 (I 5) 'Selig ihr Blinden...'

4 October 1890   E♭ major   d'–f''

Blessed are you blind who cannot see the charms that kindle our fires; blessed you deaf, who can fearlessly laugh away the laments of lovers; blessed you dumb, who cannot tell women of your heartache; blessed you dead, who have been buried! you will have rest from the pangs of love.

Wolf takes this text very seriously. To counterbalance the hyperbole of the verses he gives them a strong foundation of music expressing an unshakeable conviction of the truth of the sentiments expressed. Over a persisting pedal point the accompaniment marches like an army of anti-feminist crusaders treading through four-note descending scale-passages in an unrelentingly square four-in-a-bar crotchet rhythm. The effect is of determination, strength, simplicity and set purpose throughout, with a suggestion of organ tone to match the biblical echoes of the poem. This treatment gives the words a tone of straightforward sincerity and makes them almost believable. The first strain is announced as an uncomplicated diatonic statement in voice and piano, rising in pitch and gaining in chromatic intensity as the song proceeds. At last at 'selig ihr Toten' (blessed you dead) the music invests all that has gone before with a new solemnity. High sustained notes now toll out in treble as well as bass; the vocal line strains at the top of its tessitura, in a last long lament. The piano postlude allows itself a moment of brief grieving before recovering control as the strong descending scale-passages, gestures of self-denial and abnegation, take charge again and end the song.

NOTES 1. For the original *rispetto* 'Beati ciechi voi che non vedete', see Marcoaldi, p. 139.

2. As in 193, the earnest treatment redeems the exaggerated text. When Wolf gives such verses a more impassioned and serious expression than they have strength to bear, as in *Wehe der* (179) and *Verschling' der Abgrund* (231) the resulting imbalance mars the musical integrity of the song.

3. Some light may be thrown on the motivic significance of the musical material by a comparison between e.g. 'selig ihr Stummen' here and bars 17–19 of *Karwoche* (38), which are also about keeping silence ('und senkest schweigend' etc). There too the persistent pedal points (motif 39) have religious connotations; so has the ending here on the subdominant, like an unresolved Amen.

192 (I 6) 'Wer rief dich denn...'

13 November 1890   F major $d^{b\,1}$–$g^{b\,11}$

Who called you here, then? who sent for you? Who told you to come, if it is a burden to you? Go to the love that pleases you more, go where your thoughts are. Just go where your dreams and thoughts are; I'll gladly absolve you from coming to me. Go to the love that pleases you more. Who called you here then? who sent for you?

This is a fine example of the way in which Wolf treats the often trivial material of the Italian poems, interpreting the text and interfusing it with new emotion by subtleties of illustration and vocal stress. The piano prelude is a gesture of defiance. The voice is then directed to sing its opening questions scornfully; they are punctuated by sharp little chordal interventions, like thwarted gestures of foot or fist. There follow some trivially cheerful phrases from the piano, simulating unconcern. They cease as the voice falters at 'wenn es dir zu Last' (if it is a burden to you). The 'wenn' is stressed and sustained, to add the meaning – *if* it is a burden to you, as it were giving the person addressed a chance to say it is not. That chance is not taken, and the music resumes its assumed insouciance. Yet no sooner has it recovered than it is made to falter again, with a dying fall at 'wo du die Gedanken hast' (where your thoughts are), a slight hesitancy at 'will ich gern dir schenken' (I'll gladly absolve you) and finally, most movingly of all, at the last words. Here with the plainest of harmonies and vocal lines the music inadvertently drops its guard and is suddenly in tears. The piano postlude recovers and restores the singer's defiant stance.

NOTES 1. For the original Tuscan *rispetto* 'Chi ti ci fa venir, chi ti ci chiama?', see Tomasseo I, p. 293.
  2. Wolf was never afraid of writing song-music that seemed banal if the poetic and interpretative context justified it, as here. What may seem trivial equivalents for defiance and nonchalance are seen to be masterstrokes of depiction standing for simulated defiance, pretended cheerfulness. This procedure stands at the outer limit of song-writing; it would hardly be possible to take it any further while remaining in the domain of musical expression. But Wolf's touch was never surer than in the first part of the Italian Songbook, and here the device is used with great

effect. For another song where the music deliberately contradicts the words, see *Wie soll ich fröhlich sein* (217).

3. The motif of defiance (simulated or real) has been heard in *Ritter Kurts Brautfahrt* (97); that of cheerfulness (piano, bars 4–5 etc) has some parallel in the companionable thirds of motif 16, but is otherwise unprecedented. The snapping dissonances, motif 34, recall *Treibe nur mit Lieben Spott* (150). The prelude has a rasp in its tone like the cobbling in *Wie glänzt der helle Mond* (186) written a few months earlier.

193 (I 7) 'Der Mond hat eine schwere Klag'...'

13 November 1890   E♭ minor   b♭–d♭"

The moon has raised a serious complaint, and has made it known to the Lord. She feels that she cannot continue to stand in the sky above, because you have robbed her of her radiance. She says that when she last mustered the ranks of the stars, the full count was incomplete; you had stolen two of the loveliest – those two eyes of yours, whose light has blinded me.

The poem is no more than a quaint conceit, whether in Italian or German. But Heyse's artful subjunctives, 'wolle', 'habest' and so on, lend the lines a touch of added dignity and solemnity, like a legal document. Wolf, as so often in this songbook, goes further still, and treats the text with hushed reverence and awe. His musical response to verses about the beauty of a woman's eyes was always heartfelt. Here the setting suggests that he found these sentiments not merely believable but compelling.

In the piano part, the simple chordal pattern of falling two-bar phrases in an unchanging slow dotted-crotchet-plus-quaver rhythm suggests the grieving yet resigned mien and gestures of a pavane for lost stars. The depth of the singer's underlying emotion is hinted at in the accented word 'du' (you) and the momentary warmth of major harmony at 'Glanz' (radiance), the first imitation of the poem's real meaning. The pavane resumes as before, but when this same meaning is again adumbrated, at 'zwei von den schönsten' (two of the loveliest), the music moves with inevitable rightness into the sweetness of the major key. And when the point of the verses is revealed, at 'die beiden Augen dort' etc, those words are hushed, the pervading rhythm remains unchanged; yet, by the simplest of harmonic means – a few chromatically altered notes, a poignant discord or two, a slight shift of tonality – the music seems momentarily to falter and fight for control until the quiet final chord of the brief postlude is reached.

NOTES 1. For the original Tuscan *rispetto* 'La luna s'è venuta a lamentare', see Tigri, p. 22.

2. The details repay close study. The stepwise falling melodic line of the accompaniment is close kin to the sorrow-motif 22. For one single moment (immediately after the first 'du') that fall is made more precipitate, by the incorporation into the piano part of the vocal falling sevenths that express grieving resignation at 'erhoben', 'kund gemacht' and 'verblendet'. Otherwise bars 1–2 are repeated, at 3–4, 5–6, and once again, a minor third higher, at 9–10 and 11–12. The transition to three sharps here, from the prevailing six flats, forms the dramatic climax of the lunar lawsuit's court-scene; but the contrast should not be exaggerated, for the new key-signature is essentially a convenient way of notating the closely-related key (in Wolfian terms) of G♭ minor. The following Schubertian change to the major on the same tonic thus resolves not only the preceding four bars but the first eight; and this cumulative effect throws into yet bolder relief the surprising clashes and the subdominant treated as tonic with which the song ends, giving the sense of a worshipful Amen, final acceptance after great tribulation.

3. There is a similar ending on the subdominant, together with the interrelation of E♭ and G♭, in *Selig ihr Blinden* (191); the tone of hyperbole (and, for what it is worth, the mention of blindness) is common to both texts. An even closer analogue occurs in *Kennst du das Land* (94), at 'Kennst du den Berg und seinen Wolkensteg', again with G♭ minor notated enharmonically as F♯ minor.

4. The chordal rhythm ₵ ♩. ♪♩. ♪ has also already been heard in the first *Peregrina* song (45, note 3), the words of which are also about the beauty of a woman's eyes (cf. 44, note 5); *Peregrina II* (46, note 2) also has the flat-sharp notational ambiguity.

194 (I 8) 'Nun lass uns Frieden schliessen...'

14 November 1890   E♭ major   e♭'–e♭''

Let us make peace, my dearest life; already we have quarrelled too long. If you will not yield, I shall; how could we two make war to the death? Kings and princes make peace, and should not lovers thirst for it? Princes and soldiers make peace, and should it elude two lovers? Do you think that where such great lords succeed, a pair of contented hearts can fail?

The text, with the patterned repetitions that characterize this songbook, has a simple lulling effect of soothing reassurance. Wolf overwhelms it in music of matchless sincerity and serenity. In the piano part, softly-moving broken chords are interspersed with tenderly-falling strands of melody that match or echo the vocal line, which in turn sensitively reflects the cadence of the words and the lilt of the accompaniment. There are also moments of heightened emotion, where the stepwise vocal melodies and generally diatonic piano part briefly diverge into a falling sixth or seventh among faintly perplexed or disturbed chromatic harmonies, at the questioning phrases 'auf den Tod bekriegen?' (make war to the death?) and 'zwei Verliebten wohl missraten?' (elude two lovers?). The final question is tenderly hesitant; the piano postlude offers a tranquil and reassuring rejoinder. 'Of course we cannot fail', it says softly; 'of course we cannot'.

NOTES 1. For the original Tuscan *rispetto* 'Facciam la pace, caro bene mio', see Tommaseo I, p. 261.

2. The construction is typically taut. Piano bars 1–16 are repeated as 17–32, with a slight difference between 11–12 and 27–8 occasioned by the varied vocal line. The three-note falling phrase heard in the postlude echoes the peace-making motif that has unobtrusively sounded in the right hand throughout most of the accompaniment, e.g. in bars 4–8, set to subdominant harmonies with minor inflexions at 'Fehde' (quarrel). Such a phrase occurs in the voice part only once, at the word 'ergeben' (surrender), the verbal equivalent of the musical meaning. Its postlude version (cf. bars 8–11, 24–7) includes a hint of a converging inner voice as in Wolf's love motif 13.

3. The use of the diminished seventh harmony for rhetorical questions ('bekriegen?', 'missraten?') and the dominant seventh for real ones ('dürsten?', 'vollbringt?') is highly Schumannian (motifs 33 and 32). The persistent pedal points are motif 39.

4. For a possible sequel to this song see 205, note 2.

195 (I 9) 'Dass doch gemalt...'

29 November 1891   F major   c'–g♭"

If only a picture were painted of all your charms, and a heathen prince found it. He would honour you with a great gift; he would lay his crown in your hands. His whole kingdom to its furthest bounds would have to follow the true faith. It would be proclaimed throughout the land that all must become Christians and love you. Straightaway all the heathen would be converted and become good Christians, and love you.

As in 193 above, an innocuous and rather stilted poetic conceit is treated with burning intensity. The song presents the verses as a series of thoughts passing through the mind and turning into music as they pass. It is as if every moment of every bar were a new and immediate quickening in response to a great love. There is no prelude; the voice is impatient to begin. Broken chords and a breathless vocal line in crescendo announce the first idea as if it had just at that moment occurred to the singer. Then the voice hushes at 'fände' (found), distracted by the imagined beauty of that picture and the instant impression made on its discoverer. An increased intensity of emotion is conveyed by the chromatically changing piano chords; the vocal line inclines and bows as the crown is removed and given in homage. At the renewed quietude of repeated left-hand octaves after 'in deine Hände' (in your hands) the song comes to a half-close. But now (and again the music suggests that a new and striking idea has just occurred) the octaves become chords mounting in insistent repetition over a strong bass line, sustaining the voice's pronouncement of a complete national conversion to the furthest borders. This is briefly but tellingly symbolized in a four-bar phrase that spans the entire compass of the song, traversing an octave and a half from the lowest vocal note to the highest. A culminating crescendo clearly foretells some new and significant pronouncement. Voice and right hand have repeated notes or chords like a town crier in every street in the land; the left-hand accented theme offers a clarion call to attention. Each of these small-scale but vivid images is again a new idea, further intensified by an excited quickening of the musical pulse and then by its solemn retardation. With a return to the first tempo the vocal climax is reached with a ringing proclamation 'Christ soll ein Jeder werden' (all must become Christians). The music suddenly and briefly hushes, as if its mission were accomplished; as if, amid all the panoply and excitement, the occasion for it had been almost forgotten and then remembered – 'und dich lieben' sings the voice softly, with that last word tenderly lingered out. This is the emotional climax of the song. It is again followed by repeated octaves, this time on the keynote in what sounds like a full close. Another composer might have treated the final couplet as a further dynamic culmination. Wolf's different way – yet another original idea – is infinitely more expressive and convincing. What follows is the music of proclamation, now mysteriously muted into a quiet statement giving the sense of 'Yes, that is just what *would* happen; they would all become good Christians and love you'. The postlude muses on that Madonna face and the faith it inspires; the final chord reverts to the song's first chord, ready to repeat an endless paean of praise.

NOTES 1. For the original Tuscan *rispetto* 'Le tue bellezze fossero dipinte', see Tommaseo I, p. 42; also Tigri, p. 21.

2. The accent on the left-hand octave A in bar 19, missing in some Peters editions, is restored by the *Kritische Gesamtausgabe*. Note how this form of what might be called the proclamation motif, beginning in bar 15, is itself converted in the brief postlude; the triumph of bar 19 becomes the humility of bar 27.

3. This song marks the beginning of a new creative period. Like *Der Tambour* (17), which began the Mörike outburst, it typically teems with invention. But the more limited framework of the short Italian lyric form demands a tauter and integrated construction, a masterly achievement which repays close study.

4. For the verbal theme see 44, note 5; for the harmonies in the last line see 167, note 3.

325

196 (I 10) 'Du denkst mit einem Fädchen...'

2 December 1891   B♭ major   d'–f''

You think to catch me with a thread, to enthrall me with a glance. But I've already caught others who flew higher than you, so don't trust me, when you see me laughing. I've already caught others, never doubt it. And I am in love – but not with you. [I am in love, but not with you.]

The essence of the lyric is compressed into the music, drop by drop. Even the tiny piano prelude suggests the kind of overture that consists of a pot-pourri of themes from the opera. There is self-conscious pride in the slow double-dotted rhythm, followed by a hint of flaunting trickery as the home key is unexpectedly inflected and graced with lingering staccato chords. The opening words yield the idea of loosely-dangling threads of melody in the piano part. At 'ich fing schon andre' (I've already caught others) these drooping strands tighten and connect back to the rising assertive themes heard in the prelude – the motif of the catcher, not the caught. They relax again for the words of warning, but soon incorporate a rising inflexion or two in the right hand, as if the singer were gaining in confidence; and the self-assertion returns with renewed vigour as the right rôles are reasserted; 'schon andre fing ich', the singer again proclaims. The following words are repeated for extra effect. The first 'I *am* in love – but not with you' begins decisively – 'Ich bin verliebt' on swelling accented tones – and then suddenly adds in a rippling anticlimax of quick and quiet notes 'doch eben nicht in dich'. For the second 'verliebt' the voice goes swooning up an octave in pretended bliss, and then breaks into outright laughter for the rest of the phrase. 'So there' says the piano, and the song is over.

NOTES 1. For the original Tuscan *rispetto* 'Ti pensi di legarmi con un filo', see Tomasseo I, p. 273.

2. The music again has a compelling originality. Its few themes in few bars crackle with invention, and it is not surprising that this song follows 195 as the second of a new, though short-lived, creative phase.

3. Again the miniature construction is noteworthy. Thus the falling sixth of the prelude etc is reversed into the rising interval at 'nicht traun', which is then extended into an upward octave at 'lachen'. That idea underlies the vocal line's octave leap at the second 'verliebt', which is tense with the suppressed laughter released in the rising sixth of the final 'in dich' and instantly echoed in the bar of postlude, after which the confident rising fourth ends the song exactly as it began.

4. The prelude may be compared with that of *Geselle, woll'n wir uns* (200), with its analogous falling interval of the diminished sixth – in that context also a brief evocation of deception and chicanery.

197 (I 11) 'Wie lange schon...'

4 December 1891   F minor   e'–f''

How long I have always yearned – oh, if only a musician loved me! Now the Lord has granted my wish and sends me one, all milk and roses. And here he comes, with a delicate air, and droops his head, and plays the violin.

The verses have a certain absurd charm of their own; but the music gives them a whole new dimension of sympathy and humour. The piano begins with slow drooping wistful phrases repeated an octave higher or lower

 etc,

the melodic and rhythmic shape of which, in a variety of ingenious transformations, dominates the song. There is a lesson in song-writing encapsulated in this three-note motif, which offers a perfect musical equivalent for the theme of the words – a simple basic idea taking a somewhat unusual form. A slight syncopation, a sighing effect, and a chromatically altered note together effect this metamorphosis, which imparts to the whole song its characteristic savour of affectionate burlesque. These little phrases in the piano part moan feelingly as they move in sympathy with the plaints of the vocal line throughout the first page. But with the answering of the maiden's prayer a delightful change comes over the music. The left hand of the piano, in measured staccato semiquavers, points out the delicate new arrival on the scene. In the right hand the little sighing phrases appear in a new rhythm.

Their speed, suddenly doubled, denotes a quickening of interest; like the singer, they have become decidedly less languid and more alert. Over this accompaniment the voice sings its grateful phrases, now flowing out without distraction or hesitation and reaching their highest point with the melody of the original germ-theme at 'sanfter Miene' (delicate air). At the last words, 'die Violine', the piano takes over. Now the song ends with an entrancing postlude, one of Wolf's finest comic inspirations. It is a vivid vignette of the young violinist playing his specially rehearsed little piece 'with great difficulty and hesitancy', as the composer's direction requires, and conscious of the ever-present possibility of a sudden appalling wrong note. In an agony of indecision, the snatched accents are misplaced on the second or third beats before being triumphantly allocated to the first. Thus encouraged, the soloist ends con bravura with a trill. It has to be approached rather nervously and performed slowly and laboriously, as the composer again indicates; but the subject of this shy serenade is presumably in an uncritical frame of mind. That interpretative point, and indeed the whole effect, can however easily be obscured or even marred if the postlude is performed as an independent piano solo and not as an integral part of the song.

NOTES 1. For the original *rispetto* 'Oh quanto tempo l'ho desiderato', see Tigri, p. 72.

2. In the first (as in the Peters) edition, the minim chord and minim rest of the last bar double the 2/4 time to 4/4, no doubt by an inadvertence induced in Wolf's mind by writing a slow trill on the penultimate prolonged semiquaver. But the *Kritische Gesamtausgabe*'s amendment of this bar to a crotchet chord and a crotchet rest seems arguable or even dubious. The length of the postlude, both as music and as character-study, might well require two full minims for its resolution.

3. Wittingly or not, Wolf is here engaged in self-parody. The main theme is a burlesque of his own frequent equivalent for moods of sorrow and deprivation, namely the three-note falling motif 22, here furnished with an expressive augmented second. It is significant that this interval is heard twice only in the voice part – at 'ein Musikus' and 'sanfter Miene', which together define the song's meaning.

4. The singer herself seems to be imagined in the music as a very young girl – perhaps a contemporary of the heroine of the parallel *Ich esse nun mein Brot* (210). There are also faint echoes of *Das verlassene Mägdlein* (19). Thus the vocal line at 'immer mein Verlangen' recalls 'Träne auf Träne dann'.

5. The young violinist's solo may be interpreted as an affectionate allusion to a charming melody that occurs briefly in the Schubert song *An eine Quelle* D530 (bar 17ff.), also about the shyness of young love.

198 (I 12) 'Nein, junger Herr...'

7 December 1891   G major   d'–f''

No, young sir, this won't do at all; people should try to behave properly. You think I'm good enough for everyday, don't you? But you look out for something better at holiday time.

No, young sir, if you go on transgressing like that, your daily girl will be handing in her notice.

As usual, Wolf has looked behind the words to the mood. Here he discovers, under the ostensible gaiety, a hint of distress. But it is only a hint; nothing can be allowed to trouble for long the delightful lilt of this music, and cheerfulness prevails. The prelude announces the vivacious rhythms that characterize the song. The main theme, in voice and piano at the first words 'Nein, junger Herr', to the sound and sense of which it is designed to correspond, is subtly varied to accord with the overtones of the voice part. The right hand adds a falling sixth, already unobtrusively anticipated in the left hand a bar earlier, with the effect of a further confirmatory gesture of hand or head; 'no indeed, this will never do', and this is cunningly woven into the texture throughout. Both melody and accompaniment are set swaggering about parodistically at 'Feiertagen' (holiday time), the sound of Sunday best as distinct from workaday wear. The first strain recurs with the opening words. Now comes a brief but overt suggestion of distress as the tempo is held back. But it was not wholly serious and may even have been merely simulated. The music recovers its poise at the end of the voice part and goes dancing off in a laughing postlude.

NOTES 1. For the original Tuscan *rispetto* 'Giovinottino, non si fa così', see Tommaseo I, p. 283.

2. The falling sixths are heard augmented at bars 6 (right hand) and 13 (left hand) perhaps with a suggestion of the deception of motif 20. The frolicking at 'Feiertagen' has the typical F♯ major tonality of motif 40.

3. For some reminiscences of the main melody see 166, note 3.

199 (I 13) 'Hoffärtig seid Ihr...'

8 December 1891   F♯ minor   e♯'–f♯''

You are haughty, lovely child, and you treat your suitors arrogantly. If you are spoken to, you scarcely deign to reply, as if a kindly greeting would cost you too much effort. Yet you are no Alexander's daughter, no kingdom will be your dowry. Then if you don't want gold, take dross; if you don't want love, take disdain.

As so often in this songbook Wolf throws new and revealing light on the verses. These suggest merely petulance and peevishness; and this tension is tellingly conveyed by the fiery pace of the music, the vehemence of the vocal line and the jabbing octaves of the piano part (often in aptly contrary motion). But at the words 'als kostet' Euch zu viel ein holder Gruss' (as if a kindly greeting would cost you too much) the mood is suddenly mollified. The prelude's angry motif starts and then stops, as if unable to maintain its malice; the spikiness of the staccato quavers is smoothed into long slow chords; the voice falters in wistful tenderness.

When the angry phrases resume, words and music have been enriched by this almost involuntary admission of continuing love. But such a procedure has its dangers, and the composer no less than his imagined character has perhaps been caught in two minds. Wolf himself sought to mitigate the violence of his original setting of the final words and their aftermath; on second thoughts he deleted a four-bar postlude in which both hands strike out in gestures of rage and frustration. The resulting truncated version, ending on a single sharp final chord that is heard to break off the relationship, is still so brilliantly effective that it risks offering too great a contrast. The singer has an exacting task in making an artistic unity of such rage and such tenderness in twenty brief bars. But a successful performance can offer the most telling of tributes to Wolf's command of range and contrast within the miniature form.

NOTES 1. For the original Tuscan *rispetto* 'Bella che troppo in alto vi tente', see Tommaseo I, p. 239.

2. The deleted postlude, quoted in the *Kritische Gesamtausgabe*, would have furnished some striking examples of motif 27. Instead, all that gestured anger is forced into the last two chords, which are meant to sound like sharp slaps feel. There are similarly motivic threats of violence from the piano at 'Zinn' and then in the voice at 'Willst du nicht'. At the key-phrase 'Als kostet' Euch' etc, bars 8–9, is the love-motif 13. The contrary motion in voice and piano *passim* symbolises conflicting emotions.

3. The song may be considered as the male counterpart of *Wer rief dich denn* (192).

200 (I 14) 'Geselle, woll'n wir uns in Kutten hüllen...'

5 December 1891   D major   d'–f''

Friend, shall we disguise ourselves in friars' cowls – and leave the world to him who delights in it? Then we'll go knocking from door to door on the quiet: 'Alms for a poor monk, for Jesus' sake.' 'O dear father, you must come again later, when we've taken the bread out of the oven. O dear father, just come again later, a young daughter of mine is lying ill in bed.' 'And if she is ill, then let me go to her, lest she should die unprepared. And if she is ill, then let me in to see her, so that she can make her confession to me. Close door and window, so that no one disturbs us, while I'm hearing the poor child's confession!'

The character of the bogus friar with his pretended concern for the spiritual welfare of young girls might well have stepped from the pages of Chaucer or Boccaccio. The composer, in music as attractive as it is ingenious, presents a richly comic yet inoffensive commentary on

330

boundless fraudulence and guileless piety. The contrast is unified and deployed in quasi-narrative form by successive variations of the brief theme

announced as the beginning of a short prelude. In that context it exudes a false geniality. After the monstrous hypocrisy of 'die Welt dem lassen, den sie mag ergötzen' (leave the world to him who delights in it) it slides about in unctuous chromatics in both hands, like the self-congratulatory rubbing of fat greasy palms. Then its first two notes are heard in the piano left hand knocking on the imagined door, first tentatively and then with confident insistence, at 'dann pochen wir an Tür' etc. And the theme reappears, with added wheedling, at 'gebt einem armen Mönch' (alms for a poor monk). Now the voice of the gullible parent replies – 'O lieber Pater' etc. But the basic quaver rhythm and texture already established in the previous bars remain unaltered. It is thus made clear that this section is not solely an impression of the actual words and tone to be expected, but a heartless parody of them by the bogus friar. When his own voice is heard again at the first 'und ist sie krank' (and if she is ill) the original theme returns in the piano left hand, very pleased with itself. At the second 'und ist sie krank' it begins a rollicking so outrageous as practically to constitute a breach of the peace. Then, as if suddenly aware of the danger of giving the game away, it relapses into a more general tone of sanctimonious humbug. The imagined errand of mercy successfully completed, the theme trots off in the piano postlude in search of an actual victim.

NOTES 1. For the original Venetian *vilota* 'Compagno mio, vustu che andèmo frate', see Dalmedico, p. 41.

2. The main motif has overtones of deceit and deception also audible in other songs, e.g. *Du denkst mit einem Fädchen* (196, note 4). Its characteristic diminished sixth also typifies the lecherous and treacherous Corregidor in Wolf's opera of that name, from its first bar onwards. The sliding chromatics of the piano interlude after 'ergötzen' are motif 20. The evocative use of staccato at 'Ein Töchterlein', where the music as it were pricks up its ears, scarcely able to credit its good luck, is also motivic.

3. There are interesting and perhaps revealing resemblances between this song and that perfect piece of true piety *Wie glänzt der helle Mond* (186) dated eighteen months earlier. The parental voice in this song (e.g. at 'Ein Töchterlein' etc) sings in the tones of the devout believer in 186. The central figure here has a distinct musical affinity (e.g. at 'gebt einem armen Mönch') with the figure of St Peter in the Keller song; further, they both have rapping motifs. The earlier themes of piety are here cruelly caricatured. See also *Dank des Paria* (115, note 3).

331

201 (I 15) 'Mein Liebster ist so klein...'

3 December 1891   F major   e'–g♭''

My sweetheart is so small that without bending down he can sweep my room with his curls. When he went into the garden to pick jasmine, he was terrified by a snail. Then when he sat down indoors to get his breath back, a fly knocked him spinning; and when he came to my window a bluebottle smashed his head in.

A curse on all flies, gnats and bluebottles, and whoever has a sweetheart from Maremma! A curse on all flies, gnats and midges, and on all who have to stoop so low for a kiss!

The men of Maremma are proverbially tiny. But this setting is not a protest; it is a love-song, full of affectionate teasing and pretended dismay. Some of this transformation is effected by the amorous liveliness of Heyse's last line; the idea of stooping for a kiss is an invention not found in the original Italian. In the music, the picture of the minuscule lover and his misfortunes is treated with a certain dignity as well as humour; Wolf, after all, was himself a very small man.

The prelude anticipates the piano part at the mention of having a sweetheart from Maremma. This music, with its tiny intervals and finicking rhythm, clearly illustrates the idea of smallness; but it is far from being merely pictorial. As the direction 'sehr zart' suggests, the mood is expressive of the relationship between the singer and her lover. The voice begins with a tender melody as small in its intervals as it could well be, while the diminutive piano themes stretch and gesticulate upwards in vivid and amusing pantomime. The comic episodes are graphically treated in voice and piano, complete with buzzing wing-beats and sudden collisions. Finally the two climaxes of frustrated exasperation at 'Verwünscht sei'n alle Fliegen' (a curse on all flies) melt into a revealing tenderness at the last words 'so tief muss bücken' (must stoop so low). The postlude, thus encouraged, gains in confidence if not in stature; and there is a happy ending in which two chords, long and short, are solemnly united by the sustaining pedal.

NOTES 1. For the original Tuscan *rispetto* 'E lo mio damo è tanto piccolino', see Tigri, p. 280.

2. The constructional use of the smallness motif 3 is noteworthy. Thus the piano part at 'und wer ein Schätzchen hat aus den Maremmen', bars 50–3, becomes bars 3–6 of the prelude, introduced and echoed by further minor seconds. These are heard buzzing in diminution for the flies' wings at 'da warf ihn eine Fliege' etc. That basic interval is deliberately stretched upward for added graphic effect in the piano right hand in bars 10–17, audibly wishing itself taller. The whip-lash runs before and after 'stiess eine Bremse' are also overtly depictive.

3. See also *Ihr jungen Leute* (202).

202 (I 16) 'Ihr jungen Leute..'

11 December 1891   C major   e'–f''

*You young men marching off to war, you must take good care of my
sweetheart. See that he bears himself bravely under fire; he was never in a
war before, in all his life.*

*Never let him sleep in the open; he's so delicate, the consequences could
be serious. No, don't let him sleep out under the moon; he'd perish, he just
isn't used to it.*

The verses, though no doubt ironically intended, emerge in their musical
guise as pleasantly teasing and affectionate, just as in the previous song;
and the juxtaposition may be meant to suggest that they are again
addressed to the same lad by the same girl. Wolf matches them here with a
small-scale tune arranged as a para-military march. This is introduced
and interspersed with some rather diffident drum-taps, and later on
becomes for a moment or two decidedly dejected before recovering its
modest confidence and marching staunchly off into the distance. The
voice picks out and sings the various delightful melodies latent within this
evocative background. As in the previous song, what we hear is a
relationship, almost a duet, between the singer's dismayed concern for her
lover and his own rueful discomfiture; this idea, and the wit and freshness
of its treatment, typically add a new dimension to the miniature song-
form and turn a lyric trifle into an enduring masterpiece.

NOTES 1. For the original Tuscan *rispetto* 'Giovanettini che andate alla guerra',
see Tommaseo I, p. 183.

2. *Sie blasen zum Abmarsch* (174) is also worth comparing, this time as a more
serious treatment of the same theme of departure, again complete with military
march. The companionable thirds that go quickstepping through the piano part
of both songs are motif 16; the horn passages of motif 8 here (e.g. at 'er ginge
drauf' and in the postlude) provide a trumpet counterpart to the insistent drum-
beat as well as suggesting the open air and (in the lugubrious harmonic inflexion
at 'drauf') its possible perils. Perhaps it was the open air connotations of this motif
that led Wolf to write an analogous postlude in the otherwise wholly unrelated
Schon streckt' ich aus (213) five years later. The augmented chords at 'freiem
Himmel schlafen' and 'möchte sich bestrafen' well exemplify the bathetic
significance of motif 23.

3. At the marked tempo of crotchet = 104 only a virtuoso can give the necessary
crisp precision to the drum-tap rhythm ♩ ♪ ♫ ♩ ; it seems sensible to slacken the
speed if necessary in order to tauten the imagery. The rhythm itself may be
thought, by analogy with its counterpart in *Der neue Amadis* (108), to suggest the
idea of playing at soldiers.

4. The interlude after 'Leben' recalls the piano part at 'echte Blum' und Perl' in
Der Glücksritter (75, note 2); the common denominator is the carefree swagger of
soldierly bearing, whether genuine or parodied.

203 (I 17) ·'Und willst du deinen Liebsten...'

4 December 1891   A♭ major   e♭'–f♭''

And if you would see your sweetheart die, then do not wear your hair in tresses, my dearest. From your shoulders let it float down free; it looks like threads of pure gold. Like golden threads stirred by the wind, how lovely your hair is, how lovely she who wears it! Gold threads, silk threads uncounted – how lovely your hair is, how lovely she who combs it!

The lyric suggests the speaking of an incantation or magic spell as a most potent love-charm. The gently spread piano chords offer a feeling image of gossamer strands slowly teased or combed apart; the composer's direction 'weich' (soft) connotes yieldingness or smoothness to the touch. In the first two bars, only the first chord of each bar is arpeggiated, as a hint of what is to follow; the vocal line is solemnly motionless. But when the secret is divulged, at 'trage nicht dein Haar gelockt' (do not wear your hair in tresses), the arpeggios sound out freely and frequently, lifting and flowing, while the voice falls and rises in the fullest accord with the fervency of the wish expressed: 'lass von den Schultern frei sie niederwehen' (From your shoulders let it float down free). Then the music, like the singer, returns to the rapt contemplation of the opening strains, at the imagined vision of pure gold. With the further intensified description 'wie goldne Fäden, die der Wind bewegt' (Like gold threads stirred by the wind) the soft arpeggios, quickened and embellished, are made to waft and float in a supreme matching of image and sound. As the lyric insists on 'gold' and 'schön', like a litany, brighter sharp-key tonalities are threaded through the harmonic texture, culminating in the mysteriously remote chord heard at 'ungezählt' (uncounted). Then the music, again matching the singer's mood, reverts to the real world of the home key of A♭ major, ending as it began with an almost spoken invocation from the voice and a brief moment of adoring love from the piano postlude.

NOTES 1. For the original Tuscan *rispetto* 'Se vuoi vedere il tuo servo morire', see Tommaseo I, p. 78.

2. The piano rhythm of the first page, used in diminution on the second ♩ ♩ ♩ becoming ♪♩ ♪ etc at a reduced tempo), has the self-surrendering submission of motif 1. The piano melody is a theme associated by Wolf with the idea of adoration; its flattened sixth is brought out as an added expressive detail in the piano postlude (cf. motif 11). The sharp-key notation within the A♭ major signature may be compared with the analogous effects in *Schon streckt' ich aus* (213). At 'ungezählt' the harmonic contrasts are juxtaposed in the two dominant

sevenths a semitone apart characteristic of the mystery of motif 19.

3. The clear association between arpeggios and the gesture of hair-combing was earlier exemplified in *In dem Schatten meiner Locken* (148, note 3): motif 28.

204 (I 18) 'Heb' auf dein blondes Haupt...'

12 December 1891   A♭ major   f'–f''

Lift up your blond head and do not sleep, and do not be beguiled by slumber. I have four important things to say to you; you must not miss a single one of them. The first is that my heart is breaking for you; the second, my wish is to belong to you alone; the third, that to you I commend my salvation; the last, my soul loves you alone.

The piano begins with a persistent 12/8 crotchet-quaver rhythm in four-part chords yet full of unobtrusive melody which develops into singing right-hand octaves whenever the voice part comes temporarily to rest, whether at the end of a phrase as at 'Schlafe nicht' (do not sleep) or on a prolonged word, such as 'Schlummer' (slumber). This gives the effect of continuous shared melody, as befits the emotions and the scene portrayed. But the musico-verbal correspondence goes deeper still. The verses stress the need for wakeful and alert attention. At the same time this beautiful love-song is almost a lullaby, reaching a *forte* only five times in twenty-two bars, and then only for a beat or two. So the piano part almost enacts the role of a listener to the singing voice, emerging receptively from sleep, attending, echoing and then relapsing. This long chain of shared and responding melody is linked by the unbroken rhythm, down to the closing phrase 'dich allein liebt meine Seele'. Here the climax of the song is reached, as so often with the Italian lyrics, in a hushed murmur; and just for one brief moment the piano rhythm relaxes, as if to devote especial attention to that last word, 'soul'. The postlude softly offers the melody that lay hidden unheard at the heart of all the accompaniment throughout, as if to say that the important message has been truly received and understood.

NOTES 1. For the original Tuscan *rispetto* 'Alza la bionda testa, e non dormire', see Tigri, p. 72.

2. The rhythm and barring need careful handling in performance. When the hidden and dispersed melody is finally heard overt and entire in the postlude, its stress has shifted a bar, from the second beat to the first. This may be a Wolfian way of showing that the music has by then become (so to speak) fully awake and aware; and on any interpretation it successfully diversifies Heyse's blandly iterative iambs without sacrificing their lulling effect. Nevertheless the accentuation occasionally runs counter to the sense. This is felt most clearly at

'Herze bricht', where the musical accent makes the singer say that his *heart* is breaking, instead of, more sensibly, that his heart is *breaking*. Perhaps one should play and sing without any strong stress except where the cadence of the words demands it.

3. Another mild puzzle of accentuation occurs at the word 'vier', which Wolf has specially marked for emphasis. But there seems to be no discernible point in the fact that there are to be *four* items, and the off-beat accent here surely need not be too strongly stressed.

4. The opening bars of the song (and its postlude) have the narrative-reflective harmony of motif 21.

5. There is a detectable affinity between the final phrase ('das letzte' etc) here and in *Auch kleine Dinge* (187) at 'und duftet' etc – another reason for supposing the latter song to be a love-song.

205 (I 19) 'Wir haben beide...'

16 December 1891   E♭ major   b♭'–f''

We have both been silent for a long time; all at once speech came back to us again. The angels that fly down from heaven, they brought peace again after war. God's angels have flown down, they brought peace in their train. Love's angels came in the night and have brought peace to my breast.

In this masterpiece the contrast between sullen silence and tender speech is made movingly vivid and true. The first few bars evoke the numb sadness of estrangement. The piano rhythm is slow, tolling, in drooping octaves. The harmony is uncertain and obscure. The vocal melody is a weary monotone. Each separate element yearns for expression and fulfilment; each gradually thaws to give a hint of coming new life. Then after the word 'wieder' (again) the music takes wing. Quickening rhythms come beating in to voice and piano; the tense harmonies resolve into simple chords, with an effect of warmth and brightness; new melodies appear in the voice and in both hands of the accompaniment. The sonorous imagery embodies both the relief of peacemaking and its angelic symbolism; the piano in particular is made to sound simple yet seraphic, in a repeated four-note motif

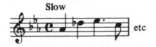

which now gently invades and dominates the music, like the angels in the poem. At the second mention of the peace that they bring and instil, 'mit ihnen ist der Frieden eingezogen', the key-changes have reached the tonic of E♭ major for the first time in the song, with an ineffable sense of coming home. At the last syllables of that phrase the voice falls to its lowest note and then suddenly soars to its highest on the first syllable of 'Liesbesengel' (love's angels), again in a brief but graphic evocation of the central image, further depicted by the piano's outspread chords. The piano musingly repeats the angel-motif, and then closes with an expression of perfect peace.

NOTES 1. For the original Tuscan *rispetto* 'Ha tanto tempo ch'eravamo muti', see Tommaseo I, p. 264.

2. The sense of the music is the amazed tenderness expressed in *Nun lass uns Frieden schliessen* (194), 'how could we have quarrelled, you and I, how is that possible?' In the one word 'wieder', bar 4, this mood is marvellously concentrated. The rising minor third is almost a question; and it echoes the questioning of the same interval at the two central moments of the earlier song, to which this one could be a natural sequel.

3. The downward curve of the piano opening bars recalls the sorrow motif 22; the outspread arpeggios are an analogue of motif 28; there is an occasional suggestion of the loving tenderness of motif 14 (e.g. piano treble and tenor voices, bar 12); the flattened sixth at 'Frieden', bar 17, and again in the postlude, has the peacefulness of motif 37.

206 (I 20) 'Mein Liebster singt...'

12 December 1891   G minor   d'–f''

My lover is singing outside the house in the moonlight, and I must lie listening here in bed. I turn away from my mother and weep tears of blood that never run dry. A broad stream I have wept by the bed, I cannot tell for weeping whether day has yet dawned. A broad stream of tears I have wept with longing; the tears of blood have blinded me.

A world of drama and passion is made explicit in the tiny compass of this masterly song. Wolf adds a new dimension to the words by incorporating the lover's serenade into the piano part. This is so bewitchingly tender and sad, and so independent in construction, that it might well pass in a solo performance as one of the finest of Chopin's mazurkas – a genre which it strongly recalls in mood and texture, without being in any way derivative. No sooner has its right-hand melody begun than the singer recognizes and identifies it: 'Mein Liebster singt'. The vocal line is equally expressive and independent throughout. Yet the song is a perfect unity; the voice of the lover and the thoughts of the listening girl are one single shared sorrow.

NOTES 1. For the original Tuscan *rispetto* 'Amor, che passi la notte cantando', see Tigri, p. 2.

337

2. The two strands of song and serenade are most subtly interwoven. Thus the vocal phrases overlap the right-hand melodies in both directions, usually following as if in involuntary response ('Liebster', 'Weg von der Mutter', the second 'Strom am Bett') but once eagerly anticipating the piano's entry, at bars 20–2. Each component has independent and varying phrase-lengths that never once coincide, a construction which is itself evocatively symbolic of the situation depicted. The guitar-patterns contain sadly-echoed repetitions (bars 3–6, 8–9) which are themselves echoed (e.g. by the interpolated bar 21) and prolonged (e.g. by the added refrain at bars 28–9) to suggest the frustrations of time passing and time wasted. In the postlude the serenading strains dissolve into the night in anticipation of the similar effect at the end of *Schon streckt' ich aus* (213): a refinement of the processional exits favoured in earlier songbooks.

3. Some of the structural features are puzzling. Thus it seems very unWolfian for the same phrase 'den breiten Strom am Bett' to be allotted such strongly contrasting accentual patterns, without any clear verbal point, as here at bars 20–3 and 30–1; and the left-hand arpeggiation is not entirely consistent, e.g. in its omission at bar 16 (so in the *Kritische Gesamtausgabe* as well as Peters).

4. If thematic kinship within Wolf's *œuvre* is any guide, the piano part at e.g. bars 8–9 suggests that the burden of the serenade is a passionate plea for elopement; this music has evident affinities with the piano part of *Und schläfst du mein Mädchen* (173), dated more than two years earlier.

5. Another 'mazurka' theme is heard in *Tief im Herzen trag' ich Pein* (169).

207 (I 21) 'Man sagt mir...'

23 December 1891   A minor   e'–f''

They tell me your mother disapproves; then stay away, my dear, respect her wishes. Oh, dearest, no, don't respect her wishes, defy her, visit me just the same, in secret. No, my dearest, take no notice of her at all, defy her, come more often than before! No, don't listen to her, whatever she says, defy her, my love, come every day!

From a characteristic piano motif

which resounds obsessively throughout, and a vocal line that freely follows all the inflexions of the words, Wolf has created music that explores every possible aspect of the mood of the singer of these verses, from petulance to anger, from tenderness to exuberance. The surrender of the opening lines is only pretended; from the very first bar the piano part is defiance itself. But somehow it is a child's defiance; a stamp of the foot, a thwarted gesture. As the voice sings ingratiatingly 'So bleibe weg, mein Schatz' (then stay away, my dear) the accompaniment's gestures in both hands grow louder and more insistent, accurately predicting the immediate change of mind 'Ach Liebster, nein' (oh, dearest, no). Then the voice becomes pleading and wheedling at 'besuch' mich' (visit me), and also, with the help of some sliding chromatics from the piano, conspiratorial, at 'im Stillen' (in secret). Voice and piano now move together through warmth to passion, with the quoted theme given a slight upward turn and added rhythmic interest. At the exultant conclusion, the word 'alle' (every) is sustained in crescendo for two bars over a fourfold quickening repetition of the defiant motif. The postlude's high-spirited conclusion culminates in a major chord, perhaps suggesting that the situation is not so desperately serious after all.

NOTES 1. For the original Tuscan *rispetto* 'M'è stato detto che tua madre 'n vuole', see Tigri, p. 263.

2. The piano part at 'Stillen' recalls that at bar 6 of *Geselle woll'n wir uns* (200), dated some three weeks earlier. A few other passages suggest a thematic use of sliding chromatics in association with the idea of deceit (motif 20). For some different equivalents for 'defiance' see 134, note 5: and compare motif 27.

3. The end of the postlude has something of the ebullient élan of the parallel passage in *Ich hab' in Penna* (232), and perhaps something of the same coquettish significance.

208 (I 22) 'Ein Ständchen Euch zu bringen...'

10 December 1891   C major   c#'–g''

I've come here to sing a serenade, if the head of the household doesn't find that unacceptable. You have a beautiful daughter; it might well be better not to keep her indoors too strictly.

And if she's already in bed, then kindly let her know on my behalf that her true love has passed this way, who has had her on his mind by day and by night, so much so that in every daily tally of twenty-four hours I miss her for fully twenty-five.

Wolf perfectly matches the poised and self-possessed swagger of the verses, and adds an ironic bantering tone of his own. The lightly tuneful vocal cadences are instantly and emphatically reiterated among the carefree strumming of the accompaniment, at 'kam ich her' (I've come here), 'ungelegen' (unacceptable), 'Töchterlein' (daughter), and so on as if the guitar were an applauding accomplice emphatically echoing each sentiment expressed. At 'dass ihr Getreuer' (that her true love) the guitar-playing begins to dance and race to the song's zestful conclusion. The serenader is clearly very amused by his own humorous exaggeration, with an exultantly prolonged top note giving the sense of italicization at 'fünfundzwanzig' (twenty-five) and an even longer extension of the final 'fehlt' to show how very much she is missed. The guitar figuration laughs and capers with glee in the postlude before disappearing into the distance.

NOTES 1. For the original Tuscan rispetto 'Io son venuto a farvi serenata', see Tommaseo I, p. 120.

2. The mood of badinage is closely akin to that of Thyrsis in Die Spröde (111) and shares his strumming accompaniment. The opening bars here have the narrative strain of motif 21; at the words 'und liegt sie schon im Bett' etc, where it becomes clear that there is to be no meeting, the piano left hand offers what is almost a parody of the separation or loneliness motif 15.

3. For the guitar music and its special effects, see Ach, im Maien war's (166, note 4); the postlude's dwindling and diminuendo both denote disappearance, as in the final flights of Schumann's Papillons, op. 2.

209 (I 23) 'Was für ein Lied...'

30 April 1896   Bb major $e^{b\,1}$–$e^{b\,11}$

What kind of song shall be sung to you, that would be worthy of you? where can I find it? I'd like best to delve it from deep in the earth, never before sung by any creature; a song that no man or woman, not even the oldest, has ever heard or sung until this day.

From these unpretentious verses Wolf has fashioned a great lovesong, itself the answer to the question posed by the first line. It was the last of the Italian songs to be composed, and its selection as the first of Book II was no doubt intended as an act of deliberate homage to Melanie Köchert. The music is instinct with tenderness; the composer's mind is clearly dwelling as much on the woman to whom the desired song is to be dedicated as on the song itself. Indeed the prelude says as much. Although sure of its rhythm, which is all-pervasive in the music of this period, it is at first uncertain of its key. But then, like a thought taking possession of the mind, it establishes beyond doubt, in one of Wolf's best-loved cadences, a home tonic. In this key the piano begins to muse, tentatively trying out melodies possibly suitable for such a song. Against this background the voice offers its own tender and devoted thoughts. The devotion is exemplified by the treatment of the words 'deiner würdig sei' (worthy of you). Here the first syllable of 'deiner' is lovingly stressed and sustained, giving the sense of – 'worthy of you? how could it be, however beautiful?'. The tonality deepens in the piano part at the words 'Am liebsten grüb' ich es tief aus der Erden' (I'd like best to delve it from deep in the earth), and then comes sighing up again to resume its musing at 'Ein Lied, dass weder Mann noch Weib' (a song that no man or woman). Here it joins with the haunting vocal melodies which in searching for and describing a beautiful song themselves become such a song. At the end the postlude restates its original musing accompaniment as a piano solo. The left hand is still creating new melodic lines to weave into the texture as if obscurely dissatisfied with the results achieved. But listeners will be satisfied.

NOTES 1. For the original Tuscan *rispetto* 'Non so quale canzona mi cantare', see Tommaseo I, p. 11.

2. In the piano's main theme is a hint of the adoration of motif 11, with the sixths sounding together. The narrative-reflective motif 21 is also present in a refined form. For the pervading rhythm, no doubt also expressive, see *Wenn du mich mit den Augen streifst* (224, note 4).

3. The piano prelude is comparable with that of *Schon streckt' ich aus* (213), dated only a month earlier. Each has the same underlying musical idea of invocation or conjuration. An earlier reminiscence, also no doubt unconscious, is the kinship of the vocal phrase here at 'Am liebsten grüb' ich' etc with that at bars 5–6 of *Peregrina I* (45, also perhaps inspired by Melanie Köchert); the two poetic ideas run parallel.

4. The song well exemplifies one of Wolf's main expressive uses of harmony; the emotional climax comes with the divergence from the main key at bars 9–12. The four-part texture here as elsewhere in the late Italian songs (cf. *O wüsstest du*, 230) suggests string-quartet writing. It is instructive to compare bars 5–6 with 13–15; their identity is varied at only one note, the third in the tenor part of each bar, in order to avoid a clash with the new vocal line.

210 (I 24) 'Ich esse nun mein Brot...'

25 March 1896   E♭ minor/E♭ major   b♭–f''

I no longer eat my bread dry; I have a thorn stuck in my foot. In vain I look around to left and right, I find no one who wants to love me.

If only there were a little old man to show me a bit of love and respect. I mean, that is to say, a well-set-up honourable old man of about my own age. I mean, to be entirely frank, a little old man of about – fourteen.

A footnote to Heyse's text explains the first line; the bread is now wet with tears. Otherwise the point of the verses, such as it is, lies in the last word. But Wolf takes a much more sympathetic view of them; he lavishes every refinement of his mature artistry on their sleazy humour. In the first section, the drooping semitones in their mourning minor tonality sob and sigh with an exaggerated mock-turtle pathos which though ironical is not unreal. The piano interlude's grieving theme that accompanied the previous words 'keinen find' ich, der mich möchte lieben' (I find no one who wants to love me) is then suddenly converted into the major and used as a small-scale processional march tune of the utmost charm and good humour, with a touch of parodied stiffness in joint and muscle, to match and illustrate the wishful thinking of 'wenn's doch auch nur ein altes Männlein wäre' (if only there were a little old man). The vocal melodies too suddenly broaden and relax like a smile at the idea of finding a suitable sweetheart. The music is now full of rhythmic life and movement, as if the singer had first of all been imagined as sitting about and moping despondently, then rallying to rise and march about pantomimically, then warming to her theme in the explanatory sequences beginning at 'ich meine nämlich' (I mean, that is to say), deliberately delaying the dénouement, and finally striding off to an effectively calculated throwaway exit line. Wolf introduces this unexpected pronouncement 'so von vierzehn Jahren' with great dramatic resource, and follows it with a spirited comment from the piano, all in the final five bars.

NOTES 1. For the original Tuscan *rispetto* 'Non posso più mangiarlo il pane asciutto', and the source of Heyse's annotation, reproduced by Wolf, 'nämlich: mit Tränen befeuchtet' ('ma con lagrime: così diciamo mangiare il pan pentito'), see Tommaseo I, p. 234.

2. This song and its companion piece *Wie lange schon* (197) on similar themes and with similar structure are basically serious-minded, musically speaking; it is a travesty of the composer's intention to treat them as comic songs in the ordinary sense, even though the sadness motif 22 is parodied in each (here in the minor section).

3. The piano part at 'ganz zu offenbaren' is as frank as the words, in its playful insistence on the smallness motif 3; the major march theme at 'wenn's doch auch nur' etc has much the same tone as in the earlier pantomime song *Epiphanias* (104).

211 (I 25) 'Mein Liebster hat zu Tische...'

26 March 1896   F major   c'–g''

My sweetheart invited me to dinner, yet had no house to receive me, no fuel, no stove for boiling and roasting, and the cooking pot itself had long since broken in two. Even the smallest cask of wine was lacking, there was no question of using any glasses; the table was mean, the tablecloth no better, the bread rock-hard and the knife quite blunt.

The craftsmanship of this song is again impeccable. Every possible point is made, from the mildly protesting piano prelude through moods of mounting indignation to the strong sense of ludicrous outrage expressed at the last words of this lamentable history and the final outspoken keyboard commentary. Such points as the rock-hard chords at 'das Brot steinhart' and the right hand's gesture of helpless hacking with a blunt knife readily lend themselves to effective and enjoyable interpretation. But the joke has fallen just a little flat in the composer's mind, and his own musical provision is neither as lavish nor as fresh as usual.

NOTES 1. For the original Venetian *vilota* 'El mio moroso m'a invitato a cena', see Dalmedico, p. 141.

2. The structure though aptly laid out on broad lines (thus bars 9–10 are essentially bars 5–8 a fifth higher) has its subtleties of detail, such as the neat diminution of the theme at 'der Tisch war schmal' etc (bar 18; cf. the tenuto melody in bars 7–8).

3. But there is perhaps overmuch reliance on stock thematic material. The prelude recalls *Begegnung* (20); the parallel sixths may also suggest a meeting, by analogy with motif 16. The chromatics of bar 3 hint at the idea of deception (motif 20). The staccato accompaniment figure that first appears in bar 6 is borrowed from the postlude to *Jägerlied* (16); the common factor may be the open-air scene, unexpected and unwelcome in the present context. For more obvious reasons the song, especially in its last four bars, is in debt to *Spottlied* (89). The physical gesturing of the postlude is motif 27.

212 (I 26) 'Ich liess mir sagen . . .'

28 March 1896   C minor   c'–a♭''

I made enquiries and I was told that handsome Toni is starving himself to death. Ever since love has tormented him so cruelly, he eats seven loaves per molar. After meals, to fortify his digestion, he consumes a sausage and another seven loaves. And if Tonina doesn't ease his pain, there'll shortly be an outbreak of famine and starvation.

Much of the commentary on the previous song seems relevant. Here too the verses present a problem. Their pawky dead-pan humour is refractory, even inimical, to musical expression. The setting has to sound suitably glum and lugubrious without actually being so; but since sound is the only mode of being that the piano part possesses the funereal pace and thematic invariance of its music may well prove a burden too leaden for the singer to lift. Again there are agreeably graphic points, such as the ominous rumbling of the trills throughout, and the perceptible quickening of interest, shortly followed by a motif of gulping hemidemisemiquavers, each time the consumption of loaves is mentioned. But although Wolf crams his song with apt expression, the result has not been generally found any too palatable.

NOTES 1. For the original Venetian *vilota* 'Me xe stà dito, e me xe stà contà', see Dalmedico, p. 139.

2. The music recalls *Der Schäfer* (107) in key, tempo and mood; the verses too are similar in theme. See also *Was soll der Zorn* (218, note 4).

213 (I 27) 'Schon streckt' ich aus . . .'

29 March 1896   A♭ major   e♭¹–e♭¹¹

No sooner had I stretched out my weary limbs on my bed than you appeared before me in vision, my dear love. At once I leap up, put my shoes back on, and go wandering through the town with my lute.

I sing and play so that the streets resound. Many a girl is listening; I have soon passed by. Many a girl has been moved by my song, while already the sound of my singing and playing is wafted away on the wind.

In some of the 1896 Italian songs (e.g. 211, 212, 218) Wolf seems to be using stock procedures without any perceptible new creative impulse. The inference might be that his powers were declining, if it were not for the fact that there also dates from this period a whole succession of resplendent masterpieces. This is the first of them in date order. For sheer beauty of sound and perfection of organization it has few parallels. As with all great work, however, its surprises and delights are not all revealed at first hearing.

The first surprise comes at the first chord of the piano's slow introduction. The key-signature of four flats is immediately contradicted by two chromatic alterations. As a result the ear hears an allusion to a chord in a remote sharp key. It is as if the serenity of A♭ major were being troubled by some bright dream. Peacefulness is achieved as the voice enters with its recollection of tranquillity at 'schon streckt' ich aus'. But at the word 'Bildnis' (vision) the remote chord already briefly hinted at shines out in a sustained arpeggio for a moment before fading back into the basic tonality. Now the tempo quickens perceptibly, and more arpeggio chords are heard, at 'Gleich spring ich auf' (At once I leap up). These chords link the coming serenade with the vision that inspired it. They become more gently insistent as the voice lilts on its way to the word 'Laute' (lute). Then after a bar of reflective interlude the serenading begins. Now the home tonality is firmly established, with a sustained tonic pedal, strolling rhythms, and limpid melodies; the listener's attention is thus entirely centred upon the figure of the lone walker in the night, singing and playing his songs of love and longing. Even here, at this pitch of art, Wolf is still inventing and re-creating fresh nuances of mood at every bar. Thus at 'so manche lauscht – vorüber bin ich bald' (many a girl is listening – I have soon passed by) the unexpected G♭ on 'lauscht' magically suggests the idea of intent listening to a half-heard melody, while the semiquavers at 'vorüber bin ich bald' flit elusively past like that melody itself and its maker in the night, a notion further enhanced by the added key-change at the final phrase. In the postlude, little snatches of serenade are heard wafting away on the wind.

NOTES 1. For the original Tuscan *rispetto* 'E m'ero spolto per andare a letto', see Tigri, p. 101. His text and translation are given in full on pp. 312–13 above.

2. The two G flats in the voice at 'Glieder', tied in the Peters edition, should surely be separate, as in the *Kritische Gesamtausgabe*. Such word-setting is a typically Wolfian miniature evocation of the text, gently stretching and relaxing from one note to the next.

3. The small-scale theme and variation treatment of the material is also carefully tailored to the meaning and emotion of the lyric. The same basic motif is heard first drowsing at bar 3

then in diminution rousing and walking at bar 7ff

and then drifting dreamily into

which is in turn decorated and softened for the final singing and playing

from bar 13 onwards.

4. The reverential rhythm that accompanies the serenading from that bar to the end is motif 1. The mediant modulations of the middle section, motif 24, are elsewhere heard in contexts associated with changes of light. Perhaps Wolf

thought of this song as taking place in successively brighter moments; the darkened room (A^b) the moonlit streets (C, E), the singing finally dispersed by the winds of dawn (A^b, C). The opening bars have the flattened sixth in A^b elsewhere associated with the idea of sleep (motif 37). The serenade's thirds at bars 13, 15, 17–18 etc may suggest the companionable mood of motif 16, while its horn passages at 14, 16, 20 etc may evoke feelings of freedom and the open air (motif 8). The semiquavers at 'vorüber bin ich bald' are comparable to those of 'sei es entwichen' in *Heut' Nacht erhob ich mich* (227), with the same notion of swift transition.

5. For a parallel to the piano prelude see *Was für ein Lied* (209, note 3); for parallels to the piano postlude, see *Ihr jungen Leute* (202, note 2) and *Mein Liebster singt* (206, note 2).

214 (I 28) 'Du sagst mir...'

30 March 1896 E^b major $b^{b\,1} - f^{b\,11}$

You tell me I'm no princess; well, you're not exactly of the Spanish blood royal yourself. No, my dear, when you get up at cock-crow it's to work in the fields, not ride in State coaches. You mock at my lowly station; but one can still be noble though poor. You mock at my having no crown or crest; but all you have to ride on yourself is Shanks's pony.

In other Italian songs (e.g. the next two) on the theme of social or personal disparity there is a sensitive tenderness or an aggressive mockery (sometimes both) underlying the verses, and Wolf has been able to concentrate on these emotions and recreate them musically. In such respects however the present lyric is comparatively deficient. The relationship between the singer and her lover is mainly that of good-humoured teasing, and the mutual ironies tend to cancel each other out. Further, the poetic blend of whimsical humour with rather self-conscious gentility ('noble though poor') makes an unpromising subject for musical portraiture. But Wolf's mastery counterbalances and even outweighs such disadvantages. The earnest tone of the first staves in voice and piano merges imperceptibly into the hint of mocking cock-crow in the mordents after 'Hahnenschrei', with a touch of trill for waking and rousing, and four accented semiquavers for footing it into the fields as the voice sings pointedly 'nicht in Staatskarossen' (not in State coaches), to a vocal line ending in a long drop designed to bring the thought down to earth with a bump. The verse construction of two quatrains turning from seriousness to mockery in the last line of each permits, even demands, a strongly symmetrical structure. But the musical moments which were so brightly evocative for the daybreak scene seem less relevant and effective for the final riposte 'und fährst doch selber nur mit Schusters Rappen', even when rounded off with a soft chuckle or two and a decisive 'so there' from the concluding chords of the postlude.

NOTES 1. For the original Tuscan *rispetto* 'Tu vai dicendo ch'io non son regina', see Tommaseo I, p. 238.

2. Conceivably, the rigidly symmetrical framework is a model of the *tu quoque* theme of the lyric. On any analysis the structure is interesting. Each half of the song has eight bars (not counting the last of the postlude); each is similar to but never exactly the same as its counterpart, in both voice and piano.

3. The strong accents at 'nicht in Staatskarossen' are motif 27.

4. Some of the material (e.g. bar 2) reappears in *Gesegnet sie das Grün* (225, note 4), or perhaps conversely was drawn from that source.

215 (I 29) 'Wohl kenn' ich Euren Stand...'

9 April 1896   C major   d'–f''

Well I know your station in life, which is no mean one. You had no need to descend so low as to love so poor and lowly a creature, when the handsomest of all must bow before you. You easily surpassed even the handsomest men, so I know all too well that you are only trifling with me. You are making game of me, as people have tried to warn me; but oh, you are so handsome – who could be angry with you?

This song of humble and hopeless adoration is one of Wolf's most original conceptions. The fluid string-quartet texture of the piano part is typical of many of the later lyrics, and it lends an added air of detached remoteness to the already unwordly feeling-tone of the music. At the same time the passionate emotion in and behind the words is also faithfully mirrored in the intensity and compression of five or more independent melodic lines in voice and piano, and the harmonies to which they give rise. In this way the poem's quasi-religious blend of deep devotion with self-abnegation is made audibly manifest. At first the voice is heard sharing the tenor or 'viola' part of the accompaniment; but soon the two levels diverge, as if in illustration of the poetic theme. The heartfelt piano melody descends down the keyboard until the words 'brauchtet nicht so tief herabzu steigen' (no need to descend so low), and then rises to start again, with the same insistent downward trend; a speaking likeness of separation and renunciation. At the halfway point, the brief interlude just before 'Die schönsten Männer leicht besiegtet ihr' (You easily surpassed even the handsomest men), the mood changes from resignation to tenderness, to encompass both the moods expressed in the lyric. But there is no halt or deviation in the continuing musical flow, into which the new feeling is

347

wholly absorbed. Unity is further achieved by a small-scale reminiscence: the assuagingly tender movement of the quaver triplets in the piano right hand recalls the rising and falling fourths of the vocal line at 'nicht so tief' (not so low). The music reaches a restrained climax at 'Ihr seid so schön' (you are so handsome) with a lingering top note to beautify that last word; then the voice falls almost to its lowest point in a final gesture of submission. After this the lulling accompaniment figuration breaks off abruptly as though needing a moment or two for control. The postlude sums up the song by combining the loneliness of the first melody with the subservience of broken triplet chords.

NOTES 1. For the original Tuscan *rispetto* 'Conosco il vostro stato, fior gentile', see Tigri, p. 137.

2. 'Herabzusteigen' here echoes 'die müden Glieder' of 213. The Peters edition's ties should surely be omitted here also (and again at 'zeigen' in bar 8) as the *Kritische Gesamtausgabe* indicates. For a harmonic echo, see *Was soll der Zorn* (218, note 4).

3. The left-hand piano melodies in the first page here and in *Auch kleine Dinge* (187) are very close to each other and to the loneliness of motif 15 in their emotive effect.

4. The fluid melodic lines in four parts recall the string-writing in late Schumann chamber music, or the later Wagner orchestra *passim*.

216 (I 30) 'Lass sie nur gehn...'

30–31 March 1896   G minor   d'–f''

Let her go then, she who acts so haughtily, like the magic herb in a field of flowers. You can see what her bright eyes are aiming at; a different man pleases her every day. She carries on just like Tuscany's river that every mountain stream must follow; she carries on like the Arno, as it seems to me, now with many followers and now with none.

A footnote to Heyse's text explains the simile; in the hot summer months the river Arno is deserted by its tributaries. Perhaps Wolf's music just fails in its efforts to irrigate a rather barren text. Although the construction is as taut and epigrammatic as ever the ideas and their treatment seem far from inspired or even original, at least on the first page. But at the words 'Sie treibt es grade wie Toscana's Fluss' (She carries on just like Tuscany's river) Wolf puts his thematic material to more effective use. This second section is no doubt that part of the accompaniment which, as Wolf told Melanie Köchert in a letter next day, had called for extremely detailed working-out. The demisemiquaver runs of imperious caprice are converted into sudden surges of power; repeated quavers add a strongly-flowing current of rhythm. Under the voice's fervent declamation, the left hand sings the melody of the opening words: 'lass sie nur gehn'. At 'sie treibt es wie der Arno' (she carries on like the Arno) an added right-hand theme mockingly quotes the piano part already heard at 'das Wunderkräutlein auf dem Blumenfeld' (the magic herb in a field of flowers). Here the tributary motifs stop their continuous rise, and descend in dramatic contrast; accented minims interrupt the previous flow of left-hand melody. The course of the music is left high and dry. In the postlude the characteristic stream of metaphors is heard running downhill and debouching in the distance.

NOTES 1. For the original Tuscan *rispetto* 'Lassatela passar che fa la brava', see Tommaseo I, p. 275.

2. 'Das Wunderkräutlein' is aptly graced by the mystery motif 19; at bars 2 and 3 the piano's sliding chromatics have something of the deceit motif 20.

3. The demisemiquaver runs for extra rhythmic impetus or as images of a strongly-flowing current of wind or water sound Wagnerian in origin (cf. cellos and basses *passim*).

217 (I 31) 'Wie soll ich fröhlich sein...'

12 April 1896   G minor   d'–f#''

How shall I be happy, and even laugh, when you always spurn me so openly? You come to see me only once every hundred years, and then as if you had been ordered to. Why do you come, if your family is against it? Set my heart free, and then you can go your way. Live at home with your people in peace, for whatever Heaven wills must come to pass here below. Dwell in peace at home with your family; for the will of Heaven shall come to pass.

The song is a masterpiece of construction; and had the verses been only a little more evocative it might have been a masterpiece at the emotional level also. As it is, Wolf distils every drop of meaning and feeling from the text without quite achieving the sum of pure quality required to match the major marvels of the Italian Songbook.

'Wie soll ich fröhlich sein', the song begins. The piano part is confined to measured minims so that these words can stand out. They are separated by a significant pause from the next phase 'und lachen gar' (and even laugh), to hint at the total impossibility even of composure, let alone laughter. Between the two phrases the right hand reiterates 'how shall I'. Now this sadly falling theme infiltrates into the piano part. After the word 'unverhohlen' (openly) it emerges in undisguised insistence, at a rather faster tempo, as a complete embodiment of the whole first phrase. Thus, as the vocal argument continues, the piano is heard saying to itself 'Wie soll ich fröhlich sein' in varied pitches and inflexions but always with a final tone that shows it is a rhetorical question, even a statement – 'I shall never know happiness without you'. The rhythm of these words in German

c ♪ ♩♩ ♩. ♩ ♩ dominates the accompaniment like an involuntary confession. There are traces of not only grief but grievance, almost petulance. After 'alle hundert Jahr'' (every hundred years), 'anbefohlen' (ordered to) and 'was kommst du' (why do you come) a new piano

motif ♩. ♬ makes a brief gesture of impatience. But this disappears as soon as an explanation for the absence is offered; it must be the family's fault, not really the lover's. He is forgiven, despite the piano's accusing accents. The music even belies the words at 'dann magst du weitergehn' (then you can go your way). A very decisive start in voice and piano is made to falter tenderly in a lingeringly delayed note and a sudden descrescendo; the thought of parting is not so easy to bear as the singer supposed. Similarly in the following passage; 'Daheim mit deinen Leuten' (at home with your people), says the voice sternly, but the little drooping right-hand phrases add their wistful cadence of 'wie soll ich fröhlich sein'. The vocal line concludes with free recitative in a final attempt to convey complete conviction. In vain; as the voice utters its last sustained note of vehement renunciation, the postlude proclaims with even greater passion the rhythm and the sentiments of the opening words.

NOTES 1. For the original Tuscan *rispetto* 'E come vuoi ch'io faccia a stare allegra', see Tommaseo I, p. 225.

2. The falling 'wie soll ich' phrases *passim* have the sadness of motif 22. The accusingly accented notes are motif 27. The dominant ending, designed to leave the question open, is motif 31.

3. Several of the Italian songs suggest the background of a family feud, the fate of a village Romeo and Juliet. Thus in *Man sagt mir* (207) the direct invitation to defy the parental ban represents what the singer of this song really means but is too proud or shy to say. The theme of *Wer rief dich denn* (192) is also relevant.

218 (I 32) 'Was soll der Zorn...'

20 April 1896   C minor   d♭'–f''

Why this rage, my love, that inflames you so? I am not aware of any sin at all. Oh rather take a well-sharpened knife and step towards me and pierce my heart. And if a knife will not avail, then take a sword, that the fount of my blood may gush heavenward. And if a sword will not avail, then take the dagger's steel, and wash all my anguish away in my life-blood.

In some of the late Italian songs there seems to be a slight but perceptible waning of Wolf's creative powers. Usually the music is as masterly as ever, but sometimes the song-writing techniques veer somewhat awry, so that procedures which in earlier contexts were subtle and inspirational seem to risk becoming formular and bizarre. This song is arguably a case in point. It seems odd to select these masochistically melodramatic verses for musical treatment, and odder still to transpose their supinely surrendering tone into something more like a threat. True, there is much menace implicit in the poem; but there it lurks off-stage. In this music it looms large; and not even Wolf could convey, in a mere twenty bars, the ideas of emotions and responses so wholly opposed as the anger and the submission here described.

NOTES 1. For the original 'Caro amor mio, non mi far l'adirato', see Tommaseo I, p. 345.

2. The confusion at the half-bar (compare bars 3 and 4 with bar 11), and the resulting uncertainty of accentuation (why 'tritt zu *mir*'?) may suggest, as in some of the Spanish songs, that the piano part is preconceived. If so, its remarkable prolongation and extension of bar 3 to make bars 9–12 may well be deliberately motivic; the right hand continues its protestations of incomprehension and innocence while the voice insists on punishment.

3. For the cyclically repetitive patterns of the right-hand melody here at bars 9–10 and again at 12–14 see *Mühvoll komm' ich und beladen* (143, note 5). Here it sounds decidedly more of a mannerism than a deeply-felt theme.

4. The piano part recalls, in the same key, a harmonic progression (Ic V7 I in C minor, with an added A♭ on the first chord) found in each of two slightly earlier songs – 212 and 215, and always at the climactic point (bars 15–16). Here the idea sounds like a somewhat jaded echo. But it may be worth noting that all three verbal contexts share the same basic concept (whether serious or ironical) of final awakening to sad reality, ie. the minor counterpart of motif 36.

5. The ominous demisemiquaver runs gathering to a sforzando have a Wagnerian ring (cf. among many examples Alberich's brooding vigil that begins Act II of *Siegfried*). The analogues with *Lass sie nur gehn* (216, note 3) may reinforce the obvious assumption that the sin of which the singer here stands accused is infidelity.

219 (I 33) 'Sterb' ich, so hüllt in Blumen...'

13 April 1896   A♭ major   c'–f''

If I should die, then shroud my limbs in flowers. I would not have you dig a grave for me. Lay me down against those walls where you have so often seen me. There lay me down, in rain or wind; I die gladly if it is for you, beloved child. There lay me down in sunshine and rain; I die joyously if I die for your sake.

Here is a late masterpiece in which the music once again transcends the verses. The left hand has a syncopated A♭ octave pedal point throughout, in gentle allusion to the off-beat rhythm allotted to the opening words 'Sterb' ich'. The mood thus created is one of amorously musing reverie; the music is far from funereal in intent. Over this background the piano right hand and the voice hover and float, pursuing their separate but engaging ways in lifting and dipping lilts of sustained melody. The tranquil resignation in the piano's falling fifths, the easy and natural flow of the voice's declaration of love, are alike deeply felt, as if the text had touched responsive chords in the composer's mind. The song follows this raptly dreaming course until the first mention of the love that has inspired it, at 'gern sterb' ich, ist's um dich' (I die gladly if it is for you). Then the piano's falling fifths are decorated with a caressing theme which though essentially a restatement of the original idea invests the music with new rhythmic and melodic life. The accompaniment figures briefly resume only to change again, as the loved one is mentioned for the second time at the final phrase; here, at 'ich sterbe lieblich' (I die joyously) the right-hand melody floats and falls as before in blissful tranquillity, and goes lingering on half-heard within the lower register of the piano postlude. The high note at the final 'deinetwegen' serves to show that this quietly climactic concluding phrase is the ground from which the whole accompaniment has flowered. As the continuous left-hand rhythm intones 'sterb' ich', so the continuous right-hand melody sings 'deinetwegen' (for your sake).

NOTES 1. For the original Tuscan *rispetto* 'Se moro, ricopritemi di fiori', see Tomasseo I, p. 348. It also appears in Tigri, p. 315, under the heading of 'sorrows of betrayal and abandonment'. Wolf's setting however surely envisages a serene adoration, with a key and syncopated octave rhythm that recall the 'Liebestod' of Wagner's *Tristan und Isolde*.

2. This left-hand rhythm in Wolfian terms is a novel and compelling variant of the self-surrender of motif 1. The open-air feeling of motif 8 makes a brief but apt appearance at the request to be allowed to remain above ground, after 'Grab mir grabt'. The flattened sixth in A♭ major as an image of sleep (here on the word 'Grab') is motif 37.

3. In that last respect, and in general mood, there is some affinity with *Bedeckt mich mit Blumen* (172, note 2) where the same last wish is expressed, and the heady blend of love and death amid flowers is even more Tristanesque in both words and music.

220 (I 34) 'Und steht Ihr früh...'

3–4 April 1896   E major   b–e''

And when you rise from bed in the early morning, you chase all clouds from the skies, you charm the sun up over the hills, and cherubs vie to appear and bring your shoes and clothes straightaway.

   Then, when you go out to holy mass, you draw everyone along with you, and when you near the sanctuary, your glance lights up the lamps. You take holy water, make the sign of the cross, then moisten your white brow, bow down and bend the knee, oh with what grace and blessedness all this becomes you! With such grace and blessedness has God endowed you, who have received the crown of beauty! With such grace and blessedness you walk through life; the palm of beauty was bestowed upon you.

The ideas of waking and walking, chiming and charming, imbue the music. The piano comes to life with an easy succession of single quavers. They rise up, and another melodic line is added in the left hand, together with repeated bass notes. Then the voices chimes in, reverently restrained at first, but becoming gradually brighter and freer as the piano goes pealing up through Wolf's beloved mediant modulations, from the opening E major through A♭ major at 'die Sonne lockt Ihr' (you charm the sun) to C major at 'bringen Schuh' (bring your shoes). It seems that the composer's imagination has been so seized by the scene and emotions described that his music takes on the worshipping tones of a church service, with summoning bell-notes and organ pedals, long before Mass is mentioned. After the brief visitation from ministering angels the piano's carillon rings out in octaves in the higher register. Then they stoop down to the terrestrial level of E major again, with the single-note church bell theme also brought down to earth with a more solid texture and changes rung in the pealing order. Here the resuming voice reverently reiterates its lowest note, at 'Dann, wann Ihr ausgeht' (Then, when you go out). The piano figurations and vocal melody are taken through the same progressions as before, this time with a processional effect as open fifths are set walking in the bass: 'so zieht Ihr alle Menschen mit Euch fort' (you draw everyone along with you). The voice is sweet and solemn, hushing into sustained six-part organ and choir chords at 'Weihwasser nehmt Ihr' (you take holy water). In the reprise at the first 'Wie hold und selig' (with such grace and blessedness) the lines of single bell-notes sound out softly as before in right and left hands, while the voice has some of Wolf's loveliest melodies, culminating in the closing words 'der Schönheit Palme ward an Euch gegeben'. These are sung strongly at first, to an accompaniment of minim arpeggios like triumphant harp-strains. But then voice and piano alike suddenly hush gently on the word 'Euch' (you) in a last involuntary tribute before the postlude's chiming reappears to lilt upwards and end the song.

NOTES 1. For the original Tuscan *rispetto* 'E la mattina quando vi levate', see Tommaseo I, p. 53; also Tigri, p. 23.

2. The motif that resounds through the piano part conveys among its chiming effects the adoration of motif 14. Bars 13–16 (about a journey to Mass) are closely akin to the basic figuration and rhythms of *Nun wandre Maria* (139, about a journey to Bethlehem). The increasingly bright mediant modulations with which this song is illuminated (motif 24) are no doubt partly a response to the details of the text; clouds are dispelled, the sun rises, angels appear, lamps are lit. But in the context of religious observance and reverence they seem also to indicate as it were an intensification of spiritual light. It is noteworthy that the modulations pivot on the flattened seventh of each successive tonality, a note which with its subdominant connotations is here associated (as so often in Schumann) with the idea of worship, whether sacred or secular or both.

3. The same emotion animates the next song, *Benedeit die sel'ge Mutter* (221, note 3), especially in those opening words; the corresponding vocal melody is, deliberately or not, drawn from the piano accompaniment figure here (e.g. the first six notes of bar 2).

4. The poem's seventeen lines on the sole theme of adoring love instead of the usual six or eight results in an elaborately-wrought monothematic structure which repays study, especially in its almost total derivation from the opening bars.

221 (I 35) 'Benedeit die sel'ge Mutter...'

21 April 1896   E♭ major   d'–g♭''

A blessing on the happy mother who bore you so sweet, so elect in beauty; my yearning wings its way to you. You so gracious of gesture, you the fairest on earth; you my jewel, my bliss; a blessing on you, my sweet. When I yearn from afar and contemplate your beauty, how I tremble and groan past concealing! In my heart I feel rebellious flames that destroy my peace; oh, madness seizes me!

[A blessing on the happy mother who bore you so sweet, so elect in beauty; my yearning wings its way to you. You so gracious of gesture, you the fairest on earth; you my jewel, my bliss; a blessing on you, my sweet.]

The first section is simple and diatonic; the second, complex and chromatic; and the third is the first repeated note for note and word for word. This is a unique procedure in Wolf, and not wholly a successful one. If the unbridled passion of the contrasting section is made convincing, the restraint of the recapitulation brings too great a contrast.

But the problem can be mitigated if not entirely resolved by interpretative art; and the serene beauty of the first and last pages is its own justification. As in the previous song, the musical mood is devotional, even hymn-like, with a quiet four-part chordal movement. But we are to infer a hidden undertone of pain and poignancy; the secret fires soon to blaze out are already flickering in the transient discords heard each time the loved one's beauty is directly mentioned and admired, at the first 'so lieblich' (so gracious) and again at 'die Holdeste' (the fairest). In between those two moments the piano part, which has been unobtrusively lifting and brightening in pitch and texture ever since the bass-clef prelude, emerges in right-hand treble octaves, the highest of which softly stresses the first word of the phrase 'du, so lieblich von Geberden' (you, so gracious of gesture) in an aptly gracious gesture of its own. The contrasting middle section about the passion induced by frustrated yearning is constructed almost entire from the piano part's falling phrase previously heard repeated in the voice part at 'meine Sehnsucht fliegt dir' (my yearning wings its way). After the prodigious climax at 'ach, der Wahnsinn fasst mich an' (oh, madness seizes me) the groans and sighs of thwarted love are heard calming and relaxing into a reprise of the opening strains, with a final heartfelt echo of 'benedeit bist du' in the postlude.

NOTES 1. For the original Italian text 'Benedetta sia la madre', see the *Italienisches Liederbuch*, pp. 225 and 272, where Heyse calls it a Venetian popular song. It does not figure in the anthologies which served as sources for all his other translations. The repetition of the first eight lines is not his but Wolf's.

2. This rather artificial ABA contrast is further emphasized and exemplified by the main thematic components of each; devoted love (motif 14) in the major section and passionate love (motif 13) in the minor, as the text requires. The groaning interlude before the reprise, after 'fasst mich an', is composed of the sorrow motif 22.

3. See *Und steht Ihr früh* (220, note 3); the resemblance is further heightened by the two-octave rising and returning of the piano part, though with no clear motivic connotation in the present context.

222 (I 36) 'Wenn du, mein Liebster...'

24 April 1896   G♭ major   d♭'–g♭''

When you go up to heaven, my dearest, I shall come to meet you, bearing my heart in my hand. Then you will embrace me lovingly, and we shall fall at the Lord's feet. And if the Lord sees our love's anguish he will make one heart of our two loving hearts. He will join our two hearts into one, in Paradise, shone about by the radiance of heaven.

This song suffers somewhat from being too palpably a reworking of material already used to better effect in its earlier counterpart, 224. The piano accompaniment here is laid out on similar lines, but rather less sensitively and flexibly; in particular the right-hand theme tends to recur too regularly and emphatically, in almost every bar. The voice part seems too manifestly subordinate to the accompaniment, without overmuch independent melodic life of its own; thus there is no clear verbal reason for the prolongation of 'entgegen', or for the different rhythmic treatment of the same indefinite article at 'Ein Herz' and 'Einem Herzen'. The climax here sounds too deliberate a parallel to the analogous passage in 224, while the grandiose postlude here with its exultant tremolandos may well be thought to lack the more purely musical appeal of the hushed conclusion of the earlier and more original work. The comparison applies also to the original verses, whence the difference of response no doubt derives. This lyric is less tender, more theatrical. It is also a woman's song, in which Wolf, for all his objectivity, less frequently succeeds in sounding the same depths of intensity that he attained in the men's songs of the Italian volume.

NOTES 1. For the original Tuscan *rispetto* 'Quando, bellino, al cielo salirai', see Tigri, p. 237.
    2. Among further parallels with 224 (q.v.), all no doubt deliberate, is the continuous rhythm c ♩ ♫ ♫♫ at almost the same metronome marking (crotchet = 48 or 54) with a similar climax at bars 15–16 and a four-bar postlude within the same twenty-bar-framework. But it seems odd that Wolf, having thought of the two poems as expressible in the same musical terms (they have the literal language of the heart in common) and provided such analogous settings, should then have failed (despite his practice in other songbooks) to link the two by juxtaposition.

223 (I 37) 'Wie viele Zeit verlor ich...'

2 April 1896   G minor   d'–e♭''

How much time I lost in loving you! If only I had loved God in all that time, I should have had a place allotted to me in Paradise by now, where a saint would sit at my side. And because I have loved you, and your sweet fresh face, I have forfeited the light of Paradise; and because I have loved you, my sweet violet, I shall never now gain Paradise.

Were these verses intended as a serious complaint – 'you have sundered me from heaven', or as a gallant compliment – 'you are more beautiful than Paradise itself', or as affectionate teasing – 'I could have had a saint at my side instead of just another sinner'? To judge from Wolf's music, his interpretation was deeply serious. As in *Der Mond hat eine schwere Klag'* *erhoben* (193) he has taken what was no doubt designed as a courtly fancy or conceit and turned it into a cry of despair and delight together. The transcending effect is achieved by the humblest of means; as Wolf told Melanie Köchert in a letter the following day, the poem 'is treated quite simply in the accompaniment and kept very naïve in tone'. Hushed repeated chords gather to a small sigh of regret and then resignedly accompany the moving melody of the vocal line. The whole music is then suddenly but unobtrusively shifted to a lower register in both voice and piano, to mark off the next thought as it were in parentheses of pitch; 'hätt' ich doch Gott geliebt' (if only I had loved God) is thus uttered as a reflectively murmured aside. The opening strains resume at their original level for 'ein Platz in Paradies' and reach their highest point for the exalted state of sitting saint-high in beatitude. Here the piano part's texture takes on a pious tone, like the strings of a Bach church cantata, with no more than the merest hint of parody or irony. At 'und weil ich dich geliebt' (and because I have loved you) the accompaniment again rejoins the voice at its down-to-earth or realistic level, in deliberate allusion to the preceding parallel passage 'hätt ich doch Gott geliebt'. So the cherishing phrases continue, in poignant contrasts helplessly torn between the loss of a heavenly Paradise and the gain of an earthly one. After the raised tones of intended reproach at 'Paradieses Licht' (light of paradise) the sudden decrescendo interposes an involuntary forgiveness; and again after the last 'geliebt' the contemplated protest falters because of the tenderness that invades the vocal line at 'schön Veigelein' (sweet violet) and overflows in the postlude's sad repeated phrases and quotations with their eloquent effect of 'verlor ich, verlor ich, ... komm ich nun nicht ins Paradies hinein'.

NOTES 1. For the original Tuscan *rispetto* 'E quanto tempo ho perso per amarte!', see Tommaseo I, p. 226; also Tigri, p. 145. The heading is 'Bitter Reproaches' in the former source and 'Unhappy Love' in the latter.

2. The postlude's falling phrases have the regretful and deprived sadness of motif 22; the evocative contrasts of register in voice and piano are also designedly motivic. The treatment of 'schön Veigelein' recalls 'mit ew'gem Licht' in *Gesegnet sei durch den* (190), and so do the minor seconds before 'verscherzt' ich mir' here (cf. 'Er schuf das Meer'). Perhaps the two passages were intuitively linked by the mention of Paradise in both poems.

3. Similarly the opening first-beat discord here (motif 34) recalls that in *Mir ward gesagt* (188), with the connotation of tears in each context. The structure of the present song is subtly fashioned from the same chord, here G minor with added E♭ not only as interconnecting harmony ('Wie viele', 'Gott geliebt', 'Ein Platz', 'dich geliebt', 'verscherzt' ich mir des') but also as melodic line ('hätt ich

doch Gott geliebt in all der', 'und weil ich dich geliebt, schön frisch Gesicht').
Note also the musical identity between those last two passages, as well as their
unifying function.

224 (I 38) 'Wenn du mich mit den Augen streifst...'

19 April 1896   G major   d'–g''

*When your gaze strays over me and you laugh and then look down and
sink your chin on to your breast, I beg you to give me a sign first, so that I
can curb my heart; so that I can curb my heart and keep it tame and quiet
when it wants to leap up for great love; so that I can retain my heart
within my breast when it wants to break out for great joy.*

The great love and joy of the poem are metamorphosed into the music by
great art. Voice and piano begin together, without preamble. The vocal
line and the right-hand octave melodies are individually separate yet
interconnected; they symbolize the cause and effect described in the poem.
'Wenn du mich mit den Augen streifst', sings the voice followed a bar later
and a fifth or twelfth higher by the piano in a canon beginning at the word
'streifst' (strays), as if to suggest a dazed reaction of delayed delight, an
involuntary imitation. The vocal line always retains its independence, at
first by its hint of separate accentuation and then by going its own way.
There is no direct imitation of looking down or lowering the gaze within
the relevant phrase; but the succeeding drop of a seventh at 'Zeichen
machst' (give a sign) continues the impression of tender dalliance. At this
moment the left-hand chords that have unobtrusively furnished the
persistent but gently yielding rhythm that informs the entire song change
from two notes into three. Meanwhile the voice and right-hand melodies
have become even more independent, though each always sustains and
enhances the other in a vivid musical metaphor of intense shared
experience. The intensity grows still further, in pitch and tone; the piano's
expanding sequences are reinforced by occasional four-note chords in the
left hand. Finally the vocal climax is reached on a top note at the first
syllable of 'ausbrechen' (break out); and then, continuing and crowning
the cause-and-effect imagery, the piano melody in turn finds its own
separate culmination, whence its final downward noddings and musings
make a memorable and evocative postlude.

NOTES 1. For the original Tuscan *rispetto* 'Quando incontri i miei occhi, e fai un
riso', see Tommaseo I, p. 70; also Tigri, p. 78.
   2. The persistent unifying bass rhythm is the reverential motif 1. Here it recalls
An die Geliebte (44, notes 2, 4 and 5), another example of the power and depth of

Wolf's response to the idea of physical beauty, especially of face and eyes. His frequent letters to Melanie Köchert show that she was much in his mind as he composed Book II of the Italian songs. But it seems mistaken to infer (with the *Kritische Gesamtausgabe*) that this was the song mentioned in his letter to her of 19 April 1896 as a radically revised version; see 225, note 2.

3. The independence between voice and piano extends almost to a notional difference of time-signature; thus the opening vocal line makes good sense construed as 3/4 time, with stresses on 'Augen', 'lachst', 'senkst', as distinct from the accompaniment's 4/4.

4. The depth of feeling in this music seems to have made a profound impression on the composer's own mind. Its rhythm c ♩ ♫ ♫♩ and the harmonic progression at the last words are heard again in later songs with similarly heightened emotive effect. The rhythm pervades both the rather derivative companion piece *Wenn du mein Liebster* (222) and the masterly *Was für ein Lied* (209). The harmony (motif 36) reappears at the last words of both 222 and (in the same key as here) *Wohl denk' ich oft* (240).

225 (I 39) 'Gesegnet sei das Grün...'

13 April 1896   A major   e'–f#"

Blessed be green and whoever wears it! I shall have a green dress made for me. The fields in springtime wear a green dress too; and the darling of my eyes wears green. To dress in green is the huntsman's custom; my love too is clad in green. Everything looks lovely in green; from green all sweet fruits grow.

Wolf burnt the first manuscript of this song, but later reconstructed it from memory and revised it to make the present version. Perhaps it still retains traces of the reasons for his original dissatisfaction. The first bars in particular sound somewhat jaded. But their contrast with the ensuing spring-song strains, at 'Ein grünes Kleid trägt auch die Frühlingsaue' (The fields in springtime wear a green dress too) is thereby much enhanced. Here the limpid melodies in voice and piano have a springtime freshness and the accompanimental rhythm takes on a new liveliness. After a tenderly melting chromatic interlude that contemplates the 'Liebling meiner Augen' (darling of my eyes) a chiming motif starts up in the piano part, matched by a hint of vocal horn-call, e.g. at 'Jäger Brauch' (huntsman's custom); the piano too, in its small-scale antiphonal interplay between the two hands, offers a miniature sketch of hunting-horns in couples. The springtime music recurs at 'Das Grün steht allen Dingen lieblich an' (Everything looks lovely in green). Finally the chiming figures return and ring out meditatively in the postlude.

NOTES 1. For the original Venetian *vilota* 'Sia benedeto 'l verde e chi lo porta', see Dalmedico, p. 19.

2. In noting that Wolf subscribed the comment 'Phönix Nr. 1' and 'Phönix Nr. 2' at the end of this song and the next respectively, the *Kritische Gesamtausgabe* adds that the meaning of these expressions is unknown. But the first sentence of commentary above is surely sufficient explanation for both. Further, Wolf's own remarks in letters to his friend Heinrich Potpeschnigg are equally clear and conclusive; he had consigned two weaker songs to the stove (15 April) but kept them in memory, and later so revised and improved them that they 'arose from their ashes like shining phoenixes' (20 April). His retention of the original date of composition on each song however suggests that the metamorphosis was more an efficient resuscitation than a miraculous rebirth.

3. Horn passages akin to the open-air motif 8, with accented dominants, stand for 'der Jäger'. Their hints of motif 14 here and in the postlude recall *Benedeit die sel'ge Mutter* (221) and the matutinal chiming of *Und steht ihr früh* (220), two other songs of benediction; perhaps the notion of bell-notes was associated in Wolf's mind with early morning and hence with springtime freshness, like his vernal key of A major – also chosen for the Keller spring song *Wandl' ich in dem Morgentau* (184), the Goethe spring song *Frühling übers Jahr* (113) and the spring chorus that begins the unfinished opera *Manuel Venegas*, dated 1897.

4. The thematic connections between the first four bars of this song and of *Du sagst mir* (214) may mean that Wolf thought of both as being sung by the same character. But the resemblance seems more accidental, as though despite his revisions Wolf were still recomposing the first four bars of the earlier song in the belief that this was a new inspiration.

226 (I 40) 'O wär' dein Haus durchsichtig...'

12 April 1896   A minor   e'–e''

I wish yòur house were transparent like a glass, my dear, when I tip-toe by! Then I should always see you within; how I should gaze at you with all my soul! How many looks my heart would send you; more than there are drops in the March river! How many looks I should send across to you; more than there are drops showering down in the rain!

The accompaniment figuration announced in the piano prelude

is heard throughout this delicate and delightful song except at the word 'vorüberstehle' (tip-toe by), when the music tip-toes too.

360

The effect of this persistent main motif is to create a vivid impression of glassy transparency and glittering clarity. Through this background material passes a fine-drawn line of sheer melody. There is no separate climactic moment in the voice part; it and the piano are fused into the same substance.

NOTES 1. For the original Tuscan *rispetto* 'Vorría che la tua casa tralucesse', see Tigri, p. 126.

2. It seems fair to infer from Wolf's own annotation 'Phönix Nr. 2' that this and 225 (not 224) were the songs destroyed but remembered and revised: see 225, note 2.

3. The worshipping rhythm of motif 1 sounds throughout. The first motif exemplified above is found nowhere else in Wolf. But his early Heine song *Sterne mit den gold'nen Füsschen* has somewhat analogous figures of treble demisemiquavers clearly used as equivalents for the Romantic imagery of bright stars moving in step (cf. motif 25); and he regularly uses bare octaves and fifths in contexts suggesting transparency, (motif 35). The present amalgam is so eloquent that it seems to have the additional property of mirroring the inner feelings of the singer; thus it is extended by a quaver as soon as the idea of glancing across is introduced in the text, after 'wie blickt' ich dann nach dir mit ganzer Seele', etc. In the following bars the piano part recalls the postlude to *Und willst du deinen Liebsten* (203) and its adoring motif 11.

4. The structure is also significant; the parallel four-bar phrases (cf. bars 2, 6, 10 and 14) are preceded and followed by the piano figure in its highest register, as if to suggest that some transient gleam of sunlight on an upstairs window had inspired both the lyrical and the musical reflections.

227 (I 41) 'Heut' Nacht erhob ich mich...'

25 April 1896   D minor   c#'–f''

Tonight I rose at midnight and found that my heart had secretly slipped away from me. I asked: heart, where are you storming off with such force? It said: it had absconded only to see you. Now see how it must be with my loving; my heart absconds from my breast to see you.

The lyric is a typically high-flown conceit designed to explain the serenader's presence beneath the balcony; hence perhaps Wolf's alignment of it with the next two songs in the Italian volume. In his setting however anything that might be thought of as strained or artificial about the verses is forgotten; with this music, the poem is great art. Exquisite melodic lines in voice and piano are given extra poignancy by their reticent string-quartet texture. The heart of the song lies in the harmonies through which these melodic lines are passed, becoming dark and bright by turns. The piano begins with meditative octaves broadening into D-minor chords, all in a slow march tempo, the music of nocturnal walking and reverie. To make the imagery explicit, these two bars are repeated as the voice sings its opening words. Their germ-cell of three notes rising in step is now heard stealing away sidelong in the piano part at 'fortgeschlichen' (slipped away). But at the words 'stürmst du so mit Macht' (storming off with such force) the same motif is powerfully declaimed by voice and piano chords together. Now the soft reply wells out warm and bright over a chord of D major; here the germ-cell is inverted into the stepwise falling tones of a humble and a contrite heart, which blurts out 'sei es entwichen' in much quicker semiquavers, to illustrate both a nimble departure and a breathless confession. This inversion persists in the piano part, while the vocal melodies rise up to the original lifting motif at the words 'entweicht der Brust' (absconds from my breast), which parallel the previous 'stürmst du so mit Macht'. Similarly the last vocal phrase, with its untranslatable but vital change from the polite 'Euch' of the heart's reported speech to the tender 'dich' of the heart's direct assurance, is musically related to its earlier appearance at 'nur Euch zu sehn'. The postlude muses on the falling theme of the assuaged and acquiescent heart, and sketches out, first in the right hand and then in the left, the melodic shape of the last words 'dich zu sehn'.

NOTES 1. For the original Tuscan *rispetto* 'Stanotte a mezzanotte mi levai', see Tommaseo I, p. 118; also Tigri, p. 102. In each context the heading is 'Serenate'.

2. The joining and dividing melodic lines of motifs 13 and 14 sound throughout the song; the postlude has a hint of the open-air motif 8.

3. It was to be expected that this setting would be related to *Wenn du mich mit den Augen streifst* (224 – another unruly heart) and *Schon streckt' ich aus* (213 – another walking serenader). The harmony at 'Nur Euch zu sehn, es entwichen' here is comparable to that at 'ausbrechen will vor grosser Lust' in 224, while the quickening at 'sei es entwichen' is akin to the treatment of 'vorüber bin ich bald' in 213.

228 (I 42) 'Nicht länger kann ich singen...'

23 April 1896   A minor   e'–e''

(*The serenader*)
I can sing no longer, for the wind blows strong and taxes my breath. Also I fear that time passes by profitlessly. If I were really sure, I should not now go back to bed. If I really knew, I should not now be walking home and losing this lovely time in loneliness.

229 (I 43) 'Schweig einmal still...'

23 April 1896   A minor   e'–f''

(The listener)
Do be quiet, you odious babbler out there, your damned singing makes
me sick. Even if you kept it up until daybreak you'd never achieve a
passable song. So do be quiet and get to bed; really, I'd rather be
serenaded by a donkey.

The poems of this song and 228 are separated in the Heyse source book;
but Wolf commented to Melanie Köchert in a letter on the same day, 'the
two pieces unmistakably belong together'. In fact, they do not; but the
idea proved an inspiration. The two songs are brilliantly interwoven with
ironic cross-reference. Perhaps the second could be understood in
isolation sufficiently well to justify separate performance. But the first
loses much of its meaning and its very real poignancy (and hence on its
own makes an ill-chosen encore piece) unless we also hear the cruel
sequel. Both stand high in sheer quality; in the musical expression of
dramatic irony they surely stand supreme in the Lied. Instead of depicting
the actual situation, Wolf deals separately with each of two very different
attitudes towards it. Thus we never hear the melody of the serenade itself,
though we can guess at its contours, which are cognate with those of the
main melody of Wolf's own *Italian Serenade* for string quartet; he may
have felt personally involved, as an actor in the imagined scene. What is
heard in the piano prelude of the second song is an exasperated and ill-
natured parody of that melody. It is not the song so much as the singer
that is getting on the nerves of his reluctantly captive audience. The
resulting resentment is vented on what was no doubt an inoffensive and
unpretentious serenade, which is held up to ridicule by a heartless
burlesque

already containing a hint of hee-haw at the end, and accompanied by a
tedious and wooden strumming. The same theme is heard in the
accompaniment of the first song thus

Here the faltering phrases are teased apart and are left floating in the air, only to blow away in the wind with a weary pathos like leaves of rejected manuscript. This pathos is notably enhanced by the sensitively-inflected vocal line and by our anticipation of the ungrateful reception the serenade is about to receive. The falling intervals that recur in each song, whether augmented fourths or minor sixths or sevenths, suggest a donkey's bray. That point is made explicitly in the second song by the word 'Esel' in the last line, and by the grotesque braying of the piano part at that point and then in the postlude. It is made implicitly in the first song, where the falling sixth quoted above occurs at the word 'singen'; our serenader is already made to appear a bit of an ass. But this song is far from comic in its effect. The fragmentary phrases in the piano, the gasping accents in the voice to show the stress within the words at 'macht den Atem was zu schaffen' (taxes the breath), the dramatic irony and its expression in the aloofly classical texture of the music, all suggest an other-wordly passion wholly wasted on a mundane recipient whose instant reaction in the second song is to double the speed of the music, as if to say 'for heaven's sake get on with it'. Its enjoyably caustic and down-to-earth style represents the total negation and rejection of the wistful magic and strangeness previously heard. Thus these two contrasting songs, deftly fashioned from the same themes in the same key- and time-signatures, are uncannily apt in illustrating the ill-assortedness, at least on this particular occasion, of the two characters concerned.

NOTES 1. For the two original Tuscan *rispetti* 'Non posso più cantar, che tira vento' and 'Stattene zitta, brutta cicalina', see Tommaseo I, p. 127 (also Tigri, p. 107) and Tigri, p. 3 respectively.

2. The metronome marking of *Nicht länger kann ich singen* should be corrected from the Peters edition's crotchet = 86, which is hardly the stipulated 'langsam', to the *Kritische Gesamtausgabe*'s crotchet = 46, as in the autograph.

3. The main theme of Wolf's own *Italian Serenade* for string quartet written in May 1887,

may be related, e.g. in its falling semitone and falling sixth, to the themes quoted above, whose three rising notes in the first song may be designed as a thematic link with *Heut' Nacht erhob ich mich* (227). In 229 the sharp mocking appoggiaturas are motif 4; the trills and mordents too are an expression of shrill and biting sarcasm. Such effects recall the flouncing and finger-snapping of *Klinge, klinge* (147). The braying motifs are a refined version of the effect already used in 237, in the same key.

230 (I 44) 'O wüsstest du...'

26 April 1896   E minor   e'–f''

Oh if you only knew, you false traitress, how much I have suffered at
night for your sake. While you lay in your locked house, I spent my time
outside in the open.

The rain was my rose-water, the lightning my only message of love; I
played at dice with the storm while I kept watch under your eaves.
Beneath your eaves my bed was laid, with the sky spread above as my
blanket. The threshold of your door, that was my pillow – poor wretch
that I am, what I have had to endure!

This song has some thematic connections with the previous three,
suggesting that Wolf thought of the poem as the complaint of the unlucky
serenader in 227 and 228 above, once he had discovered from 229 how all
his efforts had been received. Even so, the real key still seems to be
missing. The poem is a passionate lament for lost love and wasted time.
But the mood of this song is no more than wry, with an almost austere
detachment from the sense of the words. The constant staccato implies the
light touch of ironic persiflage. So does the almost parodistically accusing
accented declamation of 'du falsche Renegatin'. So does the final
departure of the postlude, as the singer remembers the moments of his
nocturnal sufferings out in the cold, heard earlier in the piano left hand at
'litt zur Nacht' (suffered at night) and 'im Freien zugebracht' (spent
outside), and finally transformed into a briefly mimed exit indicative of
baffled frustration. So, above all, does the insistent recurrence of the main
motif heard from the first notes of the piano and drawn from the last notes
of the voice at 'aussteh'n müssen' (had to endure) as if in ruefully
querulous repetition of the poetic theme of tireless perseverance. But such
a procedure has musical hazards, which are not wholly avoided; and here,
far more than usual in Wolf, the impression is one of absolute music
conceived instrumentally having no need of words and contributing little
to the text used.

NOTES 1. For the original Venetian *vilota* 'Se ti savessi, o falsa renegada', see
Dalmedico, p. 116.
    2. The structure is the logical outcome of a trend already discernible in the
Spanish songs; the independence of the accompaniment nearly parts company
with the verses. The vocal line here has the air of being grafted on to a pre-existing
piano solo. The latter's ABA form is mainly musical, not poetic. The middle
section, for all its deft interweaving of motivically illustrative ideas for 'Regen',
'Blitz', 'Sturm', in pointilliste miniature, offers a contrast not found in the lyric.
The A sections and postlude with their persistent pedals and predictable

recurrences (thus bar 1 is also bars 5, 9, 24, 28 and 33, while the main motif is omnipresent) far outdo the text in monothematicism.

3. The main theme's staccato has some affinity of mood with Wagner's *Siegfried* Act I, where the Mime-motif reiterates its sufferings for Siegfried's sake.

231 (I 45) 'Verschling' der Abgrund...'

29 April 1896   D minor   f'–a''

May a chasm engulf my lover's cottage; may a lake foam there in its place. Let the heavens shower lead shot over it, let a snake dwell in its foundations. Let a poisonous snake dwell there, to poison him who was unfaithful to me; let a snake dwell there bloated with poison and bring death to him who thought to betray me!

The vehement piano part is powerfully evocative of cataclysm and portent. It begins with violent heaving and shaking; the tumult subsides, only to reveal the threatened snake suddenly conjured up in the music. At its first mention the long crawling trills begin to shake with passion and poison, while the right-hand runs slither menacingly down. In the postlude the left-hand octaves rear and strike, the tremolandos writhe in loud agony and incontinently expire. Given a dramatic soprano of sufficiently malignant demeanour, and the fine quality of ringing *forte* needed for the high A on 'Tod' (death), together with a pianist capable of disguising the abject banality of much of the material, this song could appear to rank among Wolf's most impressive creations; but not otherwise.

NOTES 1. For the original Tuscan *rispetto* 'La casa del mi' amor vada in profondo', see Tommaseo I, p. 338.

2. The Wolfian inspiration shows ominous signs of running dry towards the end of his last productive phase and indeed of his creative life as a whole. Here he audibly draws on earlier sources, e.g. the Spanish songs; *Blindes Schauen* (155) for the blind rage expressed in the dotted rhythm ♪♪♩ and *Wehe der* (179) for the Isolde-like themes of woman scorned, complete with top A. The postlude recalls the hysterical outburst that ends *Das Köhlerweib ist trunken* (185). The quasi-glissando snake-like runs and the menacingly vibrant ·trills are also manifestly motivic.

232 (I 46) 'Ich hab' in Penna...'

25 April 1896   F major   c'–a''

I have a lover who lives in Penna, another in the plain of Maremma, one in the beautiful port of Ancona, for the fourth I must travel to Viterbo; another lives yonder in Casentino, the next with me in my own town, and I have yet another in Maggione, and four in La Fratta, and ten in Castiglione!

The Italian Songbook culminates in a brilliant firework display for voice and piano, combining prodigious effectiveness with peerless musical quality. The words count for little beyond their cumulative effect; the music adds the notion of irrepressible and irresistible ebullience. The bouncing piano part begins neutrally enough with strumming thirds in the left hand. The entry of the voice with its gleefully elated melodic lines prompts the piano's right hand to join in conspiratorially, with discreet canonic echoes. There is a brief mock climax before and after 'Zum Vierten muss ich nach Viterbo wandern' (for the fourth I must travel to Viterbo), with the twofold effect of heightening both the musical and the dramatic interest. But the feigned close is in a dissatisfied minor key; four are far too few. The effect hereabouts is that of a naughty child's gleeful recital of some small misdeed to an indulgent parent. 'Ask what happened next' implores the music, similarly excited; very pleased with itself at 'ein andrer wohnt in Casentino dort' and again reaching a temporary climax before going on – 'and there's yet another ... there's four!' (here a whole bar's pause, like an excited child taking a deep breath) ... 'there's *ten*!'. On this last word the voice rings out bright and exultant over the repeated quavers with which the song began, now in full emphatic chords in both hands; and so with the words 'in Castiglione' the voice ends. Then the piano part in turn bursts out into a riot of merriment; the virtuoso effect alone is unforgettable. Unfortunately it is often inaudible as well, since after a properly spirited performance the audience too will have broken out into delighted applause at the ostensible full close of the voice part. The postlude must be heard, not only for its astounding musical brilliance, but also for its dramatic point. A total tally of twenty-one lovers, no less, it comments – and she doesn't care twopence for any of them.

NOTES 1. For the original Tuscan *rispetto* 'Ce l'ho un amante alla città di Penna', see Tigri, p. 179.

2. The skipping sense of childlike excitement is enhanced and propelled by the little bouncing bass-notes on the off-beat (motif 1) in bar 11ff; the dancing staccato and the climactic progression at 'Fratta ... zèhn 'etc are also expressive

(with the latter, cf. motif 36). Both the difficulty and the effectiveness of the postlude may derive from its quasi-orchestral layout, reminiscent of the dazzling scintillations of the Wagner string band.

3. This felicitous blend of melodic charm and dramatic point is vividly Mozartian. Its words may have suggested Leporello's catalogue aria 'Madamina' in *Don Giovanni*; and hence its tripping downward scale passages, here at 'wieder einen hab' ich in Maggione'. Wolf interprets his inspired character-drawing as a miniature Donna Juana.

VIII. The last published songs
Three songs to words by Reinick

233 Gesellenlied (*The apprentice's song*)

24 January 1888   C major   d♯'–g''

'Masters don't fall from heaven'. And that's a great blessing! There are far too many of them here already; if yet another troop of them fell from heaven, how all those masters would thrash us apprentices, however masterly our work was.

'Masters don't fall from heaven'. And, praise be, no masters' wives either. Oh please dear heaven, if there's one grumbling away up there, preserve her in bliss so that she doesn't fall down to earth to plague us!

'Masters don't fall from heaven'. No masters' daughters either! That I've known for a long time, of course; and yet – what a joy it would be if a young and pretty and cheerful one fell for me, and would be my sweetheart!

'Masters don't fall from heaven'. That's my comfort in this world. So I shall strive to become a master myself, and then if I can find a wife, I can make here on this earth a heaven from which a master won't fall [from which a master won't fall].

Reinick in this unpretentious vein writes acceptable light verse, which pleases and amuses the composer who in turn makes his good-humoured enjoyment audible. Wolf in early 1888 was well placed to appreciate the proverbial expression that no man is born master of his craft. Each verse begins 'Kein Meister fällt vom Himmel'. This is aptly set to a heartily bluff tune, with a pompous musical truism as accompaniment. As the voice part continues the piano proceeds to a deft parody of the opening phrase, demonstrating by a revised rhythm, a lightening of the texture, and a little added trill, that the following reflections on this theme are not going to be unduly solemn. And instantly the left hand reminds listeners of the entry of the masters in Wagner's *Die Meistersinger von Nürnberg*. 'Schon viel

369

zu viel' (far too many of them already) sings the voice, in accents of alarm, soon justified by whiplash right-hand runs that point to a good hiding. In the second verse singer and piano raise their voices in unison at 'Ach lieber Himmel' in an impassioned appeal to heaven to retain any masters' wives who may happen (exceptionally, the song suggests) to be there. The third verse brings the greatest delight of all. The idea of the master's young daughter clearly held a special appeal for Wolf. 'Jung und hübsch und munter' (young and pretty and cheerful) the poem describes her. So does the music, in a sprightly dance of staccato semiquavers. The ebullient vocal melody and the scintillating piano part vie together in high spirits and then melt together in tenderness at 'wollt mein Herzlieb sein' (would be my sweetheart). The imagined charms and their effect on the singer are thus simultaneously, and most memorably, re-created. The final verse perhaps relies overmuch on themes and treatments which have already been allotted to the second verse and are less effective, indeed less clearly relevant, in the later context. But they make a resounding conclusion, well deserving of the instantaneous applause which the absence of a postlude boldly solicits.

NOTES 1. The mood and style show an affectionate apprenticeship to Wagner. The strongly-marked left-hand rhythm in bars 5, 7 etc is meant to recall the opening bars of the overture to *Die Meistersinger von Nürnberg*. The vocal line at 'Gottlob, auch keine Meisterin' echoes Sachs's 'so mach' ich den Burschen gleich zum Gesell' in Act III scene 4. That promotion was solemnized by an admonitory thump. Perhaps masters' wives exercised similar prerogatives; some such specific allusion may be intended.

2. More generally, the whip-like runs to illustrate beatings (also a *Meistersinger* motif) are recalled in *Selbstgeständnis* (64) with its analogous verbal context. Note also the companionable thirds of motif 16 at 'wollt' mein Herzlieb sein'.

234 Morgenstimmung (*Morning mood*)

8 September – 23 October 1896 (arranged for chorus and orchestra 12–17 December 1897)   C# minor/E major   b#–g#''

The night will soon be brought to an end; already I feel morning breezes blow. The Lord speaks: 'Let there be light!'.
   Then what is dark must pass away.
   From the canopy of heaven through the whole world the angels fly in joyous exultation.
   The sun's ray flames through the cosmos.
   Lord, let us strive, let us conquer.

At this time Wolf, without knowing it, was showing the clinical signs of incipient brain syphilis. Within a year he was incurably insane. Yet all the last songs (this and 238–242) are finely structured and eloquent. They arguably lack powerful original invention; but that failing was an occasional feature of Wolf's work at all stages, whenever the chosen poem failed to thrill and inspire him as it should. Here perhaps is the converse case; Reinick's poem appeals for the wrong reasons. True, it reads well enough at first glance, as an account of some fine lordly feeling. But the actual words are pedestrian and pretentious; and the music re-creates their general aspiring tone and tenor, rather than their actual substance. A revealing letter to Hugo Faisst* announces success at last in this setting, which had been preoccupying Wolf for some time. He had suddenly seen that the poet's title, 'Morgenlied' (Morning song), was inappropriate for both form and content; rebaptized 'Morning mood', it had instantly proved more amenable to musical treatment. In other words the text had become a pretext for Wolf's own morning mood of new optimism, instead of being the *raison d'être* of the music. Despite this handicap the setting achieves a strong and true rhetoric. It begins in the nocturnal C♯ minor. But after 'es werde Licht' (let there be light) the darkness is dispelled with a bright high note and a glittering piano tremolando. The night music briefly recurs at 'was dunkel ist' (what is dark) only to brighten again in successive mediant modulations as the poet's all too dazzling vision intensifies from dawn through jubilant angelic choirs and a universal flare of sunlight to the supreme triumph of the whole creation. The climax at the word 'siegen' (conquer), spread over some four bars of moderate 6/8 time with a sustained top G♯ from the voice and exultant fanfares from the piano can sound inspiring in performance.

NOTES 1. Here is one of the clearest examples of rising mediant key-change (e.g. from 'freudejauchzend': E major, A♭ major, C major and E major again) as an image of increasing luminosity, motif 24.

2. The postlude's spiritual intoxication recalls the more mundane variety evoked in some of the *Westöstlicher Divan* songs, e.g. the left hand octaves and syncopations of *Sie haben wegen der Trunkenheit* (122). At the mention of angelic flight, after 'Vom Himmelszelt ... die Engel ... fliegen', the interlude recaptures the analogous flights of fancy expressed in similar language ('Engel ... herabgezogen ... eingeflogen') in that much humbler song *Wir haben beide* (205). The setting of 'Sieg' here has the same top note in the same key and partly the same harmonies as in *Der Genesene an die Hoffnung* (13); perhaps Wolf could still hope or believe, even eight years later, in one of his remitting phases, that he might yet triumph over his own illness and be cured.

3. In fact he would soon be incarcerated in Dr Svetlin's asylum, suffering from delusions of grandeur; it was there that he rebaptized this song again as the even more magniloquent *Morgenhymnus* for chorus and orchestra.

---

* 25 October 1896

235 Skolie (*A stirrup cup*)

1 August 1889   B major   f#'–a''

Hand me the goblet full of foaming wine, give me your blossoming lips to kiss, strike the soul-inspiring strings!

A blaze of courage burns in my goblet, fires of love glow on your lips, flames of life flare from the strings.

Wave of battle, hurl me into the surges! Waves of love, lift me to the clouds! Foaming billows of life, exultantly [exultantly] I greet you!

Wolf's music, lacking the austere technical refinement and control of his last period, does nothing to redeem Reinick's vapid and pretentious verses. There is fiery and surging bravura here in abundance, together with ample opportunity for dramatic effect; and the song finely sung and played would win deserved plaudits. But the music is all too accurate in its reproduction of Reinick; Wolf has captured not only the spirited élan but also the witless bombast of the poem.

NOTES 1. The repetition is Wolf's, not Reinick's.

2. At 'Woge des Kampfes' appears the energy of motif 5 within the manliness of motif 6.

3. The prelude, the piano part at 'Saiten' and the accented notes at 'im Pokale', are dull echoes of *Der Rattenfänger* (96); the intoxicating fires (bars 22–3, 26–9) are pale reflections of *Trunken müssen wir alle sein* (120).

4. No doubt it was a mood of ebullience that prompted Wolf to the composition of this derivative song, and a mood of more realistic appraisal that led to its suppression. But in 1897 his psychic upswing was even more urgent and his critical faculty somewhat in abeyance; hence perhaps his choice and composition of the Reinick poem in 234 above, the recollection of this earlier setting, and his elated publication of both.

Four songs to words by Heine, Shakespeare and Byron

236 'Wo wird einst...'

24 January 1888   F major   c'–f''

Where will the weary wanderer one day find his last resting-place? Under palm-trees in the south? Under lime-trees by the Rhine? Shall I be buried by foreign hands somewhere in the desert, or shall I rest in the sand of some sea-coast? No matter; God's heaven will surround me there as here, and at night the stars will hover above me as funeral lamps.

Heine's lines are inscribed on his gravestone in Paris. The reason for their appeal to Wolf, even in a depressive phase, is far from clear; and at the beginning of 1888 he was soon to start the spectacular upsurge of the Mörike songs. Perhaps this song was earlier work undergoing revision at that time. There are several other Heine settings dated between 1878 and 1881 which Wolf preferred to leave unpublished; his selection of this one for publication seems more readily attributable to his melancholia in 1897 than to its musical merits, whatever its date of composition. The Wolfian motivic touches are unmistakable but uninspired; and the verbal accentuation is atypically awry throughout.

NOTES 1. The reflective motif 21 is at bars 1–2 etc; the emphatic questioning on the dominant sevenths (at 'sein', 'Rhein?' etc) lingered out by rhetorical pauses, is motif 32; the staccato points of light at 'Totenlampen ... die Sterne' are the star-motif 25.
  2. For a reworking of the piano part at bar 3 etc see *Schlafendes Jesuskind* (37, note 14). Similarly the brief requiescat in the postlude may have been in Wolf's mind when he came to write the vocal melody for 'ruhig sein' in *Dereinst, dereinst* (168), which also has evident verbal affinities with Heine's text.
  3. Perhaps the frequent pauses confound the time-signature, which demands flexible interpretation to avoid a stressed first beat on such words as 'in' (bar 6), 'an' (bars 8 and 14), 'und' (bar 20).

237 Lied des transferierten Zettel (Bottom's song from 'A Midsummer Night's Dream')

11 May 1889   A minor   d#'–a''

> *The finch, the sparrow and the lark,*
>   *The plain-song cuckoo gray,*
> *Whose note full many a man doth mark,*
>   *And dares not answer, nay.*

The song is introduced in Shakespeare thus (Act III, scene 1):

(Re-enter Bottom with an ass's head...)
Quince: Bless thee, Bottom, bless thee! Thou art translated.
Bottom: I see their knavery, this is to make an ass of me, to fright me if they could. But I will not stir from this place, do what they can; I will walk up and down here, and I will sing, that they shall hear I am not afraid.

Wolf's German text is Bottom over-freely translated, by A. W. von Schlegel. It takes the second verse (quoted above) of Shakespeare's sprightly lyric 'The ousel-cock so black of hue' and expands it into two rather flat-footed quatrains which spell out in some detail the significance of the cuckoo-call that mocks married men and also explicate Bottom's 'nay' with added choruses of explanatory hee-haws. Wolf had considered *A Midsummer Night's Dream* as the basis of an opera libretto; his exquisite setting for solo, chorus and orchestra of the fairy song *Ye spotted snakes with double tongue* in Act II, scene 2 is also dated 11 May 1889. This explains why, in one of the great song years, he turned aside between the Goethe and Spanish volumes to produce this agreeable but secondary work. Even so, Bottom's uneasy bravado finds no particular expression in this music, which is related to the words rather than the situation; Wolf was wise to concentrate on song rather than opera. The piano part of the second verse for example is crammed with cuckoo-calls, which like the hee-haws are Schlegel's rather than Shakespeare's, and in either context lyric rather than dramatic.

NOTES 1. As in *Rat einer Alten* (53) the acciaccaturas not only chirrup like the birds but cackle with laughter, motif 4 (e.g. before 'lacht darob' in verse 2).

2. The braying begins, quite unobtrusively, in the piano prelude; its later unbridled burlesque effect, in the left-hand octaves and a taxing vocal line that yodels repeatedly in a falling diminished twelfth, is unique in the Lied. The nearest parallel is Wolf's own more restrained keyboard equivalent for a donkey's bray, in the same key and similar harmonies, at the end of *Schweig einmal still* (229), dated seven years later.

3. The piano part may have been orchestrally conceived (e.g. in the four-part wind or string band staccato of bars 9–12).

238 'Sonne der Schlummerlosen...'

29–31 December 1896   C$^\sharp$ minor   c$^{\sharp}$'–e''

Sun of the sleepless! melancholy star!
Whose tearful beam glows tremulously far,
Thou show'st the darkness thou canst not dispel;
How like thou art to joy remembered well!
So gleams the past, the light of other days,
Which shines but warms not with its powerless rays;
A night-beam Sorrow watcheth to behold,
Distinct but distant – clear, but oh, how cold!

239 'Keine gleicht von allen Schönen...'

18–25 December 1896   B major   c$^{\sharp}$'–d$^{\sharp}$''

There be none of Beauty's daughters
  With a magic like thee;
And like music on the waters
  Is thy sweet voice to me:
When, as if its sound were causing
The charmèd ocean's pausing,
The waves lie still and gleaming,
And the lull'd winds seem dreaming:

And the midnight moon is weaving
  Her bright chain o'er the deep;
Whose breast is gently heaving,
  As an infant's asleep;
So the spirit bows before thee,
To listen and adore thee:
With a full but soft emotion,
Like the swell of Summer's ocean.

The words of both these Byron poems are quite literally as well as deftly translated (by Otto Gildemeister (1828–1902)); yet Wolf finds in them more than is readily apparent in a reading of the English originals. The first is a set of album verses addressed to the moon; the second a much-loved anthology piece. They well illustrate the classical and romantic aspects of Byron. Wolf very typically finds an essence in each and re-creates it. The first lyric is stripped and left shivering in clear cold music; the second is wrapped up in warm and sumptuous material. Each is imagined quasi-pictorially. In 238 the thirds in each hand are now close, now widely separated, while the voice is in contrary motion (first *forte*, then fading); 'deutlich, doch fern' (distinct but distant), just as the poem says. At 'wie Tränen zittern, schimmerst du von fern' (literally, as tears tremble, you shimmer from afar) the droopingly sad left-hand phrases rise and shine in a high arpeggio. At the last vocal phrase the sung melody contrasts the bright top note with the cold lowest note, on 'hell' and 'kalt' respectively; here and in the postlude the staccato piano chords high in the keyboard suggest the cold gleam of moonlight. Throughout the song, a recurrent syncopated rhythm intimates the sad-hearted nocturnal unrest that is the theme of the verses. The second song also has a characteristic rhythmic figure, derived more directly from the words. 'Keine gleicht von allen Schönen', the German text begins. At 'Schönen' (beauties) the piano echoes the vocal line; its rhythm tells us that the first word in the voice has been expressively lingered out to stress that *no one* can compare with such beauty. That effect is further enhanced by Wolf's prolongation of the first syllable of 'zauberhafte' (magic), and the way in which he matches his translator's treatment of the word 'dir!' (to thee) as a separated exclamation of quiet wonderment. At 'wie Musik auf Wassern' the piano melody is set floating over a wave-motion of semiquaver arpeggios, like music on the water. These are gradually stilled, again as the words suggest, until at 'eingelullte Winde träumen' (lull'd winds are dreaming) the piano interlude expresses only a hint of movement, which in turn broadens to a further swell and surge from voice and piano, as the opening melodies with a new aspiring rhythm recur to end the song. This strongly depictive music in both 238 and 239 gives the impression of two adjacent canvases in a gallery; a cold winter moonscape and a warm summer seascape, each of flawless academic perfection. They may nevertheless both be felt to lack that richness and originality of deep inward life that Wolf at his most characteristic never fails to display.

NOTES (to 238) 1. At bar 4 the piano left hand has very appropriately the sorrow of motif 22 in a context suggesting the wakefulness of motif 17; the lulling arpeggio chord for 'schlummern' is motif 28. The closing bars have the star-motif 25 of *Wie glänzt der helle Mond*, also 'kalt und fern'; its C♯ minor with *tierce de Picardie* ending (= D♭ major) is a nocturnal key for Wolf. Perhaps 'moonlight' was among the associations here.

2. The recurrent rhythm has a hypnotic Wagnerian effect comparable with the 'Liebestod' in *Tristan und Isolde*; but it is no doubt derived from Wolf's own reminiscence of his own *Alle gingen* (167), also about wakefulness at night. The thirds in both hands offer a foretaste of *Alles endet* (241) in the same key, also about mortal transience.

3. Cf. Loewe, Op. 13 no. 6; Schumann, Op. 95 no. 2; Mendelssohn, Op. posth (each setting has a different translation).

NOTES (to 239) 1. In the piano postlude is an analogue of the night and sleep motif

18, here reminiscent of the end of *Verschwiegene Liebe* (68). There are occasional hints of the mediant key-change of motif 24 (C major–A♭ major at 'wann der Mond die Silberkette' etc).

2. The added left-hand semiquavers of bar 7ff. have a floating effect analogous to their appearance in *Und willst du deinen Liebsten* (203).

3. Again the Wagnerian atmosphere is palpable; without any clear echoes, the music is Tristanesque in spirit.

The Michelangelo songs

Michelangelo Buonarroti (1475–1564) was not only sculptor, painter and architect but a considerable poet. Wolf had intended to set several of the translations (*Die Gedichte des Michelangelo Buonarotti*, Berlin, 1896) by Walter Robert-tornow (*sic*) (d. 1895) but only the following three were satisfactorily completed.

A fourth, *Irdische und himmlische Liebe*, was destroyed as substandard before the composer's breakdown in September 1897.

240 'Wohl denk' ich oft...'

18 March 1897   G minor/G major   c–e'

I often think of my past life as it was before my love for you. Then no one paid heed to me, each day was lost for me. I thought that I would live wholly for song, and also escape from the throng of humankind... Today men speak my name, whether in praise or reproof; and everyone knows that I am here!

In a letter to Oskar Grohe (24 March 1897) Wolf quoted the German text, noted that the verses were addressed by Michelangelo to a friend, and added:

> The music for them, which begins with a mournful introduction and maintains that tone up to the penultimate line, unexpectedly assumes a robust character (developed from the previous motif) and concludes solemnly with triumphal fanfares, like a flourish of trumpets sounded for Michelangelo in homage by his contemporaries.

Wolf's involvement with the poem and identification with its hero are alike clear. At the same time he typically imagines and describes a quasi-dramatic scene; and this element of objectivity is further stressed by his choice of the bass clef for the voice part and his recorded comment to a friend 'Of course the sculptor must sing bass'. The prelude's melancholy quaver octaves sing out soulfully in the lower register; then the accompaniment turns into a sad four-part reverie about past life, in the style of the Italian Songbook. The independently meditative vocal melodies are made to sound like dignified speech. Thus in 'wie es, vor meine Liebe für dich, war' (as it was before my love for you) the commas are metamorphosed into quaver rests that thoughtfully separate the loving adverbial phrase from the matter-of-fact main clause. At 'ein jeder Tag verloren' (each day was lost) it is the piano's turn to add cadences and inflexions suggestive of spoken or sung comment; the right hand seems to repeat 'verloren, vergangen', while the voice singles out and stresses the word 'ganz' (wholly) to show how whole-hearted and protracted the intense inward devotion to song had proved to be. And how rewarding, the music then implies; for that same falling phrase is then transformed into the major in full chords for both hands. A strong tonic major chord is heard, for the first time in the song, at 'da bin' (am here), making fame and presence suddenly vivid before the voice reaches its final ringing climax on the highest note at 'alle Leute!' and stands back to receive the postlude's homage in a paean of exultant fanfare.

NOTES 1. The German text translates the seventh complete stanza 'I'vo pensando al mio viver di prima' of a long poem of which ten other stanzas and some fragmentary lines survive. 'Gesang' (song) in the German text, like 'rima' in the original Italian, means poetry. The stanzaic form *ababababcc* in iambic pentameter audibly reminds Wolf of the analogous verses in Heyse's *Italienisches Liederbuch* and hence recalls his own Italian musical style.

2. The piano part at 'ein jeder Tag verloren' etc is the sorrow motif 22, in a guise reminiscent of the postlude to *Wie viele Zeit verlor ich* (223). It is incorporated into the final triumphant section as e.g. the first three accented quavers in the right hand of bars 16 and 17. In bars 11–14 the sorrow motif lends itself to the cyclic treatment already noted in *Mühvoll komm' ich* (143) and *Was soll der Zorn* (218) as indicative of inward intensity or obsession.

3. The harmonies at 'da bin, wissen alle Leute' (motif 36) have been heard before, in the same key, in the comparably climactic bars 15–16 of *Wenn du mich mit den Augen streifst* (224); there are other affinities with Italian love-songs. The change from sorrow to exultation here owes something to love, as the poem says, as well as to renown; but the resemblance may mean, more ominously, that Wolf despite his enthusiasm in letters to friends (e.g. 'Gesangsstücke nach Gedichten von Michelangelo, zu denen mir ein paar wahrhaft sublime Einfälle verhalfen', to Grohe) was no longer capable of wholly original invention.

241 'Alles endet, was entstehet...'

20 March 1897   C♯ minor   F♯ – c♯ '

Everything ends that comes into being; everything, all around, passes away. For time flies and the sun sees that everything, all around, passes away; thought, speech, grief and joy.

And our grandchildren have vanished like darkness in daylight, like haze in the breeze. We too were once men, glad and sorry, just as you. And now we are lifeless here, are but clay, as you see. [Everything ends that comes into being;] everything, all around, passes away.

Wolf continues his letter to Oskar Grohe, quoted in 240 above:

> But the second poem strikes me as more significant, and I believe it's the best of all my botchings. If it doesn't affect you to the point of losing your mind, then you've never had one. It really is something that might drive one crazy, and at the same time it has an amazing, truly classical, simplicity. You'll be astounded. I'm literally afraid of this composition, because it makes me apprehensive about my own sanity.

These are ominous forebodings; Wolf would indeed be incurably insane before the year was out. And the personal involvement noted in the previous song is clearly continued here, both in the choice of poem and its treatment. The last sentiments he had just set, a day or two earlier, were 'everyone knows that I exist'. Now his music has to add 'but everything that exists must pass away'. The result is indeed, just as Wolf claimed, a strange and terrifying masterpiece. Perhaps the setting, in following the poem, goes beyond mortal reach. It is among the dead, speaking the language of the dead. That language seems almost forgotten through disuse. Dark octaves grope for expression; lifeless chords strain agonized after some semblance of melody. The voice enters muffled and discordant as if disembodied; 'Alles endet, was entstehet; alles, alles rings vergehet'. The stepwise incantation moves inexorably downwards throughout that phrase, ending on the lowest vocal note. Now a faint metrical pulse begins to beat. Gradually a spark of life kindles and glows in the music. The piano's bass octaves resuscitate, in a more animated rhythm, the melodies that lay latent and inert in its earlier minim chords. The pulse and tempo quicken further at 'und die wir zu Enkeln hatten' (our grandchildren). There is even a glimpse of emotion at 'wie ein Dunst im Windeshauch' (like haze in the breeze). Then in the warmth of E major, now heard for the first time, there is real human regret, the more moving for its simplicity of expression, at 'Menschen waren wir ja auch' (we too were once men) and the following major-minor contrasts for 'froh' and 'traurig'. But now the warmth dies out of the music; the lifeless language resumes in ominously bare octaves at 'und nun sind wir leblos hier'; and the implacable vision of dry bones singing returns until in the postlude death itself dies away.

NOTES 1. The original Italian text begins 'Chiunque nasce a morte arriva'; the German version in Wolf's source-book bears the title 'Gesang der Todten'. He sets only its first twelve lines, of which he repeats the first as his own penultimate.

2. There is the sadness of motif 22 in the right hand at bars 9–10; the left-hand movement beginning in those bars, under repeated notes in the right, is an analogue of motif 17; the questioning inflexion of the dominant at 'so wie ihr' and the following bar of piano interlude is motif 31. The bare octaves are clearly motivic, uniquely here as ubiquitously in Brahms, in the sense of *memento mori*; so are the brief right-hand accents indicating a sudden small gust at 'wie ein Dunst im Windeshauch'. C♯ minor was Wolf's tonality for music of night and darkness; the opening octaves recall the menace of the prelude to *Der Genesene an die Hoffnung* (13) in the same key.

3. Again the articulation of the music is noteworthy. The bare bones are (a) a rising semitone, (b) a rising third or sixth, (c) a falling semitone, together constituting the main theme heard in the minim chords of bars 5–8, and in diminution in the left-hand crotchet octaves of 9–14, reinforced by the right hand at 11–15, and returning to the left at 18 and 20. The left-hand notes heard in that latter bar are rearranged in melody and rhythm to make the new idea at 21–4. The prelude is (a); the postlude has the main theme on the off-beat in the left hand and (a) + (b) inverted in the right. Analogous patterns are discernible *passim*.

4. The content and organization of motif and structure at first seem to offer striking confirmation of Wolf's own view that he was again inspired (see 240, note 3). But this music for all its depth and intensity is essentially a reworking of the thematic material of *Seufzer* (34); and it may be revealing, if there is any personal element in each, that Wolf saw his impending dissolution in terms of sin and punishment in hellfire.

242 'Fühlt meine Seele...'

22-28 March 1897   E minor/E major   A–d'

Does my soul feel the longed-for light from God, who created it? Or does the radiance stem from some other beauty, in this vale of tears, that breaks into my heart, awakening memories? Is it a sound or a dream-vision that all at once fills my eyes and heart with inexplicable searing torment that brings me to tears? I do not know. What I long for, what I feel, what guides me, is not in me. Tell me, how shall I attain it?

Only by the grace of another can it be vouchsafed to me; I have brooded on that thought ever since I saw you. I am torn between yes and no, between sweet and bitter; and for that, my dear lady, your eyes are to blame.

The German text is far from clear; but great sorrow and great love are clearly its original inspiration, and Wolf's music expresses them finely. The brooding prelude seems to be slowly groping its way out of darkness. As the voice enters, the right hand leaves its insistent obsession with the same three notes and begins to sing counter-melodies; the left-hand thirds gradually emerge from the lower register and provide a supporting rhythm. Unobtrusively the first page has risen two octaves in pitch, gained several degrees in dynamics, greatly enhanced its rhythmic interest, and increased in melodic expressiveness; the listener has the feeling of a monumental force lifting and sustaining this music, seeking enlightenment. As the voice's questioning becomes more insistent at 'Ist es ein Klang, ein Traumgesicht' (Is it a sound or a dream-vision) the key moves into the major and the piano begins to sing, in Wolf's own highly personal language, of passionate and enduring love. These themes rise to a climax, then halt and fall back on repetition as if encountering some baffling obstacle. 'Ich weiss es nicht', sings the voice, resignedly; I do not know. Now ensues a series of depictive masterstrokes. The searching music of the first page was dominated by the tonality of E minor, with voice and piano melodies moving mainly slowly and stepwise. The later love-themes incline to E major, with a fuller chordal accompaniment and wider-ranging melodic phrases. In what now follows at 'was ich ersehne' (what I long for) the piano right hand significantly combines the minor tonality and sparse texture of the first themes with the quickening rhythms of the second. Thus the two ideas of seeking and love, already unified by the left-hand rhythm ♪♩ ♪ , are now taken onwards as one single fervent quest. First half the truth is perceived; slowly and almost reluctantly; 'ist nicht in mir' (is not in me). Then the searching themes resume in the keyboard and climb ever higher, in a fantasia of staccato semiquavers, to a climactic vantage-point; the moment of waking expectancy, of awaited revelation. Then it is as if the truth is realised and accepted, with an acquiescence of deep bass semibreves. Voice and piano return to their first themes at 'Mir zeigt es wohl' (it can be vouchsafed). That problem once definitively resolved, the love-themes are recalled, suffused with major warmth, and bursting out in overwhelming intensity until the final words 'daran sind, Herrin, deine Augen Schuld' and the cherishing postlude. This is not a perfect work, nor is it easy to grasp at first hearing. But its craftsmanship is so highly-wrought, its emotion so intense, that a man might be immortal for having written this one song. It was Wolf's last.

NOTES 1. Michelangelo's sonnet 'Non so, se s'è la desiata luce' seems to have been addressed to a young man; the translator's sex-change to 'Herrin' from 'Signior' was presumably designed to make the poem seem more suitable to the public, and no doubt in fact made it more settable for Wolf. The German text sounds garbled in other ways. Thus the sonnet form limps, because the fifth and seventh lines have each lost a foot following the composer's quite uncharacteristic omission of 'ist es' before 'Ein Traumgesicht' and substitution of 'in unbegreiflich glüh'nder' for the original 'mit einer unbegreiflich glüh'nden' before 'Qual'. Further, the enjambement of the Wolfian declamation obscures the retained rhyme-scheme (Licht, Strahl, -tal, bricht, etc).

2. The staccato semiquavers at 'erwerbe' are akin to motif 26; the following suspended dominant sevenths are motif 32. The unifying rhythm is the aptly self-surrendering motif 1; the love-music, e.g. at bars 12–13, is a finely characteristic example of motif 13.

3. Again there is some evidence that this song was not a wholly original inspiration; thus the love-music is taken over from the *Peregrina* songs. The second of those (46) has the beauty of a woman's eyes as its theme; see also 44, note 5. The confused emotions here may well be related to Wolf's own devoted love for his married mistress Melanie Köchert. In his source-book the text is headed 'Deiner Augen Macht'; and its reference to 'eines And'ren Huld' could hardly have failed to elicit a personal interpretation.

4. For what it is worth, there is the coincidence that the vocal lines of Wolf's last song and Brahms's last song (*O Tod, wie bitter bist du,* at 'wie wohl tust du') end in the same year with the same notes in the same key.

Annex

Three songs from Ibsen's
The Feast at Solhaug

In late 1890 the chronically impecunious Wolf accepted a commission from the Vienna Burgtheater to compose incidental music for a planned Ibsen production. But like most subsequent commentators (including William Archer and in later years Ibsen himself) Wolf was wholly unimpressed by the play; and its interspersed choruses in their German translation by Emma Klingenfeld (1846–?) failed to offer any sufficient source of inspiration, whether on their own merits as lyric verse or in relation to their dramatic context. After a year's intermittent toil and two postponements he had glumly ground out five choruses, two instrumental preludes, and the three following solo songs, all unrealistically scored for orchestral forces and skills far beyond the theatre's resources. The scaled-down and truncated versions performed when the production at last opened in November 1891 made little impression; the play itself had only a short run. Wolf's growing reputation secured the publication of his score (Heckel, 1897) and the subsequent inclusion of the three solo songs, in his own arrangement for voice and piano, among the complete Peters edition, where they figured for some years in a miscellaneous volume of *Lieder nach verschiedenen Dichtern* (Songs from various poets). But they still found little favour, and when they were tacitly allowed to lapse their absence from the advertised tally of 245 songs seems to have been largely unnoticed, let alone regretted.

They now deserve reappraisal and revival. Wolf himself, a notoriously austere judge of his own work, was not dissatisfied with his finished score considered as theatre music. Inspired or not, the solo songs considered as 243–5 below were created by a great master at the height of his powers, and are hence far from negligible. Their so-called arrangement for voice and piano is thoroughly characteristic of the Wolfian keyboard idiom, and no doubt represents the original conception of the music before it was adapted and extended for full orchestra.

384

243 Gesang Margits (*Margaret's ballad*) (Act I, scene 3)

7–23 January 1891   G minor $d'-g^{b\,''}$

Mountain-king rode out far and wide through his domains – how sadly my days pass by; he sought to woo the fairest maid – oh, my lamenting will never end!

Mountain-king rode up to lord Hakon's gate; there stood little Kirsten, combing her hair. Mountain-king courted the slender girl, clasped her with a silver belt about the waist. Then Mountain-king led her home; he adorned her with ten golden rings.

Many a year came and went; there sat Kirsten in the mountain all that time. The valley has birds and the glory of flowers – how sadly my days pass by; in the mountain is gold and endless night – oh, my lamenting will never end!

In the play, Margaret's song is among the many dramatic devices designed to show how sour on her tongue the taste of her own marriage has always been. Ibsen's imagery of binding by silver chains, fastening with golden rings, in poignant contrast with longed-for freedom among sunlight and flowers, displays his heroine as a bird in a gilded cage. And indeed, as she confesses to her childhood sweetheart Gudrun on his unexpected return to the homeland, she has lived in tormented frustration ever since she married Bengt Gauteson for his money. But among the dramatic devices is that of irony; for Bengt himself has nothing of the powerful tyrant about him; on the contrary, he is a weak and malleable figure wholly dominated and manipulated by the Lady Macbeth character of Margaret herself. So Ibsen's legendary mountain-king (who reappears far more memorably in *Peer Gynt*, especially in Grieg's incidental music) also represents Margaret's wish-fulfilment dream of a hero and champion who will liberate her from her fatal frustration. In Wolf's music as in Grieg's the kingly themes are virile as well as sinister; and both aspects are here presented as the products of Margaret's own perfervid imagination.

The song begins with two bars of funeral march, with a right-hand rhythmic figure briefly extended to make the 'Mountain-king' theme, under the prolonged final note of which the wistfully rising 'Kirsten' motif struggles to make itself heard. At 'so traurig vergeh'n die Tage' (how sadly my days pass by) the Mountain-king theme is coiled and constricted into a vivid image of frustration. There is a flash-back trumpet call as if from heralds at the castle gates on the dire day when the dread suitor rode up 'vor Herrn Hakons Tor'; every second of the sorrow and tedium since that time is remorselessly eked out in the music. Much inventiveness is lavished on the sonorous portrayal of incompatibility (one theme stifled by the other, or both opposed in contrary motion) and of mourning (the whole song unified by the persistent rhythm of a funeral march). But it cannot be gainsaid that in the absence of a dramatic dimension to sustain interest some of the musical material sounds as apt to induce tedium as to represent it.

NOTES 1. The word in bar 34 should read 'silbernem', not silbernen' as in the first edition.

2. Some of the thematic material recalls *Wo find' ich Trost* (43); the idea of a *mésalliance* conveyed by a funeral march was heard in *Bei einer Trauung* (63); the open fifths of the cortège conjure up *Die Geister am Mummelsee* (59). A thematic depiction of incompatibility also occurs in *Seltsam ist Juanas Weise* (149). The dramatic character-study effect of one musical figure dominated by another was to be more vigorously exploited in *Der Corregidor* (1895), notably in the jealous monologue of Tio Lukas, Act III scene 1.

3. The weeping semitones at 'klein Kirsten' and 'umfing ihr' are the sorrow motif 22.

4. The Mountain-king theme here is a striking though no doubt involuntary reminiscence of the opening *Allegro con brio* of Beethoven's Piano Sonata Op. 111, a work in which the musically imaginative Wolf may well have heard intimations of grim and fateful power.

244 Gudmunds erster Gesang (*Gudmund's first song*) (Act I, scene 11)

30 October 1891 (revised 12 November 1896)   G major   B—E$^\flat$ ' (d'—e$^\flat$ '')

I wandered alone on the hillside, lost in thought; all around, the birds were twittering in the wood. So clearly their knowing song resounded: listen, listen, how love burgeons in the heart. It grows like the oak-tree, over long years; it is nourished on sorrow, on dreams and song; it germinates quickly, in the most fleeting hour, and strikes root in the depths of the heart.

Gudrun Alfson sings this song soon after his reunion at Solhaug with Signë, a childhood playmate now grown to be a woman and suddenly recognised by the blueness of her lovely eyes. She has guarded his harp as a keepsake and now returns it to him 'as bright as of yore'. We are to understand from the lyric in its dramatic context that as their eyes meet there is love between them, to the fury and despair of Signë's sister Margit, of whose unhappy marriage we heard in the first of these songs and of whose jealousy we shall learn in the third. Gudrun strikes some preluding chords and then sings; Wolf's accompaniment is scored for harp and strings accordingly. The vocal melody begins ingratiatingly; soon the right hand is trilling softly in response to the mention of bird-song, at 'da zwitscherten' etc, and the tonality brightens into E major. There is a moment of recitative at the repeated injunction 'hör' an' (listen) as if those words were confidingly spoken. Then love is described; and the vocal line at 'Sie wächst wie die Eiche' (It grows like the oak-tree) is made to rise, first to a smaller and then to a wider interval, a miniature model of growth and development, with dominant roots in the bass. For the efflorescence of love the melodies in voice and piano flow out more freely, all sigh and echo in the canonic imitations, sun and shade in the changing harmonies, with still deeper roots heard in the left hand. As a further unobtrusive underlining of the musical metaphor, the voice falls to its lowest note at the last phrase 'im Herzensgrund' (in the depths of the heart). The postlude sings the last couplet tenderly over again to itself, a love-song without words that finally fades in a few soft harp-flourishes.

NOTES 1. In the original publication (Heckel 1897) the first version of this song misprints 'ihr lustiges' (their merry) for 'ihr listiges' (their knowing) at bar 14.
   2. Wolf's 1896 revision, with the voice part transferred from bass to treble clef, deliberately tautens the construction. The thematic connection between the harp flourishes of the postlude and the birdsong figurations at 'da zwitscherten' etc is strengthened, and the latter are elaborated; the recitative effects are integrated more closely with the accompaniment; the harmony is rarefied and the accentuation refined. But the result arguably entails more complexity than the lyric requires or can sustain; and the earlier version may be preferred as both fresher in itself and more congruent with the verses.
   3. F♯ major for 'so hell erscholl' suggests motif 40; the convergence of voice and inner right-hand melody at 'Sie wächst wie die Eiche' is the love motif 13.

245 Gudmunds zweiter Gesang (*Gudmund's second song*) (Act II, scene 8)

7 March 1891   A minor/A major   e'–e''

I sailed over the water and far away; when I came back to my homeland I wooed the fairest maid. But the elf-woman looked on with rage; never, said she, shall his dear love go to church with him.

   Listen, you elf-woman, forget your grievances; if two hearts love each other, you can never part them [you can never part them].

As before, the lyric has mythological overtones; the elf-woman is drawn from the same northern folk-lore as the Mountain-king of 243 and the soothsaying birds of 244. The song is again linked with the dramatic action; Gudmund will woo and win Signë despite the jealous opposition of her sister Margit, who will indeed have reformed and recanted in time to bless the happy pair as the final curtain falls. But Wolf's setting seems to derive its point of departure rather from the voyage envisaged by the opening words. Although the main theme of the poem is rooted in terra firma, homeland and household, the music feels free to sail away in the easy lilting wave-motion established in the four-bar prelude, scored for wind band. Muted strings take up the story as the voice enters; the mood is one of veiled memory and reminiscence which is then revealed in a typical modulation as a recent and joyous moment, at the words 'freit' ich die schönste Maid' (I wooed the fairest maid), signalled by a flourish of carefree horns. Then the texture is thickened to express the complications of the plot, with its dramatic conflicts of jealousy and rage. Here the strident orchestral *tutti* strains threaten to overload the song-frame, in the piano interlude after 'mit ihm zur Kirche geh'n' (go to church with him). But the music relaxes into an affable simplicity with the ensuing transition to the major at 'Hör' an, du Elfenfraue', almost foretelling the eventual reconciliation with Margit; and the final page of postlude is its own happy ending, in which the discontentedly travelling accompaniment-figure of the opening phrase with its minor muted strings finally comes home as a burst of major melodies joyously surrounded by the full orchestra. In the last few bars all this triumph is suddenly hushed and simplified, at a typically Wolfian stroke, into the music of quiet domestic bliss.

NOTES 1. The final repetition is Wolf's, not Ibsen's.

2. There is a faint hint of the Mountain-king theme from 243 at 'in die Ferne weit'; perhaps Wolf was involuntarily recalling Margit's 'über die Lande weit'.

3. The compound time recalls other songs of sailing: *Ich fuhr über Meer* (154) with its first-line verbal echo, and *Als ich auf dem Euphrat* (126). There are also some affinities of mood with the A major of that latter song, and similarly with *Wandl' ich in dem Morgentau* (184) and the much later *Gesegnet sei das Grün* (225). The final four bars, described above as evocative of domestic bliss, strikingly anticipate the hearthside love-duet 'In solchen Abendfeierstunden' from Act II scene 1 of *Der Corregidor*.

4. The jubilant change to F♯ major at 'freit' ich die schönste Maid' is motif 40.

Index A   The songs

(The serial number allotted to each song is shown in parenthesis; all other numbers refer to pages, with the main reference shown in bold type)

389

Index B   General

397